ILLINOIS CLASSICAL STUDIES, VOLUME I

ILLINOIS CLASSICAL STUDIES

VOLUME I
1976

Miroslav Marcovich, *Editor*

UNIVERSITY OF ILLINOIS PRESS
Urbana Chicago London

Preface

Illinois Classical Studies (ICS) is a serial publication of the Classics Departments of the University of Illinois at Urbana-Champaign and Chicago Circle which contains the results of original research dealing with classical antiquity and with its impact upon Western culture. ICS welcomes scholarly contributions dealing with any topic or aspect of Greek and/or Roman literature, language, history, art, culture, philosophy, religion, and the like, as well as with their transmission from antiquity through Byzantium or Western Europe to our time.

ICS is not limited to contributions coming from Illinois. It is open to classicists of any flag or school of thought. In fact, of sixteen contributors to Volume I (1976), six are from Urbana, two from Chicago, six from the rest of the country, and two from Europe.

It is a pleasant duty for me to express here my sincere thanks to Dean Robert W. Rogers for his generous moral and material support, without which this serial publication would not have been possible. I also thank my advisers, Professors Mark Naoumides, Revilo P. Oliver, Ann Perkins, Theodore J. Tracy, S.J., and Luitpold Wallach, for helping me greatly with their wisdom and time.

Urbana, July 4, 1974   M. MARCOVICH, *Editor*

Contents

viii Contents

1

The Status of [æː] in Attic Greek

One of the best known features of Attic-Ionic is the sound change by which inherited long *ā* was raised to long open *ę̄*. This change took place in all environments in Ionic. In Attic, it either did not take place after the sounds written EIP or, according to others, it did take place there too but was later reversed in this special environment. C. D. Buck describes the change as having occurred gradually and adds: "There was once a period, still reflected in some inscriptions of the Ionic islands, when the new vowel was not yet fully identical with the general Greek H, that is, it was even more open. But in general, the H in both syllables of Attic-Ionic μήτηρ had the same sound."[1]

The new and more open vowel to which Buck refers is [æː], which is usually assumed as a necessary first stage of the change from long *ā* and which subsequently became identified with the long open *ę̄* derived from inherited long *ē*. Buck wisely does not venture to say how long a period this intermediate stage lasted. W. Sidney Allen is even more cautious,[2] observing only that the development of *ā* to [εː] probably proceeded via a stage [æː], which in turn may be represented by some Ionic inscriptions of the Cyclades. Here the sign H was at first used only to stand for the vowel arising from original long *ā*, whereas the sign E continued to be used for the vowel derived from original long *ē*. This graphic device is found, for example, in a famous archaic inscription in meter from Naxos, beginning with the words NIKANΔPH M'ANEΘĒKEN, "Nikandre dedicated me."[3]

---

[1] *Comparative Grammar of Greek and Latin*, 10th impression, Chicago, University of Chicago Press, 1966, pp. 85–86.

[2] *Vox Graeca, The Pronunciation of Classical Greek*, Cambridge, Cambridge University Press, 1968, p. 70.

[3] IG XII.V.2; see C. D. Buck, *Greek Dialects*, Chicago, University of Chicago Press, 1955, pp. 189–190.

The last vowel of the name Nikandrē is written with H as originally from long *ā*; the third vowel of *anethēken* is written with E as originally from *ē*. This handy graphic distinction, unfortunately for the thesis of the present article, was not observed in Attica, although the sign H occurs occasionally in Attic inscriptions prior to the official adoption of the Ionic alphabet in Athens in 403 B.C. Before that date the sign E represented both short and long *e*.

Is it possible to define more closely than Buck has done the period in which [æː] had not yet merged with [ɛː]? The attempt has been made in several recent publications to which I shall presently turn. To anticipate, it seems to me that the most reasonable hypothesis is that [æː] emerged in Attic-Ionic around 900 B.C. and was retained in Attic until about 400 B.C. The main scope of this paper is to defend this assumption against two counterarguments: (1) that a five-level scheme for Attic long front vowels cannot have existed by reason of phonological impossibility and (2) that there is no epigraphic evidence for the sound [æː] in Attic inscriptions. I should further note that I am accepting provisionally the special argument of Oswald Szemerényi,[4] based on what seem to me to be very sound proofs that *ā* moved to [æː] in all environments, but that when following the sounds written EIP it later moved back to *ā*. This is referred to in the literature as the Attic "Rückverwandlung," and it is important but not essential to my own argument.

Logically, whether the stage [æː] existed for centuries or for only a short period, if it was ever found in the inventory of sounds, there would be every reason to include it as a member in good standing among the sounds of Attic-Ionic. Buck prefers not to do so. Many recent authorities do posit a specific change from *ā* to [æː], which Michel Lejeune[5] puts as early as the end of the second milennium and the beginning of the first milennium B.C. E. Risch[6] suggests the tenth to ninth century B.C. Antonín Bartoněk comments gracefully that "the contemporary investigators often seem to favor very early chronological estimates, chiefly those among them, we may say, who belong to the most outstanding experts in Greek phon-

---

[4] "The Attic 'Rückverwandlung,' or Atomism and Structuralism in Action," in *Studien zur Sprachwissenschaft und Kulturkunde, Gedenkschrift für Wilhelm Brandenstein*, herausgegeben von Manfred Mayrhofer *et al.* (Innsbrucker Beiträge zur Kulturwissenschaft, 14), Innsbruck, 1968, pp. 139–157.

[5] *Traité de phonétique grecque*, Paris, Klincksieck, 1946, p. 17. In the latest revision of this book, now called *Phonétique historique du mycénien et du grec ancien*, Paris, Klincksieck, 1972, p. 235, n. 2, he claims that the change is earlier than the eighth century.

[6] "Die Gliederung der griechischen Dialekte in neuer Sicht," *Museum Helveticum*, 12 (1955), pp. 61–76; esp. p. 65.

ology."[7] The issue involved here is the requirement that the change of $\bar{a}$ to [æː] must antedate the reemergence of Attic long $\bar{a}$ by compensatory lengthening; such compensatory lengthening itself is hard to date. On the other hand, the earliest Attic-Ionic evidence to document the sound change is the genitive singular form, Ἀφροδίτες from -ᾱs, in an inscription dated about 700 B.C. from the Euboian colony of Pithekoussai.[8] Eduard Schwyzer, therefore, to be on the safe side, sets the date for the change as late as the eighth to seventh century.[9] I prefer here to follow Risch and Bartoněk in setting the date earlier than Schwyzer allows, and specifically at around 900 B.C., but again this is not essential to my argument.

W. Sidney Allen will have none of this. He claims[10] that the maintenance of a distinction involving [ɑː], [æː], and [ɛː] is improbable on general phonological grounds. While a system with five long front vowel phonemes is not impossible transitionally, he maintains that this is exceedingly rare and unlikely to have survived for long. Trubetzkoy, he adds, found this in only one Swiss and one African dialect. But as Bartoněk pointed out,[11] the system can be equally well pictured as a four-level system, with [ɑː] and [æː] placed on the same level, as shown in Diagram 4.

In this connection, the prior development of the long vowels has been displayed in Diagrams 1 through 3. The long vowels of Common Greek are shown in Diagram 1, representing the inherited Indo-European long vowels. Diagram 2, the post-Mycenean long vowels, displays a further differentiation of $\bar{e}$ and $\bar{o}$ into more open and more closed varieties. Diagram 3 shows the shift on which we are concentrating of [ɑː] to [æː] on the assumption that it was affected in all environments.

To get back to Allen's theoretical objections, I might say that the three-way contrast which he considers a fine distinction, [ɑ], [æː], and [ɛ], occurs in short vowels in many languages, including English. Even in the long vowels, I have turned up a curious analogy with the Attic-Ionic long vowels, as shown in Diagram 4, in a language not noticed by Allen. According to a recent analysis by John S. Austin,[12] the Danish long vowels show four heights:

hvide, "white,"   [viːðə]
hvede, "wheat,"   [veːðə]
væde, "wet,"   [vɛːðə]
vade, "wade,"   [væːðə]

[7] *Development of the Long-Vowel System in Ancient Greek Dialects*, Prague, Státní Pedagogické Nakladatelství, 1966, p. 99.   [8] SEG XIV 6043.
[9] *Griechische Grammatik*, I–II, Munich, 1939–1950, C. H. Beck, I, p. 233.
[10] *Op. cit.*, p. 70, n. 2.   [11] *Op. cit.*, p. 105.
[12] *Topics in Danish Phonology* (unpublished Cornell University Ph.D. dissertation), 1971.

Diagrams to Illustrate the Evolution of the Long Vowels

1. Common Greek long vowels.

2. Post-Mycenean long vowels.

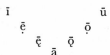

3. Attic-Ionic long vowels, about 900 B.C.

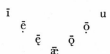

4. Attic-Ionic long vowels, about 800 B.C.

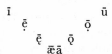

5. Attic long vowels, about 600 B.C.

6. Attic long vowels, about 400 B.C.

It is also interesting to see that long *ā* alternates with [æː] in this system but only in the environment of an *r* sound. The arguments drawn from phonological probability work both ways, and Allen's examples, like my counterexamples, really are no more than suggestive parallels.

Leslie L. Threatte's argument is weightier.[13] He calls attention to the absence in Attic of any epigraphic evidence for [æː], but this absence is by no means the crushing proof he believes it to be. All he has really established is that there is no distinctive grapheme for [æː], something quite different. As linguists well know, many important phonetic and phonemic distinctions are not represented in spelling, whether in ancient or modern alphabets. It happens that in modern English we use the symbol *a* to cover both the sound of [a] in *father* and that of [æː] in *man*. According to Björn Collinder, the short *e* symbol in Hungarian covers two distinct sounds not differentiated in the writing system except in that used by linguists like himself: one sound is short [ɛ]; the other is short [æː]. This is a dialect feature, since in a large northeastern area and in Budapest the [ɛ] has been lost.[14] Both these situations, the English and the Hungarian, to be sure are only casual parallels to the Greek one, but the similarity is striking and they suggest a somewhat similar explanation for the Attic phenomena.

Reference to Diagram 3 shows that once all long *ā*'s had been shifted to [æː], there would have been no need to create a new grapheme for [æː], because then there was no contrast between [æː] and [ɑː]. At this point the *a*-grapheme would have been sufficient, although in fact there is no evidence for literacy at this period. I am assuming here, as I mentioned before, that Szemerényi is correct in postulating this shift even when *ā* followed the sounds represented by EIP.

About 800 B.C., although that date also is admittedly subject to some caviling, a new long *ā* appeared in the Attic-Ionic long vowel system, as shown in Diagram 4. This was the result of the loss of a nasal following a short *a* sound with subsequent lengthening. Thus the feminine nominative singular adjective *pansa*, "all," became *pāsa*, the accusative plural of the feminine demonstrative, later to become the definite article, *tans*, became *tās*. There was now a contrast between the new long *ā* and the [æː], which had developed from the earlier long *ā*, and the way was now open for the [æː] to move further in the direction of [ɛː]. William F. Wyatt, Jr., speaks of the new long *ā* as triggering this development,[15] although he notes, as I must also note, that Risch dates the emergence of the new long *ā* as posterior to the merger of [æː] and [ɛː].

Szemerényi suggests[16] that with the emergence of new long *ā*, the more

[13] "A Second Look at the Dual Pronunciation of *Eta*," *TAPA*, 100 (1969), 587–591.

[14] *Survey of the Uralic Languages*, 2nd ed., Stockholm, Almqvist & Wiksell, 1969, p. 367.

[15] "The Prehistory of the Greek Dialects," *TAPA*, 101 (1970), 557–632; esp. p. 602; for Risch's view, see the article cited in note 6 above, p. 64.

[16] *Op. cit.*, p. 154.

open allophones of [æː] in Attic, by which he means those that followed
the sounds represented by EIP, moved toward [ɑː] and merged with it, as
already described. If he is right, the stage then would have been set, as the
use of writing was disseminated, for subsequent use of the *a*-grapheme to
cover the new long *ā*, plus the further new long *ā*'s resulting from this
Rückverwandlung. If he is wrong, the *a*-grapheme in any case would
cover the new long *ā* and, on this hypothesis, the unchanged long *ā*'s
which followed EIP. By like reasoning, the grapheme E, and later H, was
available both for long [æː] and inherited [ɛː] until both sounds were
completely merged in the latter.

When this change was completed is a matter of further controversy.
While few scholars would disagree with Diagram 6 as a representation of
the Attic long vowels around 400 B.C., Diagram 5 as of 200 years earlier is
subject to challenge. Bartoněk, quite to the contrary, thinks [æː] had
become [ɛː] by 700 B.C.[17] Here I prefer to follow Szemerényi's lead[18] and
set the date for the completion of this change much later, namely, during
the fifth century. Like Szemerényi, I am impressed by the arguments
advanced by R. Whitney Tucker[19] and drawn from the usage of Attic
playwrights. Up to the end of the fifth century, they displayed complete
competence in substituting a non-Attic long *ā* for Attic long [æː] in choral
lyric and choral passages of tragedy. To put it this way is somewhat to beg
the question. A more cogent version of the argument would be that the
tragic poets had no lexica of non-Attic forms to consult, and yet their
success cannot be mere chance. No doubt the stage tradition counted for
something, but the most reliable explanation is that the poets still in their
own speech differentiated between [æː] and [ɛː], that is, that contrary to
what Buck states they regularly said not [méːteːr] but [mǽːteːr], even if the
writing system was not capable of rendering this important distinction.

Cornell University

[17] *Op. cit*, pp. 139–140.   [18] *Op. cit.*, p. 148.
[19] "On the Dual Pronunciation of *Eta*," *TAPA*, 93 (1962), 490–501.

2

On The Meaning of ἐφήμερος

MATTHEW W. DICKIE

The account which Hermann Fränkel gave more than a quarter of a century ago of the meaning of the word ἐφήμερος has never to my knowledge been seriously questioned.[1] It has indeed won wide acceptance.[2] In Fränkel's view the word did not originally mean "lasting for a day" or "short-lived," but "subject to the changing day" or "variable."[3] Men are called ἐφήμεροι not because they are believed to be short-lived but because in the early archaic period men began to believe that their character or personality was at the mercy of the changes which each day brought.[4] Such an outlook on life was part and parcel of that feeling of helplessness in the face of fate which, it is held, was so pervasive in Greece in this period.[5] The belief that man's outlook on life in the early archaic period was radically different from his outlook in the so-called epic period, a view made fashionable by a number of German-speaking scholars, has recently been called into question.[6] It is perhaps time therefore to subject to a

---

[1] "Man's 'Ephemeros' Nature according to Pindar and Others," *TAPA*, 77 (1946), 131–145 = *Wege und Formen frühgriechischen Denkens*, 2nd ed., Munich, 1960, pp. 23–39 (slightly altered in German edition). Page references to the article in its *TAPA* version will be given before those to the German version. Fränkel also discusses the matter briefly in *Dichtung und Philosophie des frühen Griechentums*, 2nd ed., Munich, 1962, pp. 148–150.

[2] For example, by M. Treu, *Von Homer zur Lyrik*, Munich, 1955, pp. 225 f.; R. W. B. Burton, *Pindar's Pythian Odes*, Oxford, 1961, pp. 191 f.; D. C. Young, *Pindar, Isthmian 7*, Leiden, 1971, p. 31; and most recently by G. M. Kirkwood, *Early Greek Monody*, Ithaca, 1974, p. 221, n. 35. W. J. Slater in his review of Young, however, in *Gnomon*, 45 (1973), p. 198, criticizes the inadequacies of Fränkel's account.

[3] P. 131 = p. 23.   [4] Pp. 140 f. = pp. 33 f.

[5] P. 136 = p. 29. On this feeling of helplessness see Bruno Snell, *Die Entdeckung des Geistes*, 3rd ed., Hamburg, 1955, p. 106.

[6] K. J. Dover in *Archiloque: Entretiens sur l'antiquité classique*, tome X, Geneva, 1964, pp. 197–212, argues that we should not assume, because Archilochus or some other early poet is the first person we know to give expression to a certain attitude, that he did not

reappraisal Fränkel's two propositions that ἐφήμερος originally meant "changing as the day" and that men are called ἐφήμεροι because their character was thought to alter with changing circumstances.

In this paper I shall try to show that the passages containing the word ἐφήμερος which Fränkel adduces in support of his interpretation of that word do not in fact lend such support. I shall argue on the basis of the evidence we have that there are no grounds for thinking that "varying as the day" is the basic meaning of ἐφήμερος and that men are called ἐφήμεροι because they are thought to vary as the day.

The first passage containing the word ἐφήμερος which Fränkel cites in support of his contention that the word when applied to men means "varying as the day" is Pindar, *Pythian* 8.95 f.[7] In his view the context lends no support to the rendering "short-lived" and, in fact, it is clear from the context that the word has nothing whatsoever to do with the brevity of human life. What Pindar is supposed to be saying in this passage is that the human spirit is subject to abrupt shifts—it is sometimes confident and sometimes despondent. So, Fränkel concludes, Pindar in calling men ἐπάμεροι at this point must be speaking of their variability. A second reason is given for taking the word in this way. It is that the words which follow ἐπάμεροι, τί δέ τις; τί δ' οὔ τις; σκιᾶς ὄναρ/ἄνθρωπος mean that men are everything in succession and that there is nothing which they are not. The fact that he is nothing fixed makes man "a dream's shadow," that is, something which changes rapidly. These words Fränkel believes are tantamount to a definition of what it is for a man to be ἐφήμερος.

A paraphrase of the poem from v. 75 onward is necessary. Those who think that men achieve success through their own devices are fools. That does not lie in man's control. A *daemon* sometimes raises a man's fortune up and sometimes depresses it. A list of the victories of the athlete whose fame Pindar is celebrating follows. That leads to a description of the unhappy homecomings of those whom he has defeated. In contrast to their wretchedness is the man whose spirit soars after some recent success. But that which gives joy to men lasts only a short time before it is shaken to the ground. Then comes the word ἐπάμεροι followed by, "What is anyone? What is anyone not? Man is a dream's shadow." Pindar's main theme in this passage is the inconstancy of human fortune. He illustrates that theme with a reference to the present success of the *laudandus*, Aristomenes, and

---

have predecessors. H. Lloyd-Jones, *The Justice of Zeus*, Berkeley and Los Angeles, 1971, pp. 36–54, shows that much of what is supposed to be peculiar to the early archaic age is to be found in Homer.

    7 Pp. 133 f. = pp. 25 f.

his opponents' misfortunes. Pindar does not say that that which causes men grief lasts for only a short time. Only that which gives joy is short-lived. This is in accord with the bleak view he expresses elsewhere about the prospects for uninterrupted human felicity.[8] It is wrong to say then that Pindar in this poem is writing about the abrupt shifts of mood to which men are subject. He is writing about the inconstancy of human fortune and the brevity of human felicity.

The parallels that we have for the words immediately after ἐπάμεροι lend support to this interpretation. The image of a dream's shadow is a way of talking about powerlessness and helplessness.[9] In the *Prometheus Vinctus* Prometheus is asked what help he expects from ἐφημέριοι and whether he does not perceive their dreamlike weakness.[10] Contemplation of Ajax's misfortunes in Sophocles' *Ajax* leads Odysseus to say that men are nothing but images or empty shadows.[11] By that he means that the gods can over-turn human good fortune without the slightest difficulty. Cassandra laments that even a shadow can upset human prosperity in the *Agamemnon* of Aeschylus.[12] As for the question, "What is anyone? What is anyone not?" it is better taken in this context to be another way of describing man's powerlessness in the face of fortune. Pindar does not mean by it that man is everything but that he is nothing at all. In the Sixth Nemean Pindar says that man is nothing at all.[13] He is at that point drawing a contrast between the power of the gods and the powerlessness of men. The Chorus in *Oedipus Rex* after seeing Oedipus' fall from great good fortune are moved to declare that they count the race of men as nothing at all.[14] Finally, Aristotle in the *Protrepticus* combines both ways of talking about man's feebleness when he says, "Everything which seems great to men is only shadow-painting (σκιαγραφία). Whence it is correctly said that man is nothing and none of the things of man are secure."[15]

What we have then in this passage of Pindar are some commonplace reflections on the nature of human fortune. There is nothing to warrant Fränkel's claim that ἐπάμεροι here means "with moods that vary as the day." If that is what the word means here, then Pindar is guilty of having introduced an irrelevant element into his train of thought. Thus the con-

---

[8] *Pythian* 3.85 f.

[9] J. Jüthner, *Wiener Studien*, 54 (1936), pp. 142 f., correcting the interpretation of L. Bieler, *Wien. St.*, 51 (1933), pp. 143–145.

[10] Aesch. *P.V.* 546 ff.   [11] Soph. *Aj.* 125 f.   [12] Aesch. *Ag.* 1327 ff.

[13] Vv. 2 ff.: διείργει δὲ πᾶσα κεκριμένα/ δύναμις, ὡς τὸ μὲν οὐδέν, ὁ δὲ/ χάλκεος ἀσφαλὲς αἰὲν ἕδος/ μένει οὐρανός.

H. Jurenka, *Philologus*, 58 (1899), p. 349, also compares these passages. *Pythian* 3.84 ff. also is relevant here.

[14] Soph. *O.R.* 1186 ff.   [15] Fr. 10a Ross.

text excludes Fränkel's rendering. It is true that the context does not compel us to take the word to mean "creatures of a day." However, that is a wholly appropriate way of referring to mankind under the circumstances.

A consequence of changing circumstances determining man's mood, according to Fränkel, is that man's perception of reality becomes blurred.[16] In this way Fränkel accounts for a number of passages in which men who are addressed as ἐφήμεροι are said to be ignorant or foolish. Semonides fr. 1 D. is paraenetic in tone. It begins with a boy's being addressed and told that Zeus controls everything and disposes of it as he pleases. Men lack knowledge but ἐφήμεροι we live as the beasts of the field completely ignorant of how god will bring each thing to fruition. But hope and confidence give nurture to all men as they attempt that which will not be fulfilled. Some men wait for the next day to come, some for the next year. There is no one who does not think that he will become rich. But old age, disease, war, drowning and suicide cut men down before they achieve their aims. So, the poet concludes, we should not love evils and torture our hearts by concerning ourselves with misery.[17] What we have in this poem is an exhortation to put aside long-term plans and to live for the moment. Fränkel's method of analyzing the meaning of ἐφήμερος in this poem and elsewhere is to assume that some word or words in the immediate vicinity of the term reflect some part of its meaning. This is a dangerous assumption. In the case of this passage it is almost certain that Semonides did not think that men's outlook on reality was blurred by emotional instability. The reason for their ignorance is that as men they can have no idea what Zeus or the gods intend for them since the purposes of the gods are inscrutable and they are given no clue as to what the gods will do. This is standard Greek theology.[18] In Pindar's Eleventh Nemean we are told that although no clear signs come from Zeus as to what will be, men nonetheless

---

[16] Pp. 136–138 = pp. 29–31.

[17] L. von Sybel, *Hermes*, 7 (1873), pp. 361 f., believes that the poet at vv. 20–24 is advising against the pursuit of the things which hope encourages a man to pursue and which turn out to be evils. But it may be that the poet is simply advising against persisting in mourning past misfortunes, just as Pindar does at *Isthmian* 8.5–15. So also D. Campbell, *Greek Lyric Poetry*, London and New York, 1967, p. 186, who compares Semonides Fr. 29.13 f. D. R. Reitzenstein, *Philol.*, 57 (1898), pp. 42–45, classifies the poem as *Trostgedicht*. Wilamowitz, *Sappho und Simonides*, Berlin, 1913, p. 273, sums up the poem's intent with the verses inscribed on the silver skeleton which graces Trimalchio's table: *Totus homuncio nil est./ Ergo sic erimus cuncti postquam nos auferet Orcus./ Ergo vivamus, dum liceat esse bene.* (Petr. *Sat.* 34.10).

[18] Cf. Hes. *Erg.* 483 f.; *Hom. hymn. ad Cer.* 250 f.; Solon. Frr. 1.63 ff. and 17 D.; Mimn. Fr. 2.1 ff. D.; Theogn. 133 ff.; Pind. *Ol.* 7.24 ff.; *Pyth.* 10.59 ff.; *Nem.* 6.4 ff.; Aesch. *Suppl.* 91 ff.; 1037 f.

are ambitious and desire to do many things as their limbs are bound by shameless hope.[19] This is the same point which Semonides makes.

It is difficult to determine how pointed ἐφήμεροι is when used in a passage such as this Semonidean one. It may be that it is no more than a synonym for θνητοί or βροτοί. However, the presence of the topic of the brevity of human life in a number of other poems dealing with the enjoyment of present pleasures and the avoidance of hopes for the distant future encourages one to think that ἐφήμεροι may be pointed in this poem and mean "short-lived." The brevity of human life is emphasized in Semonides fr. 29 D., a poem on the *carpe diem* theme. Bacchylides 3.73 ff. deals with these same themes, and significantly there men are referred to as ἐφαμέριοι (v. 76).

Of the other passages which Fränkel subsumes under the same heading as Semonides fr. 1 D., Pindar, *Nemean* 6.6 ff. does not help his case.[20] There ἐφαμερίαν very clearly means "by day" as against "by night." Two fragments of Pindar are too brief to give any indication of what ἐφήμερος means in them. In fr. 182 Snell it is lamented that ἐφήμεροι are deceived and do not know. It could simply be the condition of mortals who have no knowledge of what the gods intend their fate to be which is being lamented here. In any case there is no reason to think that what we have is a definition of some aspect of the word's meaning. In fr. 157 Snell Silenus addresses Olympus as a hapless ἐφήμερος who speaks foolishly in boasting of his possessions. Again there is no reason to think that there is any necessary connection between being ἐφήμερος and being foolish. After all, it would be foolish for a man as a creature of a day to boast of his possessions. The context in which Antinous insultingly addresses Eumaeus and Philoetius as ἐφημέρια φρονέοντες at *Odyssey* 21.85 as they weep at the sight of their master's bow does not exclude the possibility that the point of the insult is that the two servants can only think of that which is immediately at hand and are unable to take stock of the further consequences of their behavior. Their short-sightedness prevents them from seeing that their weeping will upset Penelope. But even if the expression does mean "thinking thoughts which vary as the day" it hardly follows that ἐφήμερος when used of a man will mean "varying as the day." Theognis 485 f. advises that in drinking a man should not let his belly master him as it does an ἐφημέριος λάτρις. The traditional rendering "day-labourer" is dismissed by Fränkel on the ground that it does not fit the context.[21] But the traditional rendering makes good sense. A day-labourer

---

[19] Vv. 43 ff. The conjunction of human hope and ignorance of the divine will is a commonplace, to judge from Semonides, Pindar, and Theognis, vv. 133 ff.

[20] Pp. 137 f. = pp. 30 f.   [21] P. 138 n. 25 = p. 31 n. 2.

is a man whose belly governs what he does. It is because he has to fill his belly that he is forced to undertake the demeaning tasks that he customarily performs.[22]

A further aspect of the way in which the meaning of ἐφήμερος develops from its original sense of "varying as the day," according to Fränkel, is its being used of voluntary adaptation to circumstances.[23] The context demands that we take the word to mean "short-lived" in two of the passages which are cited as examples of this aspect of the word's use. Theognis, 963 ff., advises against praising a man before knowing him well on the grounds that many men put on an ἐφημέριος spirit. But time, Theognis continues, shows the true character of each. That is, a man can give an impression for a day or a short time of being trustworthy, but his true character will be shown over a long period of time.[24] Theognis, 665 f., says, "We all grieve for you in your misfortune, Cyrnus, but another's troubles are something that is ἐφημέριον." This is a commonplace to judge from Pindar, *Nemean*, 1.53 f., "His own cares press upon everyone alike but straightway the heart is free of sorrow when it is another's care." What Theognis is saying, then, is that our concern for the misfortune of others lasts only for a short time.[25]

Fränkel places τερπνὸν ἐφάμερον at Pindar, *Isthmian*, 7.40, under the heading of voluntary adaptation to circumstances and takes the phrase to mean "joy that comes day by day."[26] David C. Young in his monograph on that poem adopts Fränkel's interpretation.[27] I shall argue that that is the correct interpretation of these words. At v. 39 of the poem Pindar prays that divine envy may not disturb the calm which now prevails and in the following line he gives as a reason his quiet progress toward old age and death pursuing τερπνὸν ἐφάμερον as he goes. Then, in contrast to this mode of life, he speaks of those who look to the far-distant and as an example of that sort of man cites Bellerophon and his unsuccessful attempt to fly to heaven. The moral that Pindar draws is that a most bitter end awaits that which is sweet but contrary to right. What has to be established is that such a train of thought is in harmony with what Pindar says elsewhere on the subject of what is the appropriate way for mortals to conduct themselves.

In speaking of the success of those whom he celebrates Pindar is wont to say that they have reached the limits of human felicity and that they

[22] So also B. A. Van Groningen, *Théognis, le premier livre*, Amsterdam, 1966, *ad loc*. It is Odysseus' shameless belly which forces him to beg and seek demeaning work (*Odyssey* 15.344 f.). Cf. Ap. Rhod. 1.1172 ff.

[23] Pp. 138–140 = pp. 32 f.   [24] So Van Groningen, *ad loc*.

[25] Van Groningen, *ad loc*.   [26] P. 139 = p. 32.   [27] Young, *op. cit.*, p. 31.

should neither attempt to go further nor should they even think that they can go further.[28] The far-distant thus becomes a figure for that which is forbidden to mortals. In contrast to it there is that which is at foot or nearby or close to home.[29] Things which belong to this category are what it is appropriate for mortals to pursue. That which is at foot seems to be identical with that which comes day by day. In the Tenth Pythian at vv. 61 ff. Pindar recommends seizing that which lies at foot since it is impossible to conjecture what will happen in a year's time and in the Eighth Isthmian at vv. 12 ff. exactly the same advice is given. In other words, what is at foot is that which circumstances present us with, which it is plausible to infer is another way of speaking of that which comes day by day. In the First Olympian at v. 99 f. Pindar declares that the good which comes day by day is the highest which comes to each of mortal men. The implication of the passage is clearly that any other kind of good is wrong. For these reasons I think that Fränkel's interpretation of τερπνὸν ἐφάμερον is correct, though I have reached that conclusion by a different route from that which he followed.

There are two other instances of the word which Fränkel relegates to an appendix, which should be dealt with here.[30] One of the consequences of the plague at Athens, according to Thucydides, 2.53.2, was that men thought it right to take a speedy enjoyment of that which they possessed as they believed that their bodies and possessions were ἐφήμερα.[31] "Short-lived" or "of a day" makes excellent sense in this context. Antiphon the Sophist, DK 87 B 50, says that the life of men is like a watch for a day (φρουρᾷ ἐφημέρῳ) and is in length like a single day, so to speak (ὡς ἔπος εἰπεῖν), in which we look up to the light and then hand it on to our successors. Fränkel claims that Antiphon uses ὡς ἔπος εἰπεῖν here to apologize for his novel use of ἐφήμερος meaning "short-lived," which Fränkel believes is a late development of the word's use. But what Antiphon is apologizing for is the boldness of his comparison of life to a single

---

[28] Ol. 1.113 f.; 3.43 ff.; Pyth. 10.27 ff.; Nem. 3.19 ff.; 9.45 ff.; Isthm. 4.29 ff.; 6.10 ff.

[29] Ol. 3.43 ff.; Pyth. 3.19 ff.; 3.59 ff.; Nem. 3.30 f.; 3.75; Isthm. 4.29 ff.

[30] Pp. 142–144 = pp. 36–39.

[31] In dealing with this passage and such passages as Eur. Heracl. 866; Diphil. Fr. 45 K.; Men. Fr. 324 Körte, and Plut. Mor. 1090 B, Fränkel (pp. 142 f. = pp. 36 f.) takes ἐφήμερος to mean "unstable," "uncertain," a meaning which he derives from the sense "variable." There is no need to posit such a meaning since it is possible to translate the word in all of these passages as "short-lived." Simonid. Fr. 527 PMG: οὐκ ἔστιν κακὸν/ ἀνεπιδόκητον ἀνθρώποις· ὀλίγῳ δὲ χρόνῳ/ πάντα μεταρρίπτει θεός, compared with Diphil. Fr. 45 K.:

ἀπροσδόκητον οὐδὲν ἀνθρώποις πάθος,
ἐφημέρους γὰρ τὰς τύχας κεκτήμεθα

and with Eur. Heracl. 866, tends to confirm that the word in these passages means "brief."

day. This is the way in which ὡς ἔπος εἰπεῖν is normally used.[32] Antiphon's comparison of life to a day's guard duty which we then hand on to others is of obvious importance in determining why men are called ἐφήμεροι since it lends support to the view that they are so called because man's life was thought to be short.

In sum, what has been argued is that Fränkel has adduced no cogent reason for taking ἐφήμεροι when used of men to mean "creatures who vary as the day" and that the various passages which he brings forward in support of his contention that the basic meaning of the word is "varying as the day" do not in fact provide such support. The conclusions which, I think, should be drawn from the passages which have been analyzed is that ἐφήμερος may mean "by day," "from day to day," and "lasting for a day" and that no priority of meaning can on the basis of the evidence that we possess be assigned to any of these meanings. Even if it were possible to determine what the original sense of the word was, it does not follow that that would be of any help in establishing why men are called ἐφήμεροι.

University of Illinois at Chicago Circle

[32] Kühner-Gerth, *Gr. Gramm.*, 3rd ed., II, p. 508.

3

The Parodos of Aristophanes' *Wasps*

TIMOTHY LONG

Recent criticism has attempted to rehabilitate the evaluation of the construction of Aristophanes' *Wasps*.[1] The great difficulty in defending the quality of the play is the relationship of the first part with its theme of "juryitis" to the second with its attempts to reeducate Philokleon. This essay, however, confines itself to the parodos and is concerned both with a recent suggestion regarding the text which has gained limited acceptance and with demonstrating a dramatic connection between the parodos and the remainder of the first half of the comedy.

The parodos can be divided into four sections. In the first (230–247) the chorus gradually assembles as the koryphaios, accompanied by his son, singles out individual colleagues and urges them to greater speed.[2] It is

---

[1] U. von Wilamowitz-Moellendorff, "Über die Wespen," *SPAW* (1911), 472 (= *Kleine Schriften*, [1935], i, 298), and A. Lesky, *A History of Greek Literature* (New York, 1966), 435, are among the severest critics. P. Mazon, *Essai sur la Composition des Comédies d'Aristophane* (Paris, 1904), 80, is the most enthusiastic of the older critics. Among more recent favorable critics are C. H. Whitman, *Aristophanes and the Comic Hero* (Cambridge, 1964), 156–161; L. Strauss, *Socrates and Aristophanes* (New York and London, 1966), 132–35; D. M. MacDowell, *Aristophanes: Wasps* (Oxford, 1971), 4–7; T. Gelzer, "Aristophanes," *RE*, Sup. 12 (1971), 1449, 27 ff.; J. Vaio, "Aristophanes' Wasps: The Relevance of the Final Scenes," *GRBS*, 12 (1971), 335–351.

[2] Grammatical peculiarities, e.g. 230 and 233, repeated commands and supposed logical disjunctions, as between 239 and 240, 258 and 259, were interpreted at the end of the last century as indications of conversational exchange between individual members of the chorus. Cf. F. Bamberger, *De carminibus Aeschyleis a partibus chori cantatis* (Marburg, 1832); R. Arnoldt, *De choro Aristophanis quaestiones scaenicae* (diss. Königsberg, 1868), 11 ff., and *Die Chorpartien bei Aristophanes* (Leipzig, 1873), 7 ff.; C. Muff, *Über den Vortrag der chorischen Partien bei Aristophanes* (Halle, 1872); G. Hermann, "De choro Vesparum Aristophanis," *Opuscula*, viii (Leipzig, 1877), 253–267; F. G. Allison, "A Proposed Redistribution of Parts in the Parodos of the *Vespae*," *AJPh*, 1 (1880), 402–9; C. Robert, "Zu Aristophanes Wespen," *Hermes*, 44 (1909), 159–160. Wilamowitz, *SPAW*, 486, n. 1,

still dark as the chorus enters and so the son of the koryphaios carries a lamp to light the way. In the second section (248–272) the chorus leader tells his son to trim the lamp. The boy does this clumsily and is scolded and struck by his father. The lad threatens to desert his father and leave him to stumble on his way in the dark if he does not stop his abuse. The father swears he can punish anyone he pleases, and then, in an ironic double-take, he slips in the mud. That mishap occasions a meteorological excursus. He ends his reflections by marveling at Philokleon's absence and calls on his fellow jurors to summon their colleague from the house. The third section (273–290) is the first song of the assembled chorus. They speculate on what may be keeping as dependable and formidable a juror as Philokleon from joining them and then tempt him to participate in the prosecution of another traitor. In the fourth section (291–315) the son asks his father for a present, to which the father at first agrees but then— learning that the son wants ἰσχάδες—refuses.[3] When the son protests that he will no longer accompany his father, the koryphaios reminds the boy that he must support a family of three with his juror's dole. The parodos ends in a paratragic threnody. The son asks his father if the family can buy dinner if the courts do not sit. The father can't guarantee it, and the son answers with a lament from Euripides' *Theseus*, undercut by his father.

---

strongly opposed this "*Chorzersplitterung.*" The phenomena which had led Hermann to derive this theory were not so inconsequential as Wilamowitz would have us believe. They are now explained by maintaining that the chorus does not come into the orchestra as a group but instead slowly assembles there. P. Haendel, *Formen und Darstellungsweisen in der Aristophanischen Komödie* (Heidelberg, 1963), 35: "Die Orchester ist also nicht der Ort des Einzugs, genau genommen, sondern der Ort der Versammlung des Chors, der sich allmählich formiert." See also E. Roos, *Die tragische Orchestik im Zerrbild der altattischen Komödie* (Stockholm, 1951), 151–52.

3 Wilamowitz' paraphrase of 291–294 (*SPAW*, 489) represents the unquestioned interpretation of translators and commentators: "Vater, willst du mir wohl was kaufen?" "Gern, wohl Murmeln?" "Nein, Feigen schmeckt süsser." The boy's answer (ἥδιον γὰρ) can hardly be an acceptable reason for preference if the suggestion made by the father is a set of dice. Where the reading ἀστραγάλους now stands in our text, there was once the accusative plural of the word for some item of food neither so expensive nor sweet as ἰσχάδες. One logical candidate is the last meaning of ἀστράγαλος in Liddell and Scott: a leguminous vegetable. Dioscorides, *De Re Medica* 3, 61, offers ten possibilities for the plant, beginning with ἀστράγαλος· οἱ δὲ ἰσχάδες. Hesychius Alexandrinus, *Lexicon*, ed. K. Latte (Copenhagen, 1963), s.v. ἀστραγαλή, offers another word which would fit: ἀστραγαλή· ἡ τῆς ἴρεως ῥίζα. Theophrastus, *HP*, i, 73, describes the root: ἰδία τῆς ῥίζης φύσις καὶ δύναμις τῆς ἰνδικῆς συκῆς. MacDowell, 175, remarks that the devastation of Attica must have made figs a rarity: "All the same, the fact that the old juror regards them as an expensive luxury is a sign that he is very poor indeed." Either the juror volunteers his son a cheap substitute for ἰσχάδες, or else Aristophanes is playing a pun on the more usual meaning of ἀστράγαλος.

The scene concludes as Philokleon leans out his window and addresses his companions.

The separation of the two dialogues between the father and his son has long been regarded as disturbing.[4] Srebrny has suggested a transposition of verses which would produce one connected dialogue between the two.[5] He maintains that originally the second dialogue between the father and son (291–315) followed immediately upon the meteorological discussion ending at 265, forming one extended conversation. At the end of the dialogue came the remaining tetrameters (266–272) which urge the chorus to call Philokleon from the house. The chorus then sang its invitation to Philokleon to join it (273–290), which was followed immediately by Philokleon's answer (316 ff.). The effect of this alteration is to make the action of the parodos more direct. The chorus enters, there is a continuous conversation between the father and son, the chorus calls its companion from his house, but he answers that he cannot join them. Now this suggested change has found formal support. Russo has pointed out that a metrical pattern typical of Aristophanes' parodoi results from the proposed rearrangement.[6] He observes that in the parodoi of the *Peace* (301–336) and of the *Wealth* (253–289) Aristophanes uses consecutive pairs of "moduli" of eighteen tetrameters. If Srebrny's suggestion is adopted, a somewhat similar pattern will be formed by the tetrameters of 230–247 and 248–265. MacDowell, in his edition of the *Wasps*, does not rearrange the verses of the parodos, but he admits that he was sorely tempted by Srebrny's suggestion and Russo's corroboration.[7]

The objections are more forceful. The chief factor which held Mac-Dowell back from adopting Srebrny's suggestion in his edition was metrical. Verses 230–247 are catalectic iambic tetrameters, but 248–272 are ἀσυνάρτητα Εὐριπίδεια, or syncopated catalectic iambic tetrameters. Unlike the pairs of eighteen tetrameters in the *Wealth* and the *Peace*, the two sections in the *Wasps* would be in different meters. In the end, MacDowell elects to consider the syncopated verses as a unit and not to divide them into two sections.[8]

[4] See E. Brentano, *Untersuchungen über das griechische Drama* (Frankfurt, 1871), 178, and J. van Leeuwen, *Aristophanis Vespae* (Leiden, 1893), ad loc.

[5] S. Srebrny, "Aristophanea," *Eos*, 50 (1959/60), 44–45, independently of van Leeuwen.

[6] C. F. Russo, "Le Vespe Spaginate e un Modulo di Tetrametri 18 × 2," *Belfagor*, 23 (1968), 317–24.

[7] MacDowell, 169. F. Perusino, *Il Tetrametro Giambico Catalettico* (Rome, 1968), 35, n. 1, accepts Srebrny's and Russo's suggestion.

[8] On the syncopated iambic tetrameter catalectic see *Hephaestionis Enchiridion*, ed. M. Consbruch (Leipzig, 1906), 53, 5–11; A. Rossbach and R. Westphal, *Metrik der Griechen* (Leipzig, 1867), 203; Wilamowitz, *Griechische Verskunst* (Berlin, 1921), 231.

That is a commendable decision, but there are other reasons as well for retaining the text as transmitted. Philokleon's answer to the chorus is difficult to reconcile to this interpretation (φίλοι, τήκομαι μὲν πάλαι . . ., 316–317). Πάλαι is disastrous for Srebrny's argument. Philokleon has in fact heard the chorus and has been listening, and there is evidence in the text that he does not answer when he first hears himself being called. Moreover, this is consistent with the dramaturgy of the parodos in Aristophanes. As has been mentioned, the great virtue of the proposed change would be that the action of the parodos would become more direct; however, the action of the Aristophanic parodos is often neither logical nor direct. In the *Acharnians*, the chorus enters at 240 and declares its intention to attack the man who would betray his city and strike a separate treaty (235), but when Dikaiopolis actually appears (241), the chorus postpones its attack and lies in ambuscade until 280, while its enemy's family conducts its procession. Similarly, the chorus in the *Wealth* comes on the scene to be informed by Kario that his master is going to restore the sight of *Wealth* (257–289), but then the theme of the play is interrupted by the kind of interlude that is typical in the action of the parodos. Kario and the chorus alternate in verses of a parody first of Kyklops and his goats, then of Kirke and her man-swine (290–321). After that episode, the chorus returns to the theme of wealth for a few lines (322–334) before Blepsidemos enters. It follows that we should not expect one course of action to be carried straight through the parodos. Instead, the entry of the chorus and the father's conversation with his son may well be interrupted and taken up again, the call of Philokleon from his house may, by parallel with other models, at first remain unanswered and only yield results after some delay.

More important than these metrical and dramaturgic considerations is the question whether the parodos has any function in the play other than that of supplying an entrance for the chorus and a choral interlude to separate the prologue from the first agon. Wilamowitz' opinion still holds

---

J. W. White, *The Verse of Greek Comedy* (London, 1912), 231, nn. 1 and 2, lists nine examples. O. Schroeder, *Aristophanis Cantica* (Leipzig, 1909), gave in addition *Ach.* 1210, now discounted. I would suggest adding to White's examples *Clouds* 1114 and 1212, *Birds* 635, and *Peace* 1023. MacDowell is correct in keeping the verses as a unit. These verses represent by far the bulk of the examples of this meter in all of Aristophanes. The most unusual feature of *Wasps* 248–272 is that here we have twenty-five of these syncopated meters uninterrupted, one after another, and in a dialogue. The longest other single passage in this meter is *Frogs* 441–444, with only four verses. Verses 248–272 should be regarded as a unique metrical phenomenon, and on these grounds be allowed to remain a unit.

as the standard position on this point: "Die Parodos, die freilich mit der Handlung so wenig zu tun hat wie mit dem Wespenkostüm des Chores, ist ein Kleinod aristophanischer Kunst. . . ."[9]

The clue to this relationship lies in the use of the young boys who accompany the chorus during their entrance.[10] There are many choruses of old men in Aristophanes, but this is the only one which needs the assistance of juveniles. I should like to suggest that the use of the sons to escort their fathers creates a comic symbol of the central thrust and inspiration behind the play. At the midpoint of his career Aristophanes played with the theme of adult education. The comic paradox of the *Wasps* consists in the fact that it is the son who reforms and then instructs his father, the son who sees clearly the evils to which his father is blind, and the parodos is a concrete analogue for this central improbability. The physical infirmity of the jurors and their inability to find their own way represent both the results of and the reasons for the abuse which they receive from the demagogues, and their need for guides reflects their abject dependence and reliance. The sons of the chorus are attempting the same difficult task as Bdelykleon: to lead and guide their fathers. Their age, however, does not permit them Bdelykleon's more forceful actions in his attempts to aid Philokleon. For the imagery of the play, the important element in the entrance of the chorus is not the old men's speed but their misdirection, and the attempts of their sons to convert it.

This is in direct contradiction to the interpretation put on the character of the boys by Wilamowitz. He views them not as faithful guides who stay with the old men despite cantankerous refusals and beatings, but as scamps bent on mischief who deceive their fathers. Tangled in the manuscript difficulties around βόρβορος (259) and the problem of the meteorological ramblings which follow, he decides that the son has simply played the father for a fool once again: "Vortrefflich wie der Junge dem Alten bloss

9 Wilamowitz, *SPAW*, 314–315.

10 K. J. Dover, *Aristophanic Comedy* (London, 1972), 124 and 134, remarks that the use of boy singers and juvenile parts was a popular practice of drama in the 420s. C. Beer, *Über die Zahl der Schauspieler bei Aristophanes* (Leipzig, 1844), 49–50, suggested that there were only three boys, and identified them with the sons of Karkinos who appear at the end of the play. Wilamowitz, *SPAW*, 476, n. 1, drew attention to the fact that they are sent away later, ostensibly to fetch Kleon, but in fact to take away the cloaks which their fathers have shed. That seems to imply a larger number, and conjectures vary. J. Richter, *Aristophanis Vespae* (Berlin, 1858), 62: "sive tres sive quattuor sive quattuordecem"; Gelzer, 1450: "mindestens drei"; MacDowell, 19, vacillates; C. F. Russo, *Aristofane Autore di Teatro* (Florence, 1962), 197, offers a number and a reason for the boys' presence: "Questi fanciulli, che saranno almeno tre, hanno tecnicamente la funzione di animare la non aggressiva parodo dei vecchi coreuti."

einen Schabernack gespielt hat. . . ."[11] It is true that the son demonstrates boyish irresponsibility in the trimming of the lamp, but his father immediately reprimands him, showing that he, unlike Strepsiades, is slave to neither servant nor son. The son's threat to desert is idle, and a few lines later he warns his father of the mud on the street. Despite earcuffs, the refusal of their requests, and displays of magnificent nastiness by their fathers, the boys remain to lead them, until they are sent to fetch Kleon (409), their last dutifully performed act. This is not at all like another Aristophanic son, Pheidippides, who, when he threatens to leave his father, is as good as his word. Bdelykleon, Pheidippides, and these boys constitute the entire genus *filius* in Aristophanes, and if, as is the case with Pheidippides and the sons in the parodos, they irritate their fathers at one moment and come to their aid the next, and if their assistance ends as an annoyance, the fault lies not with them but is the outcome of their fathers' delusions.

There is also a technical relationship between the parodos and the remainder of the play. The parodos supplies the concrete justification for the argument in the agon which Aristophanes supports. When Philokleon delivers his epirrhema (548–619) he uses as a general outline the passage of the juror's day, and attempts to prove that the juror lives a life fit for a king. The juror's greatest pleasures are contained in the last section of the speech (605–620), emphasized by the fact that Philokleon almost forgets them (οὗ 'γὼ 'πελελήσμην . . ., 605). His triumph is his family's welcome when he returns with his three obols. His daughter and wife kiss and feed him, and the reason for the warmth of their reception is the money he brings with him. Of this he will not be deprived. Bdelykleon's rebuttal (650–718) is a tissue of economic chauvinism. He disregards the earlier parts of his father's discourse and concentrates on this last section. He suggests that the old man compute the total income of the city and then compare the pittance which the jurors receive. The reason for the discrepancy is, of course, the same rapacious demagoguery which Philokleon himself supports. The son ends his speech with a picture of what the financial condition of the jurors could be.

---

11 Wilamowitz, *SPAW*, 488. The same attitude is found in V. Coulon, *Aristophane* (Paris, 1948), 1, xvi. The notion that the boy deceives his father derives from the fact that the Ravennas reads βόρβορος and the Venetus βάρβαρος. Hermann, 257, suggested that μάρμαρος was the correct original reading, and was supported by Wilamowitz. F. Nencini, "Appunti aristofaneschi," *SIFC*, 1 (1920), 106–107, puts forward a startling explanation for μάρμαρος, but one which can only be supported when the word πέλεθος is also present. R. Cantarella, *Aristophanis Comoediae* (Milan, 1954) and MacDowell both dismiss Hermann's conjecture. See also Srebrny, 42, n. 1; A. von Bamberg, *De Ravennate et Veneto Aristophanis codicibus* (Bonn, 1865), 32.

What we have in the parodos is the proof that Philokleon is deluded in his self-conception, and that Bdelykleon is correct.[12] The other jurors resemble Philokleon in all things save one: his apparent affluence, or at least his son's. From Philokleon's mouth we hear only once of financial hardship, in verse 171 when he says that he must take the mule to market and sell it because it is the first of the month and the bills are at hand. That is pure ruse, another trick for the advocate's menace to escape confinement. For dramatic purposes Aristophanes has had to make Philokleon unaware of the financial miseries which his colleagues suffer. Philokleon's conception of his own life and the actual life of the other jurors—the rhetorical construct and the economic reality—are as different as light and dark, Sybaris and Akharnai. A recent critic portrays the sons of the parodos as willing accomplices in their fathers' symbiosis with the demagogues.[13] But Philokleon's picture of his daughter's reaction to his return and his reception by his wife is illusory; the boy's complaint at the end of the parodos is the accurate portrayal of the familial condition. The parodos is the dramatic method by which Aristophanes underlines the economic folly of the litigious, and to do it requires a concrete picture vivid enough to overpower the self-aggrandizing misconception of Philokleon and his fellow fathers.[14]

Indiana University

[12] Aristophanes frequently arms his favored principal in the agon with corroborating evidence from the earlier action of the play. For example, in the *Knights* one of the servants tells the other that the Paphlagonian has stolen a tidbit called Pylos (54–57). Kleon is sure to throw that accomplishment, that is, the servant's, up in the face of the Sausage Seller in the agon, and he inevitably does (836–840). The force of his contention has already been destroyed by what the audience learns listening to the prologue.

[13] Strauss, 115–116: "Although the insufficient lighting as well as the gnawing hunger give rise to a heated exchange between one of the wasps and his son, father and son are at peace with each other. The ordinary old juryman and his son, in contradistinction to Philokleon and his son, need each other; the child would starve without his father's earning the juryman's pay, and the father would not be able to earn that pay without the help of the child carrying the lamp."

[14] Some of the material in this essay is from my dissertation *The Parodos and Agon of Aristophanes' Vespae* (Princeton, 1971).

4

The Problematic Mention of Hippocrates
in Plato's *Phaedrus*[1]

HANS HERTER

Σ. Ψυχῆς οὖν φύσιν ἀξίως λόγου κατανοῆσαι οἴει δυνατὸν εἶναι ἄνευ τῆς τοῦ ὅλου φύσεως; Φ. Εἰ μὲν Ἱπποκράτει γε τῷ τῶν Ἀσκληπιαδῶν δεῖ τι πιθέσθαι, οὐδὲ περὶ σώματος ἄνευ τῆς μεθόδου ταύτης (*Phaedr.*, 270 C). "Do you believe that it is possible to know, in a measure worth mentioning, the nature of the soul without (knowing) the nature of the whole? . . . If one must trust Hippocrates the Asclepiadean, such understanding even of the body is not possible without this method."

This often discussed passage (perhaps too often) raises the question of its relation to the extant Corpus of the Hippocratics. For more than a century no progress has been made on this question, if we give credence to the complaints of R. Joly, who in a recent publication proposed a "modeste tentative" in order to reconcile the factions.[2] It seemed obvious that a

[1] This paper was read first in Freiburg im Breisgau and in Graz and then, in an enlarged form, at Princeton and in Urbana. I am greatly indebted to Professors Homer A. Thompson and Luitpold Wallach for having improved the English version of the paper, and I am deeply obliged to my American friends, especially at the Institute at Princeton and the National Endowment for the Humanities, for the generous hospitality which my wife and I enjoyed during three months in 1973. I also recall with gratitude the delightful weeks we spent at the University of Illinois in Urbana.

[2] R. Joly, *Rev. ét. anc.* 58, 1956, 204 ff. (Joly[1]) and (more cautiously) *Rev. ét. gr.* 74, 1961, 69 ff. (Joly[2]), compare *Recherches sur le traité pseudo-hippocratique du régime*, Paris, 1960, 183 f. For his solution compare note 54 below. Lit. see Joly[2], 69 ff., continuing A. Diès, *Autour de Platon* 1, Paris, 1927, 24 ff. (compare 425, 3). H. Cherniss, *Lustrum* 4, 1959, 139 ff. A. Hellwig, *Untersuchungen zur Theorie der Rhetorik bei Platon und Aristoteles* (Hypomnemata 38), Gött., 1973, 181 ff. Moreover, A. Nelson, *Die Hippokratische Schrift περὶ φυσῶν*, Diss. Upps., 1909, 91 ff. E. Hoffmann, Annex to E. Zeller's *Philosophie der Griechen* 2, 1[5], 1922, 1072 ff. A.-J. Festugière, *Hippocrate. L'ancienne Médecine*, Par., 1948, 62 ff., 74. Compare now M. Isnardi Parente, in E. Zeller-R. Mondolfo, *La filosofia greca*, 2.3.1, Florence, 1974, 494 ff.

witness as early as Plato testifies to an authentic idea of the genuine Hippocrates. Already the famous *philologus inter medicos*, Émile Littré, has used the testimony of Plato in order to ascribe the interesting essay on Ancient medicine to the celebrated chief of the Coan school himself.[3] Later on individual scholars continued to make their own choice of single treatises or groups of treatises in the *Corpus Hippocraticum*, convinced that these treatises and no others were closely connected with the method described by Plato and therefore authentic.[4] In the present century scholars at first became more cautious and ceased identifying Plato's statement with a fixed original.[5] Subsequently, however, the treatises

[3] Edition 1, 295 ff. (2, p. XV f.; XXXIV ff.; 214; 4, p. 656 ff., 1; 7, p. XI). Against Littré F. Z. Ermerins, *Allgemeine Literatur-Zeitung*, Halle, 1839, 3, 220 ff. *Hippocratis reliquiae* 2, Utr., 1862, p. XXVIII ff. Appreciation of Littré's work Diès, *loc. cit.*, who shows how in the course of time Littré withdrew from Plato's testimony. Th. Gomperz, *Phil.* 70, 1911, 213 ff. = *Hellenika* 2, Leipz., 1912, 324 ff. (*Anz. Akad. Wien*, Philos.-hist. Kl., 47, 1910, 22 f.), tried again, on the strength of new arguments, to identify the method of the Platonic Hippocrates with the reasoning of the author of Π. ἀ. λ. in ch. 20, on which already Littré had relied, only to find many opponents, especially W. Capelle, *Herm.* 57, 1922, 247 ff. (compare F. Tocco, *Atene e Roma* 14, 1911, 70 ff.; H. Gossen, *PW* 8, 1814; more favorably F. E. Kind, *Burs. Jahresber.* 158, 1912, 141 ff.). Finally, F. Steckerl, *Class. Phil.* 40, 1945, 166 ff., renewed the view of Littré, starting from Meno's report. P. Kucharski too, *Rev. ét. gr.* 52, 1939, 301 ff., allowed for Π. ἀ. λ. (compare note 32 below); likewise C. Fredrich, *Hippokratische Untersuchungen*, Berl., 1899, 6; A. Palm, *Studien zur Hippokratischen Schrift περὶ διαίτης*, Tüb., 1933, 106; W. Jaeger, *Paideia* 2, Berl., 1944, 34; R. Hackforth, *Plato's Phaedrus translated with Introduction and Commentary*, Cambr., 1952, ²1972, 151; J. S. Morrison, *Class. Quart.*, N. S. 8, 1958, 216; G. Cambiano, *Riv. Filos.* 57, 1966, 284 ff. (compare note 32 below); also H. Nohl, *Sokrates und die Ethik*, Tüb., 1904 (Diss. Berl., 1904), 45 ff., who accepts Π. ἀ. λ. as genuine (on p. 39) with Ed. Meyer, *Gesch. d. Alt.* 4, 207; 210 f. (4, 1⁵, 846, 1; 851 f.). See H. Herter, *Sudh. Arch.* 47, 1963, 276, 3 (*Kleine Schriften*, Münch., 1975, 199, 87). Hellwig 182, 14a (sub a and b).

[4] Π. ἀ. ὑ. τ. was proposed by Ermerins (1839) and Chr. Petersen, *Hippocratis nomine quae circumferuntur scripta ad temporum rationes disposita* 1, Hamb., 1839 (with *Epid.* I; III and *Aph.*, sect. 3); Π. φύσ. ἀνθρ. was suggested by F. S. Meixner, *Neue Prüfung der Echtheit und Reihenfolge sämmtlicher Schriften Hippokrates des Grossen* 1, 1 and 2, Münch., 1836–1837; W. H. Thompson, *The Phaedrus of Plato with English Notes and Dissertations*, Lond., 1868. F. Poschenrieder, *Die platonischen Dialoge in ihrem Verhältnisse zu den hippokratischen Schriften*, Progr. Metten, 1882; Π. ἑβδ. instead was preferred by J. Ilberg, *Griechische Studien H. Lipsius dargebracht*, Leipz., 1894, 26 ff., and with emphasis by W. H. Roscher, *Über Alter, Ursprung und Bedeutung der hippokratischen Schrift von der Siebenzahl*, Leipz., 1911, 116 f.; *Die hippokratische Schrift von der Siebenzahl*, Paderb., 1913, 99 ff.; 117.

[5] Fredrich, 1 ff. (H. Schöne, *GGA*, 1900, 654); H. Diels, *DLZ* 1899, 13; *Herm.* 45, 1910, 126; *SB Berl.* 1910, 1140 ff.; J. Ilberg, *Neue Jahrb.* 13, 1904, 406 f.; U. v. Wilamowitz, *SB Berl.* 1901, 15; 23; *Platon* 1², Berl., 1920, 462; F. E. Kind, *Burs. Jahresber.* 158, 1912, 141 ff.; 180, 1919, 5 ff.; H. Gossen, *PW* 8, 1810; Nelson, *l. c.*; J. Geffcken, *Griechische Literaturgeschichte* 1, Heid., 1926, 268; 2, 1934, 119; Jaeger 2, 34; J. L. Heiberg, *Einleitung in die Altertumswissenschaft* 2², 1912, 424; *Geschichte der Mathematik und Naturwissenschaften,*

Π. ἀέρων ὑδάτων τόπων and Π. ἱρῆς νούσου (and several others), the so-
called meteorological group of the Corpus, as well as Plato again presumably furnished proof of the real views of Hippocrates.[6] But the problem is not finished: even at the present time, which works of the great
Coan[7] are genuine is a point at issue.

In the meantime the problem as to the passage of the *Phaedrus* has become more complicated. L. Edelstein[8] eliminated it by changing the
interpretation of the expression τὸ ὅλον, as had been done previously by
some scholars and long ago by Hermias. Hitherto most readers had taken
"the whole" in the sense of "universe." Thus they understood the passage
to mean "it is not possible to know the nature of the soul or of the body
without knowing the nature of the universe."[9] Edelstein, however, was of

---

Münch., 1960, 94; W. H. S. Jones, *Proceed. Brit. Acad.* 1945, 104 f.; 118 f.; *Hippocrates with
an English Translation* 1, Lond., 1957, XXXIII ff.; compare *Philosophy and Medicine in
Ancient Greece*, Baltimore, 1946, 16 ff.; already Ermerins, in his edition, *loc. cit.* (compare
note 62 below). M. Wellmann, *Burs. Jahresber.*, Suppl. 124, 1905, 147, denied any publications of Hippocrates (for some time also Wilamowitz), but he changed his mind in
Herm. 64, 1929, 16 ff.

[6] K. Deichgräber, *Die Epidemien und das Corpus Hippocraticum*, Berl., 1933, 149 ff.;
compare Wellmann, *Herm., loc. cit.*, and Palm, 102; M. Pohlenz, *Hippokrates*, Berl., 1938,
74 ff.; F. Robert (see Cherniss, 140). Nestle, compare note 10 below; Hellwig 182, 14a
(sub d). Formerly I myself had the meteorological aspect in view (*Ciba-Zeitschrift* 8, nr. 85,
1957, 2819 ff.).

[7] Finally, L. Bourgey, *Observation et expérience chez les médecins de la Collection hippocratique*, Par., 1953, 88 ff. (compare 196, 1), restored a fair harmony of the Platonic
passage with the Π. ἀ. ἰ. and the meteorological group, even with all the rational treatises
of the *Corpus*. Similarly M. Vegetti, *Riv. Crit. Stor. Filos.* 21, 1966, 37 ff.

[8] Περὶ ἀέρων *und die Sammlung der hippokratischen Schriften*, Berl., 1931, 118 ff.; 129 ff.
(*PW*, Suppl. 6, 1318 ff.; *Amer. J. Phil.* 61, 1940, 226 ff. = *Ancient Medicine*, Balt., 1967,
116 ff.). Against (Gomperz and) Edelstein argues A. Rehm (–K. Vogel), *Einleitung in die
Altertumswissenschaft* 2, 5⁴, Leipz.-Berl., 1933, 26; further compare Palm, 104, 22; Jaeger,
2, 365, 54. Hellwig, 186 ff., discusses Edelstein's view within the frame of the entire
dialogue (compare Pohlenz, *Hippokrates* 114, n. 1 to p. 75).

[9] Galenus, *CMG* 5, 9, 1 p. 55, 16; compare 53, 26. Littré, 1, 298 ff. Hier. Müller,
Translation, Leipz., 1854; K. Lehrs, *Translation*, Leipz., 1869; B. Jowett, *Translation*, 1871;
Ilberg, *l.c.* and *Neue Jahrb.* 13, 1904, 406; Gomperz and Diels, *l.c.*; Roscher, *l.c.*; Gossen,
loc. cit.; C. Ritter, *Translation*, Leipz., 1914, 139 f., 131; and *Inhaltsdarstellung, Jahresber.*
Tüb., 1913–1914, 13 (*Platon* 2, 40); H. v. Arnim, *Platos Jugenddialoge*, Leipz.-Berl., 1914,
218 f.; M. Pohlenz, *Herm.* 53, 1918, 404 ff. (*Kleine Schriften* 2, Hild., 1965, 157 ff.); *Der
hellenische Mensch*, Gött., 1947, 175 f.; *Hippokrates*, 74 ff.; Wilamowitz, *Platon* 1², 462;
Hoffmann, 1082 ff.; Capelle, 251 f.; 256; *passim*; F. Überweg and K. Prächter, *Die
Philosophie des Altertums*¹², Berl., 1926, 282; J. Stenzel, *Platon der Erzieher*, Leipz., 1928,
248; Wellmann, *Herm.* 64, 1929, 21; J. Mewaldt, *DLZ* 1932, 258; L. Robin, *Platon
Oeuvres complètes* 4, 3, Par., 1933, XLVII. CXLVIII f.; Deichgräber, 149 ff.; H. Wanner,
Studien zu Περὶ ἀρχαίης ἰητρικῆς, Diss. Zür., 1939, 75 ff.; Kucharski, *loc. cit.*; Jaeger,
Paideia 2, 33 f.; 365, 54; 3, 1947, 266; A. M. Frenkian, *La méthode hippocratique dans le*

the opinion that τὸ ὅλον is nothing but the whole of the soul or the whole of the body. Now Plato's meaning was that it is not possible to know the nature of the soul without the whole of the soul, or the nature of the body without the whole of the body.[10] Consequently, we are faced with a dilemma, and the meaning of Plato's words for the Hippocratic question changes according to our choice. Therefore, the sense of the passage is not a Hippocratic problem but falls under the jurisdiction of the Platonists. We must explain the statement of Plato within the context of the dialogue, irrespective of the Hippocratics.

When we follow further discussion of Socrates and Phaedrus, we get at first sight the impression that Plato nowhere considers the universe. Thus Edelstein's interpretation seems acceptable. The true orator who wishes to influence the soul of the hearer cannot dispense with the knowledge of the whole of that soul, and the true physician must know the nature of the

---

Phèdre de Platon, Bucarest, 1941. Diller, *Gnom.* 18, 1942, 84, 1 (*Kleine Schriften zur antiken Medizin*, Berl., 1973, 205, 68); *Herm.* 80, 1952, 406 f. (67 f.); *Jahrb. Akad. Wiss. Lit. Mainz* 1959, 275 f. (93 f.); Festugière, 62 ff.; O. Regenbogen, *Miscellanea academica Berolinensia* 2, 1, 1950, 212 f.; Bourgey, 90; 91, 1; Joly[1], 205 ff.; J[2]., 79 ff.; Herter, *Ciba-Ztschr.*, *loc. cit.*, 2819. Sudh. *Arch.* 42, 1958, 85; Morrison, *Class. Quart.* 52, 1958, 216; P. Friedländer, *Platon*[2] 3, Berl., 1960, 218 f. (with n. 29 on p. 469); D. Mannsperger, *Physis bei Platon*, Berl., 1969, 62; 98; 260; Cl. Gaudin, *Rev. ét. anc.* 72, 1970, 340 ff.; Hellwig, 182 ff. "Weltganzes" Geffcken 2, 119 (but according to Democritus). Several authors confine the ὅλον to the environment, see note 53 below.

[10] Hermias, in *Phaedr.*, p. 245, 5 ff. Couvreur; H. N. Fowler, *Translation*, Lond.-New York, 1913; Edelstein, *loc. cit.*; Abel Rey, *Thalès* 2, 1935, 48 f.; *La science dans l'antiquité* 3 (*La maturité de la pensée scientifique en Grèce*), Par., 1939, 435 ff.; W. Kranz, *Phil.* 96, 1944, 193 ff. (*Studien zur antiken Literatur und ihrem Fortwirken*, Heid., 1967, 315 ff.); *Empedokles*, Zür., 1949, 351, 10; *Kosmos* 1, Bonn, 1955, 41 f., 23; W. J. Verdenius, *Mnem.*, Ser. 4, vol. 8, 1955, 286; G. Cambiano, *Riv. Filos.* 57, 1966, 284 ff. (compare note 32 below); G. J. de Vries, *A Commentary on the Phaedrus of Plato*, Amst., 1969, 234 f.; compare Hellwig, 183, 16a. G. M. A. Grube, *Plato's Thought*, Lond., 1935, 213 f., thinks of the individual souls and bodies; Hackforth, 149 ff., of the human soul and body generally. Steckerl, 167, paraphrasizes: "the whole somatic sphere"; still this sphere reaches to the heaven. The same holds good for the "Gesamtnatur" (Gomperz) or for the *physis* "in general" (Morrison). Less clearly Fredrich, 3 f.; 8 (compare Pohlenz, *Herm.*, *loc. cit.*, 405, 1; 406 f. = *Kl. Schr.* 2, 158, 1; 158 f.). W. Nestle, *Herm.* 73, 1938, 17 ff. (*Griechische Studien*, Stuttg., 1948, 538 ff.); *Vom Mythos zum Logos*[2], Stuttg., 1942, 232 f., believes that the ὅλον in itself denotes the special whole, and only indirectly ("mittelbar") has the meaning of exceeding the σῶμα. Likewise Nohl, 45 ff.; Palm, 102 ff.; Friedländer, 469, 29; P. Mesnard, *Rev. thomiste* 54, 1954, 145 f.; H. Kesters, *Tijdschr. voor filosofie* 26, 1964, 53, 31; P. Plass, *Symb. Osl.* 43, 1968, 16, 10; M. Vegetti, *Riv. crit. stor. filos.* 24, 1969, 17 ff. Kl. Oehler has expressed a similar opinion in the discussion of my paper at Princeton. Restriction of the sense "étude de toute la nature" to the sense "étude de toute nature," according to Diès, 429. J.-H. Kühn, *System- und Methodenprobleme im Corpus Hippocraticum*, Wiesb., 1956, 84 ff., interprets τὸ ὅλον in both directions.

whole of the body. When we remember that previously there had been
discussion of the "great" *technai* generally, the analogy continues, and we
would say with Edelstein that the technician must attain a "general conception of the object he treats" ("eine Allgemeinvorstellung von dem
behandelten Gegenstand"), but not at once of the universe. The common
usage of the word τὸ ὅλον is not against this view, because the term can
signify not only the *cosmos* but also a special whole, if that relationship
emerges from the context.[11]

But we do not get off so easily. Not by chance have most readers in
modern times—and likewise the ancients—understood the whole to mean
"the universe." K. Deichgräber was right in censuring the tautology[12]
which results from Edelstein's conception: it is impossible to know the
nature of the soul without knowing the nature of the whole soul! The
nature of the soul is identical, or nearly identical, with the nature of the
whole soul! Furthermore, τὸ ὅλον, as Edelstein takes it, does not occur
again in the following discussion.

On the other hand, when we go backward in the context, we find a point
of contact for τὸ ὅλον as equal to "universe," although here also the matter
is not without difficulties.[13] Socrates (269 E–270) explicitly declares that
all the "great" *technai*, insofar as they would rise above the level of a mere
routine (τριβή), need something he calls ἀδολεσχία καὶ μετεωρολογία
φύσεως πέρι (idle talk and "meteorology" about nature).[14] This is im-

[11] Edelstein, 131, 1; Hackforth, 150, 2; C. M. J. Sicking, *Mnem.* 16, 1963, 225 ff.;
Joly[2], 83, 2; Hellwig, 187 f., 26; 202, 67. Deichgräber, 151, shows that here τὸ ὅλον, if
unaffected, can mean only the universe; Edelstein's interpretation would require such
an exact expression as: ἡ τοῦ ὅλου τῆς ψυχῆς φύσις or sim. (Rehm, *loc. cit.*; Joly[2] 83, 1).
For ὅλος see H. J. Kraemer, *Arete bei Platon und Aristoteles*, Heid., 1959, 138 (especially in
Aristoteles) and K. S. Wallach, *Glotta* 45, 1967, 23 ff. Cambiano, 287 ff., asserts (erro-
neously) that Plato does not use τὸ ὅλον as universe but in quotations (*Lys.* 214 B, and
Gorg. 508 A); thus he eliminates the naturalistic interpretation in our passage. *Charm.*
156 BC has been compared since Littré and Thompson (Edelstein, II. ἀέρων 131, 1;
Frenkian, 18; 36; I. Düring, *Aristoteles*, Heid., 1966, 416 f., 103); but this passage is at
most an adequate parallel for Edelstein's view (Festugière, 64 f.; Hackforth 150, 2).
Compare note 35 below.   [12] Kühn, 88, 1; 92; Hellwig, 191, 32.

[13] Pohlenz, *Hipp.* 74 ff.; Joly[1], 205 f.; Joly[2], 79 ff.; Hellwig, 188 ff. Nevertheless, Joly[2],
82 f., suspects in 270 B "un léger détour de la pensée."

[14] Gomperz deleted καὶ μετεωρολογία, but the combination is confirmed by Plut.,
Pericl. 5 (τῆς λεγομένης μετεωρολογίας καὶ μεταρσιολεσχίας), compare Diels, *SB Berl.* 1910,
1141, 1. Formerly the words φύσεως πέρι were believed spurious (Pohlenz, *Hipp.* 78), and
Diels would read ἀδολεσχίας φύσεως πέρι καὶ μετεωρολογίας (compare Capelle, 251, 2;
252, 1; Joly[2], 81 f.); Kranz, 193 (315), also was of the opinion that the addition φύσεως
πέρι was incompatible with μετεωρολογία, if understood in the proper sense (compare
note 17 below). But φύσεως πέρι is tolerable because it belongs to both of the substantives
(compare Capelle, 251, 2).

portant concerning rhetoric and medicine. The two expressions are derogatory, the one quite unequivocally, the other provisionally. These expressions correspond to the limited horizon of the people and are used by Socrates with an ironical smile. He is hinting at the narrow grasp of the many, in order to stress the needs of the arts which he advocates himself; for what the people despise is in fact correct.[15] In Plato's Politicus the inventive technician is called μετεωρολόγος ἀδολέσχης τις σοφιστής, clearly, likewise from the vulgar viewpoint, and in the Cratylus, 401 B, also the creators of language are denoted as μετεωρολόγοι καὶ ἀδολέσχαι but not φαῦλοι.[16] We do not want to speak of the ἀδολέσχαι, but the μετεωρολόγοι are important for our argument. They go beyond the earth to the sublunar phenomena and do not confine themselves to the whole of the human soul or body.[17]

Further on we hear that Pericles advanced greatly in the art of oratory when he began frequenting the school of Anaxagoras and perceived the nature of νοῦς. He was acquiring not oratory, but something additional from outside, and that was just the μετεωρολογία φύσεως πέρι.[18] The νοῦς which Anaxagoras brought into philosophy was not the human,[19] but the

[15] Edelstein, 132 ff.; Festugière, 63; Kühn, 86; Mannsperger, 255 ff. Compare Ritter, Translation, 139; 129. See now G. J. de Vries, Mededel. Ned. Akad., Afd. Letterk., N.R. 38, 1 (1975) 15 f.

[16] Otherwise babblers are despised by Plato (compare also Erast. 132 B). See Hellwig, 117; 196 f.; also H.-G. Ingenkamp, Plutarchs Schriften über die Heilung der Seele, Gött., 1971, 126. In our passage ἀδολεσχία is dismissed, but μετεωρολογία is retained in its positive sense.

[17] Edelstein's view is endangered by μετεωρολογία (Capelle, 251 f.; less so, Deichgräber, 149,2). Therefore, he understood it (p. 134) in a metaphorical sense: "in die Höhe steigende Untersuchung" (similarly, I suppose, Steckerl, 169,2); so also Wilamowitz, Griechisches Lesebuch 2, 2⁴, Berl., 1923, 230: "verstiegene Erhabenheit" (Hackforth, 150, "high-flown speculation" or "tall-talk"; Kranz, 193 f. [315 f.]: "erhabene Redeweise"). Already F. Schleiermacher had translated: "etwas von jenem spitzfindigen und hochfliegenden Geschwätz." Against these attempts Joly¹, 205 f.; Joly², 81 f. The word retains the connection with the real μετέωρα; see generally Capelle, Phil. 71, 1912, 414 ff. (PW, Suppl. 6, 315 ff.); Kucharski, 310,1; H. Erbse, Herm., 82, 1954, 405 ff.; H.-J. Newiger, Metapher und Allegorie, Münch., 1957, 55 ff.; 63 ff.; Herter, Sudh. Arch. 47, 1963, 271 (Kl. Schr., 195); Cl. Gaudin, Rev. ét. anc. 72, 1970, 332 ff. C. W. Müller, Die Kurzdialoge der Appendix Platonica, Münch., 1975, 62 f. Compare note 21 below.

[18] Anaxag. A 15 D.-Kr. and Lanza. The remark is not critical (so Bourgey, 94 f., 4), nor ironical (so Steckerl and others), nor "half playful" (so A. E. Taylor, Plato, Lond., 1926, 314,2; likewise Jaeger, 2, 33, and others). Mannsperger, 255 ff., finds in it polemic irony against the insufficiency of Anaxagoras and Pericles. "Selbstironie," de Vries, 233 (compare Friedländer, 469,30). See Kucharski, 319 f.; Hellwig, especially 195 ff.

[19] Hackforth, 150 f., and Kranz, 195 (316 f.), hypothetically. Kühn, 86 f., credits Anaxagoras with diaeresis; compare Edelstein, PW, loc. cit., 1320. Compare also G. E. J. Mooren, Plutarchus' leven van Pericles, Diss. Nijm., 1948, 113; E. Meinhardt, Perikles bei Plutarch, Diss. Frankf., 1957, 26 ff.; 77 f.; 86 f.

cosmic intellect.[20] Plato often includes cosmology in meteorology.[21] With this we are in the sphere of the "universe," which he mentions a little later in the passage we are discussing.

It must be conceded that the cosmological element does not extend throughout the entire discussion of the dialogue; it emerges incidentally here and there.[22] Therefore, we might renew our doubts concerning the significance of τὸ ὅλον and thus find ourselves again at our starting point. We would get then into the circle of extracting the true Hippocrates from the Platonic passage and then explaining this same passage by the *Corpus Hippocraticum*.[23] Ought we to end by accepting Edelstein's interpretation, as some scholars have done, for instance G. J. de Vries in his recent commentary on the *Phaedrus*?[24] The problem cannot be solved definitively unless help is available from the outside; we need, so to speak, an Archimedian point to move the question.

In fact, there is a passage in another dialogue of Plato, namely, in the *Timaeus*, not in the great cosmological exposition of the Pythagorean Timaeus, but in the report on Atlantis and primeval Athens made by Critias, who himself is relying on Solon's report which purports to have been brought from Egypt. The passage has been overlooked by the interpreters of the *Phaedrus* because it is outside of their purview. I have often read the passage myself without thinking of the parallel in the *Phaedrus*, and I have read the *Phaedrus* without thinking of the *Timaeus* passage. Add to this the fact that the passage in question is not dealing with Hippocrates but with the old Egyptians. It is the priest of Sais who speaks and explains to his listener Solon that 8,000 years ago Athena had founded in Egypt an establishment corresponding to the establishment which she had inspired the old Athenians to set up a thousand years earlier, that is, 9,000 years ago. In proof of this statement Plato enumerates three relics from early times, namely: (1) the constitution of the three estates (professions), (2) the arming with shield and spear, and (3), we read on p. 24 BC, τὸ δ' αὖ περὶ τῆς φρονήσεως, ὁρᾷς που τὸν νόμον τῇδε (sc. in Egypt) ὅσην ἐπιμέλειαν ἐποιήσατο (sc. ὁ νόμος) εὐθὺς κατ' ἀρχὰς περί τε τὸν κόσμον, ἅπαντα μέχρι μαντικῆς καὶ ἰατρικῆς πρὸς ὑγίειαν ἐκ τούτων θείων ὄντων εἰς

[20] Hellwig, 196 ff. If we read νοῦ τε καὶ ἀνοίας, then Plato had added the opposite in a schematic manner, as he often does; but if νοῦ τε καὶ διανοίας is right, then he is hinting at the intellectual function of the cosmic *Nûs*. Kranz, 195 (316) argued that the great arts cannot altogether treat the nature of the universe; but, as we shall see, Platonic science always extends to the boundaries of the world, if not to the ideas.

[21] Pohlenz, *Hipp.* 114, n. 2 to p. 74. Compare note 17 above.

[22] Pohlenz, 75 f.; compare Joly², 83 f.; I should like to say more about these references in due time.

[23] Kucharski, 306.   [24] De Vries, 234 ff. Compare note 10 above.

τὰ ἀνθρώπινα ἀνευρών, ὅσα τε ἄλλα τούτοις ἕπεται μαθήματα πάντα κτησά-
μενος.

We have here a characteristic sample of Plato's old-age style, which I
cannot analyze in brief. The very personification of the law (νόμος) belongs
to this style. I paraphrase as follows: the goddess (Athena naturally) has
somehow given rise to a law (νόμος) in the intellectual sphere, and from
the first (without any preliminary steps), this law has taken care of the
universe (κόσμος) in such a manner that the law found out all things including the art of the seers (μαντικῆς) and medicine, which serves for the
purpose of health, starting from all that which is divine (ἐκ τούτων θείων
ὄντων) to the use of human circumstances; so the law acquired all the
relevant knowledge. With the phrase ἐκ τούτων θείων ὄντων the speaker
goes back to the cosmos. The universe is divine not only on the whole, but
also in the multiplicity of its ingredients, that is, it is animated and
governed by gods. Proceeding from this universe the law has invented the
sciences for things human, μαντικὴν καὶ ἰατρικήν, and moreover other
related sciences.[25] These sciences have to do with man and his concerns,
but they get their principles from the contemplation of the cosmos into
which human life is inserted. Here we have the medicine we were searching for, the medicine which treats mankind not without knowledge of
τῆς τοῦ ὅλου φύσεως and which even starts from the nature of the ὅλον. To
be sure, the correspondence is not perfect, insofar as in the *Phaedrus*
Socrates is speaking of Hippocrates, while Critias in the *Timaeus* is reporting the same things about Egypt, dating back 8,000 years ago, or rather
9,000 years, since these sciences, as he says, had existed in Old Athens. But
for Hippocrates and Egypt there is a common denominator, namely
Plato. We have to interpret Plato on the basis of his own views, putting
aside Hippocrates and Egypt. After all, we are dealing with a Platonic not
with a Hippocratic or Egyptological question.

At first we must pay attention to the fact that medicine is put together
with μαντική. When we recall the disregard often found in the *Corpus
Hippocraticum* for the art of the seers,[26] we may suspect that the juxtaposition is not favorable to medicine. But in Plato's view μαντική is no
doubt an imperfect form of knowledge;[27] yet it is to some extent appre-

[25] The great sciences of the *Phaedrus*? The doctrine of the ideas is unknown to the
Egyptians. Compare Herter, *Palingenesia* 4, 1969, 116 ff. (*Kl. Schr.*, 286 ff.).

[26] II. διαίτ. ὀξ. 8. But since Aeschyl., *Prom.* 484 ff., the μαντική is often side by side
with medicine.

[27] P. Friedländer, *GGA* 1931, 250 f. (*Studien zur antiken Literatur und Kunst*, Berl., 1969,
90 f.); *Platon*2 2, 70; P. Louis, *Les métaphores de Platon*, Thèse Par. (Rennes), 1945, 139 ff.;
R. J. Collin, *Class. Quart.* 46, 1952, 93 ff.; W. J. Verdenius, *Arch. Gesch. Philos.* 44, 1962,
132 f.; 136; K. Gaiser, *Platons ungeschriebene Lehre*, Stuttg., 1963, 245; 401,214; compare

ciated, provided that the really inspired χρησμῳδοί and μάντεις are separated from others.[28] This art regulates the intercourse between gods and men,[29] and therefore the seers are represented in both ideal states of Plato.[30] Thus in the *Phaedrus* medicine also is treated seriously, although with the reservation that it is in keeping with true reason, ἀληθὴς λόγος.[31] Without irony Socrates (270 B) introduces or rather reintroduces medicine and points out that medicine has the same manner (τρόπος) as rhetoric. Thus we are allowed to transfer to the body what Plato further on says of the 'soul.

In what way do the methods of medicine and of rhetoric resemble one another? Plato tells us in his next sentence: the diaeresis is common to the two disciplines,[32] namely, the method of dividing a primary concept into

---

Rhein. Mus. 110, 1967, 327 ff.; C. Zintzen, *Kl. Pauly*, s. v. *Mantik*, 971; C. W. Müller, *l.c.*, 55 f.; 123 f.; 216 f.

[28] *Ion* 534 D; *Meno* 99 C; *Politeia* 364 B; *Nom.* 908 D; Aristot., *N.E.* 4, 13, 1127 b 19 ff. (See A. Rivaud, in his edition of *Tim.* and *Critias*, Paris, 1925, 198, 2.) Compare *Phaedr.* 242 C; 248 DE; *Tim.* 71 D ff. (compare O. Apelt, *Translation*, Leipz., 1922, 182 nn. 257–259 to this passage). A. W. Argyle, *Class. Rev.* 20, 1970, 139.

[29] *Symp.* 188 CD.   [30] *Politic.* 290 C; *Nom.* 772 D; 871 D; 914 A.

[31] True reason is not linked with Hippocrates (so Vegetti 14, and others), but controling instance is (Hoffmann, 1074; compare 1083; Edelstein, 121,1; Hellwig, 183,16; 184 f.; 204). The irony of Socrates is not directed against Hippocrates (so Rivaud, 114 f.), but against Phaedrus' belief in the absolute authority of Hippocrates, although he is chief representative of the medicine (Pohlenz, *Hipp.* 77). Compare Joly[2], 89. The expression εἰ συμφωνεῖ is misunderstood by Pohlenz, 114, n. 2 to p. 76 (for συμφωνεῖν, "logisch vereinbar sein," see H.-P. Stahl, *Herm.* 88, 1960, 427 ff.).

[32] See 273 DE; 276 E–277 A; 277 B. Thus it is useless to pile up, as Bourgey 88 ff. does, (compare Joly[2], 90) similarities between medicine and rhetoric, or to stress (as Kucharski did) the rationality of the two disciplines. A. Virieux-Reymond ("Current Problems in History of Medicine," *Proceed. 19th Internat. Congr. Hist. Med.*, Basel, 1964, Basel-New York, 1966, 195 ff.) emphasizes with Kucharski the "relations causales" of the Hippo-cratic-Platonic method, and consequently he loses sight of the *Phaedrus* (compare also Vegetti, 16 f.). Deichgräber, 151; Jaeger, 2, 33 ff.; Kranz, 196 (317); Gaudin, 342 f., also Edelstein (*PW*, *loc. cit.*, 1318 ff.; *Am. J. Phil.*, *loc. cit.*) allow for the *diaeresis*, especially Hellwig, 217 ff. The influence of Hippocrates on the Platonic *diaeresis* is stressed by Bourgey, 91; 95 f. Gaudin (340 ff.) makes Plato turn away from Anaxagoras to Hippo-crates. Kucharski, 350 ff. (*Les chemins du savoir*, Paris, 1949, 129 ff.; 227 ff.; 346 ff.; *Rev. ét. gr.* 74, 1961, 388 ff. = *Aspects de la spéculation platonicienne*, Par.-Louv., 1971, 177 ff.; *Rev. philosophique* 1964, 427 ff. = *Spéculation*, 259 ff.) emphatically declares that the *diaeresis* is common to medicine and rhetoric. Yet he tries to establish not only the old method of ascending from the sensual phenomena to their ideas, but also two new methods, the dichotomic *diaeresis* and *synagoge*, and the Hippocratic reduction of larger concepts to narrower ones. In the *Phaedrus* he finds these two methods side by side; but it is hard to understand his statements (Vegetti, 21, distinguishes three "prospettive teoretiche"); finally, he sacrificed the cardinal point, the relation of the *diaeresis* to the universe. Similarly, for the sake of the *diaeresis* Cambiano, 284 ff., abandoned the universalistic

two or more subordinate concepts, and these again into others, and so on. Plato claims a diaeretical method for rhetoric of the kind already possessed by medicine. There are concepts (εἴδη) which can be divided and subdivided and others which are not so complex but which are simple and which can no longer be divided. Thus diaeresis ought to clarify whether the soul is πολυειδές or ἁπλοῦν, and similarly with respect to the body, and generally with respect to the object of inquiry in every science.[33] If the object is simple, one can at once enquire in its δύναμις (potency), in both the active and passive sense, that is, the effect it exerts upon other objects and the effect of other things upon it. If, on the contrary, the object is not simple, one must first of all determine its εἴδη (species) and explore these one by one in order to know how each one acts and reacts. It was acknowledged long ago that Plato has in mind a doctrine of the different constitutions of the soul. Therefore, in the field of medicine the methodological likeness is to be found in the well-known constitutions of the body,[34] but—strange to say—this idea has been overlooked in the research dealing with Hippocrates.

The misunderstanding of the term πολυειδές is very dangerous; here εἴδη are not μέρη.[35] The πολυειδές is not to be divided into its organs or humors, for in that case the soul ought to be divided into the reasonable part (λογιστικόν), the passionate part (θυμοειδές), and the greedy part (ἐπιθυμητικόν). In the diaeresis every concept is a whole, not part of a whole. When soul and body are divided, there do not result parts which

interpretation of τὸ ὅλον (compare note 11 above). Frenkian too pays attention to the *diaeresis* and treats the nosology of the first part of Π. διαίτ. ὀξ. "sous toute réserve"; thus he was able to state properly an opposition between the *diaeresis* and the universal medicine. In fact, there is a difficulty here to be solved, as Deichgräber had pointed out. Thompson, 124, was not far from the truth while stating: "the general law of the One in Many, which holds alike in Nature and in Thought." I hope to be able to contribute a little to the elucidation of this question.

[33] That is the φύσις of the object (271 A 7 f.). Gomperz, *Anz. Ak. Wien*, Phil.-hist. Kl., 47, 1910, 22, wrote ὑπό του in 270 D 5 and 7. For 271 A, compare Hellwig, 217, 104.

[34] Compare Hoffmann, 1082 ff.; he believes that the method aims at the health. Kranz, 199 f. (319), also considers the doctrine of the constitutions, but not for the rhetoric. The types of life (248 D) did occur to Pohlenz, *GGA* 1916, 280, 1, but only to be abandoned. Compare *Ciba-Ztschr.* 8, n. 85, 1957, 2829.

[35] Since Littré many scholars were inclined to incur into this confusion, especially v. Arnim, 219 ff.; P. Frutiger, *Les mythes de Platon*, Paris, 1930, 91, 1; 2, and others. Kranz, 198 (318) f., relying upon *Charm.* 156 BC, was looking for the Hippocratic conception of the totality of the body without showing how this view was to be applied to the soul. Compare note 11 above. The reciprocation of the parts may cause differences of physical or psychical types, as v. Arnim and Steckerl suppose; compare also Kühn, 87 ff., and Hellwig, 204 ff.

have no vital power of their own, but different species of body or soul which yield different kinds of men.

Thus we comprehend Plato's programmatic question in this way: do soul and body have many εἴδη (species), or is either of them a simple εἴδος, everywhere homogeneous (save nonsignificant variants in the world of our senses)? Only in this way does the program correspond with the discussion that follows, and only so entirely and precisely. Further on, Plato assumes types of souls and claims for each type a specific sort of speech fit to impress a particular sort of hearer and no other. Plato states explicitly that soul is πολυειδές; as to body, it goes without saying that it is πολυειδές (271 A). Plato is demanding a doctrine of the constitutions for the soul analogous to the medical doctrine of the constitutions which had existed long before and which therefore did not need special explanation.

Nor do we miss such an explanation, but as to the soul, we might want to learn what are the species Plato has in view; in the *Phaedrus* he is only speaking generally and programmatically. We find traces of such an approach in other works. For instance, in the *Politeia*, 435 E–436 A, Plato characterizes three kinds and temperaments (εἴδη τε καὶ ἤθη) represented by individual persons as well as by entire peoples. In specific cases the parts of the soul play a certain role in accordance with their predominance in behavior: the northerners (Thracians, Scythians, etc.) are distinguished by the preponderance of the passionate (*thymoeides*), the Phoenicians and Egyptians by the greediness of gain (φιλοχρήματον = *epithymeticon*), and the Greeks by the desire for learning (φιλομαθές = *logisticon*). Or take the *Politicus*; here Plato teaches a doctrine of the temperament amounting to a blend of the diverse types which produces εὐοργησία (good talents). Read the description of the character of the guardians in the *Politeia* or the portraits of the citizens of the decaying constitutions, and you shall see Plato's tendency toward typology.[36] Within our dialogue itself we find the list of human tempers and directions of life (248 DE); here the typical moment becomes especially manifest in the formations ending in -ικός, in the beginning by a slow transition, lover of philosophy or beauty or the musical and erotic (in the Platonic sense), φιλοσόφου ἢ φιλοκάλου ἢ μουσικοῦ τινος καὶ ἐρωτικοῦ. It also is worth observing, how in 252 C ff. the different types of soul react differently toward the idea of Eros, and in 259 CD the individual μουσικοί behave differently toward the different Muses. In view of the multiplicity of types of character it must have been difficult to fix types of speech suited to them. In what way Plato solved the problem, and whether he solved it at all, we do not know.

As to the medical theory of constitutions, Plato makes no hints in the

36 Further samples in Hellwig, 209 f. Compare Steckerl, 170.

Phaedrus, since he could assume that it was known. In the *Timaeus* he has nothing pertinent, because there he was content with the general conditions of the human body, which fundamentally are everywhere the same in spite of all the differences. But in the *Phaedrus* 268 A ff., he gives us to understand that he knows εἴδη of body; here someone is boasting that he is able to carry out the usual practice of medicine and also to teach others, but he is questioned by the true technicians (τεχνικοί), whether he knows when, to what degree, and for which people he must proceed in each case. Plato uses the somewhat indeterminate expression πρὸς οὕστινας, which is appropriate for single patients to be attended to in a special manner; but it also is suitable to types of patients who are subject to uniform attendance.[37] Unfortunately, Plato does not engage in details. He dispenses with examples and does not determine exactly the point where a type is passing over into individual cases, a difficulty inherent in the method of diaeresis on the whole.

In all probability the dislike of the ἄπειρον, the infinity of possibilities, and variabilities has induced Plato in the quoted passage of the *Timaeus* to remove medicine as far as possible from the θεῖα, just as in the case of the μαντική, which was likewise driven to enter into the endless multiplicity of actual cases. Nevertheless, there was behind the two disciplines "the whole," and within the frame of this ὅλον not only medicine but also rhetoric has to move. This ὅλον reaches far over the human sphere into the cosmos. For in Plato's view it is not only men who have body and soul, but also the cosmos and its powers. The universe of our phenomenal world is (contrary to the world of ideas) material, but governed psychically. This fact does not exceed all that which is expressly treated in the course of the dialogue; it fits into the frame of the diaeresis insofar as both body and soul have certain εἴδη which extend beyond mankind to the gods.[38] The human psyche is an inferior issue *en miniature* of the psychic substance, by which the higher beings are formed, and the human soul is proportionate to its body as the godlike astral soul to its material *substratum*. Thus rhetoric and medicine and generally all the "great" arts presuppose a context embracing the whole Cosmos with all things within. These arts inquire what acts upon what thing and in what manner, not only in the limits of mankind, but also among the εἴδη of soul and body of the powers outside up to the highest. As to rhetoric, the crucial point is which *eidos*

---

[37] Herter, *Sudh. Arch.* 47, 1963, 272 f. (*Kl. Schr.*, 196 f.).

[38] Hellwig, 212 ff.; compare v. Arnim, 176 ff.; 218 f.; Hoffmann, 1081; Pohlenz, *Der hellenische Mensch*, 175 f.; *Hipp.*, 75; Joly[2], 83 ff.; O. Wichmann, *Platon*, Darmst., 1966, 229 f. Edelstein, *PW, loc. cit.*, 1320 f., is at pains to keep the divine element away from the passage in the *Phaedrus*.

of speech works upon which *eidos* of soul. In this respect, after all, Plato could not stop here, at the mankind; in the central myth about the heavenly journey of the souls he had emphasized the peculiar affinity of the types of human souls each with its proper god. But from this very myth results that the souls of the gods are included in the typology, as is expressly stated in 245 C. Consequently, in 273 E–274 A the technician of speech (τεχνικὸς λόγων πέρι) is asked how one must address the gods or each god properly: with this motif the prayer is introduced into the true rhetoric.[39]

As the Platonic psychology exceeds the ὅλον of the human psyche, so also Plato's physiology and pathology rest mainly upon the connections of the human body with the universe. Body is composed of the same four elements that exist in the environment. These elements are on principle different in quality, and they work not only within the body one upon another but also inward from the outside (παθήματα, *Tim.* 61 C ff.). It is explicitly said that the different kinds of body not only exert effects, but also endure effects from bodies of other kinds.[40] Thus we see the ὅλον exceeding the human body like the soul and reaching to the boundaries of the universe. There is a beautiful passage in an early dialogue, *Gorgias,* 507 E f.: Plato celebrates the unity of the world's composition from gods to men, from heaven to earth. The same motif is indicated again in the *Meno,* 81 D, where the affinity of nature (συγγένεια τῆς φύσεως) appears,[41] and it continues to occur in Plato's writings up to "the all pervasive bond" (δεσμός) of the *Epinomis.* At the time of the *Gorgias* Plato was speaking in the manner of the Pythagoreans; later on, in the *Nomoi,* 889 B, he follows the view of the materialists, but he keeps his distance by the supposition that in the whole context a godlike principle is at work. The effects within the bodily sphere arise by movements (normal or troubled), especially when like substances are striving after like ones. There are laws prevailing in all the spheres of the universe; therefore, medical men need knowledge of the whole of nature.[42]

---

[39] Hellwig, *loc. cit.,* believes that the gods cannot be influenced by men. F. Solmsen, who discussed the whole problem with me in Madison, doubts my interpretation of the passage.

[40] Πάθη τε καὶ ἔργα of the soul already at 245 C. For the homogeneous composition of macrocosm and microcosm see Kühn, 90 ff.

[41] Herter, "Religion und Religionen," *Festschr. G. Mensching,* Bonn, 1967, 64 ff. (*Kl. Schr.,* 249 ff.). Compare H.-D. Voigtländer, *Die Lust und das Gute bei Platon,* Würzb., 1960, 157, who quotes the passages in *Gorg.* and *Nomoi.* For *Meno* 81 D see recently H. Klein, *Commentary,* Chapel Hill, 1965, 96; St. S. Tigner, *Phronesis* 15, 1970, 1 ff.; Mannsperger, 61 f.

[42] Pythagorean influence is to be verified by Archytas fr. 1, cited by Capelle, 256 ff.

In Plato's view every movement concentrates on the tendency toward the good, which pervades the whole world, but which can be disturbed by matter. Sometimes Plato's conceptions aim at parallels of macrocosm and microcosm, which A. Olerud, I believe, has somewhat exaggerated.[43] As thinking should imitate the circular movement of the universe, so does blood (*Tim.*, 81 AB); as the universe is always moving, so the soul should keep the body moving with measure, preferably by itself, that is, by gymnastic (88 C ff.). We must take advantage of the circulation, otherwise we become brutish (91 E); but if white phlegm with black bile enters the godlike circulation, it gives rise to the sacred disease (85 AB). Plato's medicine as practical experience (ἐμπειρία) remains, of course, within the narrower environment; but when it becomes science (ἐπιστήμη), especially in the *Timaeus*, it can be comprehended only within the general framework, since it reveals the general teleology of nature—in spite of the troubles caused by the erring cause (πλανωμένη αἰτία). While all things are striving after the good, the sciences engaged herein get the ὑψηλόνουν (highminded) and the τελεσιουργικόν (aiming at the ultimate).[44] Of course, necessity is important in dominating the effects (271 B),[45] but that is not decisive for Plato's trend of thought. It is simpler to say that the physician must include the whole cosmos in his method, since he has to act according to the laws existing in the whole of nature. The structure of the universe is accessible by the diaeresis, which has to arrange and determine all things in their relation one with another.

So far, I hope that the commentator of Plato's mode of thinking has fulfilled his duty; but he is taking an interest also in the question of whether Plato has rightly understood Hippocrates and how far he has done so.[46] Of course, we must not suppose that Plato is approaching Hippocrates completely unbiased, because it is known that not only Aristoteles, as H. Cherniss has demonstrated but, in a much higher degree, Plato too is accustomed to adapt what he is citing to his own purposes.[47]

Compare Kucharski, 323,1; J. S. Morrison, *Class. Quart.* 52, 1958, 216 (compare 199). Medicine belongs to astronomy, which deals with the course of the stars and with the seasons; compare Pohlenz, *Hipp.* 114, n. 1 to p. 75.

[43] A. Olerud, *L'idée de macrocosmos et de microcosmos dans le Timée de Platon*, Upps., 1951. Lit. see E. Schöner, *Das Viererschema in der antiken Humoralpathologie*, Wiesb., 1964, 13 f., 2. For the *Timaeus* see A. St. Pease, *Harv. Theol. Rev.* 34, 1941, 168, 28. Hellwig, 202 f., 67, disregards the motif.

[44] Pohlenz, *Hipp.* 76. Compare Mannsperger, 258; Hellwig, 185 f.

[45] Kucharski compares *Phil.* 28 D.

[46] For the cosmic view Plato rightly referred to Anaxagoras. Compare note 20 above.

[47] Thus, in the view of Kucharski, 309, the passage of the *Phaedrus* is a "transposition," or even a "sublimation," of the methodology of Hippocrates.

Nevertheless, the Hippocratic doctrine does not appear distorted, because the point Plato aims at is really characteristic of the Hippocrateans, namely, the doctrine of the constitutions, on which H. L. Dittmer was able to write an extensive treatise.[48] This doctrine is the kernel and the guiding idea of Hippocratic medicine, as Mewaldt (p. 10) says, and culminates in the fourfold scheme of the phlegmatic, the bilious, the sanguine, and the melancholic (of those who are dominated by phlegm or bile or blood or black bile in such a manner that in practice these four qualities are variously distributed). Of course, different constitutions react differently to the influence of the environment. Therefore, the Hippocratic has to pay attention to the outer world, since it is composed of the same substances as the human body.[49] But now the question arises as to whether Hippocrates concentrates on the ὅλον in such a manner as Plato supposes.[50] If the correspondence of macrocosm and microcosm is accentuated, the early treatise on the number seven (Π. ἑβδομάδων) becomes a principal witness;[51] but this treatise is far removed from the authentic Hippocrates. The treatise on diet (Π. διαίτης) too has a peculiar character. Here the human body is considered as an imitation of the universe (ἀπομίμησις τοῦ ὅλου: I. 10; VI, p. 484 L.).[52] On the other hand, we must pay attention to the meteorological medicine which finds the causes of the diseases in the influences of water and air and the whole environment. But as the name indicates, this environment is bounded by the meteora, that is, it is identical with the sublunar region and does not comprehend the ὅλον.[53]

[48] *Konstitutionstypen im Corpus Hippocraticum*, Diss. Jena, 1940 (compare J. Mewaldt, *Gnom.* 18, 1942, 8 ff.).

[49] Hence A. E. Taylor, *Plato*, Lond., 1926, 315, refers to the doctrine of the four humors and takes Π. φύσ. ἀνθρ. to be the pattern; but the "ingredients" are not decisive, as I have shown.

[50] The outward influences are touched upon in nearly all Hippocratic treatises, though with a different emphasis (Dittmer, 15). Bourgey, 90; 91,1; 94 presupposes astronomical influence upon the medical writers, but *Epid.* 1, 10, is the only adequate passage he cites. Compare W. Capelle, *Hippokrates, Fünf auserlesene Schriften*, Zür., 1955, 27 ff.

[51] Joly[1], 206 f.; Joly[2], 86 f.

[52] Capelle, 259 f.; Palm, 117 f.; Kucharski, 324; Wanner, 75, 34; Schöner, 34,3. Hipp., *reg. morb. ac.* 1 extr. should be excluded (Joly[2], 90).

[53] Joly[1], 207 ff.; Joly[2], 86 ff. It is not allowed to extend the ὅλον beyond the realm of the human body, but not farther than to the environment, as has been stated by Ermerins, 220 ff.; Petersen, *loc. cit.*; Ed. Meyer, *Gesch. d. Alt.* 4, 210, 1 (4, 1[5], 851, 1); Nestle; also Palm, 102 ff. Nestle, 17 f. (539 f.); (see already Diels, *Herm.* 45, 1910, 125 f.; *SB Berl.* 1910, 1141,1; compare Tocco, 70 ff.) distinguishes between meteorological medicine and natural philosophy (compare Joly[1], 208, 2; Bourgey, 91, 1); even so, the method of the *Phaedrus* cannot be dissociated from the latter. For the fluctuation of systematic and empiric methods, compare Kühn, *loc. cit., pass.*; Herter, *Sudh. Arch.* 47, 1963, 262; 276 (*Kl. Schr.*, 188; 199 f.).

Hoffmann (p. 1084) indicates that the elevation into the cosmic sphere is proper to Plato's view. Plato went beyond Hippocrates without special mention, not by mistake, but simply because he was carried away by the momentum of his thinking.[54]

Still, some passages must be pointed out which in this connection are not insignificant. To be sure, the beginning of the treatise *On Climate*[55] is not very helpful; the meteorological medicine makes allowance for the rising and setting of the stars in order to get signs of the seasons. But another passage has a larger significance, namely, the fragment of a lost treatise called in a Pseudo-Galenic dissertation:[56] ὁκόσοι ἰατρικὴν ἀσκέοντες φυσιογνωμίης ἀμοιρέουσιν, τουτέων ἡ γνώμη ἀνὰ σκότον καλινδουμένη νωθρὰ γηράσκει ("whoever practising medicine neglect φυσιογνωμίη, they grow to a dull old age, their minds rolling in the dark.") Obviously, φυσιογνωμίη is to be understood in the general sense of περὶ φύσεως ἱστορία. Thus, this passage corresponds with the passage of the treatise *On diet* I. 2 (VI, p. 470 L.), where the diseases are derived from the powerful effects of the whole world.[57] But the most significant passage is a sentence in the treatise *On human nature* (Π. φύσ. ἀνθρ. 7; VI, pp. 48–50 L.):[58] ὡς γὰρ ὁ ἐνιαυτὸς μετέχει μὲν πᾶς πάντων καὶ τῶν θερμῶν καὶ τῶν ψυχρῶν καὶ τῶν ξηρῶν καὶ τῶν ὑγρῶν—οὐ γὰρ ἂν μείνειε τουτέων οὐδὲν οὐδένα χρόνον ἄνευ πάντων τῶν ἐνεόντων ἐν τῷδε τῷ κόσμῳ, ἀλλ' εἰ ἕν τί γε ἐκλίποι, πάντ' ἂν ἀφανισθείη· ἀπὸ γὰρ τῆς αὐτέης ἀνάγκης πάντα ξυνέστηκέ τε καὶ τρέφεται ὑπ'

---

54 Joly[1], 207 ff.; Joly[2], 86 ff., believes that Plato has failed in interpreting the meteorological medicine and that he has misunderstood the ἀστρονομίη at Π. ἀ. ὑ. τ. 2 by taking the μετέωρα to mean the ὅλον (universe). Then Plato's acquaintance with Hippocrates would be reduced to a minimum. Frenkian, 38 ff., believes that Plato knew the meteorological medicine of Hippocrates only by hearsay (compare Diller, *Kl. Schr. zur ant. Med.* 122 = *Arch. Begriffsgesch.* 9, 1964, 149 f.); but is it likely that Polybus (p. 15 f.; 28; 37) would be that much mistaken? Compare note 62 below.

55 Fredrich, 5 f.; 8; 222; Nestle, 22 (545); Palm, 101 f.; Kucharski, 325; Joly[2], 87 f. Add *Epid.* 1, 10 (2, 668–670 L.); compare Kucharski, 324 f.; Bourgey, 94; 196,1; Pohlenz, *Hipp.* 114, n. 1 to p. 75. Ancient physicians prognosticated by the help of the lunar phases (Diocles, compare Pohlenz, 79). Hippocr., *Epist.* 18 (9, 382–384 L.) concerns totality, but Democritus is writing.

56 Ps.-Galenus, Περὶ κατακλίσεως νοσούντων προγνωστικά 19, 530 K.; see H. Schöne, *Deutsche Med. Wochenschr.* 36, 1910, 418 f.; 466 f. Compare H. Diels, *SB Berl.* 1910, 1140 ff.; Tocco, 76 ff.

57 Tocco, 70 ff.; Schöner, 29 f.

58 Taylor, *Plato* 315; Kranz, 199 f. (319); Pohlenz, *Hipp.* 114, n. 1 to p. 75; H. Diller, *Kl. Schr. zur ant. Med.* 94 (*Jahrb. Ak. Wiss. Lit. Mainz* 1959, 276), 122 (*Arch. Begriffsgesch.* 9, 1964, 149 f.). Joly[1], 207; Joly[2], 88 f. Compare notes 4 and 49 above. Kucharski, 336 ff., excluded Π. φύσ. ἀνθρ., formerly already Littré, 1, 296 ff., and Alb. Pettenkofer, *Versuch einer kritisch-historischen Beleuchtung des dem Hippokrates zugeschriebenen Werkes:* περὶ φύσιος ἀνθρώπων, Diss. Münch., 1837, 21 ff. Compare Diès, 31 f.

ἀλλήλων—οὕτω δὲ καὶ εἴ τι ἐκ τοῦ ἀνθρώπου ἐκλίποι τουτέων τῶν ξυγγεγονότων, οὐκ ἂν δύναιτο ζῆν ἄνθρωπος. ("For, as the year as a whole comprises all that which is warm and cold and dry and humid—for of all these things nothing would remain at any time without all of these things which are in this cosmos, but rather if anything vanished, all things would disappear; for by the same necessity altogether they subsist and are nourished one by another—likewise if anything of all that which is come together vanished from man, man could not live.") In this treatise, which is by no means eccentric, the universal connection and necessity, from which the human body cannot be excluded, is pronounced in a programmatic manner which nobody can weaken.[59] This testimony is all the more important since today the treatise is ascribed to Polybus, Hippocrates' son-in-law.[60] Thus we are led into the very milieu of the great physician. And we return to Galen, who in his commentary searched for Plato's source in this very treatise.[61]

We may be pleased that Plato's thought is confirmed at least by this unique passage, and at that by a voice from the circle of Hippocrates himself. To be sure, we do not find any treatise which would carry out the method described by Plato as fully as Π. ἑβδομάδων and Π. διαίτης, where we are far removed from the true Hippocrates. We have to concede that Plato has given greater weight to the cosmic element than Hippocrates has done in confrontation with practice. Therefore, it is scarcely reasonable to assume that Plato would have read a single treatise.[62] His statements about Hippocrates look like an *opinion courante*.[63] His medical friends could have told him, though he kept more to the Italic school than

[59] Joly[1], 209 f.; Joly[2], 88 f. (compare Hackforth, 151) objects that the author attacks medical monism and does not exceed the frame of the meteorological medicine; but his theory extends farther.

[60] At least chapters 1–8. See H. Grensemann, *Der Arzt Polybos*, Mainz, 1968 (compare J. Jouanna, *Rev. ét. gr.* 82, 1969, 555 ff.).

[61] Galen, *comm. praef.* XV, p. 4 f.; 12 ff., and 1, 42, p. 103 ff. K.; Littré, 1, 297; Fredrich, 52; Gomperz, *Phil.*, *loc. cit.*, 213; Wanner, 75,33.

[62] Compare Pettenkofer, 23 f.; Littré, 1, 299; 305 ff.; Petersen, 18 f.; Ermerins, in his edition; Diels, *DLZ* 1899, 13; Wilamowitz, *SB Berl.* 1901, 23; *Platon*, 1[2], Berl., 1920, 462,1; Nelson, *loc. cit.*; Kind, *Burs.* 158, 1912, 144; Rehm, *loc. cit.*; Diller, *Kl. Schr. zur ant. Med.* 137 (= *Gnom.* 9, 1933, 70 f.); 205 (*ebd.* 18, 1942, 83 f.); 93 f. (= *Jahrb. Ak. Wiss. Lit. Mainz* 1959, 275 f.); 122 (= *Arch. Begriffsgesch.* 9, 1964, 149 f.); Wanner, 75,33; Pohlenz; Mesnard, 145; Bourgey, 88 ff.; compare Edelstein, *Ancient Medicine*, 135 ff. Differently Fredrich, 9; Capelle, 261, compare 253; Kucharski, *Chemins*, 139 ff.; 230; Jaeger, 2, 34 f.; Joly[2], 87 ff.; Cambiano, 303. At least, Plato does not quote a single treatise; Littré, 1, 307 f. (Capelle, 250,2; Friedländer, 3, 469, 29; Geffcken, 1, 240, 8) even stated that he had developed the view of Hippocrates in his own manner; compare note 54 above. Hellwig, 183,15.

[63] Bourgey, 92.

to the Coans.[64] As matters stand, it is not likely that he had chosen the Hippocratic medicine to be his model for the cosmology.[65] The passage of the *Phaedrus* is not sufficiently detailed.[66] It is certainly not a source to provide more information than the treatises of the *Corpus* itself. What Plato says is more important for himself than for Hippocrates; methodologically it is even correct to eliminate the passage as a source when we are trying to determine the authentic views of Hippocrates.[67]

And what about the Egyptians, who are brought into the discussion by way of the *Timaeus*? Also here it is a secondary problem how far Plato's conception of foreign medicine corresponded to reality. He was in a position to know that in Egypt medicine flourished as much as did μαντική, as Herodotus (II, 84) observed; and it was *communis opinio* that from Egypt Greek visitors like Thales could get astronomical knowledge. Plato himself relates (*Phaedr.*, 274 CD) that Thoth invented mathematics and astronomy. Isocrates in the *Busiris* ascribes to the Egyptians not only astronomy together with geometry, but also a high medical art, which prescribes natural remedies. It is probable—in spite of some difficulties— that Isocrates in this essay follows Plato.[68] But this very passage is not as close to Plato as scholars believe. When we look more closely at the Isocratean passage, its Platonic character, as Ries has emphasized, is fading. We learn from Isocrates that the Egyptian priests pursue medicine, but the study of astronomy they leave to their pupils. Now this division of labor is exactly what Isocrates later, in the speech on the exchange of property (Π. ἀντιδόσεως, 261 ff.),[69] has claimed in strict contrast to Plato. Astronomy and mathematics concern the youth, not the adults, as an exercise in thinking, and he does not make the point of any practical or moral values in these sciences, though he is correcting the utilitarian judgment of Protagoras (Plat. *Prot.*, 318 DE) and of the Xenophontean Socrates (*Mem.*, IV, 7). To be sure, the Egyptian priests engage in what Isocrates calls philosophy, and within the range of this philosophy they

[64] Bourgey, 96 f., 2. Petersen, 19 n. 1, thought of "scholae" of Hippocrates.
[65] Pohlenz, *Hipp.* 76; 114 f., n. 2 to p. 76 (compare Diller, *Kl. Schr. zur ant. Med.* 123 = *Arch. Begriffsgesch.* 9, 1964, 150). Rey, *loc. cit.*; Mesnard 147; Joly², 90 (compare Kucharski, 301, 2). For Kucharski see note 32 above. Correctly Edelstein, 117 ff.
[66] Diels, *DLZ* 1899, 13; Diller, *Kl. Schr. zur ant. Med.*, 205 (*Gnom.* 18, 1942, 84).
[67] Capelle, 261; Palm, 101; Joly¹, 204.
[68] K. Münscher, *PW*, s. v. *Isokrates*, 2177 ff. (with lit.). M. Pohlenz, *Aus Platos Werdezeit*, Berl., 1913, 215 ff., believes that Plato in the first edition of his *Politeia* referred to Egypt "etwa einleitungsweise"; differently, Klaus Ries, *Isokrates und Platon*, Diss. Münch., 1959, 51 ff. (W. Burkert, *Gnom.* 33, 1961, 349 ff.). For the myth of Busiris (especially the monuments), compare S. El Kalza, 'Ο Βούσιρις, Diss. Athens, 1970.
[69] Compare Morrison, 217.

explore—besides legislation—the nature of the existing things (τὴν φύσιν
τῶν ὄντων). This expression is so vague that we cannot say whether "the
existing things" exceed the sphere of the practical philosophy of Isocrates;
in other passages of this author τὰ ὄντα do not transcend the sphere of the
object he is discussing. In Isocrates, in any case, Plato's decisive idea is
lacking, namely, that medicine and astronomy are connected. Whatever
the φύσις τῶν ὄντων may be for Isocrates, astronomy is as little included in
the philosophy of the priests as is geometry, which according to Plato must
be the scientific superstructure of practical astronomy. The Platonic conception of the unity of all sciences is not shared by Isocrates, who bears
witness to the attention which the Egyptians are paying to medicine and
astronomy, but hardly to anything else. The parallelism between Plato
and Isocrates is not sufficiently close to be explained by mutual dependence, but it suggests the supposition that at Athens the Egyptians were
credited with a natural and practical medicine. And with regard to the
undeniable relations of the Greek, especially the Cnidian, medicine to the
Egyptian,[70] we might assume that the current opinion was not unfounded.
Perhaps correlations of macrocosm and microcosm were not unknown to
Egyptians, because they held that each member of the body was cared for
by its god or was even identical with its god.[71] But I do not want to intrude
into such an alien field, because again what Plato says of the Egyptians
should be judged by the views proper to Plato himself.

In the *Timaeus* Plato attributes his own conception of true medicine—or
at best Hippocrates' conception—to the Egyptians, but we must ask why.
In this dialogue as in the *Critias* he describes the high standard of the old
Athenians who lived 9,000 years earlier and who overcame the powerful
empire of the island Atlantis. But old Athens had been devastated by an
immense flood, and Atlantis was entirely inundated. The Egyptians alone
were left behind to preserve the knowledge of the earliest events. To be
sure, Plato invented the whole history, but he established a rationale for his
account by adducing would-be scientific arguments. Above all, the
credibility of his account depended upon the reliability of the priest at
Sais who ostensibly had told the old story to Solon. For this purpose Plato
devised the following account: the goddess Athena, who was the patroness
of the old Athenians, later introduced a similar culture into Egypt. Since

---

[70] R. O. Steuer and J. B. de C. M. Saunders, *Ancient Egyptian and Cnidian Medicine*, Los
Angeles, 1959. H. E. Sigerist, *A History of Medicine* 1, Oxf., 1951, 215 ff. P. Ghalioungui,
XVIIᵉ *Congr. internat. d'histoire de la médecine*, Athènes-Cos, 1960, 269 ff.; *Magic and medical
Science in ancient Egypt*, Lond., 1963, 164 ff.; S. Morenz, *Die Begegnung Europas mit Ägypten*,
Zür.-Stuttg., 1969, 74; 76 f.; 211, 5 (*SB Leipz.* 113, 5, 1968, 86 f.; 89 f.; 125, 1). M. Kaiser,
ibd., 269 (207).

[71] Sigerist 1, 277 f.

the Egyptians were very conservative, they kept to the traditional customs and preserved at least παραδείγματα of the primordial establishment. These παραδείγματα are adduced as proof of the conditions common to the old Athenians and to the old Egyptians.[72]

Plato does not need any exact conformity between the original state and the modern state of Egypt, because of the old state only relics remained. He appeals at first to the constitutions of the Egyptians. At Athens it was known that the Egyptians were divided into classes,[73] but the accounts of some Greek authors known to us differ from each other. Plato adhered to one of the diverse traditions and was satisfied to see that this tradition somehow tallied with the classes of his ideal state. As witness for the historical establishment Plato is not of great value, but he is not primarily interested in the historical statement. The main point for him is the fact that the three Egyptian classes harmonize with the three classes of his ideal state, while his political program has no bearing on the Egyptians. The time is gone when scholars believed that Plato's ideal state was influenced by Egypt. There were critics already in his lifetime who asserted in a mocking manner that Plato himself had not invented his *politeia* but that he transcribed the constitution of the Egyptians.[74] In all probability, Plato would have refuted these mockers by stating it was not the Egyptians but the old Athenians who came earlier. Secondly, before Plato makes his statement on the Egyptian views of the universe, he observes that Athena introduced the shield and spear, and he adds that the old Athenians (and then the old Egyptians) were the first of the inhabitants of the regions about Asia to use these two weapons. Nobody has paid attention to this note: *altum silentium*. But if one has the duty to write a commentary, one cannot keep silence. Plato seems to contradict an opposite tradition which derived shield and spear from some Asiatics.[75] Thus we might be tempted to look for an historical kernel in Plato's assertion. As long as I argued in such a fashion, I got nowhere. It was only during a walk through the parks of Princeton that I found a solution, as I hope.

It is surprising that Plato mentions shield and spear and not sword or some other weapon. In fact, when we look at the monuments we are astonished to see how spear and shield characterize the equipment of the warriors in old times. The shield, of whatever kind it might be, is so

[72] Herter, *Palingenesia* 4, 1969, 131, 92 (*Kl. Schr.* 301, 92). For the meaning of παραδείγματα compare *Politeia* 561 E.

[73] Herter, *loc. cit.*, 125 (295); Kaiser, *loc. cit.*, 244, n. 6 on p. 269 f. (207, 2). The attribution of the Egyptian constitution to Busiris is arbitrary, says Isocrates (11, 30 ff.) himself, but, naturally, there was a tradition on the constitution itself.

[74] Crantor in Proclus in *Tim.* 20 D (1, 76, 2 ff. D.).

[75] Compare Herodotus 1, 171.

conspicuous, together with the spear, that the sword, if any, often does not appear. Even in Homer the ἔγχος is the proper striking weapon. Numerous representations since the Mycenaean times provide evidence,[76] and in Egypt I found the picture of warriors accompanying queen Hatshepsut on her travel toward Punt[77] and the wooden figures of Egyptian infantry from the tomb of the district prince, Mesehti, at Asyût.[78] It may well be that Plato had seen some Egyptian pictures of this kind. After all, it is well known that he overestimated the age of Egyptian monuments. But this is not the point at issue: he ascribes this equipment to the old Athenians, and only in second place to the old Egyptians. Therefore, we must seek at Athens what was decisive to him. He himself reveals the origin of his impression in the *Critias* (110 BC), where he speaks of the armed Athena and quotes the appearance and image of the goddess (τὸ τῆς θεοῦ σχῆμα καὶ ἄγαλμα) in order to prove that women at old Athens performed military service. Here we have a clear example of Plato's method of transferring a fact of his own time to old Athens 9,000 years earlier. When Plato was walking in his native town, he had occasion to look at the images of the divine patroness, and as usual Athena was armed with a shield and spear (the aegis was not suitable for his view). He could be convinced that the scheme of the goddess was original, and he imagined that Athena had given shields and spears to the old Athenians, but he was silent about the sword that Athena did not carry.[79]

Consequently, I am not much concerned about the historical background. Plato alone is again responsible for his statement. Old Athens and Atlantis are Platonic ideas, and impressions from reality that Plato inserted into his account are of secondary importance. Therefore, I conclude that he has intentionally ascribed the theory of the cosmological duty of the great *technai* to the old Athenians as well as to the old Egyptians. But all this is "Platonic," and only incidentally "Egyptian" or "Hippocratic."

University of Bonn

[76] Compare H. L. Lorimer, *Homer and the Monuments*, Lond., 1950, 132 ff.; P. A. L. Greenhalgh, *Early Greek Warfare*, Cambr., 1973; E. Kalinka, *Neue Jahrb.* 23, 1920, 40; J. P. Vernant and others, *Problèmes de la guerre en Grèce ancienne*, Paris, La Haye, 1968, esp. pp. 71 f.; 83 pl. 3.

[77] J. Pirenne, *Histoire de la civilisation de l'Egypte ancienne* 2, Neuchâtel, 1962, fig. 41.

[78] Walther Wolf, *Die Welt der Ägypter*, Stuttg., 1954, pl. 43.

[79] It is not clear whether the old Athenians in fighting with the Atlantians could do without any swords.

5

Plato, Galen, and the Center of Consciousness

THEODORE J. TRACY, S.J.

It may seem strange to suggest that Plato, the philosopher of the eternal, unchanging and immaterial Ideas, should be of any relevance to the history of the eminently practical science and art of medicine. By and large we tend to think of Plato as he is characterized by Georgio de Santillana, who writes: "The center of gravity of Plato's thought lies entirely elsewhere, in the realm of Ideas which are supposed to exist somehow beyond the world, to be contemplated only by the eye of the mind. . . . Plato's conception of science has nothing to do with anything happening in time and space."[1]

However, closer investigation turns up surprising evidence that Plato incorporated contemporary medical theory into his own writings[2] and, even more surprising, that the anatomical, physiological, psychological, and pathological theories he develops, especially in the *Timaeus*, were taken very seriously by subsequent medical authorities and had their influence upon the history of medical science in the West. It appears that Plato not only exerted his first influence upon the scientific tradition

[1] G. de Santillana, *The Origins of Scientific Thought* (Chicago, 1961), 195, 197. This impression is negatively confirmed by the handbooks on the history of medicine. We search in vain for Plato's name in the index of C. Singer and E. Underwood's *A Short History of Medicine* (2nd ed., Oxford, 1962), for example. And even a more specialized monograph like H. O. Taylor's *Greek Biology and Medicine* (New York, 1922) passes over Plato in silence.

[2] For Plato's use of contemporary medical teaching in his own account of disease, see H. Miller, "The Aetiology of Disease in Plato's *Timaeus*," *TAPA*, 93 (1962), 175–187, with bibliographical notes. For Plato's acceptance and elaboration of contemporary physiological theory, see T. Tracy, S.J., *Physiological Theory and the Doctrine of the Mean in Plato and Aristotle* (Chicago, 1969), esp. pp. 142–156.

indirectly through Aristotle,[3] but that he was recognized by later specialists in medical science as an authority in his own right.[4] And by one at least he was even preferred to Aristotle.

This striking instance of Platonic influence is the impact which he seems to have had upon Galen, the most distinguished physician of antiquity after Hippocrates. Ludwig Edelstein sums up his expert impression when he remarks of Galen that "Plato and Hippocrates were his gods; Aristotle he held in sincere respect."[5] Phillip De Lacy, in his interesting and important study of Galen's Platonism,[6] has clearly established that Galen must be considered, as he considered himself, fundamentally a Platonist, but one who drew upon the dialogues directly rather than upon the interpretations of other Platonists and exercized the right to correct or to develop Plato's doctrines in the light of his own research. Galen's esteem for Plato is evidenced by the fact that he synopsized the Platonic dialogues in eight books and composed nine other separate treatises explaining and defending various aspects of Platonic doctrine. Throughout Galen's works quotations from Plato are frequent and generally accurate, so that Joseph Walsh, in a study of Galen's writings and the influences inspiring them, is led to remark: "From very many quotations, second only in number to those from Hippocrates, it is evident Galen knew the Founder of the Academy almost word for word."[7]

That Galen was interested in Plato not only as a philosopher but also as an authority in what we call the "life sciences" is clear from his frequent references to Plato's anatomical, physiological, psychological, and medical theories. In addition to his summary of the *Timaeus* Galen wrote a commentary in four books specifically entitled *On the Medical Statements in the*

[3] Despite large differences Aristotle obviously followed Plato in many notions basic to his biology—the dual principle of material body and spiritual soul; the elemental bodies, earth, air, fire, and water; their qualities and (unlike Empedocles) their transmutability; the teleology of nature and organisms; the concept of health as dynamic equilibrium; etc. For Plato's formulation of scientific method before Aristotle, see L. King, "Plato's Concept of Medicine," *Journal of the History of Medicine*, 9 (1954), 38–48.

[4] Early evidence for this is provided by the second century A.D. medical papyrus *Anonymus Londinensis*, based in part on a collection of medical opinions attributed to Menon, Aristotle's associate. In citing two groups of medical authorities on the etiology of diseases, the papyrus places Plato at the head of the second group, reporting his views (largely from the *Timaeus*) in some 180 lines while devoting only 144 lines to the views of the other five authorities in this group. See W. H. S. Jones, *The Medical Writings of Anonymus Londinensis* (Cambridge, England, 1947), pp. 59–71.

[5] *OCD* (2nd ed., Oxford, 1970), s.v. Galen, 454.

[6] P. De Lacy, "Galen's Platonism," *AJP*, 93 (1972), 27–39.

[7] J. Walsh, "Galen's Writings and the Influences Inspiring Them," *Annals of Medical History*, N.S. 6 (1934), 148.

Timaeus.[8] Walsh has this to say of the matter: "Plato was not only the chief authority in philosophy, but his *Timaeus* was depended on in the study of physiology and biology. . . . To understand much of Galen's physiology and biology the *Timaeus* should be read, and to a physician it is one of the most interesting of Plato's works."[9]

These studies indicate clearly, then, that the influence of Plato upon Galen was profound. And there is much to be done in tracing the details of this influence upon individual works and upon various aspects of Galen's thought as a whole. However, at present I should like to consider a previous question which strikes me as interesting and equally challenging. The question is this: If, as seems clear, Galen were thoroughly acquainted with Aristotle and the other philosophers, both Greek and Roman, up to his time, why was it that he should somewhat surprisingly prefer Plato, referring to him as "the most divine Plato" and judging him "the foremost of all philosophers" as Hippocrates is the greatest of physicians?[10]

In his work *On the Natural Faculties* Galen gives his own sound principle for evaluating the work of his predecessors when he advises that to be outstanding in knowledge one must "become possessed with an ardent love for truth" and must "learn thoroughly all that has been said by the most illustrious of the Ancients. And when he has learned this, then for a prolonged period he must test and prove it, observing what part of it is in agreement, and what in disagreement, with obvious fact; thus he will choose this and turn away from that."[11]

If we assume that Galen followed his own advice, what might he include in the body of "obvious fact" that would have led him to choose Plato and turn away from Aristotle and other philosophers? Of course his motivation must have been very complex and his reasons philosophical as well as scientific. But I would like to suggest that one of the reasons for his attraction to Plato may be closely linked with Galen's investigations in neuroanatomy and their application to the center of consciousness.

We who have grown up associating the center of conscious life with the brain may find it difficult to conceive of a time when this was not obvious even to the most advanced investigators. But turning back in imagination to the fourth century B.C.—before the discovery of the nervous system, the

---

[8] *De iis quae medice scripta sunt in Timaeo*, ed. H. Schroeder and P. Kahle, *CMG*, Suppl. I (Leipzig, 1934). Only fragments are extant.

[9] See note 7 above, p. 148.

[10] Plato "most divine": *De placitis Hippocratis et Platonis* IX, 9 (Kühn V, 792); "foremost of all philosophers": *op. cit.*, III, 4 (Kühn V, 319).

[11] *De naturalibus facultatibus* III, 10 (Kühn II, 179–180) as translated by A. Brock, *Galen on the Natural Faculties* (London, 1916), 279.

distinction between veins and arteries, and the circulation of the blood—it may be easier to understand why people might question whether the center of thought and feeling lies in the head or in the heart.

The earliest pioneers of medical science in the West in fact were split on this issue. Alcmaeon of Croton, the physician-scientist commonly associated with the Pythagoreans early in the fifth century B.C., seems to have placed the center of life and consciousness correctly in the brain and sees consciousness as dependent upon it.[12] However, perhaps a generation later the physician-philosopher, Empedocles of Agrigentum, founder of the Sicilian school of medicine, identified sensation or thought closely with "the blood around men's hearts."[13] In the Hippocratic Corpus the work on epilepsy, *The Sacred Disease*, strongly asserts that the brain is the center of consciousness and intelligence (14, Littré, VI, 386–388 = Loeb, XVII, 174), while the Hippocratic treatise *On the Heart* associates intellection with that organ, claiming that "the intelligence (gnômê) of man is innate in the left ventricle and controls the rest of the soul" (10 *ad finem*, Littré, IX, 88).

In this situation Plato proposed, on rational rather than empirical grounds, that there are in man three vital principles or souls, of which the rational soul—the principle of intellectual awareness and thought—is centered in the brain; while the affective and nutritive principles are somehow "rooted" in the spinal marrow and centered respectively in the regions of the heart and of the liver (*Timaeus*, 44 D; 69 C–77 B). In the healthy individual the activities of the vital principles centered about the heart and liver are subordinate to those of the rational soul housed in the brain and are, at least indirectly, subject to its governance (see especially *Timaeus*, 69 D–70 B).

Aristotle, as we know, did not adopt the Platonic model of the human organism but instead proposed a single vital principle or soul capable of intellectual, sensitive, affective, and nutritive activities, of which the principal organ was the heart.[14] Knowing nothing of the nervous system, Aristotle had to assume that sensory impulses were carried somehow (through the blood vessels?) to the heart, where they are mediated

[12] *De Sensu*, 25 (DK 24 A 5). There is question, of course, about Alcmaeon's date. On this, and the whole problem in early Greek thought of the path and central organ of sensation and movement, see the masterful study of Friedrich Solmsen, "Greek Philosophy and the Discovery of the Nerves," *Museum Helveticum*, 18 (1961), 150–167, 169–197. On the location of the central organ, see esp. pp. 191–193.

[13] DK 31 B 105. But see note 12 above, pp. 157–158.

[14] One soul with various faculties: *De An.*, 411 A 26–B 27, 413 A 11–32; heart the principal organ: *Parva Nat.*, 468 A 13–469 A 10.

through the central sense power.[15] Motor reactions are for him inaugurated in the heart, which controls activity in the extremities through a system of sinews, called *neura* (nerves) connecting the rest of the body mechanically with the heart.[16] The controlling intellect, insofar as it needs a bodily organ, is for Aristotle dependent upon the heart.[17] The voice, by which man expresses his thoughts and feelings, is controlled from the heart.[18] The heart, he believes, is the first organ to develop in the embryo (*De Gen. An.*, 742 B 34–39). And in the mature organism the central location of the heart is seen as appropriate for the source of vital functions affecting all extremities (*De Part. An.*, 665 B 18–22, 666 A 13–16). Aristotle's view was propagated by his followers in the Peripatetic school through Hellenistic and Roman times.

This view of the heart as the center of consciousness and vital activities was also shared by Aristotle's contemporary, the physician Diocles of Carystos (fl. 320), known at Athens as the "second Hippocrates,"[19] and by Praxagoras of Cos (fl. 300), who succeeded Diocles as leader of the Dogmatic School of medicine and is credited with distinguishing veins from arteries.[20] The cardiocentric view of man gained widest popular acceptance, however, through the new philosophies of Stoicism and Epicureanism which appeared during the next century and became the dominant philosophical schools of Roman times, propagated especially through the writings of the Stoic Chrysippus of Soli, and the Roman Epicurean poet Titus Lucretius Carus.[21] Both Stoics and Epicureans,

[15] Heart the seat of the central sense power and source of the vascular system: *De Part. An.*, 647 A 25–B 8; 665 B 10–666 A 17, *Parva Nat.*, 455 B 34–456 B 12; sensation affected by the quantity of blood: *Parva Nat.*, 461 B 11–30, and its quality: *De Part. An.*, 656 B 2–6; no bloodless parts have sensation, though blood itself not sensitive: *De Part. An.*, 666 A 17–18.

[16] Motor reactions controlled from the heart through sinews: *De Part. An.*, 666 B 14–18, *Hist. An.*, 515 A 27–B 7.

[17] Even in highest operations intellect needs phantasms: *De An.*, 431 A 14–B 9, 432 A 13–14; phantasm produced by central sense power: *Parva Nat.*, 449 B 30–450 A 25; central sense power in the heart: see note 15 above.

[18] *De Gen. An.*, 776 B 12–19, 786 B 7–23, 787 B 6–788 A 10. See A. L. Peck, *Aristotle: Generation of Animals* (Cambridge, Mass., 1953), p. 592, Appendix B, No. 31: "... it is clear that the heart is the *archê* of the voice."

[19] M. Wellman, *Die Fragmente der sikelischen Ärzte* (Berlin, 1901), pp. 14–15, 122–123.

[20] F. Steckerl, *The Fragments of Praxagoras of Cos and His School* (Leiden, 1958), pp. 2–3 (his dates), 17–21 (arteries, distinct from veins, originate in the heart and terminate in "nerves" which control all voluntary movement).

[21] The Stoics: see H. von Arnim, *Stoicorum Veterum Fragmenta* (reprint, Stuttgart, 1968), II, 228, 235–244 (esp. 244, No. 894); the Epicureans: see, for example, Lucretius, II, 269–271; III, 136–144; 288–301.

though at odds on most other matters, agreed in making the heart the center of consciousness and control.

Meanwhile, some fifty years after the death of Aristotle, in the first part of the third century B.C. at Alexandria, the brilliant physician and scientist Herophilus of Chalcedon achieved the first real breakthrough in neuroanatomy, leading him to reassert the primacy of the brain as the center of consciousness and intelligence. Herophilus was the first to discover the true nature of nerves, to distinguish motor from sensory nerves, and to recognize the brain as their central organ.[22] His discoveries were further advanced by a younger contemporary at Alexandria, Erasistratus of Chios, who traced the cranial nerves to the brain itself and distinguished cranial sensory from cranial motor nerves.[23] However, though the school of Herophilus and Erasistratus continued at Alexandria, knowledge of the brain and nervous system apparently remained fairly static, and largely ignored, for more than 300 years until just before the time of Galen.[24]

Galen, born in A.D. 129, received his early education in his native Pergamum, first in philosophy and then in medicine. At twenty he moved to Smyrna for advanced studies in both fields, then to Corinth, and finally to the center of scientific medicine at Alexandria, where he completed his studies, becoming familiar with the achievements of Herophilus and Erasistratus as revived and advanced in the generation before him. He returned to Pergamum at twenty-eight and there served as physician to gladiators, a post which must have provided extraordinary opportunities for anatomical and physiological observation. Four years later he decided to seek his fortune in the capital city of the empire, and so in A.D. 162, at the age of thirty-three, he moved to Rome.

In his work on *Prognosis*, addressed to Epigenes, Galen gives details of

[22] Galen, *De usu partium*, VIII, 11 (Kühn, III, 667), *De anatomicis administrationibus*, IX, 3 (Kühn, II, 719), *De locis affectis*, III, 10 (Kühn, VIII, 212); Rufus of Ephesus, ed. C. Daremberg and C. E. Ruelle (Paris, 1879), pp. 184–185. See also Solmsen (see note 12 above), pp. 184–194, and the excellent introduction in M. T. May, *Galen: On the Usefulness of the Parts of the Body* (Ithaca, N.Y., 1968), I, 24–26.

[23] Galen, *De placitis Hippocratis et Platonis*, VII, 3 (Kühn, V, 602–604), *Hippocratis aphorismi et Galeni in eos commentarii*, 50 (Kühn, XVIII, pt. 1, 86); Rufus of Ephesus, Daremberg and Ruelle, p. 185. See note 22 above, pp. 26–28.

[24] The achievements of Herophilus and Erasistratus were preserved in the writings of Rufus of Ephesus, who flourished at the turn of the first and second century A.D. In the generation before Galen, Marinus of Alexandria and his school revived and developed the work of Herophilus and Erasistratus. These advances in anatomy and physiology were incorporated in Marinus' work on anatomy in twenty books, of which Galen made a compendium in four. Moreover, two of Galen's teachers, Satyrus and Numisianus, studied under Quintus, a younger associate of Marinus and a great anatomist in his own right. See note 22 above, I, 29–36.

his rise to prominence at Rome (2–5; Kühn, XIV, 605–630). He recalls that he was invited to the home of Eudemus, a Peripatetic philosopher who "believed my only significant ability lay in philosophical speculation, and that I was concerned with medicine as a side line" (2; Kühn, XIV, 608). However, Eudemus fell ill with recurrent fever, which provided Galen with the opportunity of serving him as a physician. When his intervention proved more effective than that of the established physicians already in attendance on Eudemus, Galen won the respect not only of his patient but also of other prominent Romans, "almost all those distinguished at Rome for position and learning," as he modestly remarks (2; Kühn, XIV, 612). These included the consul Flavius Boethus, who, like other of Eudemus' friends, was an earnest and enthusiastic Aristotelian. Upon learning that Galen was especially devoted to anatomical studies, Boethus and others asked that he explain the anatomy and physiology of respiration and voice production (ibid.). Both Aristotelians and Stoics regarded these functions as ultimately dependent upon the heart, while Galen had evidently claimed that he could demonstrate their dependence upon the brain. Eventually, then, arrangements were made by Boethus for public demonstrations and discussion. Galen refers to these as his "battle against the Stoics and Peripatetics" (5; Kühn, XIV, 626).

The sessions were convened before all those at Rome "distinguished in medicine and philosophy" and lasted several days, during which Galen demonstrated on living animals that inhaling and exhaling come about by dilation and contraction of the thorax through muscle controlled by nerves originating in the spine and that voice is produced through voluntary expiration modulated by the cartilages of the larynx, which are moved by muscles controlled through nerves originating in the brain (5; Kühn, XIV, 629–630). By these facts, demonstrated publicly, Galen felt that he had refuted the Stoics and Peripatetics and vindicated the position of Plato and Hippocrates that the center of consciousness and intellect lay in the brain, since the voice which conveys man's thoughts and feelings is controlled by nerves originating ultimately in that organ.[25] Galen reports that

25 Compare De usu partium, XVI, 3 (Helmreich, II, 386): "Because the voice, which reports the thoughts of the mind, is the most important of all the works of the soul, it must of course be produced by instruments receiving nerves from the brain . . ." This and subsequent passages from De usu partium are presented in May's translation (see note 22 above) with slight modifications. That Galen sees himself in this controversy not only as opposing Aristotle and the Stoics but also as vindicating Plato and Hippocrates will be clear from the whole tenor of his work On the Teachings of Hippocrates and Plato, where he specifically champions the position ascribed to Plato and Hippocrates, that the brain is the source of voluntary activity like voice, against that of Aristotle and Chrysippus. See, for example, De placitis Hippocratis et Platonis, II, 8 (Kühn, V, 277–278).

Boethus and the others were quite convinced and, at the request of Boethus, Galen dictated for permanent record all he had said and done on the occasion (5; Kühn, XIV, 630).

Three of Galen's principal works, begun during his first stay in Rome, are concerned with establishing the centrality of the brain and the Platonic position in various ways. First, in his work *On Anatomical Procedures* Galen records an even more famous and decisive demonstration of the controlling function of brain and spinal nerves (VIII, 9; Kühn, II, 696–698). By progressive section of the spinal chord he showed that continuity of spinal nerves and brain is needed at various levels for maintaining specific life functions. Thus, section between the first and second vertebrae brings death; between the third and fourth, arrested respiration; below the sixth, paralysis of thoracic muscles; and lower, paralysis of limbs, bladder, intestines. This exploration of the spinal chord is regarded as one of his most remarkable achievements.

Second, the largest of Galen's so-called philosophical works is written specifically *On the Teachings of Hippocrates and Plato* in nine books, of which six were completed during his first stay in Rome.[26] Galen's purpose in the work, as he tells us, is "to discuss the powers (or faculties) that govern us, whether they all originate in the heart alone, as Aristotle and Theophrastus think, or whether it is more satisfactory to postulate three sources (*archai*) for them, as Hippocrates and Plato believe" (VI, 1; Kühn, V, 505). The first five books are taken up with refutation of Aristotle, Chrysippus, Praxagoras and others who hold for the centrality of the heart, and include empirical evidence from Galen's medical experience and dissections proving that pressure or injury to the heart does not cut off consciousness and activity, while in the case of the brain they do.

In the later books of this work Galen argues positively for the Platonic and, as he claims, Hippocratic conception of man as animated by three locally distinct and mutually cooperative souls functioning through the brain, the heart, and the liver. Elsewhere he summarizes his position as follows:

I have shown in my book *On the Teachings of Hippocrates and Plato* that the brain and the spinal medulla are the source of all the nerves (the brain being in its turn the source of the spinal medulla itself); that the heart is the source of all the arteries and the liver of the veins; and that the nerves receive the psychic power (faculty) from the brain, the arteries the power of pulsation from the heart, and the veins the natural power (faculty) from the liver. The usefulness of the nerves, then, would lie in conveying the power of sensation and motion from its source to the several parts . . .[27]

[26] Galen, *De libris propriis*, 1 (Kühn, XIX, 15).
[27] *De usu partium*, I, 16 (Helmreich, I, 32–33), May (see note 22 above), I, 89.

It will be evident from this that Galen has adopted, with elaborations of his own, Plato's tripartite soul centered in brain, heart, and liver.

Finally, Plato's influence upon Galen is illustrated in another work, begun at this time and destined to become his most popular. This is his work *On the Usefulness of the Bodily Parts*, a combination of anatomy, physiology, and philosophy intended to show how the organs of man's body are perfectly suited to their functions because they were designed for this purpose by Nature and by Nature's divine Craftsman. Though Galen frequently acknowledges his debt to Aristotle's writings, especially the *De Partibus Animalium*, the basic conception of this work is Platonic, being a development of the enterprise of the *Timaeus* in showing how the goodness of the Dêmiourgos is communicated in the formation of each organ of the human body.[28] And nowhere is Galen more vigorous in his opposition to Aristotle than in his discussion of the brain (VIII, 2 ff.; Helmreich, I, 445 ff.). Aristotle's notion that the brain's function was to cool the heat of the heart is labeled utterly absurd (VIII, 2; Helmreich, I, 446). Aristotle is severely chided for not observing, or not trusting his observation, that the brain is warm to the touch (VIII, 3; Helmreich, I, 449). And to Aristotle's statement that "not all the instruments of the senses extend to the brain" Galen exclaims: "Aristotle! What a thing to say! For my part, I am certainly ashamed even now to mention the subject" (VIII, 3; Helmreich, I, 451). He then proceeds to lecture Aristotle on the origin and location of the cranial nerves, rebuking him for mistaking the function of the brain and neglecting the rest of the nervous system, and concluding that "it is impossible to explain correctly the usefulness of any part without first finding out the action of the whole instrument. Let us, then, assume for the present discussion propositions demonstrated in other works of mine. I have shown in my book *On the Teachings of Hippocrates and Plato* that the source of the nerves, of all sensation, and of voluntary motion is the brain, and that the source of the arteries and of the innate heat is the heart" (VIII, 3; Helmreich, I, 453).

These, then, are some of the considerations which suggest that Galen's investigations of the brain and nervous system were of importance in leading him to adopt the Platonic view of man over that of Aristotle and other philosophers. However we may evaluate Plato's influence upon Galen, and Galen's own influence upon the history of medicine in the

[28] See, for example, III, 10 (Helmreich, I, 174), where Galen refers to *De usu* as "a true hymn of praise to our Maker. . . . I regard as proof of perfect goodness that one should will to order everything in the best possible way, not grudging benefits to any creature, and therefore we must praise him as good." Compare Plato, *Timaeus*, 29 D 7 ff.

centuries that followed, this much at least can be said: that his demonstrations, as the champion of Plato and Hippocrates against Aristotle, the
Stoics, and others, established clearly and verifiably for future generations
the brain as a source of sensation and motion and the nerves as their
channels.[29] This was no small contribution to the basic knowledge of
anatomy and physiology upon which modern medicine depends.

University of Illinois at Chicago Circle

[29] This is not to say that the brain was universally accepted as the center of consciousness after Galen. Two centuries later a well educated intellectual like St. Augustine of
Hippo still assumes the heart as the center of life and consciousness. See his *Confessions*,
passim.

6

The Origin and Date
of the *Sortes Astrampsychi*

GERALD M. BROWNE

When Rudolf Hercher published *Astrampsychi oraculorum decades CIII*, he buried his edition in the *Jahresbericht über das Königl. Joachimsthalsche Gymnasium* (Berlin, 1863), a publication not to be found even in the British Museum. In 1901 J. Rendel Harris reprinted most of Hercher's text in *The Annotators of the Codex Bezae* (Appendix C, pp. 128–160), but even this reprint does not appear to have caught much attention.[1] Consequently, numerous questions connected with the text have remained unanswered. In particular, the problems concerning its origin and date deserve close study, and it is to these problems that I shall address myself in the present article. For a general introduction to the book of Astrampsychus and for a discussion of the method by which it was composed, I refer the reader to my paper in *BICS*, 17 (1970), 95–100. Instead of Hercher's awkward and somewhat misleading title, I shall use Björck's more convenient formulation, *Sortes Astrampsychi*.[2] I shall also refer to the author as Astrampsychus. The work is a patent forgery,[3] but continually to call its author pseudo-Astrampsychus is too pedantic and is hardly illuminating.

The questions of the origin and dating of the *Sortes Astrampsychi*, I believe, are intimately related. But before I deal with them in detail, the reader may find it useful to have a survey of previous scholarly work on this subject.

[1] E.g., even those most indefatigable of papyrologists B. P. Grenfell and A. S. Hunt failed to notice that a fragmentary papyrus which they published in 1916 as P. Oxy., XII, 1477, in fact belongs to the book of Astrampsychus. See below, p. 54 and note 5.

[2] G. Björck, "Heidnische und christliche Orakel mit fertigen Antworten," *Symb. Osl.*, 19 (1939), 95.

[3] It is so treated, e.g., in the recent work of W. Speyer, *Die literarische Fälschung im heidnischen und christlichen Altertum* (Munich, 1971), p. 81.

Hercher assigned the text to the early Byzantine period. For reasons that he did not disclose, he felt that its author wrote "graecitate ea, quam Byzantini scriptores sexto fere vel septimo post Christum saeculo professi sunt" (*Praefatio*, p. V). Following Hercher, P. Tannery stated that the work could hardly antedate the sixth century, though he conceded that the text in some more primitive form may have circulated under the name of Astrampsychus early in the Roman Empire.[4] The Swedish scholar G. Björck effectively demolished the late dating by showing that P. Oxy., XII, 1477, which the editors said was "probably written in or shortly before the reign of Diocletian," in fact comes from the *Sortes*.[5] Because the name Astrampsychus appears in an Egyptian magical papyrus (PGM, I, 8.1), and because a later redactor clearly differentiated between the part of the introduction composed by Astrampsychus and that designed for a Christian audience,[6] Björck concluded that "ein Orakelinstrument, das den *Sortes Astrampsychi* der Mss. sehr ähnlich sah, und von welchem Ox. 1477 ein Fragment ist, im römisch-heidnischen Ägypten angefertigt und schon dort und damals unter den Namen Astrampsychos gebracht worden ist."[7]

Attempts to establish a more accurate date thus far have been in vain. In *Astrology in Roman Law and Politics* (Philadelphia, 1954), F. H. Cramer

[4] P. Tannery, "Astrampsychos," *REG*, 11 (1898), 103 and 105. Tannery's arguments rest on mistaken ideas concerning the transmission of the text, as I shall demonstrate in a subsequent study.

[5] Björck (see note 2 above), p. 97. Perhaps because of international conditions at that time, this identification did not receive the acclamation it merited, and in "An Early Mediaeval 'Book of Fate': the Sortes xii patriarcharum," *Mediaeval and Renaissance Studies* 3 (1954), 52, T. C. Skeat again called attention to Björck's discovery; see also E. G. Turner, *Greek Papyri* (Oxford, 1968), p. 188, n. 59. But even now scholars fail to connect the papyrus with Astrampsychus. The following, e.g., deal with it as if it were anonymous: S. Safrai, "The Avoidance of Public Office in Papyrus Oxy. 1477 and in Talmudic Sources," *The Journal of Jewish Studies*, 14 (1963), 67–70 (I owe this reference to Dr. J. D. Thomas, University of Durham); B. G. Mandilaras, *The Verb in the Greek Non-Literary Papyri* (Athens, 1973), p. 399; O. Montevecchi, *La Papirologia* (Turin, 1973), p. 279.

[6] "Er [Astrampsychos] erscheint in den Mss. am Anfang des Ganzen als Verfasser eines Briefes an 'König Ptolemaios,' und der spätere Redaktor zieht eine sharfe Grenze zwischen seinem Werke und den christlichen Einschiebseln: . . . οὕτω μὲν οὖν ὁ Ἀστράμψυχος, οἱ δὲ τῆς εἰς τὸν ἕνα θεὸν ἀκλινῶς ἀντεχόμενοι λατρείας προσέθηκαν . . . ," op. cit. (see note 2 above), p. 98. Support for Björck's view comes from two manuscripts which were overlooked by Hercher in the first and only edition of the *Sortes*: Codex Erlangensis 89 and Codex Marcianus 336 both lack the section beginning οἱ δὲ τῆς εἰς τὸν ἕνα θεὸν κτλ. and are devoid of the other signs of Christian interference which characterize most of the manuscripts of the *Sortes*.

[7] Op. cit. (see note 2 above), p. 98.

asserts that the *Sortes* is "prior to the time of Manetho's *Apotelesmata*, i.e., prior to A.D. 100" (p. 185). This assertion, accepted by W. and H. G. Gundel in *Astrologumena* (Wiesbaden, 1966), p. 157, is simply an opinion; no evidence is presented to support it, and it is further vitiated by Cramer's confusion of the *Sortes* with the *Onirocritica* also attributed to Astrampsychus.[8]

Previous scholarship has established a terminus ante quem: P. Oxy., XII, 1477, shows that the *Sortes* was not written before the early fourth century. Two additional papyri of the *Sortes* recently have been published: P. Oxy., XXXVIII, 2832 and 2833; the second of these belongs, like 1477, to the late third or early fourth century, but it is very likely that the first is to be assigned to the third, thereby pushing the terminus ante quem somewhat farther back.[9] For establishing a terminus post quem the evidence perhaps is less straightforward. If it is rightly interpreted, it corroborates Björck's conclusion that the *Sortes Astrampsychi* was written in Egypt. Egyptian origin, as I hope to demonstrate, fixes a terminus post quem for the work.

The introductory epistle prefixed to some of the medieval manuscripts of the *Sortes* refers to Astrampsychus as an Egyptian.[10] A tradition recorded in Diogenes Laertius 1.2 that he was Persian magus living between the time of Zoroaster and Alexander the Great was either ignored or overlooked by the compiler of the *Sortes*.[11] The hypothesis that the work was written in Egypt comes immediately to mind, and this hypothesis receives some support from the occurrence of the name Astrampsychus in the Egyptian magical papyrus mentioned above. But the designation of

---

[8] The latter was published as an appendix to Rigaltius' edition of Artemidorus: *Artemidori Daldiani et Achmetis Sereimi F. Oneirocritica, Astrampsychi et Nicephori versus etiam Oneirocritici, Nicolai Rigaltii ad Artemidorum Notae* (Paris, 1603). W. and H. G. Gundel also follow Cramer in confusing the two works: *Astrologumena*, p. 157 and n. 48.

[9] It should not be assumed that 2832 was drafted early in the third century. In the edition I stated that, on paleographical grounds, the papyrus "should probably be assigned to the third century." Professor H. C. Youtie writes to me (letter of February 24, 1974): "I have made numerous comparisons with facsimiles, and I have had to conclude that your dating to the 3rd cent. is extremely likely. Perhaps if I had been dating it for the first time, I should have said late 3rd/early 4th."

[10] This is explicitly stated in the introductory words of some manuscripts: Ἀστραμψύχου Αἰγυπτίου πρὸς τὸν βασιλέα Πτολεμαῖον περὶ προρρήσεως διαφόρων ζητημάτων. In others it is implicit: βασιλεῖ μεγάλῳ Πτολεμαίῳ Ἀστράμψυχος ἱερεὺς καὶ βίβλων ἐπισφραγιστὴς ἰδίῳ δεσπότῃ χαίοειν. A detailed discussion of these and other details which relate to the *Überlieferungsgeschichte* of the *Sortes* will appear in the *praefatio* to my Teubner edition (in progress).

[11] For a discussion of the passage in Diogenes Laertius, see Björck (see note 2 above), p. 98, n. 1.

Astrampsychus as Αἰγύπτιος hardly constitutes proof that the *Sortes* originated in Egypt. Egypt always has been the land of mystery *par excellence*, and therefore the writer of such a text as the *Sortes* would be eager to associate his production with that country.[12]

However, there is other evidence to suggest a connection with Egypt. This is a matter of great importance in dating the text. In particular, two of the questions in the work deserve close attention in this connection: No. 88 εἰ γίνομαι βουλευτής, and No. 95 εἰ γίνομαι δεκάπρωτος.[13] If the *Sortes* was in fact written in Egypt, these questions fix 200 A.D. as the terminus post quem for the text. These offices were not established in Egypt until that year, when the Roman system of municipal bureaucracy was grafted onto the country.[14] The earliest papyrus of the *Sortes*, P. Oxy., 2832, belongs to the third century A.D. Egyptian origin of the *Sortes* therefore would mean that the work was written sometime in the third century.

The evidence I have in mind comes from the oracular petitions of Egypt.[15] These petitions, drafted either in Egyptian or in Greek, are small sheets of papyrus which individuals presented to local temples in the hope of ascertaining the future. As we shall see presently, they bear close resemblance to the questions in the *Sortes Astrampsychi*. The petitions are in the form of a protasis followed by an apodosis. This form is clearly visible in the Egyptian texts. The earlier of these are in Demotic and

---

[12] Compare, e.g., Ps.-Manetho, Βίβλος τῆς Σώθεως (*FGrHist.*, II, 609, F 25), which is entitled ἐπιστολὴ Μανεθῶ τοῦ Σεβεννύτου πρὸς Πτολεμαῖον τὸν Φιλάδελφον; see Speyer (see note 3 above), p. 81 and n. 8.

[13] On εἰ see below, p. 57 and note 21. In quoting from the *Sortes* I follow the earlier tradition, preserved in the papyri and in the better manuscripts, wherein the present tense is more common than the future. Hercher's witnesses prefer the future, though they achieve no consistency in this respect.

[14] See, e.g., A. K. Bowman, *The Town Councils of Roman Egypt* (Toronto, 1971), passim. Question 95 εἰ γίνομαι δεκάπρωτος may permit an even more accurate dating of the text. Although the *dekaproteia* is thought to have been introduced in 200 A.D., J. D. Thomas, in a paper delivered at the Fourteenth International Congress of Papyrologists (Oxford, 1974), argues that it did not appear until the reign of either the Gordians or Philip. He may well be right, but his view cannot be proven because of P. Lond., 1157R, "which suggests that *decaproti* existed, in some places at least, during or before the reign of Alexander Severus," P. J. Parson, *JRS*, 57 (1967), 136 f. (I am grateful to Dr. Thomas for communicating the results of his research to me before the congress.)

[15] In a paper in the *Festschrift Marcel Richard* (in press), I discuss the relationship between the *Sortes* and the Egyptian oracular petitions, without, however, entering into the importance this relation has for dating the text. The following discussion both summarizes and supplements my article. See also A. Henrichs, "Zwei Orakelfragen," *ZPE*, 11 (1973), 115–119.

belong to the Ptolemaic period.[16] One example will suffice to show the structure: "O my great Lord Soknebtynis, the great god. It is thy servant Stotoëte, son of Imḥūtep, who says 'if it is a good thing for me to live with Tanwē, daughter of Ḥape, she being my wife, send out to me this petition in writing.'"[17] These texts appear in positive (e.g., "if it is a good thing . . .") and in negative form ("if it is not a good thing . . ."), and by some process, probably sortition, the petitioner obtained the copy chosen by the god.[18]

The later Egyptian texts, in Coptic, continue the Demotic syntactical structure. Of the two texts of this type so far published, one is of special interest. Written in the seventh to eighth century A.D., it survives in two copies, one of which reads: "O almighty God, if you command me, your servant Paul, to go to Antinoou and remain there, order me through this papyrus." The other gives the alternative: "O almighty God, if you command me, your servant Paul, to remain [here] under the roof of the monastery of Apa Thomas, order me through this papyrus."[19]

The protasis-apodosis formulation which underlies the Egyptian texts is also the basis not only of the Greek oracular petitions but also, I would maintain, of the questions in the *Sortes Astrampsychi*.

The Greek petitions have been most recently discussed, with full bibliography, by A. Henrichs.[20] Most of them use εἰ, corresponding to the Egyptian parallels[21]; e.g., P. Mich. inv. 1258[22]

> κυρία Εἶσι· εἰ ἐξοῦ
> μοι γέγονεν ὁ
> πόνος καὶ θερα-
> πείαν μοι διδοῖς,
> 5 ποίησόν μοι τοῦ-
> το ἀναχθῆναι.[23]

[16] For bibliography pertinent to the Demotic texts, see Henrichs (see note 15 above), p. 115, n. 1.

[17] P. Flor., 8700 (G. Botti, "Biglietti per l'oracolo di Soknebtynis in caratteri demotici," *Studi in memoria di Ippolito Rosellini*, II, Pisa, 1955, 13); the translation is that of J. Černý, *Egyptian Oracles*, in R. A. Parker, *A Saite Oracle Papyrus from Thebes* (Providence, 1962), p. 47.

[18] E. Bresciani, P. Pestman, P. Mil. Vogl., III, *Testi demotci*, 195 f.

[19] The translation of the Coptic is mine. The text was published by H. de Nie, "Een koptisch-christelijke Orakelvraag," *Ex Oriente Lux: Jaarbericht*, 8 (1942), 615–618. The same pattern of expression appears in the other Coptic oracular petition, published by S. Donadoni, "Una domanda oracolare cristiana da Antinoe," *Rivista degli studi orientali*, 29 (1954), 183–186.

[20] See note 15 above.

[21] Henrichs (see note 15 above), p. 116 and n. 7.

[22] Published by Henrichs (see note 15 above), p. 117 f.

[23] In line 1 read ᾿Ισι and ἐκ σοῦ (see editor's comments *ad loc.*).

58   Illinois Classical Studies, I

[Editor's translation: "Herrin Isis! Falls Du mein Leiden verursacht hast und mir Heilung verschaffst, veranlasse, dass mir dieses (Billet) zurückgebracht wird!"]

The questions in the *Sortes Astrampsychi* resemble these Greek oracular petitions both in content and in structure. The following examples illustrate contextual similarity:

No. 20 εἰ ἀγοράζω τὸ προκείμενον
        PGM II 31c εἰ συμφέρει μοι ἀγοράσαι . . . [τοῦτό μ]οι δός
No. 21 εἰ γαμῶ καὶ συμφέρει μοι
        Schubart 12²⁴ [εἰ] δέδοταί μοι γαμῆσαι [τοῦ]τό μοι δός
No. 42 εἰ σώζομαι ἀσθενῶν
        PGM II 30c ἡ μὲν σοθήσωι ταύτης ἧς ἐν ἐμοὶ ἀσθενία[ς] . . .
        τοῦτό{ν} μοι ἐξένικον²⁵

The examples from Astrampsychus may be translated as if they were questions, and in terms of semantics they are in fact questions. But grammatically they are protases, to which the appropriate apodosis (e.g., τοῦτό μοι δός) has been suppressed. In other words, what we find in the *Sortes* is a direct descendant of the protasis-apodosis formulation of the Egyptian oracular petitions. It is this connection with the petitions which corroborates the view that the work was composed in Egypt.

I have attempted to explain and clarify one feature of the *Sortes Astrampsychi* by utilizing the evidence provided by the Egyptian oracular texts. If I have succeeded in connecting the *Sortes* with these texts, we may say with some conviction that the work originated in Egypt sometime during the third century of our era.²⁶

Center for Hellenic Studies, Washington, D.C.

²⁴ From the collection assembled by W. Schubart, *Zeitschrift f. ägypt. Sprache*, 67 (1931), 110–115.

²⁵ Read εἰ μὲν σωθῶ (or σωθήσομαι) ταύτης τῆς ἐν ἐμοὶ ἀσθενείας, τοῦτό μοι ἐξένεγκον. For εἰ with subjunctive see Blass-Debrunner-Funk, *Greek Grammar of the New Testament*, 372.3 with bibliography.

²⁶ An expanded version of this paper was delivered as a lecture at the University of Illinois, March 1, 1974.

7

Hephaestion, *Apotelesmatica*, Book I

MIROSLAV MARCOVICH

1. Page 1.10 Pingree (Teubner, 1973) Μὴ ταραττέτω δὲ μηδένα τὸ ἐπ' ἐνίων δυσθεώρητον διὰ τὸ πολυμερὲς τῆς τοιαύτης θεωρίας καὶ τὴν κατὰ τὸ ἐνδεχόμενον ἐπίσκεψίν τε καὶ γνῶσιν εἰς τελείας ἀκαταληψίας δόξαν τῶν τε πλείστων καὶ ὁλοσχερεστέρων συμπτωμάτων οὕτως ἐναργῶς τὴν ἀπὸ τοῦ περιέχοντος αἰτίαν ἐμφανιζόντων . . .

This text does not make sense. Read instead: Μὴ ταραττέτω δὲ μηδένα τὸ ἐπ' ἐνίων δυσθεώρητον, διὰ τὸ πολυμερὲς τῆς τοιαύτης θεωρίας, κ α τ ⟨ ά γ - ε ι ν ⟩ τὴν κατὰ τὸ ἐνδεχόμενον ἐπίσκεψίν τε καὶ γνῶσιν εἰς τελείας ἀκαταληψίας δόξαν, τῶν γ ε πλείστων . . . "Let nobody be disturbed by the fact that in some cases difficulties involving observation (because of the complexity of the astrological theory) *reduce* the investigation and knowledge (so far as they are possible) to the fancy of a complete inability of comprehension, since a great majority of general astrological accidents so clearly manifest the influence of the surrounding heaven (upon men) . . ."

As is known, Hephaestion of Thebes in Egypt is borrowing his wisdom from Ptolemy, whose *Apotelesmatica* read on page 3.12 Boll-Boer (Teubner, 1957) as follows: μήτε (sc. τις) πρὸς τὴν κατὰ τὸ ἐνδεχόμενον ἐπίσκεψιν ἀποκνοίη, τῶν γε πλείστων καὶ ὁλοσχερεστέρων συμπτωμάτων ἐναργῶς οὕτως τὴν ἀπὸ τοῦ περιέχοντος αἰτίαν ἐμφανιζόντων . . . τὸ ἐπ' ἐνίων δυσθεώρητον ἀκαταληψίας τελείας δόξαν παρέσχεν . . . As for the phrase διὰ τὸ πολυμερὲς τῆς τοιαύτης θεωρίας, it is Hephaestion's own. Compare his page 81.8, τὸ γὰρ πολυμερὲς τῆς θεωρίας ἐνταῦθα ποσῶς ἀναγκάζει πλείοσι χρῆσθαι, and page 118.26, διὰ τὴν πολυμερῆ καὶ πολυθρύλλητον αὐτοῦ θεωρίαν.

2. Page 1.18 Πρὸς οὓς ἀντιτακτέον μὲν τό τε ἐφ' ἡμῖν καὶ τὸ ἐν τοῖς πλείστοις σπουδάσμασι τῶν ἀνθρώπων, δυσωπῆσαι δὲ τῆι περὶ τούτων ἐνεργείαι . . .

Read: ἐναργείαι (= cod. A) and compare Sextus Empiricus, *P. H.* III, 135, τοὺς σκεπτικοὺς . . . δυσωπεῖ δὲ καὶ ἡ ἐνάργεια. "One should also put them to shame by the very evidence about such things."

3. Page 2.9 μηδὲ οὕτω χρὴ νομίζειν ἅπαντα τοῖς ἀνθρώποις ὡς ἐκ θείου τινὸς καὶ ἀλύτου προστάγματος μηδεμιᾶς ἁπλῶς ἄλλης αἰτίας ἀντιπρᾶξαι εἰς ἔνια δυναμένης. Evidently, the verb "to happen" is missing, to go with "to men." Thus read: νομίζειν ⟨ἀπαντᾶν⟩ ἅπαντα τοῖς ἀνθρώποις and compare Ptolemy, *Apotelesm.*, page 12.6, μηδ᾿ οὕτως ἅπαντα χρὴ νομίζειν τοῖς ἀνθρώποις ἀπὸ τῆς ἄνωθεν αἰτίας παρακολουθεῖν ὥσπερ ἐξ ἀρχῆς ἀπό τινος ἀλύτου καὶ θείου προστάγματος καθ᾿ ἕνα ἕκαστον νενομοθετημένα καὶ ἐξ ἀνάγκης ἀποβησόμενα, μηδεμιᾶς ἄλλης ἁπλῶς αἰτίας ἀντιπρᾶξαι δυναμένης . . .

4. Page 3.23 Ἀρχὴν δὲ ἐποιήσαντο ἀπὸ τοῦ Κριοῦ ἐαρινοῦ τμήματος διὰ τὸ ἐκ τοῦ νοτίου ἡμισφαιρίου ἐπὶ τὸ βόρειον τότε τοῦ Ἡλίου μετερχομένου ὑφ᾿ ὃ τέτακται ἡ καθ᾿ ἡμᾶς οἰκουμένη ἄρχειν ὥσπερ αὖθις ζωῆς καὶ τὰς βλάστας τῶν φυτῶν καὶ πάντων τῶν παρ᾿ ἡμῖν ζώιων τὰς πληρώσεις γίνεσθαι. The sentence does not make sense. Evidently, there is a lacuna in the text. Thus read: Ἀρχὴν δὲ ἐποιήσαντο—ὑφ᾿ ὃ τέτακται ἡ καθ᾿ ἡμᾶς οἰκουμένη. Ἄρχειν ⟨γὰρ τότε τὰ πάντα⟩ ὥσπερ αὖθις ζωῆς . . . Hephaestion's probable source of inspiration, Ptolemy, *Apotelesm.*, page 30.17, is different in sense: Διόπερ καὶ τοῦ ζωιδιακοῦ μηδεμιᾶς οὔσης φύσει ἀρχῆς ὡς κύκλου τὸ ἀπὸ τῆς ἐαρινῆς ἰσημερίας ἀρχόμενον δωδεκατημόριον τὸ τοῦ Κριοῦ καὶ τῶν ὅλων ἀρχὴν ὑποτίθενται, καθάπερ ἐμψύχου ζώιου τοῦ ζωιδιακοῦ τὴν ὑγρὰν τοῦ ἔαρος ὑπερβολὴν προκαταρκτικὴν ποιούμενοι . . .

5. Page 5.16 Τὰ δὲ σημεῖα· λεπτὰ τὰ στήθη μὴ σεσαρκωμένα, αἱ κνῆμαι γυμναὶ καὶ ἄσαρκοι· ἕξει σημεῖον περὶ τὸ ἀριστερὸν ἢ ὑπὸ τὴν ἀριστερὰν μασχάλην. Read: ἕξει σημεῖον περὶ τὸ ἀριστερὸν ⟨στέρνον⟩ ἢ ὑπὸ τὴν ἀριστερὰν μασχάλην and compare page 23.18, σημεῖον ἐπὶ τῶν στηθῶν αὐτοῦ εὑρεθήσεται; page 28.5, σημεῖον ἔσται περὶ τὴν ὀσφὺν καὶ ὑπὸ τὴν μασχάλην καὶ περὶ τὰ στήθη.

6. Page 7.5 = Dorothei Sidonii frag. metrica, page 92.5 Kroll (*CCAG* VI)

Ὀκτὼ δὲ* πρώτας ὁρίων μοίρας Κυθέρεια
ἐν τούτωι (sc. ἐν Ταύρωι), Στίλβων δὲ μετ᾿ αὐτὴν ἔλλαχε μοίρας
δὶς τρεῖς, καὶ Φαέθων ἔλαχ᾿ ὀκτώ, πέντε δὲ Φαίνων,
τὰς δ᾿ ὑπολειπομένας ἔλαχεν Πυρόεις μετὰ τούσδε.

---

* δὲ Housman, agn. Pingree: δ᾿ ἔλαχεν A P: δ᾿ ἔλλαχε N

Pingree adopts Housman's δὲ for the transmitted δ᾿ ἔλαχεν. But this verb is likely in the first line, as can be seen from lines 2–4. I think ὁρίων is an explanatory gloss (deleted already by A. Koechly, in *Manethonis Apoteles-*

matica, Teubner, 1858, page 114.26). Accordingly, read the first line as follows:

ὀκτὼ δὲ πρώτας [ὁρίων] μοίρας λάχεν ⟨ἡ⟩ Κυθέρεια

and compare the following hexameter ends of Dorotheus: page 5.2 = page 11.8, λάχεν ἡ Κυθέρεια; page 25.6, τέσσαρας ἡ Κυθέρεια.

7. Page 7.25 Τὸ δὲ σημεῖον· τὸ πρόσωπον πλατύ, τὰ στέρνα εὐρύτατα, ὀφθαλμὸς εὐειδής, τὰ ὦτα πλατέα . . . Evidently, read τὰ δὲ σημεῖα (as in the rest of the eleven zodiacal signs), and also εὐρύτατα, ⟨τοὺς⟩ ὀφθαλμοὺς εὐειδής. Compare pages 8.9, τῶι προσώπωι εὐειδεῖς; 9.28 = 16.4 = 30.2 τὸ πρόσωπον εὐειδής.

8. Page 8.20 . . . κατὰ μέρος δὲ τὰ μὲν προηγούμενα αὐτοῦ φθαρτικά, τὰ δὲ μέσα εὔκρατα, τὰ δὲ ἑπόμενα μεμιγμένα καὶ ἄτακτα, τὰ δὲ βόρεια πνευματώδη καὶ σεισμοποιά, τὰ δὲ νότια ξηρὰ καὶ καυσώδη. This is a description of the dodekatemorion of Gemini. It is literally copied from Ptolemy, *Apotelesm.*, page 96.10. Consequently, read: τὰ μὲν προηγούμενα αὐτοῦ ⟨δίυγρα καὶ⟩ φθαρτικά. This is confirmed by Vettius Valens, page 8.3 Kroll: ἀπὸ γ' ἕως ζ', εὔυγρα.

9. Page 8.27 Κατὰ ⟨δὲ addidi⟩ Πτολεμαῖον· Ὑρκανία, Ἀρμενία, Μαντιανή, Κυρηναϊκή, Μαρμαρική, Αἴγυπτος κατὰ χώραν. Read: Αἰγύπτου ⟨ἡ⟩ κάτω χώρα. Ptolemy (page 76.14) has Αἰγύπτου κάτω χώρα. Also compare *Rhetorii excerpta ex Teucro Babylonio* (under the same sign of Gemini), page 199.4 Boll (*CCAG*, VII): κατὰ δὲ Πτολεμαῖον Ὑρκανία, Ἀρμενία, Ματτιανή, Κυρηναϊκή, Μαρμαρική, Αἰγύπτου (R: Αἴγυπτος T V) ἡ κάτω χώρα, and Hephaestion, page 133.29, διὰ τῆς κάτω Αἰγύπτου.

10. Page 9.27 Τὰ δὲ σημεῖα αὐτοῦ· μέσος τὴν ἡλικίαν ἔσται, εὐειδὴς τὸ πρόσωπον, μέγας (P: μέσος A) τὸ σῶμα. Read: μέλας τὸ σῶμα and compare pages 10.8, ξανθὸς τὸ σῶμα; 21.9, μικρομεγέθης, μέλας; 28.4, οὐ πάνυ εὐμεγέθης, μέλας τὸ χρῶμα; 12.6, μικρομεγέθης, μελανόχρους.

11. Page 13.23 εὐεργετῶν τοὺς ὑποτασσομένους, καὶ πολλοὺς σκεπάσει καὶ κτήσεται, εὐεπίψογος δὲ διὰ γυναῖκα. Read: πολλοὺς σκεπάσει καὶ ⟨πολλὰ⟩ κτήσεται = pages 11.17, 20.18, 21.5, 26.13, 28.3, 30.9, and 27, 217.23.

12. *Dorothei Sidonii fragmenta metrica*: page 15.14

Ἑπτὰ δὲ τὰς προτέρας ἔλαχε Στίλβων ἐπὶ τῆσδε (sc. Παρθένου)
μοίρας καὶ δέκα Κύπρις ἔχει, Φαέθων δὲ κατ' αὐτὴν
τέσσαρας, ἑπτὰ δ' Ἄρης, πυμάτας δύο δ' ἔλαχε Φαίνων.

62   Illinois Classical Studies, I

Read: μετ᾿ αὐτὴν = pages 7.6, 11.9, 13.15, 27.7 (Koechly). Page 19.15

Ὑπὸ δ᾿ αὐτῶι ἔπλετο πᾶσα
Καρχηδών, Τυρίης Διδοῦς χερὶ δωμηθεῖσα,
Ἄμμωνος Λιβύη τ⟨ε⟩ ὑπ᾿ ὄμμασι Σικελίη χθών.

Read: Λιβύη καὶ ὑπ᾿ ὄμμασι. Similarly, page 11.8

ἐν τούτωι, μετέπειτα δὲ ἐξ λάχεν ἡ Κυθέρεια

read: δέ ⟨θ᾿⟩ ἐξ (Kroll), and compare pages 5.3, 37.10. Moreover, page
21.26

Ἔστρωται δ᾿ ὑπὸ τῶιδε βαθύπλουτον κλίμα Γάλλων
καὶ Κρήτη, Κρονίδαο Διὸς τροφός, ἡ δέ τε Μυσῆς
ἁρπαγίμης ὑμέναιος ἔφυ κρατερῆς Εὐρώπης

read: ἧι δέ τε, "where was the wedding of Europe." Page 22.16

Δώδεκα δὲ προτέρας Φαέθων μοίρας λάχε τούτου,
πέντε δέ τοι Παφίη, τρι⟨τά⟩τας Στίλβων μετὰ τούσδε,
τέσσαρας Ἑρμείας ἔλαχεν, Φαίνων δέ τε πέντε,
τὰς δ᾿ ὑπολειπομένας Ἄρης λάχε δὶς δύο μοίρας.

The comma at the end of the second line is unnecessary and misleading,
since Στίλβων is Ἑρμείας, the planet Mercury. Page 29.1, Ὑπόκειται δ᾿
αὐτῶι·

ἡ Ἐρυθρὰ θάλασσα
ἕως τῶν Ὠκεανοῖο ῥοῶν.

Read: [ἡ] Ἐρυθρά ⟨τε⟩ θάλασσα. Hephaestion uses "the Indian Ocean"
without the article on pages 4.20, 22.6, 29.9.

13. Page 16.2 καὶ μετὰ τὴν νεότητα εὐνοηθήσεται ἀπὸ γυναικὸς καὶ
ἐσχάτης καλῆς τεύξεται.

Read: ὑπὸ γυναικὸς = pages 14.17, 20.9, 23.5, 23.13, 26.12, 27.18, 30.1.

14. Page 19.4 Τὸ δὲ τοῦ Σκορπίου δωδεκατημόριον . . . ἔστιν οἶκος
Ἄρεως. τοῦτο δὲ τὸ κέντρον ἄσπορον καὶ πέφυκεν ὀφθαλμοὺς πηροῦν ἢ
ὑποχύσεις καὶ λευκώματα ποιεῖν διὰ τοὺς νεφελοειδεῖς ἀστέρας τοὺς παρα-
κειμένους ἐν τῶι Γαλαξίαι . . .

Read: τοῦτο⟨ν⟩ δὲ τὸ κέντρον and compare page 93.22, τὰ δὲ ἔσχατα
⟨καὶ addidi⟩ τὰ περὶ τὸ κέντρον (sc. τοῦ Σκορπίου) ποιεῖ κιναίδους, ἔσθ᾿ ὅτε
δέ τινας καὶ ὑποχύσεις ἐν τοῖς ὀφθαλμοῖς ἔχοντας διὰ τὸ νεφέλιον τὸ περὶ τὸ
κέντρον . . .; page 142.7, καὶ τῶι κέντρωι τοῦ Σκορπίου.

15. Page 20.27 ἔσται ἐν ζημίαις καὶ ἀνωμαλίαις καὶ ξενιτείαις καὶ τύχης
μετεωρισμῶι καὶ ψυχικῶς καὶ σωματικῶς ἀρρωστήσει . . .

The phrase τύχης μετεωρισμός is nonsensical. The scribe had confused Ψ

and T, thus read: ψυχῆς μετεωρισμῶι, "mental trouble" or "disturbance."
This is confirmed by pages 23.12, καὶ ψυχικὸν μετεωρισμὸν ἕξει; 207.25, ἔσται ἔν τε ἀσθενείαις κρυπταῖς καὶ νόσοις μακραῖς καὶ μετεωρισμοῖς ψυχικοῖς.

16. Page 29.4 ⟨Κατὰ δὲ Πτολεμαῖον·⟩ Φαζανία, Νασαμωνῖτις, Λυδία, Κιλικία, Παμφυλία.

Read: Νασαμωνῖτις, ⟨Γαραμαντία,⟩ Λυδία, Κιλικία, Παμφυλία = Ptolemy, page 76.29, (Γαραμαντική); Rhetorius, page 211.25, (Γαραμαντίαν), *CCAG* VII.

17. Page 30.7 . . . τραφήσεται πλουσίως καὶ διαστήσει τοὺς γονεῖς καὶ τὰ αὐτῶν μειωθήσεται καὶ δι' ἑαυτοῦ κτήσεται πολλά· ἔσται γὰρ ἐμπορικός πώς τις καὶ περίκτητος . . .

Read: καὶ τὰ αὐτῶν μειώσει (= pages 9.23, 10.4, 12.12, 25.25, 30.25) . . . ἔσται γὰρ ἐμπορικός πώς τις καὶ περικτητ⟨ικ⟩ός, and compare κτητικός, "skilled in earning."

18. Page 31.10 Ὁ μὲν οὖν Ἥλιος κατείληπται θερμαίνων ἅμα καὶ ξηραίνων. ἡ δὲ Σελήνη ὑγραίνει καὶ πεπαίνει ὥσπερ τὰ σώματα μετὰ τοῦ ἠρέμα θερμαίνειν.

Read: καὶ ὥσπερ πεπαίνει τὰ σώματα and compare Ptolemy, page 17.21, οὕτως ἄντικρυς τὰ σώματα πεπαίνουσα (sc. ἡ σελήνη).

19. Page 32.21 . . . τῆι (sc. δυνάμει) τοῦ Ἄρεως. Page 33.27, . . . τῶι (sc. ἀστέρι) τοῦ Ἄρεως.

Read the former: τῆι τοῦ Ἄρεως, ⟨οἱ δὲ λοιποὶ τῆι τοῦ Κρόνου καὶ ἠρέμα τῆι τοῦ Ἑρμοῦ, οἱ δὲ ἐν ἄκροις τοῖς κέρασι τῆι τοῦ Ἄρεως⟩ (= Ptolemy, page 23.16–17), and the latter: τῶι τοῦ Ἄρεως, ⟨οἱ δὲ ἐν ἄκροις τοῖς ποσὶ καὶ τῶι σύρματι τῶι τοῦ Ἑρμοῦ καὶ ἠρέμα τῶι τοῦ Ἄρεως⟩ (= Ptolemy, page 25.3–4).

20. Page 40.5 Περισχεθῆναι λέγεται οἷον τὴν Παρθένον Λέων καὶ Ζυγὸς περιέχει.

Read: οἷον ⟨ὅταν⟩ τὴν Παρθένον . . . περιέχηι and compare page 42.12, οἷον ὅταν ὁ τῆς Ἀφροδίτης λόγου ἕνεκεν ἑξάγωνον ποιῆι πρὸς τὰ φῶτα διάστασιν.

21. Page 49.17 . . . τῶν τε ἀλόγων ζώιων καὶ τῶν ἐκ γῆς φυομένων σπάνιν (sc. ἐμποιεῖ ὁ τοῦ Ἄρεως ἀστήρ) εἰς χρῆσιν ἀνθρωπίνην . . .

Read: τῶν ἐκ γῆς φυομένων εἰς χρῆσιν ἀνθρωπίνην σπάνιν and compare Ptolemy, page 88.6, περὶ δὲ τὰ ἐπιτήδεια πρὸς χρῆσιν ἀνθρωπίνην τῶν τε ἀλόγων ζώιων καὶ τῶν ἐκ τῆς γῆς φυομένων σπάνιν . . .

22. Page 56.7 Ἐν δὲ τῶι Λέοντι ἐκλείποντα τὸν Ἥλιον κατὰ τὴν πρώτην τρίωρον βαρβάρων στρατιὰν πολεμῆσαι τοῖς Ἕλλησι καὶ ἑλεῖν αὐτοὺς μηνύειν, κατὰ δὲ τὴν δευτέραν τρίωρον . . . , ἐν δὲ τῆι τρίτηι τριώρωι . . . , ἐν δὲ τῆι τετάρτηι τριώρωι, τουτέστι δύνοντα (edd.: δύνων A L P), βαρβάρων ἐπίθεσιν καὶ πτῶσιν σημαίνειν.

64   Illinois Classical Studies, I

Delete τουτέστι δύνων as an explanatory gloss on τετάρτη τρίωρος (i.e., between 3 and 6 P.M.). It is not to be found in the rest of the cases (pages 55–62).

23. Page 66.18   Μικρὸς δὲ καὶ στυγνὸς ἀνατείλας (sc. ὁ τῆς Σώθεως ἀστήρ) βορέου πνέοντος ἐπιστρατεύσασθαι τῆι χώραι τοὺς ἐκτὸς καὶ οὐ καλῶς ἀπαλλάξειν, τήν τε ἀνάβασιν τοῦ Νείλου καὶ αἰσίαν τῶν ὑδάτων ἐπιφορὰν ἔσεσθαι σημαίνει καὶ τὰς τιμὰς ἐλαττωθῆναι.
Read: ἐπιστρατεύσεσθαι.

University of Illinois at Urbana

8

Roman Coins as Historical Evidence: The Trojan Legends of Rome

RICHARD E. MITCHELL

Numismatics forms part of our material record of the past and deserves greater consideration than it receives from most historians. Philip Grierson once remarked that "history without numismatics is imperfect," but he also cautioned that "numismatics without history is impossible."[1] Without doubt, the most important contribution a numismatist can make is the application of numismatic evidence to the solution of historical problems. As Michael Crawford stated it: "Numismatics cannot be an end in itself, only a servant of history."[2] Herein lies the true importance of the numismatic contributions of Theodor Mommsen, E. J. Haeberlin, Harold Mattingly, Laura Breglia, Andreas Alföldi, and Rudi Thomsen.[3]

However, despite special pleading, numismatics is dependent upon the literary tradition and cannot stand alone. When a coin is the only record we possess of an event, a cult, or a state's existence, both numismatist and historian alike are virtually helpless. Tales of treaties, wars, religious celebrations, monuments, and state honors paid to individuals are only a few features from the sources commonly used to date and interpret Roman coins. Consequently, numismatic evidence is most often used to modify, confirm, or otherwise illustrate what already is known in part. For example, certain denarii of the Republic stand as *testimonia* to the importance of certain *gentes* and help us to see more clearly the significance

---

[1] *Numismatics and History* (Historical Association Publication, London, 1951), p. 15. Consideration of space requires that citations be kept to a minimum. An attempt will be made to cite works which have ample references to the primary and secondary material.

[2] "Roman Republican numismatics," *A Survey of Numismatic Research*, 1960–1965, I (Copenhagen, 1967), 161.

[3] For an excellent discussion of "160 years of research," see Rudi Thomsen, *Early Roman Coinage*, I (Copenhagen, 1957), 210–248.

of *pietas*, *mos maiorum*, and *honores* and how family claims to greatness, based upon the accomplishments of ancestors, gradually replaced the pride supposedly once felt in the *res publica*. The later denarii, especially those of the first century B.C., underline the developing role of the individual in Roman politics and the destruction of traditions we are told earlier generations held dear. From imperial coinage we see the cult of the individual focused on the emperor alone and learn of the religious and mythological foundations of the principate, the growth of ceremonies, and the development of cults; and frequently we obtain a portrait of the emperor personally and some idea of the regalia of his office.[4]

On the other hand, some numismatic evidence is earlier than any surviving Roman literary record, and while the coin types reflect the official Roman attitude of their time, the coin material has a greater claim to authenticity than the literary record since it is unaffected by subsequent rationalizations of historical developments. For example, we are all familiar with the story of how the writing of Roman history began only after Rome obtained hegemony over the Italian peninsula, was well on her way to a similar position in the Western Mediterranean, and already had considerable contacts with Eastern Mediterranean states. Indeed, Fabius Pictor's work is often explained as an attempt to present Roman development and rule in the most favorable light to a Greek speaking world.[5] Thus we know that traditional interpretations of Roman expansion and internal developments prior to the Second Punic War are, to a degree, products of hindsight and greatly affected by the contemporary events and prejudices of the writers, by the existing Greek historical and rhetorical traditions, by contemporary philosophical assumptions, and by the strong aristocratic, if not gentilic, bias of the authors. The growth of Rome's empire is presented as divine will, as the consequence of her religious, moral, or governmental excellence: a race of Cincinnati destined to rule the world. We are told by ancient and modern historians alike that the early Romans were patriotic, proud, and noble folk who were without imperial ambitions or greed until Carthage forced their hand. Similarly, in their quest for *virtus*, in their observance of *pietas* and *fides*, true Romans found their strength, and while giving aid to weaker states, had no desire or need for the higher culture and refinements known

[4] A. Alföldi, "The main aspects of political propaganda on the coinage of the Roman Republic," *Essays in Roman Coinage Presented to Harold Mattingly* (Oxford, 1956), pp. 63–95, presents a reflective, provocative, but not always successful attempt to survey the trends in Republican coinage.

[5] E. Badian, "The early historians," *Latin Historians*, ed. T. A. Dorey (New York, 1966), pp. 1–36. This is an admirable study with excellent bibliographical notes.

to others.[6] Like the old Washington Senators, the Roman senators were first in war, were first in peace and, while not last in the American League, were last in the acquisition of the economic, cultural, and artistic sophistication that characterized the civilization of their Hellenic neighbors.

The earliest Roman coins are unaffected by these later justifications or explanations for Rome's success, but they must be correctly dated and interpreted if we are to obtain historical evidence from their specific types, weights, or particular styles, which offer insights into Republican history. The coins, unlike modern specimens, do not date themselves, and they have often surrendered secrets they may never have intended to reveal. They tell a scholar who dates them to the third century things they would never dream of telling a specialist who supports their fourth century origin, and each scholar claims that the numismatic evidence fits his period. Although adequate presentation of the various theses and the evidence to support them appear elsewhere,[7] a brief survey of the scholarship and the current state of our knowledge will serve as a necessary background for our main problem. While drastic shifts in dating Rome's earliest didrachm coinage occurred in the last hundred years, all chronologies, high and low, have always rested squarely on the literary tradition.

Pliny says Rome first struck silver coins in 269 B.C. when, in the consulship of Quintus Ogulnius and Gaius Fabius, the denarius was issued.[8] Other literary evidence confirms the 269 (or 268) B.C. date but does not mention the denarius. Those who accept this "traditional" date for the denarius assume that certain heavier silver coins, without value marks, are earlier than the denarius and must have been struck elsewhere than in Rome before 269 B.C. Because Rome established permanent contact with coin-producing and coin-using cities to the south in the period from 340 to 270 B.C., the coins were generally assigned to Campanian or South Italian mints. Capua and Neapolis in particular were supposed to have been influential in the development of early Roman coinage. In this manner the coins acquired the name "Romano-Campania."[9]

[6] See D. C. Earl, *The Moral and Political Tradition of Rome* (London, 1967), p. 11 ff. and esp. the eulogy for L. Caecilius Metellus (p. 24). R. M. Henry, "Roman tradition," *Proceedings of the Classical Association*, 34 (1937), 7 ff., is still useful.

[7] In addition to Thomsen's presentation cited above (note 3), see *Early Roman Coinage*, II–III (Copenhagen, 1961), for an extensive discussion of the various theses. Compare R. E. Mitchell, "A new chronology for the Romano-Campanian coins," *N.C.*, 6 (1966), 66 ff.; "The fourth century origin of Roman didrachms," A.N.S., *Museum Notes*, 15 (1969), 41 ff.

[8] *N.H.*, pp. 33, 42–47.

[9] Thomsen, *Early Roman Coinage*, I, 19 ff., presents the ancient literary evidence important for the study of early Republican coinage and photographs and complete descriptions of all Roman coins mentioned in this essay.

The theory concerning their fourth-century Campanian origin came under attack in 1924 when Harold Mattingly wrote that metrologically and stylistically the coins ought to be dated closer together. He suggested that four mints issued the coins simultaneously. The horse's head and horse types of the Romano-Campanian coins were interpreted as copies of Punic types and were dated according to the treaty concluded by Rome and Carthage against Pyrrhus.[10] Subsequently, when Mattingly lowered the date for the denarius, he was forced to abandon his original chronology for the Romano-Campanian coins and dated the first four issues to 269 B.C. Thus Mattingly concluded there were no true Romano-Campanian coins.[11]

Early in his career, Mattingly complained that although numismatists were attracted to his position, historians remained unimpressed.[12] By the middle of the century this had changed. However, while only a few numismatists continued to support the traditional chronology, the Mattingly revolution, untouched by traditionalists, was struck a mortal blow from another quarter. Rudi Thomsen's exhaustive and penetrating study of *Early Roman Coinage* came to several conclusions which shook the foundation of the Mattingly edifice and at the same time proved the unacceptable nature of certain traditional interpretations.

Thomsen demonstrated the sequential order of the Romano-Campanian issues. The sequence is clearly shown by the metrology of the coins and is borne out by the hoard evidence.[13] The *ROMANO*-inscribed coins began with the bearded, helmeted Mars/horse's head coin, the heaviest of the group, and proceeded to the lightest, the coin with helmeted Roma/Victory attaching palm to a trophy. The latter was struck on the six scruple standard (about 6½ grammes). The coins with *ROMA* legend followed in sequence, also issued on the six scruple standard, including the early issues of the quadrigatus, the last of the Romano-Campanian coins. That the latter was replaced by the denarius during the Second Punic War, as Thomsen averred, is now clearly demonstrated by the hoard evidence from Morgantina.[14]

10 "The Romano-Campanian coinage and the Pyrrhic War," *N.C.*, 4 (1924), 181 ff.

11 To trace the development of Mattingly's argument, consult "The first age of Roman coinage," *J.R.S.*, 19 (1929), 19 ff.; "'Aes' and 'pecunia,'" *N.C.*, 3 (1943), 21 ff.; "The first age of Roman coinage," *J.R.S.*, 35 (1945), 65 ff.; and *Roman Coins* (London, 1960).

12 *J.R.S.* (1929), 20.

13 Thomsen, *Early Roman Coinage*, III, 49 ff., developed the position already advanced by L. Breglia, *La prima fase della coniazione romano dell'argento* (Roma, 1952).

14 Thomsen's *Early Roman Coinage*, II, is devoted to establishing the date of the denarius' first appearance. On Morgantina, see T. V. Buttrey, "The Morgantina excavation and the date of the Roman denarius," *Atti, Congresso Internazionale di Numismatica* (Roma, 1961), p. 261 ff.

Also thanks to a Romano-Campanian bronze overstrike of a Syracusan coin, Thomsen demonstrated that the *ROMANO* coins were still issued in the 280's, at a time when the supporters of the traditional chronology assumed the *ROMA* coins were in circulation.[15] Thomsen did not prove, however, that the *ROMANO* coin in question could not be earlier than the 280's, which must remain probable since the coin is one of only two prominent bronze issues, litra and half litra pieces, issued together with all four *ROMANO* staters.[16]

In his placement and interpretation of the earliest Romano-Campanian coins, Thomsen returned to Mattingly's origin thesis: certain types were Carthaginian inspired and date to the time of Pyrrhus' Italian adventure. Elsewhere I have shown that neither Thomsen's *terminus post quem*, i.e., 300 B.C., for the first Roman issue nor the Punic interpretation of the types is numismatically or historically defensible.[17]

According to Thomsen, the third *ROMANO* coin with youthful Hercules/she-wolf suckling Romulus and Remus types was the first silver coin struck at Rome in 269 B.C. The consuls of that year, Q. Ogulnius and C. Fabius, are reflected in the choice of types, since Ogulnius and his brother erected the statue of the she-wolf and twins on the Capitol in 296 B.C. and the Fabii considered Hercules their patron.[18] In fact, there is no reason the coin cannot be as early as 296 B.C. and, indeed, Thomsen's date for the Hercules' coin led him into a most illogical interpretation and date for the last *ROMANO* issue, the Roma/Victory.[19] Because of the similarity between Greek control letters on both the Roma coin and a coin depicting Arsinoe II, the Roma issue has long been associated with the Roman-Egyptian legations of 273–272 B.C. However, Thomsen's unreasonable date for the Hercules didrachm led him to suppose it was struck on an Egyptian standard, a statement that has not a shred of evidence to support it, while the Roma/Victory, which actually bears the physical evidence of the Roman-Egyptian contact, was issued circa 260 B.C. A date near 272 B.C. is more appropriate for the Roma/Victory,

15 Thomsen, *Early Roman Coinage*, III, 101 ff. Compare Breglia, *La prima fase*, pp. 82 ff., 127; Charles Hersh, "Overstrikes as Evidence for the history of Roman Republican coinage," *N.C.*, 13 (1953), 41, 44 ff.

16 Mitchell, *Museum Notes* (1969), p. 48 ff.

17 Thomsen, *Early Roman Coinage*, III, 93 ff. Compare Mitchell, *Museum Notes* (1969), p. 43 ff.

18 Thomsen, *Early Roman Coinage*, III, 120 ff., is based on the argument advanced by Franz Altheim, "The first Roman silver coinage," *Transactions of the International Numismatic Congress* (London, 1936), p. 142 ff.

19 For a discussion of the evidence and bibliography, see Mitchell, *N.C.* (1966), p. 66 ff., and *Museum Notes* (1969), p. 56 ff.

not only because it attests to Rome's Egyptian embassy, but because it was struck on the six scruple standard. Pyrrhus introduced this standard during his stay at Tarentum, and Rome encountered it no later than her conquest of the city in 272 B.C. Roma and Victory were particularly appropriate types for that year, and there are strong reasons to believe the Roma coin was actually struck at Tarentum.[20]

One can see that directly connected with the problem of a particular coin's date is the historical interpretation of the specific types selected for an issue, which supposedly lend support to the chronological placement of the coin material. I want to concentrate on those coins which by their types and according to modern commentary are associated with the legends concerning Rome's foundation. My primary concern is to show that the historical interpretation of the coin types which justifies locating them in accordance with a lower chronology for Rome's earliest didrachm coinage is neither defensible numismatically nor the most acceptable historically.

The use and abuse of the legend concerning Rome's Trojan origin by senate, noble, and emperor in the last two centuries B.C. are familiar to classical scholars. While specific problems remain unanswered, the general evaluation of the evidence is not much in doubt. On the other hand, the evaluation of the Trojan legend's existence and the identification of its specific features in the "pre-literary" period of Rome's existence are problems which continue to entice and perplex those interested in either the development of Rome's official state policy or in the transmission and alteration of the foundation legend in the literary tradition.

Coins have provided considerable evidence for the elucidation of the final phase of the legend's importance, and Rome's first didrachms have been used as evidence for an earlier period of the legend's development because they are both earlier than the first Roman literature and because some types feature subjects associated with Rome's foundation stories. In this area few scholars have turned numismatics into history's handmaiden as extensively as Andreas Alföldi, albeit with considerable controversy over his interpretations. His work deals with the entire length of Roman history and rarely goes unnoticed, even if his evaluation of the numismatic material and his speculation on its historical importance sometime fail to win support. This is not the case, however, in his Trojan explanation of an early Roman didrachm.[21] His interpretation is supported by no less an

[20] Mattingly, *J.R.S.* (1949), p. 68 ff., argues for Tarentum, but his stylistic arguments are not always convincing.

[21] *Die trojanischen Urahnen der Römer*, Rektoratsprogramm der Universität Basel für das Jahr 1956 (Basel, 1957), is the most important of Alföldi's publications for our purpose,

authority than Rudi Thomsen,[22] among others,[23] and for this reason Alföldi's views must be dealt with in detail.

The coin in question is the Roma/Victory didrachm,[24] for which Alföldi has offered a most ingenious interpretation and date. The Phrygian helmet worn by the female on the obverse is the key to his identification. E. J. Haeberlin[25] had suggested the helmet might contain a reference to Rome's Trojan origin, and Alföldi finds in the Trojan slave woman Rhome the probable candidate to convey such a meaning. He states that the so-called Phrygian helmet derives from the Persian tiara and that the motif generally came to serve as a trademark denoting the peoples of Asia Minor, including Trojans. While the motif is employed in exactly this generalized fashion on South Italian fourth century pottery, Alföldi insists that once the motif was borrowed by the Romans the general meaning stopped: "In Rom aber hört diese Unsicherheit auf; da kann es sich einzig und allein um den goldenen Kopfschmuck der trojanischen Urmutter des Römervolkes handeln."[26]

Alföldi is anxious to show that Roman belief in their Trojan ancestry is not simply a Greek invention, prompted by the normal Greek speculation on the origins of non-Greeks, or a late literary invention designed to denegrate the Romans as barbarians or flatter them as descendants of Homeric heroes. While only Greek sources attest to her name, Rhome's essence, not her name, emerged from the native tradition of Rome. Indeed, contends Alföldi, the Romans did not originally look to Aeneas, whom the Etruscans worshipped as their *Stammvater*, but focused on a woman as the source of their ancestry. It was natural, considering the Etruscan domination over Rome, that the *Urmutter* whose immaculate conception would give the twins to Rome, should be considered Trojan— an inheritance from the Trojan-oriented foundation story of the Etruscans which was not Greek in origin. Thus Rome's belief in her *Urmutter* is deeply rooted in Italian pre-history and her Trojan character is as old as

---

but my summary of his views also borrows from the following publications, in particular the last item: "The main aspects," *Essays in Roman Coinage*, p. 63 ff.; "Timaios' Bericht über die Anfänge der Geldprägung in Rom," *Mitteilungen des Deutschen Archäologischen Instituts, Röm. Abt.*, 68 (1961), 64 ff.; and *Early Rome and the Latins* (Ann Arbor, 1963). I justify drawing from all the aforementioned publications because Alföldi's thesis seems generally consistent, if not always clear. I trust his views are not misrepresented herein.

[22] *Early Roman Coinage*, II, 160 f.

[23] G. Karl Galinsky, *Aeneas, Sicily, and Rome* (Princeton, 1969), p. 188 f.

[24] Alföldi, *Troj. Urahnen*, Taf. III.1; Thomsen, *Early Roman Coinage*, III, 133, fig. 38.

[25] "Der Roma-Typus auf den Münzen der römischen Republik," *Corolla Numismatica* (Oxford, 1906), p. 146 f.

[26] *Troj. Urahnen*, p. 8.

the Etruscan hegemony in Latium. That the Romans eventually depicted their Trojan ancestress on a coin issued circa 260 B.C. proves to Alföldi that she had long since become flesh and blood to them.[27]

In support of his views, Alföldi argues that Aristotle's account[28] of the Trojan slave women who burned the ships of their Achaean captors and forced them to settle in Italy is older and preferable to Hellenicus' confused and combined tale which brings Rhome with Aeneas to Italy, after Odysseus, where she fires the boats of her own kinsmen.[29] Alföldi sees in Aristotle's story the original tradition concerning the *Urmutter* and finds it consistent with similar tales accepted from the Greeks by the half barbarian peoples of the West. Alföldi's arguments, as expressed in various works, are not easy to follow or organize coherently since the historical and temporal relationships between various sections and arguments are not always clear. For example, he does not specifically date Aeneas' entry (reentry?) into a position of importance in the Roman foundation story. Apparently he believes that Aeneas became important in the Roman legend as a consequence of the federal center and cult at Lavinium coming under Roman control in 338 B.C. As early as the sixth century, Etruscans introduced Aeneas at Lavinium where he was identified with the divine ancestor of the Latins. After Rome took control, a history of early Roman-Lavinian *foedera* was fabricated to justify Rome's claim to Latin leadership and to support her priority in the Trojan legend of Aeneas.[30]

Naturally, as Rome's power and influence increased, Rhome was cast in a more favorable light. Thus while in Hellenicus (circa 450 B.C.) she is a slave, by the time of Callias (circa 300 B.C.) Rhome has been given a more prestigious pedigree: wife of Latinus and mother of Rhomylos, Rhomos, and Telegonos, who found Rome and name it after their mother.[31] Her genealogy was altered to conform to Rome's increased aspirations—aspirations fully recognized by her Hellenic neighbors. As further proof of her importance, Alföldi refers to the account of Agathocles

[27] *Troj. Urahnen*, p. 9 ff.   [28] Dionys. Hal., 1.72.3–4.

[29] Dionys. Hal., I.72.2 (= *F.G.H.*, 4 F 84). Alföldi, *Troj. Urahnen*, p. 9 ff., also believes that the story of Rhome was contained in Hieronymus of Cardia and Timaeus, but there is no evidence. For the correct view that Aristotle reports Aeneas came to Italy with and not after Odysseus, see Lionel Pearson, *Early Ionian Historians* (Oxford, 1939), p. 191, n. 1; and the discussion in E. D. Phillips, "Odysseus in Italy," *J.H.S.*, 73 (1953), 57 f. Indispensable for all the problems discussed herein is W. Hoffmann, "Rom und die griechische Welt im vierten Jahrhundert," *Philologus*, Suppl. 27.1 (1934).

[30] *Troj. Urahnen*, pp. 10, 18 f.; compare *Early Rome*, pp. 176 ff., 206 ff., 251 ff., 265 ff., and 391 ff.

[31] Dionys. Hal., 1.72.5 (= *F.G.H.*, 564 F 5a). Compare Fest., 372 L. (= *F.G.H.*, 564 F 5b).

of Cyzicus,[32] who attributed the erection of a temple of *Fides* to Trojan Rhome, an act which resulted in the city bearing her name. Alföldi assumes that a Locrian coin, issued about 274 B.C., featuring a seated female (PΩMA) being crowned by another (ΠΙΣΤΙΣ), is clear evidence not only that Rome politically employed *fides* as an ethical concept at this time, but that the coin reflects an earlier, pre-existing tradition concerning Rhome's association with the temple of *Fides*. The Locrians were addressing themselves to the current Roman belief in their Trojan ancestry, centering around Rhome. According to Alföldi PΩMA on the coin is not a personification of the city but is a Greek form taken directly from the Latin (Roma).[33]

As Alföldi and countless others recognize, both Timaeus and Lycophron attest to Rome's pretentions in regard to certain preexisting features of the Trojan legend and to Aeneas' importance to the story.[34] Rome had certainly staked her claim prior to the third century. According to Alföldi, around 300 B.C., after the Romans defeated the Samnites and began moving southward into Magna Graecia, the Roman sphere was inundated by Greek culture. Consequently, while a tradition developed which claimed a purely Greek ancestry for the Romans, the question of Rome's Trojan descent became an ambiguous concept. On the one hand, its claimants used it to associate themselves with the Homeric literary tradition and thereby with Greek culture, while on the other hand, despite a tendency to minimize the differences between Greeks and Trojans, the Trojans were viewed by some as barbarians. It was natural in such a climate to find Rome expressing herself on her coins both in terms of her pretentions to Greek culture and her claim to Trojan ancestry.[35] Alföldi maintains that early Roman coin types "speak to the Greeks of Magna Graecia and they use for that purpose allegorical concepts drawn partly from the Greeks themselves."[36] The Romans did this "to show that they

---

[32] Fest., 328 L. (= *F.G.H.*, 472 F 5).   [33] *Troj. Urahnen*, p. 11 f., and Taf. XI.1

[34] A. Momigliano, "Atene nel III secolo a.C. e la scoperta di Roma nelle storie di Timeo di Tauromenio," *Rivista Storica Italiana*, 71 (1959), 529–556 (= *Terzo Contributo*, I (Roma, 1966), 23–53], has an excellent discussion of the pertinent fragments of Timaeus and Lycophron (for Lycophron, see esp. p. 47, n. 71) and a helpful bibliography (pp. 51 ff.). Alföldi (*Troj. Urahnen*, passim, and *Early Rome*, pp. 125 ff., 171 f., and 248 ff.) draws conclusions about Timaeus' work (and Lycophron's dependence upon him) that cannot be supported by the existing evidence. See also Alföldi, *Mitteilungen, Röm. Abt.* (1961), p. 64 ff.; and the entirely proper criticism of A. Momigliano, "Timeo, Fabio Pittore e il primo censimento di Servio Tullio," *Miscellanea di Studi Alessandrini in memoria di Augusto Rostagni* (Torino, 1963), pp. 180–187 (= *Terzo Contributo*, II, 649–656).

[35] *Troj. Urahnen*, p. 27 ff.

[36] "The main aspects," *Essays in Roman Coinage*, p. 65.

belonged to the same sphere of culture as the Greeks."[37] Moreover, Alföldi contends that by the Pyrrhic War, at the latest, Rome was making political use of her claim to Trojan origin. Pyrrhus, however, was chiefly responsible for reversing the process of Trojan-Greek assimulation. He portrayed the Trojans as barbarians and enemies of the Greeks. Alföldi accepts Pausanius' account of Pyrrhus' new Trojan War,[38] finding proof of it in the Pyrrhus-Achilles/Thetis coin struck by Pyrrhus in Magna Graecia.[39] Alföldi correctly points out that, according to Pausanius, Pyrrhus was reacting to Rome's claim to Trojan descent, not putting forth the idea for the first time as Jacques Perret maintains.[40] Rome's Trojan ancestry also was recognized by Sicilians. The Segestans, for example, claimed Trojan descent through Aeneas, and when they defected from the Carthaginian side in 263 B.C., they looked to the Romans as their kin: "sie wussten wohl," says Alföldi, "dass dieses Verfahren den Römern sehr erwunscht war."[41]

The later third century evidence concerning Rome's political use of her supposed Trojan ancestry, as well as the reaction of others to it, is well known and does not effect the focus of this essay.[42] Rather our concern is the Rhome coin which Alföldi asserts supplies us with "das früheste unmittelbare Zeugnis für die politische Verwertung der Trojanerherkunft in der grossen Politik des dritten Jahrhunderts durch den Römerstaat selbst."[43] It was employed "um eine vornehmere Eintrittskarte zum diplomatischen Spiel der Weltpolitik als die Rivalin vorzulegen."[44] The Rhome type obtains its significance from Alföldi's assumption that a "Dido"-type in Phrygian bonnet depicted on a Siculo-Punic coin issued a few years earlier actually served as the prototype for the Roman issue.[45] Rome was answering Dido with Rhome: the confrontation of *Urmütter*. However, by this time, Alföldi asserts, Rhome's name was no longer used and she was now called Ilia or Rhea Silvia.

[37] *Op. cit.*, p. 67.   [38] Pausanias, I.12.1. Alföldi, *Troj. Urahnen*, p. 28.
[39] Alföldi, *Troj. Urahnen*, p. 28 ff., Taf. XII.1; Thomsen, *Early Roman Coinage*, III, p. 137, fig. 39.
[40] Jacques Perret, *Les origines de la légende troyenne de Rome*, 281–231 (Paris, 1942); Alföldi, *Troj. Urahnen*, p. 14. Despite an untenable thesis, Perret's collection of the literary references is extremely helpful. Both E. J. Bickerman, *Classical Weekly*, 37 (1943), 91–95, and A. Momigliano, *J.R.S.*, 35 (1945), 99–104, have excellent reviews of Perret's work.
[41] *Troj. Urahnen*, p. 29. Compare Galinsky, *Aeneas*, p. 173, where the initiative is placed with the Romans.
[42] See Alföldi, *Troj. Urahnen*, p. 29.; and the works cited above (notes 34 and 40) for helpful notes and bibliography. Also, Galinsky, *Aeneas*.
[43] *Troj. Urahnen*, p. 32.   [44] *Ibid.*
[45] *Troj Urahnen*, p. 31, Taf. IV.1; John Svoronos and Barclay Head, *The Illustrations of the Historia Numorum* (Chicago, 1968), pl. XXXIV.8.

Romulus already existed as a fixed eponymous founder, and Rhome's identity was consequently fused with the mother of the twins. The fact that a Trojan woman was featured on the *Wappenmünzen* of the Roman Republic shows that by the First Punic War Rhome-Ilia was accepted in the official foundation story of Rome.[46] Alföldi speculates on the origins and possible early date for the meeting of Dido and Aeneas and on the central importance of Sicily in the formation of the Roman-Carthaginian struggle and its romantic parallels, and concludes that regardless of details, precedents and themes at least had been established which the earliest Roman literary figures followed and embellished. In the Dido-Aeneas tale, Naevius was merely giving a romantic poetic form to a conflict already heralded by Timaeus' synchronism of the foundation dates of Rome and Carthage as well as expressed by the coat of arms displayed on a Roman coin issued in direct opposition to the *Wappenmünzen* of Carthage and as a direct attack on the Punic foundation story.[47] Alföldi convincingly argues that such a background "could well inspire poets to embroider further on this theme."[48]

We are not concerned with Alföldi's view that Rhome-Ilia's Trojan character became too much of a liability for Rome to bear, resulting in the Hellenization of the Phrygian-Trojan helmet on Roman denarii, or with his interesting evaluation of the evidence of divine will acting through a female to herald Rome's greatness. He argues that while such alterations and transfigurations obscure the original Trojan *Urmutter* of the Romans, they do not prohibit a reconstruction of the original. In other words, Alföldi assumes that Rhome, a name known only to Greek sources, was recast as Ilia, Rhea Silvia, Roma, and Vesta among others by the Romans when they began to record their own versions of their legendary past.[49]

There are objections to Alföldi's arguments, but chiefly our concern is whether his interpretation and date for the Romano-Campanian didrachm are the most acceptable. His interpretation is based upon a series of interrelated conjectures which focus on Rhome's importance and place in the tradition, on her association with Ilia and their identification with the Roman coin type, and on the Trojan character of the latter, as well as on the Etruscan origin of the Trojan legend and its early importance in Etruria, Lavinium, and Rome. Alföldi also assumes that the "scientist" can

---

[46] *Troj. Urahnen*, p. 33.

[47] *Troj. Urahnen*, p. 31 ff., *Early Rome*, p. 158 f. Also Galinsky, *Aeneas*, p. 188: "Because it was so closely associated with Sicily, the Trojan legend of Rome took on anti-Carthaginian overtones. This is confirmed by Alföldi's ingenious observation that the Roman state had the head of its Trojan ancestress, Rhome, put on the coins struck during the First Punic War (fig. 131a)."

[48] *Early Rome*, p. 159.   [49] *Troj. Urahnen*, pp. 13, 33 ff.

unravel the perplexing "clouds of mythology" by studiously assessing their historical content.[50] By combining or emending various accounts and relating them to the archaeological evidence he obtains a personally reliable picture of the early development of the Trojan saga. His faith in the reliability of the early Greek tradition about Rome is based upon the belief that the Romans were obedient to their speculations: "Dies geschah allerdings mit einer einzigen, aber bedeutsamen Abweichung: die trojanische Urmutter wurde von den Römern nicht mehr Rhome genannt, da sie in Romulus schon einen festeingewurzelten Namensgeber besassen, sondern entweder Ilia oder aber Rea Silvia."[51]

Apparently the Romans did borrow considerably from earlier Greek accounts when they began to record their own past in poetry and prose. The Greeks were interested in Rome, particularly it seems in the legendary and regal period more than in the early Republic.[52] They may have added considerable detail and embellishments to the Roman story, sometimes certainly incorporating local names and customs into their accounts. It is also possible that they began very early to see parallels between their own historical development and Rome's.[53] In this way Greek speculation became part of the "official" Roman version which began with Fabius Pictor. Fabius, writing in Greek, not only tried to remedy the situation by presenting Roman development in a more favorable light, but he also doubtless demonstrated his indebtedness to Greek sources and helped to canonize particular features of Rome's past history which were Greek in origin.[54] However, the important question is not whether Romans were influenced by such Greek traditions but whether Trojan Rhome, or rather her essence, played a significant role in the Roman tradition, albeit converted from her original position as *Urmutter* to simply the mother of the twins. Except for his identification and interpretation of the "Rhome" coin, there is no evidence to support Alföldi's position.

Although Rhome is consistently depicted as the eponym of the city, like

---

[50] *Early Rome*, p. 250 f.   [51] *Troj. Urahnen*, p. 12.

[52] Emilio Gabba, "Considerazioni sulla tradizione letteraria sulle origini della Repubblica," *Fondation Hardt, Entretiens*, 13 (Genève, 1966), 135–169.

[53] R. M. Ogilvie, *A Commentary on Livy*, Books 1–5 (Oxford, 1965), consult the index (p. 765) for references: "Greek: episodes adapted from Greek mythology and history." Also informative is Hermann Strasburger, "Zur Sage von der Gründung Roms," *Sitzungsberichte der Heidelberger Akademie der Wissenschaften, Philos.-Hist. Klasse* (1968, 5 Abhandlung), pp. 7–43.

[54] Consult F. W. Walbank, "The historians of Greek Sicily," *Kokalos*, XIV–XV (1968–1969), 476 ff.; A. Momigliano, "Linee per una valutazione di Fabio Pittore," *Rendiconti Accademia dei Lincei, Classe di Scienze morali, storiche e filologiche*, XV (1960), 310–320 (= *Terzo Contributo*, I, 55–68), and the works cited above (notes 34, 52, and 53).

Ilia she is only a secondary character and neither could play the important role Alföldi assigns them nor could they be depicted as martial figures on coins.[55] Rhome could not have been replaced, even in name, if her position had been as central to the Roman tradition as Alföldi maintains. In fact, when closely examined, the tradition about Rhome is far from consistent in the Greek sources. She is variously depicted as Trojan, Greek, or slave; as the daughter of Italus and Leucaria or of Telephus (Hercules' son); as the wife of Latinus (son of Odysseus and Circe or Hercules), of Ascanius, or of Aeneas; and as the mother of Rhomylos, Rhomos, and Telegonos.[56] Similarly, Rhomos is presented as the son of Rhome, of Odysseus and Circe, of Ascanius, of Emathion, or of Aeneas, and like Rhome as the child of Italus and Leucaria.[57] Clearly there was no stable tradition among the Greeks for the Romans to follow, and the former freely postulated ancestors and genealogies for their invented eponymous founders. Indeed, the Greeks were so unclear about Rhome that she is closely associated with the legends of all three great wandering heroes, Hercules, Odysseus, and Aeneas. Only in the third century in one account alone is she the granddaughter of Aeneas,[58] a position equal to that occupied by Romulus and Remus in Naevius and Ennius.[59] If the Romans recast her as Ilia before 260 B.C. they also had to change her relationship with Aeneas together with her eponymous function. No direct equation between Rhome and Ilia can be made. That a third century Greek presented Rhome as the mother of Rhomylos and Rhomos (and Telegonos) is not proof the Romans had recast her as Ilia. True, Ilia, as the name suggests, may well have been considered the Trojan daughter of Aeneas,[60] but her role in the saga is very insignificant and even at an early time her fall from grace may not have been a feature of the tradition pleasing to the Romans.[61] As a vestige of the Roman *Urmutter*, Rhome would have to replace either Aeneas or Romulus, and this is precisely what Rhome does in the various Greek versions of the saga.

However, the Romulus and Remus legend is demonstrably older than the third century B.C. because a statue of the she-wolf suckling the twins was erected on the Palatine near the Ruminal fig tree in 296 B.C. and a Romano-Campanian coin struck about the same time copied the statue

[55] S. Weinstock, rev. of Alföldi, *Troj. Urahnen*, in *J.R.S.*, 49 (1959), 170 f.

[56] The ancient references are collected in C. Joachim Classen, "Zur Herkunft der Sage von Romulus und Remus," *Historia*, 12 (1963), 447 ff.; Strasburger, *Sitzungsberichte der Heidelberger Akademie* (1968), 9 ff.; and Alföldi, *Troj. Urahnen*, p. 10 ff.

[57] Consult the note above for references.

[58] Agathocles of Cyzicus, in Fest. 328 L. (=*F.G.H.*, 472 F 5a).

[59] Serv , in *Aen.*, I.273.   [60] Compare Serv., in *Aen.*, VI.777.

[61] Compare Strasburger, *Sitzungsberichte Heidelberg* (1968), p. 26 ff.

group for its reverse type.[62] Although the evidence is open to discussion, Romulus may have existed alone half a century or more earlier,[63] and Rhome may have unduly complicated the Roman tradition. For example, Rhome and Rhomos are each presented as the child of Italus and Leucaria[64] and they are obviously female and male versions of the same type of Greek speculation. One could easily claim that Rhome was recast as Rhomos and, since Rhomos may have entered the Roman tradition as Remus, that she was ultimately identified with Remus.[65] Remus was introduced into the Roman story before the statue's existence, and Callias,[66] writing about this time, displays the typical Greek disregard for the local tradition known to his contemporaries Timaeus and Lycophron[67] by combining in the same story eponymous Rhome with her eponymous sons Rhomylos and Rhomos, who found the city and name it after their mother. Like Alcimus and others before him, Callias, apparently incorporated elements of fourth century Roman beliefs, but we can not assume that his story, or any other Greek account, presents a contemporary Roman version of the foundation story unless it can be independently supported by archaeological evidence or inferred from the developed Roman version.

Thus Rhome is not unknown to Roman literature because she became identified with Ilia before the Romans began to develop their own literary tradition. She is unknown because she represents a Greek version of the city's origin and name which was in direct contradiction with the native belief centering around Romulus (and Remus?). As E. J. Bickerman demonstrated, the Greeks did not generally take into consideration local foundation stories when developing their own versions. When they first set forth Rome's foundation legend, they mainly drew "inferences from the name of the city to a person or supposed founder or foundress: Romos

[62] Ludwig Curtius, "Ikonographische Beiträge zum Porträt der römischen Republik und der julisch-claudischen Familie," *Mitteilungen des Deutschen Archäologischen Instituts, Röm. Abt.* (1933), p. 204 f.; Thomsen, *Early Roman Coinage*, III, 119 f.

[63] For the legend's development, see Ogilvie, *Commentary*, pp. 32 ff., 46 ff.; Classen, *Historia* (1963), pp. 47 ff.; and Raymond Bloch, *The Origins of Rome* (London, 1960), p. 47 ff., with pl. 6, which shows a fourth-century bas-relief from Bologna of a wolf suckling a single child.

[64] Plut., *Rom.*, 2.3: Dionys. Hal., I.72.6.

[65] Compare Classen, *Historia* (1963), p. 453 ff., with bibliographical references.

[66] Dionys. Hal., I.72.5 (= *F.G.H.*, 564 F 5a).

[67] See note 34 above. It has always seemed possible that Lycophron obtained his information directly from the Roman legates who visited Egypt in 273 B.C. Q. and N. Fabius as well as Q. Ogulnius had good reason to be well informed about Rome's legendary past and to desire to tell their story to others. I plan to develop this idea in a future publication.

or Roma [Rhome]."[68] The Romulus legend developed locally while Rhome (Rhomos and Rhomanos) remained a characteristically Greek etymological explanation.

For Greeks there was no problem with a story that included Rhome, Rhomylos, and Rhomos, but for Romans, Romulus' existence precluded belief in other eponymous characters, and the mother of the twins could not have been called Rhome. This is certainly the reason Alföldi must transform her into Ilia, but apart from his interpretation of the coin, there is no evidence the Romans adopted Trojan Rhome but changed her name. Yet what of the "Trojan" helmet worn by the female on the Roman coin? There is no reason to separate the motif from the South Italian context in which it originated and from the area where the coin is most frequently found.[69] The *ROMANO*-inscribed didrachms were all struck in Campania or South Italy, and all bear stylistic, metrological, and typological affinities with the coins of Magna Graecia.[70] Alföldi himself recognizes this[71] but prefers to seek the prototype for the "Rhome" coin in a Carthaginian specimen, not appreciating that it is more reasonable to seek the type's origin both in its nearest numismatic parallels and in territories where the Romans were most active. Both the coins of Velia,[72] which fell to Rome in 293 or 272 B.C.,[73] and those of Tarentum feature helmets which form the closest parallels to the Roman coin in question. Perhaps Cicero's reference to priestesses who came to Rome from Velia contains a clue to the significance of the Roman type,[74] but we know little of the matter. As for Tarentine coins, several depict Taras on the reverse holding a "Phrygian" helmet very like the one found on the Roman coin, but it is impossible to say if the helmet is identified with Tarentum or one of her foes. The helmet occurs on a coin from the Pyrrhic period and could possibly refer to Rome's defeat, but it is also known on earlier specimens as well as featured on the obverse of earlier Tarentine coins

---

68 "'Origines gentium,'" *Classical Philology*, 47 (1952), 65 ff., presents a most helpful and balanced discussion of the "historical" methods of the Greeks.

69 Thomsen, *Early Roman Coinage*, I, 101. M. Thompson, O. Mørkholm, and C. M. Kraay, *An Inventory of Greek Coin Hoards* (New York, 1973), presents additional hoard evidence. Compare R. E. Mitchell, "Hoard evidence and early Roman coinage," *Rivista Italiana di Numismatica*, 75 (1973), 89 ff.

70 Mitchell, *Museum Notes* (1969), p. 41 ff.

71 *Troj. Urahnen*, p. 30 f.; "The main aspects," *Essays in Roman Coinage*, p. 65 ff.

72 Alföldi, *Troj. Urahnen*, Taf. IV.5; Thomsen, *Early Roman Coinage*, III, 125, fig. 3.

73 Livy, X.54.9 (293 B.C.). K. J. Beloch, *Römische Geschichte* (Berlin, 1926), p. 430 f., makes Livy's reference an anticipation of Sp. Carvilius' second consulship (272 B.C.).

74 *Pro Balbo*, pp. 24, 55. Compare H. Le Bonniec, *Le cult de Cérès à Rome* (Paris, 1958), p. 397 ff.

where the helmet is worn by a youthful rider.[75] We can say no more than that the helmet motif was known at Tarentum, but such information is sufficient in light of previously stated arguments that Tarentum was both the mint where the Roman coin was struck and the place where its weight standard was encountered. Considering the close parallel between the Roman and Tarentine (and Velian) coins, the origin of the helmet type should be sought in the context of Roman activities in South Italy and not seen as a reaction to a Punic Dido, whose very existence at such a time is problematic to say the least.[76]

There is no literary or physical evidence that either Dido or Rhome-Ilia figures in Roman diplomatic propaganda about 260 B.C. Rather, the Roman type ought to depict a goddess, and the aforementioned Locrian coin offers better evidence for the Roman coin type's identity. The seated figure (PΩMA) on the Locrian coin does not wear a Phrygian helmet or bonnet, and there is no reason to believe she is Rhome instead of the earliest extant depiction of the personification of the city—Roma.[77] Unlike Rhome or Ilia, Roma would certainly be presented in a martial fashion if the occasion demanded. If the helmet she wears on the Romano-Campanian coin has significance, it may well carry a reference to the city's Trojan origin. From Timaeus and Lycophron we have knowledge of certain features of Rome's claim, focusing on Aeneas, Lavinium, and Romulus and Remus, and the evidence is contemporary with or earlier than the Locrian coin. It is reasonable to assume that Agathocles of Cyzicus, or his source, was guilty of combining a Greek etymological explanation for the city's name with a few accurate details of Rome's ethical pretentions which were first voiced in the Roman campaigns in South Italy in the 270's.[78] It is also possible that Agathocles translated

[75] For the Tarentine coins in question, see *S.N.G.*, *A.N.S.*, I, pl. 30, 1106–1111 (= Evans, Period VII), pl. 26, 966–973 (= Evans, Period IV), and pl. 26, 990–993 (= Evans, Period V). Compare Alföldi, *Troj. Urahnen*, Taf. IV.9–11.

[76] Compare A. S. Pease, *Publi Vergili Maronis Aeneidos Liber Quartus* (Cambridge, Mass., 1935), p. 11 ff., who believes that Timaeus did not connect Aeneas with Dido (p. 17), and even on the point of whether it was Naevius or Virgil who first did so says "an agnostic attitude is here the only safe one (p. 21)."

[77] Alföldi, *Troj. Urahnen*, Taf. XI.1. Thomsen, *Early Roman Coinage*, II, 155 ff., discusses the Locrian coin and concludes that the figure is Roma. Yet Thomsen supports Alföldi's argument: "We can not but accept his [Alföldi's] conclusion that the goddess with this head-dress on the early Roman coins must be the ancestress Rhome, or Roma in the Latin form of the name (p. 161)." I do not question that Greeks could have translated Roma into their own Rhome. The problem is Rhome's identification with Ilia and Rhea Silvia and the *Urmutter* propaganda of the First Punic War. Thomsen does not present Alföldi's position accurately.

[78] For Agathocles, see Fest., 328 L. (= *F.G.H.* 472 F 5). See the excellent discussions

Roma into a Trojan ancestress because of etymological speculations he discovered in early Greek authors. The foundation of Alföldi's belief in the original significance of Rhome is his confidence that he uncovered the Etruscan roots of the Greek tradition concerning the Trojans in Italy. The Etruscans considered Aeneas their *Stammvater*, and the sources which connect him with Rome were referring either to Etruscan Rome or to the Trojanization of the ancestral cult at Lavinium. Etruscan kings repeatedly conquered Rome, Alföldi contends, and Rome's regal hegemony is an annalistic fabrication. The true successor to Alba Longa was not Rome but Lavinium, where in the sixth century Aeneas was introduced by the Etruscans and identified with the divine ancestor of the Latins. Originally Rome would not accept either Etruscan Aeneas or his detour at Lavinium. Trojan Rhome remained Rome's inheritance until Etruria, Latium, and Lavinium were brought under control. Thereafter, Rome began to use the Aeneas legend to gain political acceptance in Latium and Magna Graecia and, by fabricating a history of her own early dominant position, placed herself at the center of the saga.[79] In pressing his argument, Alföldi must amend, combine, and alter accounts to make them conform to his thesis.[80] There is no need to discuss his "historical" reconstruction since sufficiently strong and telling arguments have been leveled against it to discredit it thoroughly.[81] Alföldi's method of ferreting out the Etruscan and Lavinian roots of the early tradition are equally objectionable. For example, Alcimus reports that Aeneas' wife was Tyrrhenia, and by stressing her Etruscan name Alföldi tries to establish the original connection of Aeneas with Etruria, not Rome.[82] True, this may be weak evidence that Alcimus knew an Etruscan name, but the name is not historical evidence that

---

of Hoffmann, *Philologus*, Suppl. (1934), p. 60 ff.; and Filippo Cassola, *I gruppi politici romani nel III secolo a.C.* (Trieste, 1962), p. 171 ff., esp. p. 175.

[79] This is a short summary of some of Alföldi's main points in *Troj. Urahnen* and *Early Rome*.

[80] He accepts the emendation of Aristotle (*Early Rome*, p. 251, n. 3), he combines several versions of the Rhome legend despite their variations (*Troj. Urahnen*, p. 10 f.), and he alters the statement of Hesiod (*Troj. Urahnen*, p. 24 f., where Hesiod's statement is connected with Alba Longa, and *Early Rome*, p. 188 f., where Alföldi is the one to "confuse the conquerors and the subjugated"). There are too many such Procrustean examples to cite completely.

[81] See A. Momigliano, rev. of A. Alföldi, *Early Rome and the Latins*, in *J.R.S.*, 57 (1967), 211 ff.: "There is a curious similarity between the method Alföldi attributes to Fabius Pictor and the method he himself uses in studying Fabius: 'Fabius was prepared to demonstrate this at any cost'; so is Alföldi. (p. 212)."

[82] Alcimus in Fest., 326 L. (= *F.G.H.*, 560 F 4). Alföldi, *Troj. Urahnen*, p. 14 ff.; *Early Rome*, p. 278 ff.

Etruscans controlled Rome in the regal period or that the legend of
Aeneas was in origin Etruscan. All the evidence cited by Alföldi can only
prove, at the most, that the legend of Aeneas was "something that archaic
Rome had in common with Etruria."[83]

Although it is true that Aeneas was popular in Etruria as early as the
sixth century,[84] there is no evidence that the Etruscans worshipped him
as their *Stammvater* or that he had a cult in Etruria. The evidence Alföldi
unearths to prove his thesis admits of more than one explanation. The
statues from Veii do not conclusively establish his extraordinary position[85]
nor does the large percentage of pottery depicting Aeneas known to have
been found in Etruria. G. Karl Galinsky is not surprised by the Etrurian
provenience of a large percentage of Aeneas pots; it is what one expects.[86]
The pottery depicting Ajax, to take a random sample, shows that the
provenience of a slightly higher percentage of them was Etruria.[87] Aeneas'
extraordinary position in Etruria remains unproven.

As for Aeneas' importance at Lavinium, his association with the cult of
Indiges is a secondary development, and the literary and physical evidence
employed by Alföldi to date his early arrival there is fourth century or
later in date as are the earliest literary references to Lavinium's importance in the Trojan legend.[88] Galinsky forcefully argues that Aeneas'
introduction is the consequence of Rome's "political and religious re-
organization of the Lavinian cults" which occurred in 338 B.C.[89] Roman
control resulted in "the Trojanization of Lavinium's Penates and their
identification with Rome's own."[90] Galinsky also asked the crucial
question: "Why would the influential Roman historians . . . who did
their best to promote Rome's claim to Trojan descent, want to defeat
their purpose by suppressing the Lavinian tradition on which this claim
was to be based?"[91] In truth, they did not suppress it, anymore than they
totally fabricated the importance of regal Rome. Thus even if Aeneas'
early acceptance in Italy can be established there is no evidence that
Rhome, not Aeneas, was accepted by Rome and, since the focal point of
the earliest Greek accounts is Rome, no reason to believe that the various

---

[83] A. Momigliano, "An interim report on the origins of Rome," *J.R.S.*, 53 (1963),
102.

[84] Alföldi, *Troj. Urahnen*, p. 14 ff.; *Early Rome*, p. 278 ff.

[85] See Galinsky, *Aeneas*, p. 122 ff., with bibliographical references.

[86] Alföldi, *Early Rome*, p. 283; compare Galinsky, *Aeneas*, p. 123 ff.

[87] See J. D. Beazley, *Attic Black-Figure Vase-Painters* (Oxford, 1956). I want to thank
my student Richard Saller for this statistical information.

[88] Alföldi, *Troj. Urahnen*, p. 19 ff.; *Early Rome*, p. 246 ff.; Galinsky, *Aeneas*, p. 141 ff.
Compare A. Drummond, rev. of Galinsky, *Aeneas*, in *J.R.S.*, 62 (1972), 218 ff.

[89] Galinsky, *Aeneas*, p. 160.   [90] *Op. cit.*, p. 156.   [91] *Op. cit.*, p. 145.

traditions establish Aeneas' priority in Etruria and Lavinium and their dominance over Rome.

While there is no evidence that Aeneas was not accepted very early by the Romans, there is very little proof that he was. The strongest arguments are in favor of considering the earliest tradition about the Trojans in Italy as a Greek fabrication. By the fourth century, however, the Trojan legend was accepted by Romans and combined with the original local, native tradition concerning Alba Longa and Romulus and contaminated by the idea of a Trojan colony at Lavinium led by Aeneas which was modeled on the story of Alba Longa.[92] Subsequent generations worked out the difficulty of Aeneas' association both with Alba and Lavinium and eventually solved the chronological problem of Aeneas' arrival date and Romulus' later foundation of the city by giving Lavinium the lead for thirty years, the Alban kings for three hundred, and Rome for eternity. No evidence or historically acceptable reason exists for placing Rhome in this development or for identifying her with Rhea Silvia and her poetic counterpart Ilia. If Rome accepted the Trojan legend early, Aeneas must not be disassociated from it. If, as seems more reasonable, it is primarily a fourth century development, then both Aeneas and Romulus are part of the story. In either case there is no room for Rhome.[93]

There are many objections to Alföldi's many arguments, but chiefly our concern is whether his interpretation and date for the Romano-Campanian coin are the most acceptable. Much that he has written is admittedly very attractive and helps to solve countless problems, despite creating more, and since we can never be certain of what the Romans believed even when they tell us, for the sake of argument we will assume that his identification of the coin is correct in order to comment directly upon his historical interpretation and date. Rhome cannot be accepted, but a Trojan *Urmutter* is a remote possibility.

If Alföldi's assumption that the so-called Dido-type was the prototype for the Roman coin is correct, his explanation that the latter was issued as anti-Carthaginian propaganda cannot stand. Indeed, S. Weinstock finds

---

[92] See Bickerman, *Classical Philology* (1952), p. 65 ff.; Classen, *Historia* (1963), 447 ff. (Die ältesten griechischen Berichte erwähnen nur Rhome, die der römischen Tradition fremd ist, p. 452); and Strasburger, *Sitzungsberichte Heidelberg* (1968), p. 7 ff., for bibliographical references and discussion.

[93] Alföldi, *Early Rome*, p. 201: "A broad stream of Etruscan influence inundated the [Roman] state religion as well as private religiosity." This is the most perplexing feature of Alföldi's thesis. If early Rome was greatly indebted to Etruscan, Latin, and, through Etruscan mediation, Greek influences, why is Aeneas not associated with early Rome but the concocted Rhome is? Why is Aeneas prominent later while there is no sign of Rhome?

it incredible that a Punic "Dido" would be used as the prototype for a Roman coin issued as a direct attack on the original.[94] Since Alföldi assumes that the Romans and Carthaginians were on the same side during the Pyrrhic War, a time nearer the emission date of the Punic coin in question, and since he accepts Mattingly's and now Thomsen's argument that the horse's head and horse-types of earlier Romano-Campanian coins were inspired by Punic coin types of Rome's ally in the Pyrrhic War,[95] then it is more reasonable to assume that the "Dido" head also was borrowed from a friendly Carthage rather than to assume the type was directed against Carthage. Indeed, the Pyrrhic War is not only a better time for the possible borrowing of the type, if Alföldi is followed, but as we shall see it offers the best possible historical context in which to place the Roman issue according to the best evidence available.

As Alföldi suggested, Rome began to make political use of the Trojan saga before the Pyrrhic War and, reacting to Rome's claim, Pyrrhus depicted himself on a coin as a descendant of Achilles and set about to wage a new Trojan War against the Trojan colonists. What better occasion for the "Rhome" issue than the Pyrrhic War or, if the Victory reverse type has significance, its successful completion? Rome's Trojan *Urmutter* would be a direct response to Pyrrhus-Achilles and his Trojan War. Add to this the fact that the Roman coin in question was issued on the reduced standard Pyrrhus introduced at Tarentum which quickly spread to other Magna Graecian cities and that the metrological evidence can be seen to support a date in the 270's for the Roman coin's issue. Moreover, as mentioned above,[96] almost all numismatics are agreed that the sequence of Greek letters on the Roman didrachm is associated in some way with a similar sequence found on coins depicting Arsinoe II, sister-spouse of Ptolemy Philadelphus. The embassy Ptolemy sent to Rome and Rome's return legation certainly provided ample evidence to support the Roman coin's 273–272 B.C. date. In addition, the closest parallels to the "Trojan" helmet type are found on Tarentine coins, some issues of which are in metrological agreement with the six scruple Roman coin. In sum, the female in "Trojan" helmet and the Victory attaching palm to a trophy are extremely appropriate subjects for such a date, and the evidence from both the coins metrology and Greek control letters are

[94] Weinstock, *J.R.S.* (1959), p. 171.
[95] *Troj. Urahnen*, p. 31 ff.; "The main aspects," *Essays in Roman Coinage*, p. 67. But Alföldi believes the horse-types have their own Roman significance. He accepts Mattingly's late dating of the earliest didrachms, but not his four mint theory.
[96] See above, 69 f.

in total agreement with the literary evidence and Alföldi's interpretation
of the Trojan ancestress of Rome.[97]

University of Illinois at Urbana

[97] A final point should be made. If the coin type in question is Rhome-Ilia, why is she
not the obverse of the she-wolf and twins coin rather than Hercules? I will address myself
to this question in a future publication.

9

Confectum Carmine Munus: Catullus 68

DAVID F. BRIGHT

Despite the constant flow of scholarship on Catullus 68, the undecided questions concerning the poem are still of the most fundamental sort. Indeed, a topic on which divergent views have apparently hardened again is the first question of all: is this one poem, or two (or even three)? The Pandora's box opened by Rode almost two hundred years ago is not likely to be closed soon; meanwhile it is possible to conduct further exploration of some of the more puzzling issues in the hope of finding solid ground and to move from there to areas where less agreement has been achieved.

In this paper I propose to examine the structure of Catullus 68, and to consider the meaning of the poem as expressed in its architecture. Of course, there have been schemes in abundance revealing the structure of this poem: it is a complex exercise in Alexandrian ring-composition,[1] but how are the rings composed? The first problem is to recognize the major divisions of the poem in order to analyze the movement of the whole. Prescott[2] adopts the simple division into three parts (A = 1–40, B = 41–148, C = 149–160) signaled by the change from second to third person and back to second in referring to the correspondent. It is also the division indicated by the most abrupt transitions of thought. There is no necessary implication in this about the unity or disunity of the poem, although Prescott makes much of the relative sophistication and structural subtlety

---

[1] K. Quinn prefers to think of 68 as "a linear structure (which is perhaps a better way to describe a poem as long as Poem 68)"; compare *Catullus. An Interpretation* (New York, 1973), p. 181 (hereafter "Quinn"). But the movement and the effect of the poem, as I hope will be clear, depends on the ring-composition being recognized and felt by the reader at each stage. In any case compare Quinn's comment on lines 89–100 (below, p. 96).

[2] H. W. Prescott, "The Unity of Cat. LXVIII," *TAPA*, 71 (1940), 473–500 (hereafter "Prescott").

of the three parts (in particular, his comment that "artificial symmetry exists only within B"[3] would not find a wide following today); and, following Skutsch,[4] he declares the poem to have formal unity in that A is prologue and C epilogue to the body of the poem. If we go no further than the observation that B is a distinct portion preceded and followed by two other structurally unrelated panels, there can be agreement; but Jachmann's criticisms of this as an architectural analysis are properly cautionary.[5]

But in a sense this scheme can be used as a means of begging the question of unity, because by *characterizing* A and C rather than (for the moment) merely *identifying* them, the unity of the poem is assumed at the outset; and it must be admitted that the problem is rather too complex for such premature conclusions.

The converse is also true. The *chôrizontes*—both those who argue that nothing but accidental or misled juxtaposition relates A to BC[6] and those who view 68 as an artistic whole clearly divided into two portions at 40/41[7]—assume an overall structure of 41–160 and seek to produce the balance of a ring composition in order to prove the assumption. Such a balance would match 41–50 and 149–160; but the break at 148/149 is as abrupt as 40/41, and a finely poised structure on these terms raises more problems than it solves. It will not allow the lament for the dead brother to stand in its present place as the center,[8] and the outer portions (41–50, 149–160) are of unequal size. The options at this point are to accept the imbalance as unimportant (i.e., the balance of theme and idea is what matters, not the form)[9] or to revamp the poem in order to produce segments of equal length. This is the approach of Vretska,[10] who removes 157–158 from their present position and places them after 139.[11] These lines are obviously a desperate problem,[12] to which I must return later.

3 Prescott, p. 476.

4 F. Skutsch, "Zum 68. Gedicht Catulls," *RhM*, 47 (1892), 138–151.

5 G. Jachmann, *Gnomon*, 1 (1925), 200–214, reviewing Kroll's edition. It should be noted that Jachmann overstates his case somewhat when he claims (p. 211) that there is no link in thought between vv. 40 and 41.

6 So Rode, Ramler, Schwabe, Baehrens, Marmorale, *et al.*

7 E.g., J. Wohlberg, "The Structure of the Laodamia Simile in Cat. 68," *CP*, 50 (1955), 42–46 (hereafter "Wohlberg"); F. O. Copley, "The Unity of Cat. 68: A Further View," *CP*, 52 (1957), 29–32 (hereafter "Copley").

8 On this problem see below, pp. 96 ff.   9 So Copley, p. 31.

10 K. Vretska, "Das Problem der Einheit von Catull c. 68," *WS*, 79 (1966), 313–330 (hereafter "Vretska").

11 He means 140, having reckoned apparently without allowance for the missing v. 47.

12 Characterized by G. P. Goold as "perhaps the most baffling passage in Catullus" ("A New Text of Catullus," *Phoenix*, 12 [1958], p. 108).

Vretska thus obtains an epilogue of 10 lines (displaying a 4–6 substructure which he finds also in 41–44/45–50); but the solution means still having an unsolved mystery after 141 and must be bolstered by removing the lament in 91–100. This is a rather complicated string of transpositions and deletions which still does not produce a satisfying pattern in all details.[13]

The safest approach, it seems, is that exemplified by Kroll[14]: examine the parts ABC separately since they are so clearly marked off from one another. Once this analysis is completed, such questions as it may raise or answer can be handled with more confidence. It is clear that B has an intricate and careful structure, and so does A. The fundamental questions thus become: (1) are the structures of A and B similar; (2) if so, does this similarity reveal anything about the underlying relationship between A and B; and (3) does C have a discernible structure or is it merely a simple close to the complexities of the rest of poem 68?

Before tackling these questions, we must venture into the mystery of the name of Catullus' addressee. By one of the more wry ironies of fate, Catullus twice insists that he wants above all to ensure that his friend's name should never be obliterated by the passage of time (43–50, 151–152), and yet it is the least clear detail of the whole poem.

Of the six places in which the name for Catullus' friend occurs or may reasonably be thought to occur (vv. 11, 30, 41, 50, 66, 150), the key is line 50. It is the only place where the name—if it is a name—must begin with a vowel. Pennisi argues that the true reading is *illi*,[15] based on a confusion of *a-i* which he also finds in v. 150 (*aliis* V *illis* Pennisi). This is tempting, because it would leave Manlius (or Mallius) a clear field; at v. 66 Mallius could be restored if necessary. But it is this lonely holdout at 50 which refuses such solutions. Catullus is stressing not merely that his friend has helped him, but that his *name* deserves to be recorded and remembered; he is making the same point at 150. It is at precisely these two places that the MSS insist on a word beginning *al-*; and at these two places a name is needed to sustain the point of the sentence. At 150 V had *aliis*, which has found its defenders[16] as well as those who, like Pennisi, would alter it to

---

[13] Vretska ends up with 10 lines at each end, and 4 passages of 22 lines each around an *omphalos* of 4 lines (vv. 105–108). Since even this *omphalos* is not a single, discrete unit, but breaks into two parts, the structure is finally unconvincing, albeit ingenious.

[14] W. Kroll, *Catull*[3] (Stuttgart, 1959), pp. 218–220.

[15] G. Pennisi, "Il carme 68 di Catullo," *Emerita*, 27 (1959), 234–235.

[16] H. Weber, *Quaestiones Catullianae* (Gotha, 1890), pp. 112–113. Weber's retention of *aliis* is alluring in another way: if it is correct, then the addressee's name does not occur at all in C, and the difficulty of A and C being in some way prologue and epilogue, distinct from B not only in style but also in grammatical person (A–C second, B third) yet using different names, is eliminated. But of course it is preferable to have a single solution accommodating all the occurrences of a name in the poem.

something quite different. Again a solution which would eliminate the proper name is tempting, but the sense of the passage resists. Indeed, the parallel between the two passages ensures, as Pennisi saw, that they must be treated alike.

There seems to be nothing for it but to accept Allius as the name in 50 and 150; and if that is so, 66 must surely follow despite the *Manlius* of GR and the *vel Manllius*—a most suspicious variant—of O *marg.* In other words, half of the passages in question must yield Allius, and in a fourth (41), Scaliger's *qua me Allius* is a more logical correction of the reading of V (*quam fallius*) than Pennisi's *qua Mallius*.

All this leaves us where most editors have been all along; the problem boils down to a suspected difference between the name in A and the name in BC. If the name in A must be Manlius (or Mallius or Manius) and in B Allius, then 68 is almost certainly not one poem. Lachmann's idea that Manius Allius was addressed by his *praenomen* in A and his *nomen* in BC presents at least two difficulties. First, if the distinction between the use of the *praenomen* and *nomen* is connected with the relative familiarity with which Catullus speaks to his friend, we should expect that the two parts in more loose epistolary style (A and C) would stand together against B[17]; and yet the split is by everyone's reckoning A versus BC.[18] Furthermore, the double gentilicium Manius (or Manlius) Allius, despite Ellis' approval, is most improbable as early as this poem. Fordyce gives further evidence on the difficulties involved in such a name.[19] Altogether, then, Manlius Allius is an unlikely person at best.

Finally it may be observed that if Allius is indeed the correspondent's name, the identification with Manlius Torquatus[20] falls at once, with the one possible escape that A may be addressed to Manlius and BC to Allius. This is improbable, and the identification is in most instances merely special pleading in order to allow greater knowledge (or the feeling of greater knowledge) about the correspondent of 68. The fact that 68 hardly squares with our other evidence on Torquatus has been brushed aside.

[17] So G. Williams, *Tradition and Originality in Roman Poetry* (Oxford, 1968), p. 230, n. 2, reads Mani in 150 to restore agreement between A and C.

[18] R. Godel, "Catulle, poème 68," *MH*, 22 (1965), 57, adds the curious, though hardly conclusive, detail that the only *praenomen* attested for the Allii is Gaius. He accepts Manlius in A and thus splits the poem into two distinct compositions; as does F. Guglielmino, "Sulla composizione del carme LXVIII di Catullo," *Athenaeum*, 3 (1915), 426–444.

[19] C. J. Fordyce, *Catullus* (Oxford, 1960), pp. 342–343; compare E. Fraenkel, *Gnomon*, 34 (1962), 261–263 for problems in Fordyce's solution as well.

[20] Defended by, e.g., Godel and Pennisi and used as the basis of elaborately specific interpretations by P. Whigham, *The Poems of Catullus* (Baltimore, 1965), pp. 36–40.

We are thus left with 11 and 30, where V read *Mali*. Some alteration is needed, no matter what view one takes of the poem as a whole. Schöll[21] (or more exactly Diels)[22] offered a solution which has attracted much criticism, but which nevertheless solves far more problems than it raises: *mi Alli*. As Prescott notes, "the metrical objections are not weighty,"[23] particularly since the elision before the sixth foot—the real bone of contention—is a not uncommon phenomenon in satire and other lesser departments of verse. Its appearance in this epistolary context should not occasion undue alarm.

Perhaps the most we can say for the moment is that the name *can* be consistent throughout the poem, and that rather than beginning with Manlius (or whatever) in A, it seems preferable to begin with Allius in BC. Viewed this way, the probability of a single name is slightly enhanced, as is the probability that the name is Allius.[24]

It may be worth recalling here the comparisons made by Helms,[25] Arnaldi,[26] and Salvatore[27] between Catullus 68 and the *Ciris*. These studies suggest that the author of the *Ciris* not only modeled his style on that of 68, but also adapted several specific phrases and the arrangement of some ideas from the whole of poem 68. This is distinct from the incidental borrowing of expressions from, for example, poem 65 or 101, and reflects rather the impression of 68 as a unified composition in the eyes of a poet not more than three generations after it was written.[28] This is a powerful incentive to accepting this unity, although the argument is often disregarded.[29]

But none of this alters the fact that poem 68 falls into three recognizable segments, and to each of these in turn our attention must now be directed.

Part A (1–40)

Almost every analysis of these 40 lines acknowledges the lament for the poet's dead brother to be the heart of the composition. That this is true

---

21 F. Schöll, "Zu Catull," *Jb.Kl.Ph.*, 121 (1880), 472–473, for 30; uneasy about 11.

22 H. Diels, "Lukrezstudien. I," *SB Ber.*, Phil.-hist. Kl. 1918², 936, n. 1; he merely accepts *mi Alli* for the poem without distinction.   23 Prescott, p. 496.

24 To simplify the logistics of this paper, I shall refer to the addressee hereafter as Allius.

25 R. Helms, *Die pseudo-virgilische Ciris* (Heidelberg, 1937), p. 7; compare also note 28 below.

26 F. Arnaldi, *Studi Virgiliani* (Napoli, 1943), pp. 215–229.

27 A. Salvatore, *Studi Catulliani* (Napoli, 1965), pp. 97–100.

28 Helms believes the composition of the *Ciris* coincided with the last years of Ovid's life, probably in the reign of Tiberius: so AD 14–17: "Ein Epilog zur Cirisfrage," *Hermes*, 72 (1937), 78–103.

29 See also below pp. 110 f. on Propertius, 2.28.

structurally can be seen readily enough; whether it is also the heart of A thematically is a slightly more open question. The poem begins with the request of Allius for consolation which Catullus elaborately rejects as a reference to his own situation. It is not easy to say immediately whether his own lament is the actual point, set in the context of his friend's request, or whether that lament is simply a part of his response buried in the larger theme of Allius' *incommoda*. The fact that his lament is repeated at the heart of B[30] strongly suggests that it is, even here, more than a subordinate part. It is the theme to which he builds and around which he organizes his thoughts in both parts. The repetition of so many lines is unexampled elsewhere in Catullus, and even in the case of individual lines repeated there is always a clear structural purpose in the device.[31] In 68 the brother passage functions almost as a chorus, pausing to reflect and expand upon the emotional content of the events described.

Given this centrality of function and of structure (there are 14 lines preceding and following this passage), what architecture can be seen in A as a whole? Certainly 1–10 stand apart. Godel[32] refers to them as preamble, and in effect excludes them from the balance which he finds in the remaining verses (11–14, 15–36, 37–40), as *grosso modo* 1–40, being one-fourth of the entirety of 68, may be excluded from the purported symmetry of 41–160. But 1–10 are not as sharply separated as this plan would suggest. They contain Allius' request for *munera Musarum et Veneris*, and they set the rest of the section in motion as it were. Finally, they comprise a single sentence, building to the *munera* (10). The rejection of this request—after due explanation—occupies an equal number of lines, 31–40, and to make this explicit Catullus marks the balancing portion with the key word *munera* (32).

By a similar device, Catullus marks off the intervening sections. Verses 11–14 constitute a transition from the pleasure he feels at the friendship implicit in Allius' request (*id gratum est mihi,* 9) to the sorrow which prevents him from fulfilling that request (*ne amplius a misero dona beata petas,* 14). The transitional lines ending with the keynote *misero* are matched by the end of the second transition back from the death of his brother to the request of his friend: *miserum est* (30).

---

[30] I leave aside for the moment the tangled question of whether 91–100 *originally* appeared in B; it is in the finished version and the self-quotation in the *omphalos* of both parts is obviously a crucial factor in our response to 68 as a whole.

[31] The most common form is the repetition of the first line of a poem as the last line: compare poems 16, 36, 52, 57: or the creation of a stanzaic pattern within a poem as in 8, 42, 64.323–381. Compare H. Bardon, *L'art de la composition chez Catulle* (Paris, 1943); *Propositions sur Catulle* (Collection Latomus, 118, Bruxelles, 1970).

[32] Godel (above, note 18), p. 53.

These key words then stake out the plan of A:

1–10   Allius' request for *munera*
  11–14   Transition from Allius' distress to Catullus' (*misero*)
    15–26   The nature of Catullus' distress: death of brother
      15–18   the joy of his youth
      19–26   the sorrow at his brother's death
    27–30   Transition from Catullus' own thought to Allius', by way of quotation from the letter, which further illustrates that the poet's lot is *miserum*, both in his own terms and in the context from which Allius writes.
31–40   Allius' request for *munera* therefore cannot be fulfilled.

This scheme takes into account all the verses, without excluding 1–10 from the symmetry (as do Godel and Prescott), and allows the key words to exercise the shaping influence they naturally would have. A recent paper by M. B. Skinner[33] accepted the overall tripartite structure but proposed a paneling effect by dividing the outer segments into 10 + 4 (1–10/11–14, 27–36/37–40). This requires viewing 11–14 as the "preliminary *recusatio*" and ignoring the clear *recusatio* in 31–32. In fact 33–40 are an amplification of that refusal (*nam*, 33), which the poet rounds off with 37–40, but he does not begin it there. Verse 37 is not as strong a division as 30/31. The panel structure is tempting but is countered by the use of keywords just noted. The same objection may be raised against Godel's simpler pattern. By taking 15–36 as the core of the letter, he blurs the essential distinctions within this block at 26/27 and 30/31.

Prescott[34] builds the whole of A around the two distinct *munera*. There is in his arrangement neither parallel panels nor ring-composition— hence his comment, cited earlier, that artificial symmetry exists only in B. He recognizes the fact that the *munera Veneris* and *munera Musarum* must be at least thought of separately (whether they are in fact two separate things may be questioned). But his elaborate exegesis while bringing out so much that is valuable, leads him to treat 19–26 as a pathetic parenthesis,[35] though functional. Thus for Prescott 15–30 (minus 19–26) deal with *munera Veneris*, 33–36 with *munera Musarum*, and 37–40 with both. The lines on the poet's brother thus serve essentially the same purpose as the apostrophe in poem 65, heightening the emotional force of the surrounding statement. But they are, as Prescott pointed out, much more functional here since they *are* the explanation for the refusal.

---

[33] M. B. Skinner, "The Unity of Catullus 68: The Structure of 68a," *TAPA*, 103 (1972), 495–512. Ms. Skinner kindly supplied me with a copy of her paper in advance of publication.
[34] Prescott, pp. 477–487.
[35] Compare Copley's comments on 91–100 (below, pp. 96 f.).

In view of the considerations the pattern I have outlined seems to represent most accurately the movement of these 40 lines. There is the further fact that the ring-composition thus obtained is matched exactly by the form of B.

There are distinct difficulties in seeking the structure of A in the antithesis of the two *munera*. That *munera Musarum et Veneris* is no mere hendiadys is clear (*utriusque*, 39); but it is equally clear that the two are interrelated. The development of poem 68 in its entirety is a working out of the connection between love and poetry, which depends in its turn upon the connection between the situations of Catullus and his friend. The link between the two situations is established at once by the figure of shipwreck used of Allius (*naufragum*, 3) and repeated by Catullus for his own troubles (*merser fortunae fluctibus ipse*, 13).[36] Moreover, the poet returns to the rescue from deadly waters in B (63–66) when describing the aid Allius had previously given. This explicit chain of images does much to bind the parts of the poem together: the present troubles of Allius (he asks Catullus for rescue), the present troubles of Catullus, and the previous pressures of love (Allius already has saved Catullus once, and Catullus is loath to refuse repayment). Because Catullus and Allius are in comparable straits, Catullus can respond to and appreciate his friend's anguish by looking at his own misfortunes.

For Catullus, the *munera Veneris* which he enjoyed in his youth were lost to him by the death of his brother, and this has resulted in the loss of *munera Musarum*. They are separate but can only exist together. So with Allius, his misfortunes in love have resulted in the loss of pleasure in the *carmen veterum scriptorum*. There is no difference in kind between Allius' loss of the ability to *enjoy* poetry in the context of love and Catullus' loss of the ability to *create* poetry. Both occurred for similar causes, and both presumably can be restored in similar fashion. Indeed the double gifts of love and poetry are so intertwined that one can prompt the other. The recovery of love (happiness is perhaps a better generic term) will free Catullus' muse or Allius' capacity to enjoy poetry; and the gift of poetry will bring back that happiness which both now miss. Catullus stresses that the *veteres scriptores* (or *vetera scripta*)[37] are unable to please Allius because he is

---

[36] It does not matter, for purposes of examining the imagery in the poem, whether Catullus is repeating a figure in 3 employed by Allius in his letter and echoing it later, or supplying this common enough figure on his own.

[37] Compare Prescott, p. 485. There is a difference in implication between these two possibilities. *Veteres scriptores* would suggest that previous writers *as such* (whether pre-Alexandrian or simply pre-Allian) are powerless to charm. *Vetera scripta*, on the other hand, implies that the poetry of the past fails to have any effect because it is not speaking to Allius' condition—it is "old hat" in terms of content (perhaps even including Catullus'

94   Illinois Classical Studies, I

under the cruel affliction of unrequited love and thus cannot be calmed
and soothed by the strains of traditional poetry. He therefore asks Catullus
to solve both problems. The notion that Catullus could do so by lending
him a book[38] is therefore impossible: Allius is not hampered by lack of a
book but by the afflictions of Venus. If Catullus is to assuage his friend's
distress it will be by a *new* poem, and that poem will be on the very subject
raised by Allius, his situation, and his banishment from happiness.

Some have rejected the relationship implied in this reading of the lines
on the grounds that Allius was only half-serious in describing his plight[39]
or that Catullus on his part did not consider Allius a close friend and
rejected him with cool distance.[40] But the tone of the poem itself is earnest
and hardly suited to a jocular and exaggerated complaint on Allius' part.
There is a decline to be sure from the figurative language of the opening
lines to the more flat descriptive quality of 33–40, but there is no con-
comitant lapse from a serious tone to one of irony or jest. Catullus wrestles
throughout with the desire to grant a friend what he cannot seem to
provide. By the same token, the idea that Allius was not a close friend,
which does seem to find some support in line 9, is at odds with the open-
ness with which Catullus shares his experiences and his deepest feelings,
including the moving address to his brother. Would any man so readily
relive such experiences by way of rejecting an unwelcome request from
a former friend? Kiessling accepted the friendship of the two men but
thought Catullus was showing the shallowness of Allius' concerns by
contrasting them with his own genuine sufferings.[41] The repeated use of
the shipwreck or troubles-at-sea figure would seem to indicate that
Catullus is *associating* his friend's difficulties with his own. No doubt
Catullus may have felt that his own trials were harder to bear than

---

earlier poetry). The plea then would be for poetry *for* and *on* Allius' condition. This I
believe to be more nearly true and to be supplied in B with the recollection of Catullus'
and Allius' past happiness; but the ambiguity may be intentional.

[38] T. E. Kinsey, "Some Problems in Catullus 68," *Latomus*, 26 (1967), 39; compare
Prescott, p. 485.

[39] G. Williams (above, note 17), pp. 230–231; compare the tone of Quinn's description: "Catullus' correspondent has sent him . . . a poem, in the form of a verse epistle,
lamenting, with suitably heart-rending rhetoric, that his girl has deserted him, and
asking for a clutch of poems from Catullus by way of consolation" (Quinn, p. 185).

[40] Kinsey (above, note 38), p. 37, n. 1: "a tone which might be adopted toward a
former friend one wanted to drop without a quarrel."

[41] A. Kiessling, *Analecta Catulliana* (Gryphiswaldiae, 1877), p. 14: Catullus writes these
lines "ut ficto eius et supra modum aucto propter amicae perfidiam dolori vera sui ipsius
incommoda opponat." Although I think this is an inaccurate impression, Kiessling is
right in his analysis of the end of the poem, "in extrema votorum pro Alli eiusque puellae
salute nuncupatione . . . consolatione sua non iam opus esse auguratur."

Allius': it is characteristic of human behavior to react thus, but this does not mean that Catullus felt Allius' request was pure melodrama. If he did feel this way, the composition of poem 68 is an absurdly elaborate response to the problem. Again the same kind of question arises as with Kinsey's approach: would Catullus, who by his own admission is severed from his Muse and surrounded by sorrow, make so earnest an effort to respond to the empty emotionalism of a friend?

In short, it seems that 68 may well be what it claims to be: a consolation sent to a good friend by one who can appreciate the friend's suffering since he has experienced it himself. But what is missing in these 40 lines is any satisfactory account of the *reason* for Allius' distress. We are told of the symptoms but not the cause. There is admittedly no compelling reason for Catullus to give these details, yet questions are raised—expectations are aroused—but not resolved. We have the figurative description of Allius' plight in 3–4 with no explication. This is not in itself surprising, but Catullus does elaborate on his own situation which is clearly intended to be in some fashion parallel or analogous to Allius'. We are left wondering how the two are related: in particular the pregnant reference to *hospitis officium* in 12 raises a question without answering it—until B, at least.[42] Catullus repeats the key word *officium* in each section at the outset (42, 150) in order to emphasize its primary importance in linking his thoughts.

But the formal balance of A does not allow us to look for any solution to these questions within its confines. The abruptness of the transition at 40/41 has not unnaturally encouraged belief in a lacuna,[43] which has taken from us the end of A and the beginning of B. This alluring solution, however, will not stand up in the face of the structural analysis. We must go in one direction or the other on the assumption that nothing is missing here. Either we have two poems, one ending somewhat abruptly and the other beginning *in mediis rebus*, or else the abruptness is a feature of the poem and merely shows in a higher degree the sort of transition to be seen elsewhere in 68.

If this second alternative is preferable, we must then look outside A for fuller indications of the relationship and experiences hinted at—which means, of course, B.

---

[42] As G. Lieberg observes, "Der im ersten Teil wichtige Gedanke, man dürfe das *officium hospitis* nicht von sich abwälzen, wird erst voll verständlich, wenn man seinen Bezug auf die Situation im Mittelteil der Elegie erkennt." (*Puella Divina*, Amsterdam, 1962, p. 156.)

[43] So L. Pepe, "Il mito di Laodamia in Catullo," *GIF.* 6 (1953), 108; previously in L. Pighi, "Inchiesta su una lettera," *Convivium*, 17 (1949), 873 ff., and V. Marmorale, *L'ultimo Catullo* (Napoli, 1952), p. 46.

Part B (41–148)

These lines have prompted most of the analytical ingenuity of recent years. That there is a symmetrical pattern, no one really doubts. The question is how the concentric rings are formed and where the center, the *omphalos*, lies. Most structures resemble that proposed by Kroll[44] in placing the lament for the poet's brother (91–100) at the center[45]; Quinn has neatly characterized the lines (he is in fact referring to 89–100) as "a kind of central nucleus, a short, plangent, self-contained elegy."[46] But recently suspicions have been voiced that these ten lines may be an intrusion into the original composition.[47] The essential complaint is that they are inconsistent with the tone of the surrounding verses: Copley notes that the lament comes naturally enough in A, but in B the poet is writing about "happy love" and the desolation expressed in 91–100 does not belong. This depends, of course, on the interpretation of the surrounding lines on Laodamia which, it must be admitted, do not uniformly depict the bliss of union: the prevailing theme of 75–106 is the destruction caused by separation from love.

The further objection is raised that 91–100 present an awkward fit grammatically and stylistically with what precedes and follows.[48] Copley suggests that *quaene etiam*, 91, shows Catullus meant these lines to be "a parenthesis or afterthought."[49] Even if this is true, it is not necessarily valid to say that "it is odd to find the central section of a pyramidal poem occupied by a parenthesis." Poem 65 has precisely this structure, and the parenthesis is on precisely this subject. The pathetic apostrophe gains rather than loses force by the abruptness with which it begins and ends. Once again, we have one of those sudden transitions, as at 41, which attract too strong a reaction in isolation.

The implication is that originally 68.41–160 was a separate poem, without 91–100, written at a time when Catullus' relationship with Lesbia was happier. When he sent 68A, a *recusatio*, to his friend, he softened the rejection—or to some degree made up for it—by sending along this earlier composition and simply inserted 91–100 as a means of unifying the two poems ("the whole poem becomes an elaboration of the *recusatio*").[50]

---

[44] Kroll, p. 219.

[45] R. Westphal, *Catulls Gedichte*[2] (Breslau, 1870), p. 82, takes 87–100 as the *omphalos* of his structure, patterned after the Terpandrian *nomos*.

[46] Quinn, p. 179.

[47] Wohlberg; Copley; Vretska; P. T. Wiseman, *Catullan Questions* (Leicester, 1968), p. 23.

[48] Compare especially Vretska, pp. 323–325.

[49] Copley, p. 31. It should be remembered that *quaene etiam* is a conjecture by Heinsius for *que vetet id* in V.   [50] Copley, p. 32.

Two problems result from this approach. First, when the lines are removed, the poem has no clear center of gravity. Copley finds the "unifying *sententia*" in 87–90/101–104[51]; Wohlberg and Vretska fixed on 105–108[52]; and Wiseman, concerned to find marriage as the heart of this and other neighboring poems, is most precise: *coniugium*, 107.[53] In short, the poem becomes a decidedly unstable affair.

Second, we are in any case almost committed to the risky position that by excising 91–100 as a later addition, we will have intact the original poem. But is this the only alteration in the second edition of the poem? Guglielmino believed that 135–140 were also added at this point,[54] which would leave a severely asymmetrical composition in the original edition. It is not impossible, of course, that the first version was asymmetrical, but the careful balance everywhere evident strongly suggests that such corresponsions were part of the very nature of the poem from the beginning. Furthermore, Copley matches 41–50 and 149–160 as introduction and conclusion to Catullus' "poetisches Opfer." Now, 149–160 fairly certainly are part of the poem at the stage at which Catullus sent it to Allius, when he would have added 91–100. We ought then to remove 149–160, and thus 41–50, from the "original" version as well—and this clearly will not do. There may well be an earlier version of 68 underlying its present condition, but we can no longer get back to it. We must, I believe, take the whole poem in its present extent as representing the offering to Allius and work with the structures thus discovered. Lines 91–100 are now the center. In a sense, any awkwardness in the transitions at 91 and 101 is even further evidence of Catullus' determination to have these lines here and of their significance in the overall scheme. The elegance of the patterns moving out from this center can only strengthen the impression that they belong and, without them, we should have a very different poem indeed.

Most of the subdivisions of B are clear and generally recognized; but there are, I think, certain refinements and further supportive arguments which may be adduced. Around 91–100 stand 87–90/101–104, introducing and concluding the theme of Troy. Verses 87–90 present Troy as the scene of death, the place which lures men to their death (*coeperat ad sese Troia ciere viros*): so in some fashion, it may be implied, Troy had drawn Catullus' brother, and the poet's thoughts (even if not his syntax) move directly to the brother's death. The balancing lines focus on Troy as an instrument of separation from home from the Greek perspective (*fertur . . . pubes Graeca . . . deseruisse focos*). So the central lines 91–100 shifted from the death

[51] Copley, p. 31.   [52] Wohlberg, p. 43; Vretska, p. 327.
[53] Wiseman, p. 23, n. 1.   [54] F. Guglielmino (above, note 18), pp. 426–444.

which claimed the poet's brother to the poet's own sense of abandonment. The personal and mythical are thus in perfect harmony and convey the same sequence of emotions found explicitly in poem 101 and symbolically in poem 64.

The next concentric circle contains, on the one side, lines 73–86 and, on the other, lines 105–118, both dealing with Laodamia's thwarted passion for Protesilaus. Once more there is a marked difference in the perspective of the two passages. The first presents the facts of Laodamia's loss, with an apparently novel twist in the introduction of the idea of guilt in Laodamia leading to the death of her husband.[55] The tragedy, it is clearly stated, was prompted by the fates, which in a sense mitigates the heroine's guilt, though it does nothing to assuage her grief. There is again a parallel to Catullus' attitude toward the death of his brother: his brother was taken by fate, and all the poet's joy, which was nourished by fraternal love, withered and perished.

The matching lines 105–118 treat the theme in a highly figurative fashion, using the labors of Hercules as an elaborate simile. The obscurity of these verses borders on the grotesque, and interpretations of the labors in this context are largely unsatisfactory.[56] What is clear from the passage is that Catullus has carefully portrayed the depths of Laodamia's love in totally symbolic terms, as contrasted with the direct account in 73–86. Yet there are verbal links between the two sections: *siccare*, 110, recalls *ieiuna*, 79, and *deterioris eri*, 114, echoes *invitis eris*, 78.

Furthermore, both sections contain metaphorical elements developed in the next concentric ring. Verses 73–86 continue the motif of water and flowing (*saturasset*, 83; *sanguine sacro*, 75, of due rite; and by contrast *ieiuna*, 79) found more fully in 57–72; the *Stymphalia monstra* of 113 constitutes the first of three bird similes, the others (*volturium, columba*) appearing in the next section, 119–134.

These sections (57–72/119–134) are not only of equal length but in fact are identical even in their substructure. Lines 119–134 deal with the ecstasy of Laodamia's love and are divided into three symmetrical panels of 6-4-6 verses:

---

[55] On the reworking of this myth see Pepe (above, note 43), although Pepe's conclusions on the role of the "pre-Indo-European Nemesis" seem extravagant. See also E. Baehrens, "Die Laodamia-Sage und Catulls 68. Gedicht," *Jhb.Kl.Ph.*, 115 (1877), 409–415, and Lieberg, p. 207 ff.

[56] For an extreme example see Whigham (above, note 20), pp. 38–39. Quinn, p. 188 says it is "almost impossible to take seriously" these lines on Hercules, and wonders whether they might represent Catullus' effort "to express his mood of disenchantment with Alexandrian cleverness."

119–124 *simile*[57] *of rescue* from the vulturine kinsman by the gift of a grandson

125–128 *simile* of birds of passion to portray Laodamia's love

129–134 *comparison of Laodamia and Lesbia,* and the *coming of Lesbia to Catullus,* which completes the figure of birds with the flitting Cupid and provides transition back to Lesbia as the focus of the next section

This structure is precisely balanced by that of 57–72:

57–62 *simile* of refreshing waters

63–66 *simile of rescue* from deadly waters

67–72 the *coming of Lesbia to Catullus,* leading to the *comparison with Laodamia* which introduces the succeeding section

Thus these parts correspond in architecture and are parallel in subject: the one tells of the ecstasy of love in Catullus, and the other concludes the love of Laodamia in the theme of ecstasy. The two pairs of similes put it beyond doubt that these sets of lines are intended to be matched; but there is still more. Catullus is telling of the help which Allius provided in arranging the meeting for the lovers. He is, in fact, the counterpart of the flitting Cupid in the figurative language of the second passage (133–134): he literally "plays Cupid" to Catullus and Lesbia.

Laodamia thus plays two distinct roles in the symbolism of the poem. She represents Lesbia in the role of beloved woman—the *candida diva*[58] of v. 70—and also Catullus in the loss of his brother. Both these themes are to apply to Allius and illustrate the bond of experience between him and Catullus. Allius' loss is put into context by reference to the more grievous deprivation of Laodamia, and the love, however truncated, which he has previously enjoyed can be seen also as a greater blessing than even the archetypal figure of love and fidelity could claim. The threads left untied at the end of A are picked up in B.

The inescapable conclusion from the parallels between 57–72 and 119–134 is that the simile in 51–56 must be separated from the similes in 57–66. The first compares the burning of Catullus' love to the heat of Aetna[59] or the hot springs of Thermopylae, the second and third (57–62, 63–66) to the relief provided by Allius' help. The fact that the first and second both deal with water has encouraged the belief that they are connected and that Catullus has allowed his imagination to lead him beyond

[57] For a valuable examination of these similes, see Williams (above, note 17), pp. 108–111.

[58] See the exhaustive treatment of this in Lieberg, esp. 188 ff.

[59] A. G. Robson, "Catullus 68.53: The Coherence and Force of Tradition," *TAPA,* 103 (1972), 433–439, presents an attractive case for reading *Trachinia* rather than *Trinacria.* The passage gains considerably in the consistency of geographical reference (and in applying throughout to Hercules), and the symbolism is not at all damaged by the change.

the limits of the comparison. F. Skutsch[60] separated them, though many (including Kroll and Fordyce) have again regarded them as continuous. Fordyce[61] adduces three objections to breaking the sentence at 56. (1) The break would be abrupt. But we have seen already a tendency toward such abrupt transitions elsewhere in the poem. When dealt with individually these sudden shifts are generally taken as signs of corruption or explained away; when taken together they seem to form a pattern reflecting stylistically the paratactic bent of mind with which the poet views his own experiences and the myths by which he illustrates them.[62] (2) The second comparison in 63–65 "makes the structure awkward and unwieldy." But as can be seen it is only by accepting the break at 56 that a balanced structure can be obtained; any other arrangement is unmanageable. (3) "Elsewhere in Catullus a simile introduced by *qualis* relates to what precedes." This is true in the three other instances Fordyce cites, but is hardly a binding rule, and in view of the architectural considerations, loses much of its force. The movement is *qualis* (57)—*tale* (66). The purpose of the two similes (57–66) is to explain the "rescue" performed by Allius. But as with the bird motif which begins in 113–115 in a minor key and is developed into the major symbolic theme of 119–134, so here the water motif which occupies 57–66 is introduced in a minor key in 54–55 (where the real point is not the water but its heat, continuing from the heat of Aetna) and tapers off in the transition to 73–86.

The next ring, therefore, is 51–56, on Catullus' agony of love, with its hint (*duplex*, 51) of ambivalence, and 135–140 on his agony at Lesbia's infidelity.[63] In this second part, the theme of *duplex* is more prominent: the poet must come to terms with Lesbia's wavering loyalty, as Juno put up with Jupiter's. As in other balanced sections, there is a shift in perspective. One member deals in highly abstract language with feelings, the other more directly with Lesbia's actions. Once again the two parts are united

---

[60] F. Skutsch (above, note 4), p. 141. Skutsch's schema for B is the same as that defended in this paper, with somewhat different evidence and quite different emphasis.

[61] Fordyce, p. 350. He also points to *Il.*, 9.14–15, the apparent source of this simile, as further indication that there should be no decisive break at 56. While the influence of the Homeric lines may certainly be felt in the language of the simile, this in no way shows how Catullus structured his verses. The evidence of the poem's concentric patterns is more immediate and overriding.

[62] See further on this below, pp. 103 f.

[63] W. Hering, "Die Komposition der sog. Allius-Elegie (Catull 68, 41 ff.)," *Wiss. Zeitschrift Rostock*, 19 (1970), 599 ff. argues (in my opinion unconvincingly) that 8 vv. have been lost after 56. He subsequently developed his idea that these missing verses, together with 51–56, formed a unit of 14 lines balancing 135–148 in their present condition (assuming no lacuna after 141): "Beobachtungen zu Catull c. 68, 41–160," *ACD*, 8 (1972), 31–61.

by verbal echo: the burning of Aetna for Catullus' agony, and *flagrantem iram*, 139, for Juno's chagrin (compare *flagrans*, 73, of Laodamia).

This leaves the outermost layer, 41–50, which serves as a preface to the whole, complete with invocation of the Muses. Its subject is in general terms Allius' gift of friendship and the need to record that special gift. There is, of course, the lacuna after 46, but not more than one line could be missing from the sentence in order to complete the thought. Something akin to the supplement *omnibus inque locis celebretur fama sepulti*[64] would work quite well. We have, then, ten lines at the beginning which must surely be balanced by an equal number at the end (141–148). The break in sense after 141 gives sufficient warning that there are verses missing, and since Marcilius first postulated a lacuna in 1604, editors have generally conceded the point. Those who have tried to make sense out of the text as it stands[65] have in some cases created even greater obscurity. Streuli[66] reviews some of the solutions offered by defenders of the present state of the text and shows that the traditional two-line lacuna is much the best answer.

Two details may be observed in support of this theory. First, the following question could be raised: Even assuming that 41–50 and 141–148 were originally of equal length, could there not be, for example, three lines missing after 46 and four after 141—or any such set of numbers? As I have just suggested, there is not really any room in Catullus' thought for more than one line after 46,[67] and if that yields ten lines, the balancing arm must also be ten lines. Besides this, the central pillar (91–100) is also of this length, and we have thus a pattern developing. In A, the opening and closing elements were ten lines each; in B, the three main points of beginning, *omphalos*, and end are all ten lines.

Second, G. P. Goold,[68] in explaining the lacunae in poem 61, conjectured an ancestor of V with 32 lines to the page. This same format could be used to account for the losses in 68, which occur 96 lines apart or—on this scheme—three pages. For example, if this hypothetical codex had the text arranged with v. 46 at the end of one page, the succeeding

64 Compare Schwabe, *Catulli Veronensis Liber*[2] (1886), *ad loc.*: supplied by corrector in D. Paris 7990, 8232, 8236. Also in Dubl. K.2.37; see W. R. Smyth, "Three Notes on Catullus," *Hermathena*, 74 (1949), 40.

65 Compare esp. G. Friedrich, *Catulli Veronensis Liber* (Leipzig, 1908), p. 473 ff.; Lieberg, p. 261; and Birt (below, note 70).

66 P. E. Streuli, *Die Lesbia-Partien in Catulls Allius-Elegie* (Urnäsch, 1969), pp. 68–74.

67 The marginal *deficit* in OG is not any sort of evidence: the scribe would observe that *a* line was lacking, and would not need to consider further—if indeed the singular is intended to mean anything more than "something missing."

68 Goold (above, note 12), p. 95, n. 2.

pages would contain [47]–78, 79–110, 111–[141^a], [141^b]–poem 69. The
lines which dropped out would thus be at the tops and bottoms of pages,
from which, through physical damage or scribal carelessness, lines may
easily be lost.[69]
What is missing? The question, of course, is unanswerable. One might
conjecture a balance to the *nec* of 141 in 141^a, and in 141^b the start of the
idea completed in 142. Kroll (*ad loc.*) notes that the *atqui* ought to mark
the start of a new theme or a new example but that two lines would hardly
be enough room in which to develop a new theme involving the direct
address (presumably Catullus would be addressing himself) of *tolle*, 142.
But *tolle* has—I believe rightly—been held suspect by many. Birt[70]
proposed *tale* as part of a reconstruction (including *custodibat*, 139) to
explain the text without resorting to a lacuna. Schöll[71] proposed *nec
gratum tremuli tollere amantis onus*, which provides balance and good sense.
All of this produces a composition of astonishing complexity. Not only
has Catullus constructed the whole of B as a ring-composition of *omphalos*
and five outer rings, but he has also built into this structure smaller cycles
identified by motifs of key words and has further linked the balancing
members with verbal echoes. The two clearest examples of this technique
are to be seen in 51–86 and 105–140. Each of these passages, as noted,
breaks into three recognizable segments: 51–56/135–140, 57–72/119–134,
73–86/105–118. In 51–86, two motifs cross each other, alternating in
prominence: 51–56 focuses on the *burning* passion of Catullus (*arderem* etc.)
and introduces the motif of *water* in a minor key, as it were (the tears);
57–72 uses the *water* motif as the principal theme, but retains in lesser
prominence the burning heat (62); and 73–86 stresses again the burning
(*flagrans*, 73, references to sacrifices), while reducing the motif of flowing
or water to a lower key (chiefly in negative terms: *ieiuna*, 79, *ante* . . .
suam . . . *saturasset*, 83).
Matching this is a slightly less thorough set of motifs in 105–140. Again,
it is *burning* which unifies the passage by linking its outer limits: 105–118
speaks of the *aestus amoris* (where *aestus* suggests the water motif of 51–86
as well as the seething heat) and introduces the *bird* motif (*Stymphalia
monstra*, 113). This latter figure occupies the whole of 119–134 (the vulture,
the dove, and by extension the flitting Cupid attending Lesbia). Verses
135–140 pick up in minor key the burning with *flagrantem*, 139 (echoing
flagrans, 73).

[69] I might add that the same interval—32 lines—separates the fragmentary 58^b from
55.12, to which place a few of the *recentiores* and many editors assign it.
[70] Th. Birt, "Zu Catulls Carmina Maiora," *RhM*, 59 (1904), 428.
[71] Schöll (above, note 21), pp. 477–478.

Furthermore, the central element of each of these subcycles, as I have already noted, is itself constructed in *aba* fashion by being divided into 6-4-6 lines, the first and second units being similes drawn from nature in each case.[72]

I have appended a schema which will make these complexities somewhat clearer:

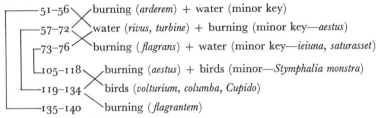

    ┌────51–56⟍ ⟋burning (*arderem*) + water (minor key)
    │   ✕
    │ ┌─57–72⟨ ⟍water (*rivus, turbine*) + burning (minor key—*aestus*)
    │ │
    │ ┌─73–76⟋ ⟍burning (*flagrans*) + water (minor key—*ieiuna, saturasset*)
    │ └─105–118⟍ ⟋burning (*aestus*) + birds (minor—*Stymphalia monstra*)
    │   ✕
    └──119–134⟨ birds (*volturium, columba, Cupido*)
       └──135–140   ⟍burning (*flagrantem*)

Thus the architecture of B is repeated at several levels and in several ways. It can be argued that the abruptness to be observed in several transitions can be related in part to the extreme—perhaps excessive—demands which so minute a structure placed on the poet. There was sometimes no smooth way to shift from one topic to the next, and the pattern, so deliberately and obviously sought, took precedence over gliding transitions. At the same time, as I mentioned earlier, this approach is essentially paratactic. Scenes are set up alongside one another, and it is in the end the reader's—and the poet's—perception of the commensurability of the real and the mythological which gives the poem its force. In short, Catullus' solution to this range of themes (brother's death, Allius' help, Lesbia, Laodamia and Protesilaus as symbolic in varying ways of all these) was this tendency to parataxis of thought, and it reveals itself not only in the sudden shifts to be observed at the seams but in the basic conception of the poem. How could all these themes, emotions, experiences and symbols be correlated simultaneously? They could not by any process of subordination and integration; but by introducing the themes in distinct panels, leading up to Catullus' most immediate concern and then considering them again[73] in the time-honored pattern of ring-composition, the poet could convey the distinctions of each as well as their

72 G. Howe, "Nature Similes in Catullus," *U. North Car. Studies in Philology*, 7 (1911), 1–15, analyzes briefly a number of nature similes including 68.55–62 (which he regards as an unbroken unit) but does not deal with the others in this poem.

73 A. Barigazzi, "L'unità dell'epinicio pindarico," *A&R*, n.s. 2 (1952), 121–136, remarks with particular reference to Pind., *O.*, 7, on the advantage of presenting events in reverse chronological order back to the critical moment and then returning in normal sequence to the present. The listener thus considers each event twice: the first sequence aims at marvel, the second at understanding. The same process is at work in Catullus, 68,

interrelationship. Laodamia is the link, and it is for her that the most elaborately figurative language is reserved.

If Laodamia is the link, however, the death of Catullus' brother is a kind of filter, and as the themes are presented a second time there is a distinct change in the way these themes are perceived.[74] I have already suggested some of the ways in which this shift operates. For example, the description of Lesbia's coming to Catullus gives almost no concrete detail —except the picture of her clicking her sandal on the threshold—but swiftly moves from the reference to Lesbia as *candida diva* on to the more elaborate scene of Laodamia's ill-fated arrival at the home begun in vain. Then Laodamia, who is introduced in a simile, is herself described in highly symbolic language in the second half of the structure (105–134). But conversely Lesbia, who at first is referred to figuratively (*candida diva*), is presented more directly in the second half, as Catullus faces his own experiences more directly, complete with their flaws and risks. The Laodamia simile allows Catullus to see his relationship to Lesbia in a cool, almost placid way. By the end of B, he is able to accept the inevitable fact that the "ideal" love he imagined in his goddess must fade and fail. Even as his brother died, and the most secure relationship in his life was shattered, so nothing in life is really safe from such disruption.

Laodamia cannot bear to part with Protesilaus: this is the theme of 81 ff. Granted that the union was irregular and ill-fated, still the separation was intolerable. At the moment of her coming to Protesilaus, thoughts of separation were farthest from her mind: the same may be said of Catullus when Lesbia came to him. But after the lines on his brother's death, a separation as sudden and shaking as that suffered by Laodamia, Catullus can accept the idea of losing his possessive grip on Lesbia with relative resignation. The second Laodamia passage refers chiefly not to the extravagant hope of the first arrival or to the agony of her loss but to the joy and depth of the love itself. Thus the intensity of the first half is mollified after the death of his brother. Laodamia becomes more symbolic, and that in terms of love rather than loss; while Lesbia, on whom the poet dared not gaze directly in the earlier lines, becomes correspondingly more concrete, her *rara furta* less calamitous.[75]

---

where in fact there is some chronological regression (Catullus and Lesbia—Laodamia and Protesilaus—the origins of the war). For further comparable features of Catullus, 68 and Pindar see G. Lafaye, *Catulle et ses modèles* (Paris, 1894), pp. 209–216.

[74] For a good discussion of this process see C. Witke, *Enarratio Catulliana.*, Mnemos. Suppl. X (Leiden, 1968), 41 ff.

[75] K. Büchner, "Catull 68.136," *MH* 7 (1950), 14–18, proposed reading *verecunde* for *verecundae* 136. Despite the mannerism of adjectives at the caesura and noun at line end, so prominent in the elegists, which may support *verecundae*, the perspective I have presented

Similarly, the lines on Troy (87–90/101–104) change in tone from the hateful, personal outburst at 87–90 to a more remote, epic flavor of 101–104 (*fertur*) despite the focus on punishment of adultery—a theme presumably close to Catullus' own thoughts.

Thus all the elements of the first half of B are built up to the death of the poet's brother, with its several levels of value, and then each is examined again. Those elements which are not personal become more remote, more symbolic. The personal element of Catullus' own experiences is faced more directly, and the poet comes to realize that his initial comparison of Lesbia to a *diva* was futile. This is surely the import of 141, *atqui nec divis homines componier aequum est.* Catullus will settle, as he must, for a human, fallible relationship. This he describes with painful bluntness in 141–148. The movement from dream and idealization to reality and practical acceptance of the way of the world is complete and is made explicit—perhaps even made possible—by his brother's death. I cannot imagine this poem in anything resembling its present shape without these central verses. They are the catalyst for the whole.

But this examination of 68.41–148 began as an exploration of the links between parts A and B of the poem. What has become of Allius? What of the poet's inability to write a *consolatio* for his friend? Catullus has taken the very reason for that inability—his recent tragic experience—and used it as a vehicle for conveying consolation to Allius. He has wrestled with his own frustrations, losses, and tottering hopes and has found the means to accept the happiness which preceded them without demanding that they continue forever. But that happiness, in part at least, depended on Allius' good offices; more to the point, it was precisely in the area of life where Allius has been wounded that he had assisted Catullus. By using a single figure, Laodamia, to symbolize both Allius' love and loss on the one hand and Catullus' love for Lesbia and loss of his brother on the other, Catullus has suggested the basic identity of Allius' experiences and his own. The resolution of the anxiety which Catullus discovers in and for himself also will apply to Allius. After working through the problem on his own terms, Catullus can return to Allius. As Laodamia served as a type for Catullus' sufferings in the loss of his beloved brother at Troy, so in one sense Catullus himself serves as a type for Allius. From the point at

here points to *verecunde.* It is Catullus' attitude toward Lesbia which is at issue here; he will be able (now) to view her *furta*—provided that they are *rara*—with restraint and discretion. He is answering the statement he made in v. 30 (*non est turpe, magis miserum est*). Büchner adduces further evidence in other elegists for this *verecundia* on the part of the poet rather than the mistress, and develops his ideas at length, *Humanitas Romana* (Heidelberg, 1957), pp. 109–133.

which reality is secured, the poet turns again to his friend and makes the
lesson explicit: this is part C.

Part C (149–160)

The transition is abrupt, as at the juncture of A and B. It is marked not
only by the sudden change of subject but also by a return to a more conventional, epistolary style, and to direct address to his friend, as in A. But
it is not as if the long intervening part B had never occurred. Catullus
carefully summarizes the whole poem in these concluding lines, *both parts
A and B.*

The passage contains, however, one of the most discussed and desperate
problems in all of Catullus: lines 157–158 which, Vretska notes, are
corrupt if they are in their proper place or, if sound, do not belong here.[76]
It is, I think, safe to say that they are not sound. Goold[77] points to the
hiatus in 158 as one of several signs of corruption; the asyndeton *dedit
aufert* is clumsy in the extreme; and what does *terram* mean? The solutions
offered for any or all of these flaws are legion.[78] One of the basic difficulties
is the reference involved. As the text now stands, 155–160 consists in a
round of good wishes to all connected with the events of the poem. Allius
and his *vita* come first and then the house and its mistress (surely not
Lesbia, whose entrance for her curtain call comes last, as befits the star)
and, after the puzzling lines, Lesbia and Catullus. Who is missing in this
list? The lines sound as if they were referring to Jupiter, but Catullus
would scarcely say "*sis felix*" to Jupiter. Kinsey feels the missing person is
Catullus' brother and emends to read *et qui principio nobis erat omnia, frater/
a quo sunt primo dulcia nata bona.* He thereby avoids the troublesome hiatus
in 158 and brings in the one person who has figured prominently in the
poem but has gone unmentioned here. But after the agonizing process
through which the poet has gone in facing his brother's death and its
implications, the salutation in this fashion seems grotesque (poem 101 is
not really a parallel) and, in any case, what would 158 mean? Cicero,
despite the good offices of Lipsius and Thompson, is unconvincing and a

---

[76] Vretska, p. 322. Hering's solution is peculiar: after considering at length the nature
of the corruption, and emending the lines, he then rejects them as interpolated ("Beobachtungen" [above, note 63], p. 42 ff.).

[77] Goold (above, note 12), p. 108.

[78] See S. Johnson, "A Fresh Solution to a Famous Crux in Catullus," *CJ*, 40 (1944–
1945), 10–18, for a review of solutions proposed up to that time; to which add Kinsey
(above, note 38), p. 45; D. F. S. Thompson, "Interpretations of Catullus, I," *Phoenix*, 11
(1957), 121–124; and Pennisi (above, note 15), pp. 223–228.

rather sudden entry into this group. If we ask who is missing, the answer is nobody.

Pennisi,[79] like Vretska, felt that the lines could not stand in their present place, but he moved them to after 154: in other words, the two couplets have been transposed at some stage, and perhaps the damage to the text occurred at that point. The strong impression that Jupiter is the referent can then stand. Verses 153–154/157–158 together constitute a promise of blessings from the gods in general and Jupiter in particular. Pennisi adduces Prop. 2.3.25–28 as in a similar vein, and he reads for 157–158:

> et qui principio nobis terram dat et aufert,
> a quo sunt primo omnia nata bona.

This leaves the disturbing hiatus. Scaliger's *nobis* for *primo* (which will have crept in under the influence of *principio,* 157) would be very satisfying but for *nobis* immediately above. Again the sequence of thought may be such as we have seen earlier, and the poet may compare Allius' situation with his own. *Vobis* 157 could provide a suitable contrast: (may the gods bless you) and he who first blessed you—from whom all gifts to us also originated. *Terram* is still peculiar; *et eram* (*te et eram* Munro) is possible. Such or similar changes produce a couplet somewhat as follows:

> et qui principio vobis et eram dat et aufert,
> a quo sunt nobis omnia nata bona.

All of this, of course, is conjectural tinkering. The fundamental notion— that Jupiter is the source of blessing—seems clear enough and is as much at home after 154 as it is intrusive after 156.

What then do we have in C? The lines fall clearly into three sections:

1. The first four lines (149–152) are a reprise on the theme of repayment and the remembrance of Allius' favors. The opening parts of both A and B are recalled here. Catullus is after all repaying Allius for his many *officia* (compare *hospitis officium,* 12, and *officiis,* 42) by giving him a *munus* (compare *munera,* 10) by which his name will never lapse into oblivion (151–152, compare 43–50). The poet further makes clear the relationship of A and B in 149–150: I have, after all, repaid you with a munus the only way I could (*ut potui*), and the *munus* is achieved in the process of this poem (*confectum carmine*). The lines confirm the process I have tried to describe in B: by the act of analyzing his own experiences and his reaction to them, Catullus has both immortalized Allius as a true friend and also shown how Allius can reconcile himself to his problems.

[79] Pennisi, p. 227.

2. This much and only this much Catullus can do for his friend, but the *foedus amicitiae* encourages the poet to predict that the gods also will repay Allius. 153–154 recall the tone of poem 76 where *pietas, fides*, and *benefacta priora* all lead to the prayer that the gods grant the favor of release from the agonies of a crumbling relationship. The second section (153–154/157–158) states this theme of repayment at the hands of the gods. These *munera* (154) are clearly of a higher order than the *munus* which Catullus can offer. Only through the *munera* of the gods can Allius attain happiness. As with the central portions of B, there is a turning back to the earlier, legendary days: in B, Laodamia is brought into prominence as a symbol of the experiences being recalled; in C, the poet predicts blessings for Allius such as were once—in those days—bestowed upon the *pii antiqui*.[80] If the general drift for 157–158 suggested above is in the right direction, Catullus will have skilfully linked at this level also Allius' lot and his own: as Jupiter sent blessings to me (and I have now recognized them for what they are), so he has sent you your happiness of earlier days, and by the same token the separation from your *vita* is part of the scheme of things. This is a crucial fact for Allius to realize, since once it is recognized the situation will seem less overwhelming—and less irremediable.

3. The poem then closes (155–156/159–160) with the series of good wishes or prayers for happiness. Catullus can now at last express, with some hope of its realization, the prayer that Allius and his *vita* may find happiness, as he also prays in the same terms for Lesbia and himself. In a sense Allius' *vita* and Catullus' Lesbia are to provide blessings for the two men as parallel to the gods' gifts of 153–154/157–158. Thus are reconciled Catullus' earlier exuberant references to his *candida diva* and his recognition that such worship is futile. The term for Lesbia in the second half of B and in C is *lux mea* (132, 160). He seems to be saying: I am happy as long as she is happy; she is at the center of my existence; but the figurative language of divinity is now gone. In a sense, 159–160 summarize the implications of the two passages on Catullus' brother and show how he has found, as it were, a new emotional center of gravity. Catullus' cry in 93 (*ei misero fratri iucundum lumen ademptum*) is answered in both B and C, as he now calls Lesbia *lux mea* (132, 160, nowhere else in his poems) instead of *diva*. Line 93 was one of the lines in the lament which Catullus altered in B (compare 21, *tu mea tu moriens fragisti commoda, frater*), and the reason for that change lies in the shift of focus from his brother to Lesbia, for which we are being prepared in 91–100.

What I am suggesting is that A, B, and C are linked by the fact that

---

[80] Lieberg, p. 262, n. 341, points to the similar turn of mind in 64.382 ff. after the main, mythologically oriented body of the poem.

they all cover the same ground in approximately the same order, but in different idioms: Allius asks for rescue and consolation, 1–10/ Allius previously rescued Catullus, 41–66/ Catullus has now returned the favor, 149–150. Allius' name is to be remembered, 43–50/ Allius' name will be remembered, 151–152. Catullus recalls the love and passion of his youth, 15–18/ Catullus recalls the love and passion of his meeting with Lesbia, 51ff. The blending of bitter and sweet in the gods' dealings with men: Venus 18/ Laodamia's fate/ *dedit aufert* or what lurks behind it, 157. The death of Catullus' brother as a turning point, 19–26/ the death of the brother, 91–100. The empty bed is *miserum* but not *turpe*, 27–30/ Lesbia's infidelity is distressing but pardonable, 135–148. The reality of the present situation, 31–40/ the real nature of Catullus' relationship with Lesbia, 141–148/ the prospects for the future, 155–160.

The three parts, though individually structured, are parallel statements. One poses the problem in plain terms, the next restates this theme in experiential and symbolic terms, and the last draws the conclusions on the theme. None is complete without the other two. The matched echoes of A and B to be found in C show that A and B cannot be divorced. The very point of C forbids its separation from B.

The junction at 40/41 is still, perhaps, the most jarring detail. It can now be seen from a different perspective. Catullus creates in A an air of expectancy, aided by the position of the conditional clause at the very end: if only there were some way . . . B then provides the release to the tension, beginning as it does so abruptly and treating not the problem of Allius' desolation but what Catullus can discuss: Allius' help for him. The invocation to the Muses imparts the impression of a beginning, but in so immediate and engaged a fashion (even allowing for starting *in mediis rebus*) that 41 cannot actually be the first line of an independent poem. The sustained elevation of tone sets B apart, and yet the very lack of transition links it to A. The neoteric style of B answers Allius' request for such poetry and shows in a way how Catullus has obviated his lack of a library: he has written on his own experiences instead of relying on the poetry of others.[81]

The structure of 68 is not unlike that of a trilogy.[82] Each piece is formally independent, displaying its distinctive architecture and style, but the theme is constantly pursued throughout the three parts. The initial

---

[81] Compare Salvatore's comment (*Studi Catulliani*, p. 103): "Nel caso del c.66, Catullo, non potendo creare, traduce; qui in 68, nell' impossibilità anche di tradurre, crea, è costretto a creare qualcose di nuovo."

[82] In a different context, Wohlberg, p. 44, suggests that the narrative of the Laodamia episode is developed like a tragedy.

statement of the theme of suffering in A, its reworking in B in quite different terms with progress toward a resolution, and the resolution itself in C provide both unity and distinctness to the parts.

The pattern of formally separate structures combining to produce a single statement with the development of a unifying theme is to be observed elsewhere in Catullus[83] and most notably in the later elegists. The practice in Propertius and Ovid has been studied in detail by K. Jäger,[84] with much evidence from other poets both Greek and Roman. The problem again is to decide whether in individual instances we are dealing with separate poems or a single poem with subdivisions. Barwick in a most provocative article[85] provided a list of examples, from Catullus, the elegists, and Martial of pairs or triads of poems. The most interesting example is Propertius 2.28, which appears in N as two poems (1–34/35–62), elsewhere as one poem. The evidence of N is not altogether reliable one way or the other, and opinion has differed drastically.[86] Rothstein's division into three separate poems[87] has attracted a consistent following, but the view that it is a single unit is supported by internal analysis.[88] As with Catullus 68, there are very abrupt transitions marked by change of situation, presumed lapse of time, and change of addressee. White's comparison to a play in four acts with an implied lapse of time between acts is a helpful approach.[89] However one may divide the poem, it is certain that all 62 lines constitute a unified treatment of a single theme, namely, the illness and recovery of Cynthia.

It is possible, indeed, that Propertius had Catullus 68 in mind as at least a partial model for 2.28. The appearance of *mea lux* (2.28.59) is striking, as Propertius only uses the expression three times, all in Book 2 (2.14.29, 2.28.59, 2.29.1), and the third occurrence is in the opening line

[83] K. Barwick, "Zyklen bei Martial und in den kleinen Gedichten des Catull," *Phil.*, 102 (1958), 284–318; also F. Stoessl, "Die Kussgedichte des Catull und ihre Nachwirkung bei den Elegikern," *WS*, 63 (1948), 102–116.

[84] K. Jäger, *Zweigliedrige Gedichte und Gedichtpaare bei Properz und in Ovids Amores* (Diss. Tübingen, 1966).

[85] K. Barwick, "Catulls c. 68 und eine Kompositionsform der römischen Elegie und Epigrammatik," *WJA*, 2 (1948), 1–15. Barwick, however, uses the evidence to suggest that 68 is two poems, though they "in höherem Sinne zusammen ein Ganzes bilden" (p. 7).

[86] Jäger 56–57 summarizes the differing views of the question. He regards 2.28 as two poems divided at 46/47.

[87] M. Rothstein, *Die Elegien des Sextus Propertius²*, I (Berlin, 1920), p. 368.

[88] See esp. R. White, "The Structure of Propertius 2.28: Dramatic Unity," *TAPA*, 89 (1958), 254–261.

[89] White, p. 260. The four divisions would be 1–34, 35–46, 47–58, 59–62.

of the next poem. Its only appearance in Catullus, as noted earlier, is in poem 68 (*lux mea* both times, 68.132, 160). Also, Propertius 2.28.33–34

> hoc tibi [sc. Iovi] vel poterit coniunx ignoscere Iuno:
> frangitur et Iuno, si qua puella perit

recall Catullus 68.138–140.[90] Beyond such isolated details, there is a similarity in the line of thought (however different the tone). Cynthia's illness is traced to an offense against the gods, specifically *totiens sanctos non habuisse deos* (6), not unlike Laodamia's offense for which she was deprived of Protesilaus. But Laodamia's sufferings and loss are transmuted, as we have seen, into a vision of the ecstasy of love, and Catullus' situation when it re-emerges from the realm of myth points to a happier solution. So Propertius promises Cynthia (15–16)

> sed tibi vexatae per multa pericula vitae
> extremo veniet mollior hora die.

The point is embellished in the Propertian manner with a series of heroines who suffered but were ultimately rescued and attained glory (in fact, divinity). The whole movement of the Laodamia passage conveys the same message. The agony is taken from our vision and replaced by joy.

In the third part of the poem (49–56) Propertius laments the death of all beautiful women of legendary times through Troy—and Achaia—to present days and then pleads for his special concern, Cynthia. The thought in particular of 53 (*et quot Troia tulit vetus et quot Achaia formas*) may find its parallel in Catullus' lament at the indiscriminate death dealt out at Troy (68.89–90):

> Troia (nefas!) commune sepulcrum Asiae Europaeque,
> Troia virum et virtutum omnium acerba cinis,

with which he leads into his particular instance, his brother.

It should be noted that Propertius in a neighboring poem (2.32) clearly had Catullus 68 in mind[91] and uses Lesbia herself as an example of license (2.32.45). The similarity in the line of thought, though handled differently and used to different purpose, raises at least the possibility that Propertius saw Catullus 68 as a unit and viewed the ideas of the poem as I have suggested. The Propertian poem would then stand beside the evidence from the *Ciris* referred to earlier, as an indication of antiquity's view of this puzzling masterpiece.[92]

University of Illinois at Urbana

90 One might add Propertius' gallant cry in 2.28.42/Cat. 68.160.

91 Propertius 2.32.29–30/Cat. 68.135–140. Compare Jäger, p. 215 and n. 83.

92 I should like to express my thanks to Professor Revilo P. Oliver, who read this paper and made many valuable suggestions.

Appendix: Schema of Catullus 68

A (1–40)

a 1–10 Allius' request for consolation   10

b 11–14 Transition to Catullus' own situation   4

c 15–26 Catullus' situation (a) 15–18 joy in youth   12
                               (b) 19–26 sorrow after brother's death

b¹ 27–30 Transition back to Allius   4

a¹ 31–40 Allius' request refused   10

B (41–148)

a 41–50 Allius' former gift of friendship   6   10

b 51–56 Catullus and Lesbia: the agony of passion   6

c 57–72 Catullus' love: the ecstasy: nature similes: refreshing water   4   16
                               rescue from deadly waters   6
                    fulfillment: Lesbia's coming

d 73–86 Laodamia's love thwarted   14

e 87–90 Troy and death   4

f 91–100 Brother's death at Troy   10

e¹ 101–104 Troy and separation   4

d¹ 105–118 Laodamia's love thwarted   14

c¹ 119–134 Laodamia's love: the ecstasy: nature similes: rescue from vulture 6   16
                               birds of passion   4
                    fulfillment: Lesbia's coming   6

b¹ 135–140 Catullus and Lesbia: the agony of infidelity   6

a¹ 141–148 Lesbia's gift of love   10

C (149–160)

149–152 Catullus' repayment of Allius and his remembrance: 4
              reprise of first parts of A and B: present

153–154/157–158 The gods and repayment: 4
              reprise of themes of central parts of A and B: past

155–156/159–160 Resolution of tension: 4
              reprise of closing sections of A and B: future

10

Poeta Ludens: Thrust and Counter-Thrust in Eclogue 3

BARRY B. POWELL

Although several scholars in recent times have attempted to elucidate the enigmatic Third *Eclogue*,[1] their work has appealed too often, I would complain, to Vergil's Hellenistic antecedents and too seldom to the poem itself. While not disclaiming the usefulness of such appreciations for defining the generic context in which Vergil composed,[2] I fear that the poem's meaning and value must, in the end, be discoverable from the dynamics of its own internal dramatic development.[3] The rules of this development, I wish to argue here, are those we find in game. For in the Third *Eclogue* Vergil gives us twin top-notch gamesters who, in a game of words, seek to overthrow one another through daring twist and lightening rhetorical legerdemain, and we, the understanding listener, will revel in the complexity and ballyhoo that accompanies each turn in a fine match hotly contested.

---

[1] H. J. Rose (*The Eclogues of Vergil*, Berkeley and Los Angeles, 1942, 40 ff.), following the lead of A. Cartault (*Études sur les Bucoliques de Virgile*, Paris. 1897, p. 127 ff.), compared the poem with its Theocritean "originals" and found it wanting. J. J. H. Savage ["The Art of the Third *Eclogue* of Vergil (55–111)," *TAPA*, 89, 1958, 142–158] saw in it an elaborate political allegory, but found no followers. C. P. Segal ("Vergil's *Caelatum Opus*: An Interpretation of the Third Eclogue," *AJP*, 1967, pp. 279–308) saw the poetry of the Third *Eclogue* as coming from a kind of tension generated between various thematic oppositions. Friedrich Klingner (*Virgil*, Zürich and Stuttgart, 1967, pp. 50–59) carefully measures the tradition and gives the best account of Vergil's debt to his predecessors. M. C. J. Putnam (*Virgil's Pastoral Art*, Princeton, 1970, pp. 119–135), owes much to Segal but discovers insidious elements in the pastoral landscape. Brooks Otis (*Virgil, A Study in Civilized Poetry*, Oxford, 1963) has some comments (particularly pp. 128–133).

[2] And for defining the context of individual poems within the book; see Otis (above, note 1), p. 128 ff.

[3] Compare Putnam (above, note 1), p. 4 ff.

Menalcas calls to Damoetas asking, "Whose herd?" (1). The question is simple, but it throws up to Damoetas that he has no herd of his own: the contest has begun. There is reproach in an *Meliboei?* But the question's precise significance is obscured within the fuzzy edge that surrounds pastoral, the realm of insinuation which lends tone or mood but does not contain objective information. Who is Meliboeus? At least, judging by Damoetas' insistent rejoinder (he twice says "Aegon"), Damoetas would rather not hear the name (2). Then Menalcas answers: "Poor beasts, that they must suffer at your hands, O Damoetas, for Aegon's inferiority to me in love" (3–6). The reply is brave, but Aegon's inferiority to Menalcas is claimed, not proven. And where is Neaera now? Menalcas puts a good face on a poor situation and then insults Damoetas for bringing the matter up at all (*hic alienus custos*, 5).

Innuendo goes with Menalcas' style, as in the vague an *Meliboei* (1); and throughout Menalcas preserves a certain decorum when Damoetas is crass. We may see in this a rudimentary characterization, but we will also recognize Damoetas' agonistic obligation as respondent to intensify the terms that Menalcas has laid down. This he does now: "Remember who you're talking to, my boy (*parcius viris obicienda*). As far as your achievement with Neaera is concerned—why everybody knows you're a pederast on the receiving end (*novimus qui te et quo*)—even the goats are embarrassed (*transversa tuentibus*)" (7–9). This *alienus custos* holds high cards of his own.

The sexual indiscretions of Menalcas may excite the disgust of man and beast, but Damoetas, Menalcas replies, is inept and an oaf: he can't milk goats, he can't even prune a vine (10–11). "O that must have been the time when (*tum*)" establishes the connection with Damoetas' volley, and "I suppose (*credo*)" identifies the adept irony by which Menalcas, false claimant to the deed (*mala vitis incidere falce novellas*), shows where the real guilt lies. This is clever but weak behind the broadside of 7–8.

Realizing a kind of advantage, Damoetas picks up from his *quo sacello* (8) with *Aut hic* (12) and, adding the charge of petty spite to pederasty (alleged again in *perverse Menalca*), Damoetas tells how Menalcas, mortified, once avenged a lover's pique in a way that speaks for itself (12–15).

An unrelenting assault requires new ground for insult (16–20). Damoetas, then, is a knave and a thief (*audent cum talia fures, pessime*), and Menalcas knows whereof he speaks (*ego vidi*). In fact, to prove that this feud is of long standing, we now learn that it was Menalcas who alerted the owner (*Tityre, coge pecus*).

This is touché for Menalcas, and Damoetas is thrust to the defensive. It was his goat anyway, Damoetas complains. He won it by playing on his pipe (21–24), a reply that nicely turns the poem toward its natural form, the singing contest. "You couldn't play a straw (25–27)," Menalcas snorts. Dameotas wagers a heifer that he can do a lot better than that (28–31). Damoetas may be cavalier to wager another man's heifer (Aegon's), but Menalcas, the younger of the two herders (compare 7), is driven into apparent retreat when he must admit the limits set to his independence by *pater* and a *noverca iniusta* (32–34). Well, he will put up a *caelatum opus* instead, wonderfully carved and never used. The reference to Conon intends to impress, but *quis fuit alter* reminds us that these men are (for the moment) common people after all, beguiling in their affectation.

Damoetas will not be impressed and mocks the offer. Cups by Alcimedon must not be all that rare, because Damoetas himself has not one but two of them (*et nobis idem Alcimedon duo pocula fecit*, 44). Nor is variety Alcimedon's forte: Damoetas' cups boast a floral motif very like that on Menalcas' cup (45; compare 38–39), and *Orpheaque in medio posuit* (46) answers *In medio duo signa* (40). Lest anyone miss the irony, *necdum illis labra admovi, sed condita servo* (47) exactly repeats 43. Having doubled Menalcas' wager, Damoetas goes on to deny its value, saying, *Si ad vitulam spectas, nihil est quod pocula laudes* (48), a quibble that unexpectedly lets Menalcas back in with "You're only trying to get out of it—all right, a heifer it is" (*numquam hodie effugies; veniam quocumque vocaris*, 49).[4] Damoetas may seem to have forced the hand of Menalcas, but, after all, if Menalcas will win (he is confident), the *noverca* will have no loss to count. And, by hedging at first, Menalcas has stopped the betting from going higher than Damoetas' original bid while preserving his self-confident image. This is a victory of sorts for Menalcas, and he seals it by calling to a passerby, Palaemon (50). If Damoetas hoped to buy the pot, he has been soundly deceived. He does not disguise his irritation: *Quin age, si quid habes* (52). Nor will this be your ordinary contest—*sensibus haec imis (res est non parva) reponas* (54), advice directed to Palaemon, to Menalcas, and to us.

Palaemon's three lines on *formosissimus annus* (55–57) give rhetorical relief, delimit the preceding informal match, and equip us with the pastoral setting. Then 58–59 mark out the terms of the formal contest (*incipe Damoeta, alternis dicetis*) and announce its inception.

The amoebean contest may be compared to the riddling folk song, wherein we seem to see something ancient, a battle of spells perhaps whose outcome, for the weaker magician, is shame or death. This urbane descendent of a primordial custom may stake no such odds, but it is not a game for amateurs. Moving swiftly, it is merciless to the unclever. According to its rules the leader (Damoetas) needs to dazzle and bewilder his opponent through versatile handling of conventional literary forms and

---

4 Segal, I take it, has not understood that a heifer *is* the prize. See above, note 1, p. 302.

through sudden shifts in subject or theme. The respondent (Menalcas) must match the leader's convention but, in some way, turn its content around. Damoetas is like White in chess, because his aggressive style and strategy develop from his being first to move. Black on the other hand— Menalcas—gains in definition what he loses in initiative; if he can only keep even, perhaps White will make that one wrong move.

Damoetas leads off slow and sure, a hymn to Zeus (60–61). *Principium* is a pun: from Zeus does the world proceed and from the subject of Zeus does Damoetas' song commence. Then, deftly, he continues in formal hymnal style (*auxesis*): having named the god, he cites an outstanding attribute (*Iovis omnia plena*). Through an oblique syllogism, whose conclusions are expressed in two sentences joined by the demonstrative pronoun in hymnal anaphora, it follows that Zeus not only nourishes all life (*ille colit terras*), but also nourishes the poet's song (*illi mea carmina curae*).

Menalcas replies to this elegant opening by declaring that he, for his part, is loved by Phoebus. If Zeus be king of all, Phoebus is lord of poetry, the subject now at hand. So Menalcas is personal where Damoetas has been abstract, which gives Menalcas' address greater force: *et me Phoebus amat*. Menalcas answers the *auxesis* by naming Apollo's special plants, a metaphor probably for his own (pastoral) poetry.

Taking advantage of his lead, Damoetas shifts to an amatory theme, perhaps picking up from his opponent's *amat* (62). "My girl Galatea wants to play games—she's running away, but not too fast" (64–65). The picture charms and provokes, but Menalcas comes back easily: "Amyntas and I—we're past playing games—I make it with him as often as I do with Delia" (66–67). Whatever Damoetas' Galatea is leading up to, Menalcas has already concluded with Delia. Amyntas, *puer delicatus*, makes two to Damoetas' one. And there is no lost motion here (*At mihi sese offert ultro*).

Damoetas pursues the theme. "I give everything to my beloved— sweets for the sweet" (68–69). Since, metonymically, his love is *Venus*, the gift will be *palumbes*. "Well I do what I can (*quod potui*)," Menalcas answers, "I've already sent apples to my boy, and tomorrow he gets more" (71). What Damoetas only has in mind, Menalcas has accomplished: as often in Greek and Latin poetry, *mala* symbolize sexuality fulfilled.

The going gets tougher with "O the things my girl has spoken—I only hope the gods are listening in" (who will see her pledges fulfilled)[5] (72–73). But the connection between 72 and 73 is obscure,[6] and Menalcas,

[5] For the interpretation see Klingner (above, note 1), pp. 55–56, n. 2.

[6] Too obscure for Servius (and his followers) who mistakes 72–73 to mean *ita . . . mecum dulce locuta est Galatea, ut deorum auditu eius digna sint verba.*

on his toes, like ourselves, must supply the missing words to follow the sense.

Menalcas' answer reveals that he takes the lines correctly. Where Damoetas formally praises (his girl promises all) but in fact complains (talk is cheap), Menalcas appears to complain when really he praises: "What's the use that you love me, Amyntas (*me ipse animo non spernis*), when your birth is so high (*dum tu sectaris apros*) and mine is so low (*ego retia servo*)" (74–75). "Poor" Menalcas—he takes his lovers from the best class.

Speaking of class, Damoetas claims it for himself in the next complicated distich. "Today's my birthday—send me your girl Phyllis, O Iollas; come the *Ambarvalia*—then send yourself" (76–77). Damoetas therefore stands as master to Iollas—so much for Menalcas' confessed servility in 75 (Damoetas scores 1 point). Birthdays are for love, and real love is between man and woman; as for pederasty (*Iolla . . . ipse venito*), that is suitable for a day of abstinence (*cum faciam vitula pro frugibus = Ambarvalia*), that is, it is as good as nothing—so much for Menalcas' sexual inclinations (Damoetas scores 2 points). Counting Galatea, Damoetas is the lover of three—so much for Menalcas' much-vaunted Amyntas (give Damoetas a score of 3 points).

Menalcas resists the attack by denying the premises upon which Damoetas has built it. Assuming, brilliantly, the identity of Iollas,[7] Menalcas shows us where that man's affections lie in *Phyllida amo ante alias* (78). *Discedere* (78) answers *mitte* (76)/ *venito* (77) and *Formose, vale, vale, inquit, Iolla* (79) deals with Phyllis' putative affections, while reserving to the last word of the distich the key to the masquerade. Damoetas, then, by Menalcas' reckoning, is odd man out.

Damoetas has other cards to play: a four-part priamel and yet another girl. "Wolves are hard on flocks, rain ruins the harvest, and wind the trees—but what hurts *me* (*nobis*) is the displeasure of Amaryllis" (80–81). The first three terms of the priamel (*lupus, imbres, venti*), cast in images from nature, establish foil for the "pronominal cap" (*nobis*),[8] which personalizes and forms a climax to the focusing device of the priamel.

Menalcas answers the terms one by one, but replaces the mood of gloom (*triste*, 80) with cheer (*dulce*): "Moisture pleases the sown seed, arbute the kid, willow the pregnant flock—but to me is pleasing Amyntas

---

[7] Here I follow the punctuation of E. de Saint-Denis (*Virgile: Bucoliques*, Paris, 1970, p. 53). "Si *Iolla* était exclu des paroles d'adieu, li ne serait pas placé à la fin du vers" (p. 114, n. 80).

[8] For the term see Elroy Bundy, *Studia Pindarica I* (Berkeley and Los Angeles, 1962), p. 5, n. 18.

alone" (82–83). Damoetas seeks to aggrandize his position by adding lover to lover, but he has thereby invited the charge of frivolity. There must be *some* advantage in having a single beloved (*dulce mihi solus Amyntas*, 82) over suffering the wrath of still one more girl (*triste nobis Amaryllidis irae*, 80).

It is Damoetas' prerogative to shift topic or motive suddenly, and now he defies the expectations of all by knocking down the very convention by which the poem exists—as if an actor stepped off the stage and into the audience, there to carry on a conversation with an eminent person un-related to the dramatic action. And the effect on us is the same: shock combined with pleasure at the unexpected intimacy. Here then in the Third *Eclogue* is no "real" country setting. We have a strictly formal literary contest, waged between Vergil and himself (and the audience) with the intent of delighting and entertaining. "Well the genre may be pastoral, but at least *Pollio* likes it," Damoetas says. "Let's have a prize (*vitulam*) for the good man" (for he has fine taste in literature) (84–85). The lines are a plug for Pollio, Vergil's tribute to his friend and fellow poet. *Quamvis est rustica*, needless to say, is ironical: a sophisticated, not simple, taste characterizes this *lector*.

Menalcas appreciates the subtlety and comes back with higher praise still. (He not only likes poetry, but) "Pollio, a *novus poeta* like Vergil, writes it himself (*et ipse facit nova carmina*)—give the good man (not a heifer but) a bull" (86–87). *Nova carmina* answers *rustica*, but the irony is gone. And *taurum* betters *vitulam* as *poeta* betters *lector*: well, a superior talent merits a richer reward.

Damoetas returns for a second try. "May he who loves you, Pollio, come where it pleases you to be; and may the honey flow for him, and the bramble bear spice" (88–89). Damoetas compliments Pollio once again, obliquely alluding to a kind of poetry that Pollio, as *novus poeta*, will have written, *viz.*, amatory verse, for which the *adunata* of 89 are standard fare. *Qui* therefore will be he whom Pollio addresses in his verse, and Damoetas-Vergil's lines amount to "May you be successful in your suit, my friend Pollio."

It is the natural role of Menalcas to mock his opponent, and now he parodies *qui te, Pollio, amat* (88) by *qui Bavium non odit* (90). He thereby preserves the form (*qui . . .*), inverts the meaning (*odit*), but also changes the subject (*Bavium*). Maevius, too, he pillories[9] and then completes the formal similarity of his couplet to 88–89 by matching Damoetas' elegiac *adunata* by *adunata* proverbial for the fool (91)—you'd have to be *that* deranged to enjoy such stuff. Damoetas in his couplet has sought to

---

[9] Compare Hor., *Epod.*, 10.2.

compliment Pollio, but Menalcas' reply, while formally a close parallel to his opponent's words, abandons Pollio entirely to attack viciously contemporary poetasters (perhaps literary opponents of Pollio). Attacking Menalcas' vituperative tone, Damoetas carries back the poem to within the usual bounds of pastoral; as if the actor returned to the stage and resumed the action of the play, but with an offhand reference to the preceding extemporization. "You who gather flowers and strawberries burgeoning on the earth" (92) are Damoetas' pretty words for "You who enjoy poetry in the pastoral genre," while "flee, lads, flee hence, a cold snake lurks in the grass" (93) tell how Damoetas see Menalcas' relationship to this world: Menalcas turns a gentleman's game into a parlous exchange of insult.

Damoetas has spoken to the lover of pastoral (*qui legitis flores*). Menalcas' surprise, therefore, is to reply as the *pastor* himself. "Careful, my sheep, don't go too far—that's a dangerous bank—you see how the ram has just fallen in" (94–95). To speak as the shepherd is an effective stroke, because of course he *is* a shepherd (at least when on stage). *Ipse aries* (95) answers *anguis in herba* (93) and embarrasses Damoetas (= *aries*) by denying to him metaphorically the surefootedness which a slippery game, like this one, requires to survive. He means "Nice try, but no success."

In the now white heat of battle Damoetas seeks no new attack, but answers Menalcas in kind. "Hey Tityrus, get your goats back from the river—when the time comes, I'll wash them in the spring myself" (96–97). The image is pastoral, but its rhetorical force amounts to "Hold on, my friend, you go too far: why destroy yourself? I'll do it for you, with my poetry (*in fonte*)." *Tityre* may recall the First *Eclogue*, but here the word is metonymy for "shepherd," thus "my pastoral friend." The figurative significance of *flumen* as "danger" has been established by Menalcas himself (95); and *capellas* reminds us that Menalcas is a goatherd (8). The metaphorical equation between the herd-*cum*-herder and poet-singer also has been suggested (94–95). But the *jeu des idées* turns finally upon *in fonte*, because, presented as an alternative to *flumen* (96) and suggested by Menalcas' own *ripae* (94), it bears the second meaning of "poetic font." He means "Back off, or you're all washed up."

To reply Menalcas begins with a close imitation of *reice capellas* (96) and then shifts radically in imagery while upholding the tone of virulent attack. "Gather the sheep, boys; if the heat stops up the milk—like just recently—we shall press in vain the teats with our hands" (98–99). We might paraphrase: "You better watch out yourself (*cogite ovis, pueri*): if you're going to get hot under the collar (*si lac praeceperit aestus*)—like just now (*ut nuper*)—I'll win the game by default (*frustra pressabimus ubera*

palmis)." Damoetas' anger—Menalcas alleges—is going to confound his
flow of wit as the summer heat stops up milk in the udder. Damoetas will
lose the match before Menalcas can win it; Menalcas' own wit will then
have no object, nothing to "work over." Here Menalcas plays the same
game that he did in 94–95. While meeting the formal requirements laid
down by his opponent (*frustra pressabimus ubera palmis* is equivalent to
omnis in fonte lavabo), he denies that his opponent has made a point at all.

Fighting fire with fire, Damoetas answers, "Alas! how thin is our bull
amidst the rich vetch! One and the same love is the ruin of herd and
herder" (100–101). The image is strictly pastoral, referring to the life of
the herd, and "poetic" in its projection of human feelings into the animal
world. But its figurative significance is "The possibilities of the genre are
great (*pingui arvo*), but your performance is wanting (*macer taurus*); your
eagerness (*amor*) ruins your poetry (*pecori*) as it disgraces you (*magistro
pecoris*)." Damoetas, in effect, calls Menalcas a "bull-in-a-china-shop."

Although by *mihi taurus* (100) Damoetas has referred to his opponent,
Menalcas refuses the assault by taking the words literally, as if Damoetas
had simply meant, "O My, I have problems in my herd—the bull is in
love." "Sure," Menalcas parries, "I have problems too—since someone
(that is, *you*) gave them the evil eye" (102–103). These may be fighting
words, but Menalcas' meaning adheres as closely to his expression as does
flesh to the bones of ailing goats (that is, *vix ossibus haerent*). So Menalcas
seems to say also that "If the inner meaning to my words in this poetic
game hangs as loosely on the external image as does the flesh on the bones
of diseased sheep—well, *you* have brought us to this pass."

Beyond such obfuscation can lie only mystery, and on that note the
contest ends. "You will be Apollo if you tell me where the breadth of the
sky is not more than three cubits" (104–105). "And I really will give you
Phyllis, if you can tell me where the names of kings are born on flowers"
(106–107). *Apollo* does recall 62, as often observed, as *Phyllida* recalls the
exchange in 76–79, therefore returning the end of the contest to its
beginning. But the riddles themselves have no answers, as proved by the
weakness of proposed solutions.[10] Klingner describes the verses correctly:
"Das Spiel wird endlich in den beiden Rätselfragen [104–107], die mit
ihrer paradoxen Phantastik—Grosses im Kleinen—doch wohl verblüffen

[10] Asconius Pedianus and Cornificius, according to Servius and Philargyrius, discover
a *jeu de mots* between *caeli* and *Caeli*, the second referring to one Caelius, a prodigal
Mantuan who lost all save three cubits of earth for his tomb. Heyne thought the reference
to be the bottom of a well. Savage argues for the hole in the temple of Juppiter on the
Capitoline (J. J. Savage, "The Riddle in Virgil's Third Eclogue," *CW*, 47, 1954, 81–83).
Compare also, J. Perrett, Virgile, *Les Bucoliques* (Paris, 1961), p. 44; M. C. J. Putnam,
"The Riddle of Damoetas," *Mnemosyne*, 18, 1965, 150–154.

und necken und jedenfalls eben spielen wollen, so leicht wie Seifen-blasen."[11] Damoetas hopes to trick up Menalcas, at last, by posing an impossible question. Menalcas, undaunted, answers in kind.

The explicitly riddling form of the last two couplets of the contest would seem to confirm that the true ancestry of this now modern and polished genre belongs to that primordial magical duel whose issue, for the lesser spellbinder, mythology preserves in the tales of Apollo-Pan[12] and Apollo-Marsyas.[13] Here, however, there is no winner. Palaemon rightly calls it a draw. Each man deserves the sacrificial animal (*vitula*, 109) and "so do all good *novi poetae* (*quisquis amores/ aut metuet dulcis aut experietur amaros*)" (109–110). It has been a good bout, well fought and rich in poetic fare (*sat prata biberunt*, 111), and now it is finished (*claudite iam rivos*, 111).

The Third *Eclogue* has long frustrated understanding because its critics, I think, when not too much given to *Quellenforschung*, have sought to dis-cover what they fancied to be "poetic virtue" in it. But by poetic, when all is said and done, they have meant something like "emotional." Somehow we are to know the *Eclogue* as poetry through the subtle re-verberations that play between original and re-creation or through alleged tensions that different levels of meaning and image generate within us, as if Vergil were a Romantic after all. But word games are played with the brain, not the solar plexus, and it is from the intense intellectuality of daring affront and bold riposte that we take our pleasure in the poet's words—not a draught for children, perhaps, who love the idle play of poignant image, but a heady liquor for men and women at the banquet of Augustan song.

University of Wisconsin at Madison

[11] Klingner (above, note 1), pp. 57–58.   [12] Ov., *Met.*, XI, 146 ff.
[13] Ov., *Met.*, VI, 302 ff.; Apollod., I, 24; *et al.*

11

An Interpretation
of Horace's Eleventh Epode

GEORG LUCK

Petti, nihil me sicut antea iuvat
  scribere versiculos amore percussum gravi,
amore, qui me praeter omnis expetit
  mollibus in pueris aut in puellis urere.
hic tertius December, ex quo destiti   5
  Inachia furere, silvis honorem decutit.
heu me, per urbem—nam pudet tanti mali—
  fabula quanta fui, conviviorum et paenitet,
in quis amantem languor et silentium
  arguit et latere petitus imo spiritus.   10
'contrane lucrum nil valere candidum
  pauperis ingenium' querebar adplorans tibi,
simul calentis inverecundus deus
  fervidiore mero arcana promorat loco.
'quodsi meis inaestuet praecordiis   15
  libera bilis, ut haec ingrata ventis dividat
fomenta vulnus nil malum levantia,
  desinet inparibus certare summotus pudor.'
ubi haec severus te palam laudaveram,
  iussus abire domum ferebar incerto pede   20
ad non amicos heu mihi postis et heu
  limina dura, quibus lumbos et infregi latus.
nunc gloriantis quamlibet mulierculam
  vincere mollitia amor Lycisci me tenet;
unde expedire non amicorum queant   25
  libera consilia nec contumeliae graves,
sed alius ardor aut puellae candidae
  aut teretis pueri longam renodantis comam.

This curious poem was called by Friedrich Leo *plane elegia iambis concepta*—a very apt description. It sounds paradoxical, and the poem is something of a paradox. Eduard Fraenkel[1] tried a slightly different approach. He thought that Horace here made full use of themes current in Hellenistic erotic poetry, especially erotic epigrams, as they are preserved in the Greek Anthology. Horace knew Asclepiades, Meleager, and Philodemus—no doubt about that—but in this particular poem, I think, he imitates, or perhaps parodies, the manner of a Roman poet. The themes may be Greek, but I think I can name the man who introduced them into Roman poetry and made them popular. It is the man who is known as the ἀρχηγέτης of the Roman love elegy. I should like to show that in his poem Horace alludes to Cornelius Gallus.

Though he never mentions him by name, Horace almost certainly was familiar with the work of Virgil's great friend. Horace's *Epodes* were written at about the time when Gallus' fame as a love poet must have reached its zenith. At about the same time, Virgil was at work on his *Eclogues*, two of which pay tribute to Cornelius Gallus.

The whole concept of love and the love-poet which emerges from the Eleventh Epode is so typical of Latin elegiac poetry that practically every line can be paralleled from Propertius, Tibullus, or Ovid. But none of them had published anything at this time. Catullus is entirely different.

I do not think it necessary to discuss our Epode together with nr. 15, although it is closely related. There, too, the poet seeks to end an unhappy love affair. Again, as Kiessling-Heinze point out, the themes can be traced back to Hellenistic love poetry. But in this case I would hesitate to connect them with Gallus.

Let us now isolate the various themes of nr. 11 and compare them to passages in the later elegiac poets. The commentaries give a few parallels, but a quick search in the *indices verborum* and concordances furnishes many more. I shall not give a complete list but select the more important ones, hoping to establish a catalogue of themes and ideas typical for Gallus:

I. The poet in love does not enjoy writing *versiculi* any more (1 f.). We should hardly compare Propertius 2, 16, 33 f., *tot iam abiere dies, cum me nec cura theatri/ nec tetigit Campi, nec mea Musa* (P, Volscus: *mensa* cett.) *iuvat*, because here the reading *Musa* is not absolutely certain. But we have an excellent parallel in Virgil, *Ecl.*, 10, 62, where Gallus himself says, *iam nec Amadryades rursus nec carmina nobis/ ipsa placent*. In the same context, Virgil's Gallus speaks of hunting as *nostri medicina furoris* (60). The concept of love as *furor, insania,* or *malum vulnus* is characteristic of our Epode (compare *furere,* 6; *fomenta vulnus nil malum levantia,* 17). Horace seems to have chosen the word *versiculi* deliberately. Of course, he is not thinking of iambs. The

1 Fraenkel, ed. *Horace*, 1957, p. 67. He draws attention to F. Jacoby's article on the origin of the Roman elegy, *Rhein. Mus.*, 60 (1905), 38 ff.

diminutive is typical for love poetry, hence for elegiac verse (compare *nugae; lusus*). The very word *versiculi* alone might indicate that Horace, in this Epode, deals with elegiac themes.

II. To be "wounded" or "smitten" by love (*amore percussum gravi*, 1) is another theme dear to the elegiac poets, though the closest parallel comes again from Virgil (*Georg.*, 2,476), *ingenti percussus amore*, where it is the love of the Muses. *Gravis amor* is fairly frequent in Propertius (2, 30A, 7 f.; 3, 8, 10; 21, 2), and Tibullus uses the adverb *graviter* in an expressive way (2, 1, 70), *a miseri, quos hic graviter deus urget*.

III. The idea that the poet is the constant target of love (*amore, qui me praeter omnis expetit*, 3) is probably as old as Anacreon, but it is certainly typical of Propertius; compare 1, 6, 23 ff.; 2, 22A, 17 f., *uni cuique dedit vitium natura creato:/ mi fortuna aliquid semper amare dedit; 34B, 57 ff. He sees himself as the victim, the martyr of passion; but on this martyrdom he builds his fame as a poet. He suffers, but he suffers in a stylish pose.

IV. If he is not in love with a beautiful woman, he is in love with a handsome boy (*mollibus in pueris aut in puellis urere*, 4). Here, again, one thinks of Anacreon, but Gallus, too, may have written homoerotic poetry, for in Virgil, *Ecl.*, 10, 36 ff. he says, *certe, sive mihi Phyllis, sive esset Amyntas,/ seu quicumque furor .../ mecum inter salices lenta sub vite iaceret:/ serta mihi Phyllis legeret, cantaret Amyntas*. Tibullus' Marathus poems may indicate at least some passing interest in boys, but nothing suggests a similar taste in Propertius and Ovid.

V. Love is a kind of madness (5 f.). We have already mentioned this concept in the song of Virgil's Gallus (Ecl. 10). There is a very close parallel to Horace's *hic tertius December, ex quo destiti/ Inachia furere, silvis honorem decutit* in Propertius 1, 1, 7, *et mihi iam toto furor hic non deficit anno*.

VI. The poet claims to be ashamed, humiliated, because he is the talk of the town (7 f.). This notion occurs frequently in Propertius; compare, for example, 2, 24, 1 ff., "*Tu loqueris, cum sis iam noto fabula libro/ et tua sit toto Cynthia lecta foro?"/ cui non his verbis aspergat tempora sudor?/ aut pudor ingenuis aut retinendus amor*, etc. and 3, 25, 1 f., *risus eram positis inter convivia mensis/ et de me poterat quilibet esse loquax*. Compare Tibullus 1, 4, 23; 2, 3, 31 f.; Ovid, *Amores*, 3, 1, 21. In some of these passages the poets express their embarrassment at being the subject of malicious gossip, but they also show a certain pride in being notorious.

VII. His behavior at a banquet shows his companions that he is in love (9 f.). This is the theme of Callimachus, *Epigr.*, 13 Pf. (*Anth. Pal.*, 12, 134), Tibullus 1, 2, and Lygdamus 6. In our text, the poet is embarrassed at having revealed too much. The symptoms are obvious.

VIII. A rich rival enjoys, temporarily at least, the favors of the lady whom the poet loves. Ever since Callimachus, *Epigr.*, 7 (*Anth. Pal.*, 12, 148), the poet's poverty is a theme of erotic verse. It may have had some basis of fact in Callimachus' life; it probably has none in the life of Tibullus, but he follows the convention; compare 1, 4, 57 ff.; 9, 7 ff.; Prop. 2, 16, 1 ff.; 33 ff.[2]

IX. The wine motive (13 f.) is not used in the same way as in Tibullus 1, 5, 37 f. and Propertius 3, 17, 3f. These passages, quoted by the commentators, are misleading. A closer parallel would be Tibullus 1, 9, 25 ff., *ipse deus . . . permisit . . .| ederet ut multo libera verba mero :| ipse deus somno domitos emittere vocem| iussit et invitos facta tegenda loqui.* It is not the topos *vinum curarum medicina*, but the theme that wine favors παρρησία. It loosens the tongue and gives the lover courage to talk freely about his sorrows, too freely, perhaps; for this reason Bacchus is called *inverecundus deus* (13). But it certainly helps to vent one's anger; compare Prop. 1, 1, 28, *sit modo libertas quae velit ira loqui.*

X. The poet seeks the help and advice, or at least the sympathy, of his friends (12, 16 f.; 25 f.). Compare Prop. 1, 1, 25 f., *at vos qui sero lapsum revocatis, amici,| quaerite non sani pectoris auxilia.*

XI. He decides to break with the woman and is told by his friend to go home; that is, not to stop at her house (19 f.), but he cannot resist. We find short-lived resolutions of this kind in Tibullus 1, 5, 1 f., *asper eram et bene discidium me ferre loquebar,| at mihi nunc longe gloria fortis abest* and Propertius 2, 2, 1 f., *liber eram et vacuo meditabar vivere lecto ;| at me composita pace fefellit Amor,* both perhaps influenced by Gallus. The very same situation (the poet magically drawn to the door of the mistress) is found in Tibullus 2, 6, 13 f., *iuravi quotiens rediturum ad limina numquam :| cum bene iuravi, pes tamen ipse redit;* and 47 f. we have the *limen durum* of Horace.

There is a break between vv. 22 and 23. The love affair with that woman seems to have come to an end. He may have returned once or twice to the *non amicos . . . postis*, but now all this belongs to the past, and he is in love with a *puer delicatus*, the "little wolf" Lyciscus. The manner in which Horace describes the attractions of this boy, *gloriantis quamlibet mulierculam| vincere mollitia*, can hardly be said to represent his own ideal. A boy who is more feminine than any woman is a slightly absurd figure in Horace's work. This might support the view that our Epode has the character of a parody.

XII. The friends are likely to disapprove of this new affair. Their first reaction would take the form of *libera consilia* ("may I be perfectly frank with you ?"), and only when he appears to be deaf to their advice will they

[2] In the lost elegy or elegies to which Horace, *Carm.*, 1, 33, refers, Tibullus seems to have complained that "Glycera" preferred a younger man to him, not a wealthier one.

switch to the harsher tone of *contumeliae graves.* But even that will be in vain.

XIII. He will always be in love (compare above, on 3 f.), and he can only drive out one love with another. This idea is familiar to us from Propertius 2, 3, 45 f. *his saltem aut* (*ut* codd., corr. Luck) *tenear iam finibus, aut, mihi siquis/ acrior, ut moriar, venerit alter amor.* Ovid makes a precept of this in *Rem.,* 462 ff. Love must ultimately triumph, there is no resistance, and this brings us back to Virgil's Gallus (*Ecl.,* 10, 69), whose song ends with the famous line *omnia vincit Amor, et nos cedamus Amori.*

The Johns Hopkins University

12

Egyptian Influence in Tibullus[1]

LUDWIG KOENEN

Introduction

Living in a time which brings distant and different cultures nearer to each other and exposes them to the influence of each other, scholars observe with growing interest how the Roman poets came to grips with the strange Egyptian culture and were influenced by it, at least from the time when Egypt became a part of the imperium Romanum in 30 B.C. As long ago as 1924, E. Norden tried to make it clear that Vergil in his fourth eclogue was influenced by old Egyptian traditions; in the present generation further research pointed to the Egyptian influence in Roman literature. In 1955, the Egyptologist A. Hermann pointed out astonishing similarities between the Egyptian and Roman form of the paraclausithyron which the lover who found no admittance into his loved one's house sang before her door, bringing offerings to the door as to a goddess.[2] In 1962, H. Fuchs

---

[1] This paper was read on three separate occasions in January 1974 at Ann Arbor, Duke, and Urbana, and its German prototype in June 1969 at Cologne and later in Bonn. I enjoyed encouragement and criticism, especially from Professors F. O. Copley, H. Dahlmann, Ph. Derchain, A. Henrichs, R. Merkelbach, J. K. Newman, and W. H. Willis, and by my friend Dr. Gumbert Ludwig, a Franciscan priest in Cairo. I thank J. G. Shelton for his help in phrasing the English version of my paper. Lately P. Grimal called the attention of scholars to the Egyptian ideas in Tibullus I, 7: "Le dieu Sérapis et le Génius de Messalla" (paper read in Paris, February 1969, and published in the *Bull. Soc. Fr. Eg.*, 53–54, 1969, 42 ff.); he follows the same line of interpretation I do, and the reader may be referred to his paper for supplementary arguments and information.

[2] A. Hermann, *Beiträge zur Erklärung der ägyptischen Liebesdichtung*, Akad. Berl., Inst. f. Orientf., 29, *Ägypt. Studien H. Grapow gew.*, Berlin, 1955, 118 ff.; for the paraclausithyron see pp. 134 ff. The offerings to the door in Plautus's *Curc.*, 71 ff. (cf. Tib. I, 2, 13 f.; Prop. I, 16, 41 ff.), are certainly a parody of Roman rites and Italian folklore (E. Burck, *Das humanistische Gymnasium*, 43, 1932, 194 ff. = *Das römische Menschenbild*, Heidelberg, 1966, 250 ff.; F. O. Copley, *Exclusus Amator*, Phil. Monogr., 17, Baltimore, 1956, 28 ff.), but this does not exclude the additional influence of Egyptian religious ideas and poetry by the way of Hellenistic mediation.

directed attention to an Egyptian parallel of Horace's Ode 3, 30: "exegi monumentum aere perennius/ regalique situ pyramidum altius."[3] Horace may have thought of Cornelius Gallus, the first Roman governor of Egypt, who fixed inscriptions describing his deeds on the walls of the pyramids.[4] But already in 1200 B.C. an Egyptian scribe on papyrus felt, quite similarly to Horace, that his work would last longer than brazen pyramids with tomb inscriptions of iron. After this parallel between Horace and the Egyptian scribe, other parallels collected by P. Gilbert in 1946 became more convincing. The "carpe diem" of Ode I, 11 and similar invitations to enjoy life follow the patterns of the Egyptian songs of the harper.[5] Obviously the Greek poets in Alexandria took up Egyptian thoughts and formulations and passed them on to the Romans. In 1968, M. West pointed to similar invitations and expressions in Hellenistic poems, and indeed U. v. Wilamowitz-Moellendorff had already taken notice of correspondences between Hellenistic epigrams and old Egyptian poems.[6]

But the Romans were influenced by the Egyptians not only through Hellenistic poems. The fact that the Greeks did not hesitate to take up Egyptian influences justified the Romans in imitating the Egyptians directly. They adopted parts of the Egyptian ideology of kingship and took over even some of its ceremonial rites. When the Roman republic was followed by the principate, the Roman emperors had to look for an ideology in order to make the new form of personal government understandable and acceptable. They claimed to renew the old Roman traditions and to keep up the old institutions, but in fact they changed them, borrowing from several sources—among them from the old Egyptian ideology of kingship, which had already been adopted by the Greek kings of Egypt. This point was rightly stressed by I. Trencsényi-Waldapfel.[7]

[3] H. Fuchs in: *Antidoron E. Salin zum 70. Geburtstag*, Tübingen, 1962, 149 ff.; cf. I. B. Borzsák, *Acta ant.*, 12, 1964, 137 ff.; I. Trencsényi-Waldapfel, *Acta ant.*, 12, 1964, 149; S. Morenz, "Die Begegnung Europas mit Ägypten," *Sb. Akad. Leipzig*, Phil.-hist. Kl., 113, 5, Berlin, 1968, 109; D. Korzeniewski, *Gymnasium*, 79, 1972, 382, n. 6.

[4] E. Maróti, *Beitr. zur alten Gesch. und deren Nachleben*, Festschr. Altheim I, Berlin, 1969, 452 ff.

[5] P. Gilbert, *Latomus*, 5, 1946, 61 ff.; cf. S. Morenz in: *Handbuch d. Orientalistik*, I, 1 Ägyptologie, Leiden and Cologne, 1970, 233 f.; but cf. also Eurip., *Alc.*, 785, and Menander, *Aspis*, 249. Gilbert already points to the above-mentioned parallel between Horace and the Egyptian scribe of 1200 B.C.

[6] M. L. West, *HSCP*, 73, 1968, 113 ff.; U. v. Wilamowitz-Moellendorff, *Hellenistische Dichtung*, I, 120 n. 1.

[7] Eléments égyptiens dans la poésie de l'age d'or, *Ann. univ. sc. Budapestinensis de R. Eötvös nominatae*, sectio phil., 6, 1965, 3 ff.; idem, *Savaria*, 3, 1965, 125 ff. (Hungarian with a German summary); cf. E. Köberlein, *Caligula und die ägyptischen Kulte*, Meisenheim, 1962; L. Koenen, *Eine ptolemäische Königsurkunde*, Bonn, 1957, 14 f.

At the same time, when the religion of the Egyptian goddess Isis conquered the Greek and Roman world, Roman poets occupied themselves
with this strange religion. In 1968 it was demonstrated that Tibullus and his
imitator Lygdamus allude to an Egyptian rite. The old Egyptian dead
had to assert before the court judging him: "I did not do this sin, I did
not do that sin." According to the Mosaic Law such "negative confessions"
were practised by the Hebrews, but later, obviously in the Egyptian tradition, also by priests and initiates of the mysteries. When Tibullus feels that
his last hour is near, he states: "parce pater! timidum non me periuria
terrent,/ non dicta in sanctos inpia verba deos."[8] Even Propertius plays
with this rite when he proclaims to the goddess of his lady's door: "te non
ulla meae laesit petulantia linguae, / quae solet irato dicere pota ioco."[9]
Later we read similar allusions in Petronius: "non templis impius hostis,
admovi dextram,"[10] which echoes Lygdamus's "nec nos sacrilegi templis
admovimus ungues"[11] and also the oath of a priest: οὐδὲ οὐ μὴ κολλήσω
τοὺς δακτύλου[ς τῷ ἱερῷ].[12] In another way Horace alludes to the mysteries
of Isis. In Ode III, 26 Venus plays the part of Isis-Nemesis, the goddess
who castigates the initiates for their former sins: "o quae beatam diva
tenes Cyprum et/ Memphin carentem Sithonia nive/ regina, sublimi
flagello/ tange Chloen semel arrogantem."[13]

Here we shall confine ourselves to Tibullus. He knew the mysteries of
Isis. His mistress had been initiated, as the poet himself states (I, 3, 27 ff.).
Her sexual relationship to Tibullus was part of her religious devotion. If
the poet wanted to please her and to win her, he had to show interest in

[8] I, 3, 51 f.; cf. ZPE, 2, 1968, 31 ff.; R. Merkelbach, ZPE, 11, 1973, 82 f.; for the
Hebrew practice cf. Deut., 26, 3 f., and 1 Sam. 12, 13 ff., and see G. v. Rad, Gesammelte
Studien zum Alten Testament, München, 1958, 281 ff., esp. 290 f.

[9] I, 16, 37 f. "ioco (Heinsius) is a certain emendation for 'loco'" Butler-Barber. The
"irato" of the codices is confirmed by I, 6, 10, "quae solet irato," where "irato" is a
wrong reading taken from I, 16, in order to replace the authentic "ingrato" preserved
only by the Itali; "dicere ioco" instead of "dicere iocum," because "quae" is the accusative belonging to "dicere." "pota" (Heinse) is as good a conjecture as any and replaces
the corrupt "tota" (cf. Sh. Bailey, Enk). I understand: "No wantonness of my tongue has
hurt you by words it is accustomed to use when drunk and scoffing angrily." Cf. Tibullus's
paraclausithyron, I, 2, 81 ff.

[10] 133, 3, 7 f.; cf. O. Raith, Studi class., 13, 1971, 112 ff.

[11] 5, 11: "ungues" conjectured by me for the corrupt "ignes" or "aegros" of the
manuscripts; cf. R. Merkelbach, ZPE, 11, 1973, 83 n. 8. For the "negative confessions"
in Roman literature see also Lygdamus 4, 15 f.; Prop. II, 28, 9 ff.; IV, 11, 41 ff., for the
corresponding positive confession, see Prop. II, 26, 3. I hope soon to demonstrate this by
detailed interpretations. W. D. Lebek refers to Stat., Silv., 5, 5, 1 ff.

[12] SB, VI, 9641; τῷ ἱερῷ] supplevi; for other suggestions see R. Merkelbach, ZPE. 2,
1968, 18 to line 8. For the "negative confessions" see also Philod., AP, 10, 21, 5.

[13] Cf. I. Trencsényi-Waldapfel, Éléments (see n. 7), 6.

her religious beliefs. He called her "Delia" with regard to the island of
Delos. But Delos was one of the main places not only of the Greek god
Apollo, but also of the Egyptian goddess Isis, whose son Horus was
identified with Apollo. In the third century B.C. the cult of Isis at Delos
was founded by an Egyptian priest coming from Memphis.[14] And Horace
showed his reverence to the Isis of Memphis in the ode just quoted, III, 26.
From the second century B.C. on, Roman tradesmen brought the cult of
Isis to Rome. In fact, this island was one of the stations along the route the
cult of Isis went from Memphis to Rome.[15] Therefore the name Delia
connects the poet's mistress not only with Apollo, the god of the poets, but
also with Isis, the goddess to whom this lady devoted herself. Thus the
name Delia itself may be taken as a symbol of the Roman love elegy,
which as poetry is devoted to the Greek Apollo, but at the same time as a
love song to the beloved girl and her religious feelings dominated by the
Egyptian Isis. The same is true for Propertius's Cynthia[16] and Lycinna,[17]
but not quite for Tibullus's second mistress, whom he called "Nemesis."

[14] *IG*, XI, 4, 1299; H. Engelmann, *The Delian Aretalogy of Sarapis*, Leiden, 1975. For
Memphis as place of Isis, see J. Bergman, "Ich bin Isis," *Acta Univ. Upsal.*, Uppsala,
1968.

[15] Delos was a free port used for transhipment by Roman merchants; there they
became acquainted with Sarapis (P. Roussel, *Les cultes égypt. à Delos*, Paris-Nancy, 1916;
cf. P. M. Fraser, *Ptol. Alexandria*, Oxford, 1972, I, 800). The importance of merchants for
the spreading of the cult of Isis is stressed by P. M. Fraser, *Opusc. Athen.*, 3, 1960, 1 ff.,
esp. 20 ff. Köberlein, *loc. cit.* (see n. 7), 70 ff. Significantly, there was a priesthood of
μελανηφόροι in Rome (L. Vidman, *Sylloge inscriptionum rel. Isiacae et Sarapiacae*, 426, 427;
cf. idem, *Isis und Serapis bei den Griechen und Römern*, RGVV, 29, Berlin, 1970, 68 ff.) as well
as in Delos (Roussel, 21, 26, 58, 95, 98, etc.; cf. Vidman, *SIRIS*, index I, p. 348 s.v.);
besides this priesthood is known in Eretria only (*SIRIS*, 75). Isis herself is μελανηφόρος in
the *Orph. hymn*, 42, 9, and in a hymn of Isidorus (*SEG*, VIII, 550, 34 = E. Bernand,
Inscr. métriques de l'Egypt Greco-Romaine, Paris, 1969, 175, 2 = V. F. Vanderslip, "The Four
Gr. Hymns . . .," *ASP*, 12, 1972, 3, p. 49 [cf. the note on p. 62]; see Th. Hopfner on
Plut., *De Iside* 58 (II, 227); R. Merkelbach, *Roman und Mysterium in der Antike*, München-
Berlin, 1962, 145, n. 6). In Preneste as well as in Delos, Isis was assimilated to Fortuna
Primigeneia (Roussel, 119 and 128). Certain devotional objects were called "Deliaca" (*Hist.
Aug.*, Alex. Sev., 26, 8 = I, 270 Hohl; cf. F. Dunand, *Bull. de la Fac. des Lettr. de Strasb.*,
Dec., 1968, 151 ff.). But for bringing Isis to Rome, other places were important too:
Sicily, South Italy, Eretria, Chalcis (Vidman, *Isis*, 95 ff.), and Alexandria, which supplied
Rome with its goods since the end of the second century B.C. (Fraser, *Alex.*, 155 f.).

[16] For the connection of Zeus Kynthios and Athene with the cult of Isis see Roussel,
loc. cit. (n. 15), 166, 187, 209; for Artemis Kynthia see, e.g., Prop. II, 34, 80; Artemis too
was associated with Isis (Roussel, 179) and identified with her (Roussel, 127 and 128,
Ἄρτεμις Ἑκάτη; cf. Merkelbach, *loc. cit.* (n. 15), 92. For the identification of Delian Apollo
with Horus, see *Chron. d'Eg.*, 67, 1959, 110 ff.

[17] Lycinna is named after Ἀπόλλων Λύκειος who at Lycopolis in Egypt was worshipped
as Horus (Macr., *Sat.*, I, 17, 40; cf. D. Wortmann, *Philologus*, 107, 1963, 157 ff.).

The goddess Nemesis had no special relations with the poets, but she was identified with Isis, as already was seen in Horace's Ode III, 26.[18] In short, Tibullus called his mistresses by such names as were given to the initiates in the course of their initiation. Many such names are to be found in literary works and in inscriptions, such as Nemesius, Memphius, Memphites, Tarsia, and so on.[19]

[18] For Isis Nemesis cf. Roussel, *loc. cit.* (n. 15), 138–140.

[19] The religious meaning of the "signa" (P. Wuilleumier, "Et. hist. sur l'emploi et la signification des signa," *Mem. prés. à l'Acad. des Inscr.*, 13, 2, Paris, 1932; cf. R. Merkelbach, *loc. cit.* [n. 15], 117 n.; L. Vidman, Isis [n. 15], 94 and 130 f.; also, P. Thrams, *ZPE*, 9, 1972, 139 ff.). Aseneth's change of name into Πόλις Καταφυγῆς [Joseph et Aséneth, ed. Philonenko, 15, 6]) has been doubted (I. Kajanto, *Supernomina*, Helsingfors, 1966; cf. H. Solin, *ZPE*, 10, 1973, 279; G. Freimuth's argumentation against explaining the poetical names of Tibullus's and Propertius's mistresses as sounding like names given to the initiates is rather superficial [Mus. Helv., 21, 1964, 90 n. 25]). *Nemesius: CIL*, VI, 12323. *Memphius:* Vidman, *SIRIS* (see n. 15), 425 and 586; cf. Dessau, 5187, 5191, and 5192. For the religious interpretation of *SIRIS*, 586, it may be relevant that the dead woman, a cult musician, was presumably welcomed to the paradise by Venus (Isis), and it was this goddess by whom Tibullus hoped to be introduced into Elysium (I, 3, 58; cf. P. Grimal, *Homm. à Deonna*, Brussels, 1957, 258 ff.). *Vere Memfiana:* Vidman, *SIRIS*, 424. *Memphitis* is the second name of Anthia, the heroine in the novel of Xenophon from Ephesus (4, 3, 6; see Merkelbach, *loc. cit.* [n. 15], 107); and the worshippers of Isis are called by Petronius: "Memphitides puellae/ sacris deum paratae" (fr. XIX). For *Tarsia* see the *Hist. Apoll. Regis Tyri* (Merkelbach, *loc. cit.* [n. 15], 165). Also names such as *Isius* (Vidman, *SIRIS*, 578), *Meliteius* (P. Wuilleumier, *Inscr. lat. des trois Gaules*, Paris, 1963, 250), *Melite* (in Ach. Tat.; cf. Merkelbach, *loc. cit.* [n. 15], 139), *Semelius* (*CIL*, XIV, 4488), *Oresios* (Vidman, *SIRIS*, 620) identify persons with Isis, alias Semele and Artemis. Other signa allude to rites: *Eugamius* (Vidman, *SIRIS*, 586; cf. *IG*, XIX, 1682 = Kajanto, 13), *Heuresius* (Vidman, *SIRIS*, 501; cf. idem, *Isis*, 94), *Thiasus*, a name used by a nauarchos at the "navigium Isidis" (Vidman, *SIRIS*, 428), *Nabe* (Dessau, 4475) and *Navigius* (*IG*, IX, 1641 = Kajanto, 66), presumably also connected with the "navigium Isidis"; *Innocentius* may allude to the "negative confessions," and when Innocentius' wife is called *Encratius*, both names may denote the morals of the mysteries (*CIL*, V, 5869 = Kajanto, 68). Even names such as *Gregorius* (Kajanto, 59 ff.; L. Moretti, *Riv. fil.*, 93, 1965, 179 ff.) and *Felix* may have been representations of the vigilance and happiness of the initiates, at least at the time when these names came into use. I hope to show soon that names such as Petronius's *Polyaenos*, the alias of Encolpius, *Circe*, and *Oenothea* are signa too. Since prostitutes were often adherents of Isis and other mysteries, one should not be surprised that they were called by names like Δελφίς, Παρθενίς (Isis), Νεβρίς, Ἀμπελίς, Βακχίς, Φοιβίς (Apollo-Horus), Παννυχίς, and Θαίς (a name which could be understood as "belonging to Isis," but certainly not always had this association; see W. Swinnen, *Chron. d'Eg.*, 42, 1967, 158 ff.); cf. the names of courtesans in Lucian's *Dial. meret.* Certainly such names as Μέμφις, Μεμφείτης, Εὑρέσιος, Θίασος, Ἴσις, Σεμέλη, Νέμεσις, Μελίτα and Μελίτιος were used as normal personal names, but not always without religious significance. Sometimes the religious significance may have been forgotten, but it was inherent and could reappear as suited the intent of the name-givers. The fact that very worldly ladies are called Mary does not exclude the use of this name by nuns in its full religious meaning.

Nevertheless, it was not only the courtesans who paved the way to the mysteries and Egyptian beliefs and rites for poets like Tibullus, but also the attraction of this religion for the Romans and some of their politicians. The mysteries of Isis succeeded against the resistance of conservative circles which in the twelve years between 59 and 48 B.C. five times destroyed the altar of Isis erected on the Capitol.[20] In 28 B.C. it was forbidden by Augustus to erect chapels of Isis within the walls of Rome, and in 21 B.C. this prohibition was expanded by Agrippa up to the first milestone. Later under Tiberius in 19 B.C., the worshippers of Isis were prosecuted. By law it was not permitted to worship new and foreign gods, not even in a private cult.[21] Nevertheless the Egyptian cults had been growing in Rome since the times of Sulla.[22] At the end of the republic men wearing the mask of the jackel-shaped god Anubis were a common sight in the streets of Rome. After being proscribed in 43 B.C., M. Volusius escaped under the protection of such a mask. Later, so did the young Domitian dressed as a worshipper of Isis (Tac. Hist., 3, 74, 1). In the time of Augustus, Fortuna's temple at Preneste became practically a temple of the Egyptian Isis, as is demonstrated by the mosaics depicting the river Nile and its miraculous land. It was already in 43 B.C. that the triumviri Octavian, Antonius, and Lepidus planned to erect a temple of Isis and Sarapis but were prevented from doing so because of the Egyptian war. The triumviri were no worshippers of Isis, but were motivated by political calculations, as can be seen in Augustus's later repressive action against the chapels of Isis. Nevertheless in 43 B.C. they gave the impression of favoring the Egyptian cult in order to please the common people. Some of the members of the Roman aristocracy were even fascinated by the new cult. Already under the reign of the last Cleopatra the Roman officer

[20] A certain T. Sulpicius was "sacerdos Isidis Capitolinae," probably before 58 B.C.; see Vidman, SIRIS, 377 = Dessau, 4405.

[21] Cic., De leg., 2, 19; cf. 21. For the ups and downs of the cult of Isis in Rome, see F. Cumont, Die orientalischen Religionen im röm. Heidentum, Darmstadt, 1959 (Paris⁴, 1928), 75 ff.; K. Latte, Röm. Religionsgesch., Handb. d. Altertumsw., München, 1960, 282 ff.; E. Köberlein, loc. cit. (see n. 7), 11 ff.; P. F. Tschudin, Isis in Rom, Aarau, 1962; V. Tran Tam Tinh, Essai sur le culte d'Isis à Pompéi, Paris, 1964, 19 ff. W. Hornbostel, Sarapis, Leiden, 1973, 361 ff.

[22] According to Apuleius the Roman college of pastofori was founded in the time of Sulla. In the sixties of the first century B.C., the curule aediles minted coins with signs of the cult of Isis, obviously because these signs were so popular that the aediles did not mind using them despite official politics directed against the cult at that time. See Vidman, Isis (n. 15), 101 ff., whose interpretation of the facts detected by A. Alföldi ("Isiskult und Umsturzbewegung . . .," Schweizer Münzblätter, 5, 1954, 25 ff.; Schweizer numism. Rundschau, 36, 1954, 5 ff.; Essays in Rom. Coinage pres. to H. Mattingly, Oxford, 1956, 94; Jb. Ant. Christ., 8–9, 1965–1966, 62 f.) is convincing for me.

C. Iulius Papius prayed together with his suite to the Lady Isis at Philae,[23] just as later, in the second century, stylish Roman gentlewomen used to make pilgrimages to this place (Juv. 6, 526 ff.). So did formerly the Greek kings of Egypt[24] and their high officers, especially the epistrategus, the governor of all Upper Egypt.[25] Cornelius Gallus, the first Roman governor of Egypt and the creator of the Roman elegy, offered and thanked the Roman gods and the Νεῖλος συνλήπτωρ in Philae for his victories over the insurgents. His inscription erected at Philae records that Gallus was installed by Augustus as the first governor of Egypt and won two battles and subdued the rebellious Thebaid, which—as is said— formerly did not submit itself to the kings of Egypt, and that he conquered five cities partly by the first assault and partly by a siege, captured the leaders of the revolt, led his army past the cataract, received embassies of the Aethiopians at Philae, put their kings under protection, and installed

23 On March 28, 32 B.C.: *OGI*, 196 = *SB*, 8427 = A. Bernand, *Les inscr. grecques de Philae*, I nr. 63. In A.D. 5 a certain Aulus Novius Faustus prayed at Philae to Isis (*SB*, 8834 = E. Bernand, *Les inscr. gr.* . . . , II nr. 153).

24 Euergetes I dedicated a chapel to Isis and Harpocrates at Philae (*OGI*, 61 = *SB*, 8859 = A. Bernand, 4); Epiphanes (*OGI*, 98 = *SB*, 8395 = A. Bern., 8) and Euergetes II (*OGI*, 142 = *SB*, 8882 = A. Bern., 17) also went to the island; one wonders whether it was not on the occasion of royal visits that the gods Isis and Horus dedicated statues to the king Philometor, after they had greeted and acknowledged him as legal king and god according to the ritual of royal visits to the temples (*OGI*, 122 = *SB*, 8879 = A. Bern., 10, Βασιλέα Πτολεμαῖον θεὸν Φιλομήτορα Ἴσις καὶ Ὧρος and *OGI*, 121 = *SB*, 8770 = A. Ber., 12 [king Philometor, his spouse and son]). Soter II went to Elephantine and performed the rites of the Nile flood: ἀποδοὺς τῷ Νείλῳ τὰ νομιζ[όμενα (*OGI*, 168; see D. Bonneau, *La crue du Nil*, Paris, 1964, 391 n. 1). See also R. Merkelbach, *Isisfeste in griechisch-römischer Zeit*, Meisenheim, 1963, 67.

25 For the epistrategus as governor of all Upper Egypt in the later Ptolemaic times see now the monograph of J. David Thomas (*Papyrologica Colonensia*, VI, Opladen, 1975). The epistrategus Demetrius visited Philae obviously on the occasion of a synode and dedicated an altar to the gods (*SEG*, 8, 788 = *SB*, 3448 = A. Bern., 20); the epistrategus Hephaistion (sic) prayed in Philae to Isis for his children (A. Bern., 44); so did the epistrategus Callimachus for the king Neos Philopator (Auletes; *OGI*, 186 = *SB*, 8398 = A. Bern., 52, and *SB*, 4084 = A. Bern., 53); and Callimachus's son, when in the same office, for Cleopatra Philopator (A. Bern., 58; cf. *SB*, 8652 = A. Bern., 57); for the epistrategus of Roman times see *SB*, 8428 = E. Bernand, 135. Also strategi were often seen praying to Isis at Philae: *SB*, 8397c = A. Bern., 38; *SB*, 8397b = A. Bern., 41; *SB*, 8668 = A. Bern., 51; *OGI*, 184 = *SB*, 8666 = A. Bern., 59; *SB*, 6116 = A. Bern., 64; *SB*, 8401 = E. Bern., 134; *SB*, 8669 = E. Bern., 149; in early Roman times: *SB*, 8410 = E. Bern., 136; *OGI*, 695 = *SB*, 8419 = E. Bern., 162. The visits of the higher officials and their suite became such a burden for the priests and the temple that they asked Euergetes II to relieve them of providing all needs for the visitors (*OGI*, 137–139 = *SB*, 8396 = Lenger, *C. Ord. Ptol.*, 51 f. = A. Bern., 19; cf. P. J. Sijpesteijn, *Historia*, 18, 1969, 110 n. 7).

a king in the North of Nubia.[26] It was the normal duty of an Egyptian king on his coronation to perform a ceremony in which he ritually subdued the rebels and, if necessary and possible, to subdue them militarily, further to visit all parts of the country including the South and, by that, to enact the unification of Upper and Lower Egypt, and to receive embassies. Before his coronation, Epiphanes conquered Lycopolis, captured the leaders of the revolt, and killed them at Memphis in the course of the ceremonies.[27] The siege of Lycopolis was enacted according to the rites: the city was encircled by dikes, and the water of the Nile flood was directed into the space betwen the walls and the dikes, thus washing out the walls and the foundations.[28] Obviously Gallus employed the same methods in his sieges,[29] and by this he performed the role of an Egyptian Pharaoh at his in-

[26] *OGI*, 654 = Dessau, 8995 = J.-P. Bucher, *Gaius Cornelius Gallus*, Paris, 1966, 38 ff. = E. Bern., 128. Later during the reign of Augustus a certain Iunius Sabinus came to Philae and took part in a festival of Isis together with the soldiers under his command, after they had won a battle probably against the Aethiopians (*SB*, 8671 = E. Bern., 159). Germanicus visited Syene too.

[27] As an allusion to this victory Epiphanes was represented as wrestler Horus defeating Seth (Baltimore Walters Art Gallery, inv. nr. 54. 1050; Athens, National Museum, inv. nr. ANE 2547); other Ptolemaic kings, among them presumably Euergetes I (Istanbul, Museum of Antiquities, inv. nr. 190) were represented in the same gesture, and it seems that it was Philadelphus who asked a Greek artist to adapt the Egyptian theme of Pharao overcoming the rebels and enemies to the language of Greek art and athletic contests, by that transforming the Egyptian ideology of kingship into Greek thinking (H. Kyrieleis, *Antike Plastik*, part 11, 1974, 133 ff. G. Grimm in a forthcoming article quoted by Kyrieleis, 136 n. 11). I daresay Theocritus wrote his Herakliskos for the basileia, the celebration of Philadelphus's birthday and installation as joint ruler, and the poet commemorates the education of young Herakles (that is, Philadelphus) in wrestling (110 f.; see L. Koenen, *Eine agonistische Inschrift aus Ägypten und frühptolemäische Königsfeste*, Meisenheim, in press).

[28] Ros. (*OGI*, 90 = *SB*, 8299 = W. Spiegelberg, *Der demot. Text der Priesterdekrete von Kanopos und Memphis mit den hieroglyphischen und griechischen Fassungen und deutscher Übersetzung*, Heidelberg, 1922, 77 ff.; cf. *SEG*, 8, 463) 21 ff. = 12 ff. = 48 ff.; King Pianchi conquered Memphis: "Memphis was taken (by) a flood of water" (J. H. Breasted, *Ancient Records*, IV, 435, §865, cf. 434, §862); and according to Heliodorus, Hydaspes employed the same methods for conquering Syene (9, 3); Schapur encircled Nisibis by the river Mygdonios which flooded the land around the walls "as the river Nile floods Egypt" (Jul. imp., *Or. ad Const.*, I, 27 B ff.; II, 62 CD). See also *Ach. Tat.*, 4, 14; Zon., *Epit.*, 12, 30 p. 156, Dind. and R. Merkelbach (s. n. 15), 134 f. and 281 ff.; idem (s. n. 24), 23 ff. and 14 ff.; D. Bonneau (s. n. 24), 81 f.; M. H. A. L. H. van der Valk, *Mnemos.*, III, 9, 1941, 97; R. Keydell, *Polychronion, Festschrift F. Dölger*, Heidelberg, 1966, 345 (but it may be clear by the implications of this note that Julian's report cannot be used for dating Heliodoros).

[29] The Nile helped him to conquer the cities of the rebels as Apollon and Philadelphos fought a ξυνὸς ἄεθλος against the Celts (Call., *hym.* IV, 171; cf. *Chron. d'Eg.*, 34, 1959, 110 f.; for similar thoughts in ancient Greece see E. Fraenkel, *Horace*, 280 ff.).

stallation,[30] especially by recording his deeds not only in Latin and Greek, but also in the holy language of the hieroglyphs. With this symbolism involved, one understands Augustus's harsh reaction.

Also, the philosophical and religious speculations of the Romans were influenced by Greco-Egyptian thought rather early. Marcus Valerius Messalla Rufus, cos. 53 b.c., connected the Greek concept of the Aion with the Aion who had his cult at Alexandria, and he transferred these ideas to the Roman god Janus.[31] But the worship of Aion in Alexandria was part of the cult of Osiris-Sarapis. Osiris, the dying and reviving god, who was closely connected with the idea of eternity, was identified with the Aion in the Greco-Roman period; he was pictured encircled by the snake which bites its own tail (Uroboros), and this was a well known symbol of eternity.[32] But particularly the other Messalla, Marcus Valerius M., the friend and patron of Tibullus, was openminded to the cult of Isis and Osiris. He was in Egypt in 30/29 b.c. and perhaps also before that in the company of Antonius, to whom he surrendered himself after the battle of Philippi. When Tibullus sang the praises of the Egyptian religion and alluded to its rites and beliefs, he could be sure of being understood not only by his mistress, but also by his patron. This can be demonstrated by an interpretation of the elegy which Tibullus recited on the occasion of Messalla's birthday, shortly after Messalla had his triumph over Aquitania in 27 b.c. (I, 7). This date is politically significant. One year before, in 28 b.c., Augustus himself had turned against the cult of Isis changing, as it were, his former favorable attitude (see pp. 132 f.).

The Proportions of Themes in Tibullus's Birthday Elegy, I, 7

In the elegy I, 7, Tibullus praises Messalla's greatness in five themes:

I. The victory Messalla had won as governor of Gaul against the Aquitanians, and the triumph which was granted to him for this (vv. 1–12; 6 distichs)
II. his governorship in Syria (vv. 13–20; four distichs)

---

[30] By all his deeds the Pharao performed the role which had been played by the gods in the beginning of time; see E. Hornung, *Geschichte als Fest*, Darmstadt, 1966.

[31] R. Reitzenstein, *Poimandres*, Leipzig, 1904, 38, 276 f., 362; Merkelbach, *loc. cit.* (n. 24), 47 n. 10.

[32] Aion-Osiris: Damascius, *Vita Isid.* fr. 174, Zintzen; vgl. L. Kákosy *Oriens ant.*, 3, 1964, 15 ff.; idem, "Zu einer Etymology von Philae: 'Insel der Zeit,'" *Acta ant.*, 16, 1968, 39 ff.

III. the Nile and a hymn to the god Nile-Osiris (vv. 21–54; 17 distichs)
IV. Messalla's sons (vv. 55 *f.*; one distich only)
V. the task of repairing the via Latina assumed by Messalla (57–62; 3 distichs)

There follows one final distich.

Seventeen distichs, that is, more than half of the whole poem, are devoted to the Nile and Osiris; the four other themes, including the final distich, cover altogether not more than 15 distichs. Obviously Tibullus thought that Messalla's trip to the river Nile was the most important event in the life of his patron, more important, for example, than his merits in the battle of Actium and even more important than his consulate on the side of Octavian himself in 31 B.C. Tibullus did not mention either of these two themes with a single word. For the triumph, the greatest event in the life of a Roman general, Tibullus reserved only a few lines. Therefore Augustin Cartault conjectured that Messalla was initiated in Egypt.[33] This could explain why Tibullus chose to praise Osiris so abundantly in his birthday poem for Messalla. The initiation into the cult of Osiris may have been regarded as the true birthday of Messalla. But this is a mere conjecture. Here it will be asked how far the detailed interpretation of the poem will guide us.

INTRODUCTION TO THE HYMN TO OSIRIS

After Tibullus has praised the triumph of Messalla, he gives short impressions of Messalla's stay in Syria, pretending to search for a theme, as Callimachus among others does.[34] Shall I sing praises of the Cydnus or the Taurus or of Palestinian Syria? Then Tibullus turns to the Nile:

    17   quid referam . . .
    21   qualis et, arentes cum findit Syrius agros,
             fertilis aestiva Nilus abundet aqua?
    [Or shall I sing, how the fertile Nile floods high in the summer, when the dog
    star causes the fields to dry and crack?]

---

[33] p. 49; see also M. Ponchont, *Tibulle*, 51; E. Burck, *Gymnasium*, 70, 1963, 90 (= *Vom Menschenbild in der röm. Literatur*, Heidelberg, 1966, 240).

[34] 13 ff.; for ex. cf. Call., *hym.* IV, 28 ff.; Pind. *Ol.* 2, 1 ff.; l. 14 echoes Call. fr. 43, 42; for other Callimachean reminiscences in these lines see A. W. Bulloch (*Proc. Cambr. Phil. Soc.*, 199, 1973, 71 ff.), who reinforces the conclusions of G. Luck (*Latin Love Elegy*, London², 1969, 83 ff. = *Die röm. Liebesel.*, Heidelb., 1961, 83 ff.) against critics not believing in much Alexandrian influence on Tibullus (e.g. F. Solmsen, *Entr. Fond. Hardt*, 7, 1960, 295; idem, *Hermes*, 90, 1962, 316). "in eodem carmine (I, 7) Tibullus passim Callimachum sequi videtur," R. Pfeiffer on fr. 383, 16.

Putting this question, Tibullus finds the theme for his poem: the miracle of the Nile flood. This introduction is a reminiscence of Callimachus. For Callimachus has praised the Nile flood thus: θηλύτατον καὶ Νεῖλο[ς ἄ]γων ἐνιαύσιον ὕδωρ (384, 27). According to the conventions of Roman literary circles, the Roman poet, now that he has paid tribute to a famous Greek model, is entitled to praise the Nile in his own way. Tibullus stresses the miraculous paradox: The inundation comes at the time of the greatest heat. It starts when the dog star Sirius can be seen shortly before sunrise for the first time, after its period of invisibility.[35] The days of the dog star are the days of the greatest heat, in which the fields threaten to dry up.

For our further thoughts it may be useful to recall the myth by which the Egyptians tried to understand the strange connection between the greatest summer heat and the Nile flood; this myth was known to the Greeks and Romans; and Callimachus among others dealt with it (fr. 811). According to this myth Seth, the god of heat, murdered Osiris. Then the vegetation dried up and the Nile had only low waters because the vegetation and the Nile were regarded as manifestations of Osiris. Isis searched for her dead husband Osiris and buried him in Biggeh, a small, inaccessible island in the area of the first cataract just opposite Philae. Isis, whose heavenly manifestation was the dog star, raised Osiris to new life. Out of his leg streamed water, that is, the Nile flood.[36] Osiris was the source of the Nile; and the Nile flood made the land fertile again. The power of the revived Osiris appeared in the inundation of the Nile.

Now Tibullus wants to deal with the miracle of the Nile flood. He does this in a long hymn to Nile-Osiris. In this hymn three themes can be distinguished:

1. The invocations by which Tibullus reveals the names of his god (vv. 23–28; 3 distichs)

2. the good deeds of the god, in which his power, his arete, comes to light (vv. 29–48; 10 distichs)

3. the final hymnos kletikos, the prayer for the appearance of the god (vv. 49–54; 3 distichs)

---

[35] This coincidence of Nile flood and the heliacal rising of Sirius has been dealt with rather often by Greek and Latin authors; see D. Bonneau, *loc. cit.* (n. 24), 43 n. 4.

[36] H. Junker, "Das Götterdekret über das Abaton," *Denkschr. Akad. Wien*, 56, 1913, 40; Th. Hopfner, *Plutarch, Über Isis und Osiris*, II, Prague, 1940 (Darmstadt, 1967), 152; R. Merkelbach, *Z.Ä.S.*, 99, 1973, 121. For the explanation of the Nile flood as the tears of Isis (Paus. X, 32, 10), see Ph. Derchain, *Chron. d' Eg.*, 45, 1970, 282 ff.

THE INVOCATIONS TO THE GOD

First we turn to the invocations to the god (vv. 23–28). Poetically pretending to search for a proper theme, Tibullus came across the miracle of the Nile flood. Therefore he opens his hymn with this miracle:

23   Nile pater, quanam possim te dicere causa
         aut quibus in terris occuluisse caput?

[Father Nile, how could I answer, for which reasons or in which countries you have hidden the head of your waters?]

The ancients could call a river "father," as we still do sometimes, and "caput" may be taken as a proper word designating the source of a river, just as we speak today of the headwaters of the Nile.[37] But in a hymn to a river god the word keeps its pregnant meaning. As we shall see soon, Tibullus identifies the Nile with Osiris in line 27. Osiris has been buried on the spot where the Nile flood comes forth. To this god the question is suitable quite literally: "Where did you hide your head?"

Tibullus feels unable to tell where and why Nile-Osiris hides his source. The ancient Greek and Latin authors discussed the questions connected with the Nile flood and its reasons very often.[38] Herodotus says: οὐδεὶς αὐτοῦ οἶδε τὰς πηγάς (II, 32). In Callimachus it is the Nile who says about himself: ὃν οὐδ᾽ ὅθεν οἶδεν ὁδεύω | θνητὸς ἀνήρ (384, 31 f.). And Horace praises the Nile: "fontium qui celat origines" (Odes IV, 14, 45).

Actually the ancients did not know the source of the river Nile. But the Egyptian priests made a virtue of necessity and taught that the Nile flood was a divine miracle, which human beings were not permitted to understand; the god withholds himself from the questioning people. For the Egyptians, the question of the Nile flood belonged to a religious taboo. We read in an old Egyptian hymn to the Nile god that he is "hidden in his form of appearance, a darkness by day, to whom minstrels have sung." And further: "He cannot be seen . . . no one can read of the mystery; no one knows the place where he is; he cannot be found by the power of writing." He loves "to come forth as a mystery."[39] According to the

---

[37] E.g., Prop. II, 15, 33 (cf. P. J. Enk's note in his commentary, Leiden, 1962, p. 223). Ov., Met. II, 254 f. (Nilus . . . occulitque caput) imitates Tibullus; see also E. Norden on Verg., Aen. VI, 360 (p. 234) and D. R. Shackleton Bailey, Propertiana, Cambridge, 1956, 112 (reg. II, 24, 5–8).

[38] H. Diels, "Seneca und Lucan," Abh. Berl. Akad., 1885, 5 ff. (for Lucan, see below); Bonneau, loc. cit. (n. 24), 135 ff.; H. Bonnet, Reallexikon der ägyptischen Religionsgeschichte, Berlin, 1952, 525 ff. (s.v. "Nil").

[39] J. A. Wilson in: J. B. Pritchard, Ancient Near Eastern Texts, Princeton, 1955, 372 ff.; G. Maspero, Hymne au Nile, Bibl. d' Et., 5, Cairo, 1912; E. Bacchi, "L'inno al Nilo," Publ. del R. Museo di Torino, 4, 1950; G. Roeder, Kulte, Orakel und Naturverehrung im alten Ägypten, Zürich and Stuttgart, 1960, 332 ff.; A. Erman, Die Literatur der Ägypter, Leipzig,

Egyptian belief, the sources of the Nile were hidden and one was not permitted to search for them. Therefore Herodotus tried in vain to ask the Egyptian priests (II, 19). They did not know a straightforward answer but possessed secret teachings which they were not allowed to tell those who had not committed themselves to a special relationship to the deity. In Lucan's 10th book, the Egyptian priest Acoreus reveals to Caesar a secret teaching about the sources of the Nile. Others may regard it as pious to be silent; Acoreus thinks it better to speak out this teaching (194 f.). He appeals to the revelation of the Nile god (286 f.).[40] Similarly, in the novel of Heliodorus, the Egyptian Isis priest Kalasiris refers to the secret teachings in a discussion with so-called philosophers: "I said all I knew and what is written in the holy books about this river and what prophets only are permitted to know and to read "[41] And according to Libanius, wise laws prohibit normal men from seeing the god Nile even when on the river, but a man like Maximus from Ephesus, who visited Egypt at that time, is permitted to open his eyes, and he may see the god and talk with him (ep. 1274, 1 ff.).

Already with his first invocation Tibullus pays attention to the mystery and the taboo connected with the god Nile. He continues in the style of a hymn with invocations which begin by anaphora:

> 25 te propter nullos tellus tua postulat imbres,
> arida nec pluvio supplicat herba Iovi.
> te canit atque suum pubes miratur Osirim
> barbara Memphiten plangere docta bovem.

[It is because of you that your land requires no showers and that no withered vegetation makes supplication to Jupiter as bringer of rain. It is of you that the foreign race sings, you that they honor as Osiris, this race which is skilled in lamenting the bull of Memphis.]

That the Nile competes with the rain is often said in the ancient literature.[42] With the Egyptians this topos can be traced back to the

---

1923 (photom. reprinted, Leipzig, 1970), 193 ff. I do not imply that Tibullus knew this special hymn, which was composed before the nineteenth dynasty, but he may have heard of such hymns, most likely by Greek mediators.

40 Lucan's Caesar would dispense with the civil war, if he could see the sources of the Nile instead (X, 191 f.; cf. n. 38).

41 2, 28,2, ἐμοῦ δὲ ἅπερ ἐγίγνωσκον εἰπόντος καὶ ὅσα περὶ τοῦ ποταμοῦ τούτου βίβλοις ἱεραῖς ἀναγεγραμμένα μόνοις τοῖς προφητικοῖς καὶ γινώσκειν καὶ ἀναγινώσκειν ἔξεστι . . .

42 Herod. II, 13; Eurip., Hel., 1 ff.; Aristoph., Thesm., 855 ff.; Apoll. Rhod. 4, 269 ff. For more instances see R. Keydell, Hermes, 69, 1934, 424; S. Sauneron, BIFAO, 51, 1952, 41 ff.; Bonneau, loc. cit. (n. 24), 129, n. 5; see also A. Hermann, Jahrb. Antike u. Christent., 2, 1959, 54.

140   Illinois Classical Studies, I

thirteenth century B.C.[43] Here I shall restrict myself to quoting one Greek poet for many. Eur., *Bacch.* 406 ff.: ⟨χθόνα⟩ θ' ἂν ἑκατόστομοι | βαρβάρου ποταμοῦ ῥοαὶ | καρπίζουσιν ἄνομβροι.[44] Similarly to this Tibullus points again to the miracle of the Nile flood: the vegetation need not supplicate Jupiter for rain as in the Erigone of the Alexandrian poet Eratosthenes Aristaeus, the king of Keos, prays to Zeus in order to be freed from the heat of the dog star.[45] With Tibullus it is then that the decisive distich follows: "te canit . . . atque miratur Osirim." Friedrich Klingner taught us how we should understand this: "It is to you that they sing, you that they honor as their Osiris."[46] The Nile is identified with Osiris.[47]

The following pentameter commemorates the lamentations for the dead

[43] In a hymn to Aton: "All distant foreign countries, thou makest their life (also), for thou has set a Nile in heaven, that it may descend for them and make waves upon the mountains, like the great green sea, to water their fields in their towns. . . . The Nile in heaven, it is for the foreign peoples and for the beast of every desert that go upon (their) feet (while the true) Nile comes from the underworld of Egypt" (*ANET* [see n. 39], 371). A similar thought is expressed in the mentioned hymn to the Nile (see n. 39) and later in a Greek amulet (H. J. Milne, *Catal. of the Lit. Pap. in the Brit. Mus.*, London, 1929, 239; cf. Bonneau, *loc. cit.* [n. 24], 410 ff.).

[44] I follow Meineke; see also Westerbrink's edition (cf. the beginning of the corresponding line, 421 ἴσα δ'); C. W. Willink (*CQ*, 60, 1966, 222 f.) suggests ἢ χθόν' ἂν (and in the corresponding line ἴσα δ'); cf. also the commentary of J. Roux (II, 388). The manuscripts offer Πάφον θ' ἂν, and this weak modification of Euripides's wording belongs to the tradition followed by Manilius (*Astr.* IV, 635, "Aegyptique Cypros pulsatur fluctibus amnis"; see J. Jackson, *Marginalia Scaenica*, Oxford, 1955, 117). It seems very doubtful whether the idea of an underground or underwater Nile connecting Egypt with islands (for Delos see Call. *hym.* IV, 206 ff.; III, 170 f. and scholion; Lycophr. 576, and schol.; Paus. 2, 5, 3; see E. R. Dodds's note on Eurip., *Bacch.*) goes back to Euripides's time, even though a similar idea of underground connections of the river Alpheios is found in Pindar (*Nem.* 1, 1; cf. Strabo 6, 2, 4 p. 270; Paus., 5, 7, 2 f.). The river Alpheios became the model for imagined connections of the Acherusian Lake (Prop. I, 11, 1 f.; cf. F. H. Sandbach, *Cl. Rev.*, 1938, 213; D. R. Shackleton Bailey, *Propertiana*, 32). In any case, Euripides had no reason to connect Paphos and Egypt by the river Nile, and one would not expect him to allude to such a connection in order to show his learning or knowledge of folklore.

[45] This has been preserved by Hyginus, p. 37, 12 ff.; see R. Merkelbach, *Miscellanea di Studi Allessandrini in mem. di Aug. Rostagni*, Torino, 1963, 469 ff., especially 518 f. R. Pfeiffer warns against this reconstruction of Eratosthenes's Erigone, but on general grounds only (*History of Classical Scholarship*, Oxford, 1968, 169, n. 1).

[46] F. Klingner, *Eranos*, 49, 1951, 117 ff. (reprinted in: *Römische Geisteswelt*, 412 ff.).

[47] Already in Pyr. 589 (S. A. B. Mercer, *The Pyramid Texts*, New York, London, and Toronto, 1952); Plut., *De Is.* 32, Νεῖλον εἶναι τὸν Ὄσιριν. For more see H. Bonnet, *loc. cit.* (n. 38), 571, and Merkelbach, *loc. cit.* (n. 15), 39; cf. also H. Kees, *Totenglaube und Jenseitsvorstellung der alten Ägypter*, Berlin², 1956, 146 f.; H. Frankfort, *Kingship and the Gods*, Chicago, 1948, 190 ff.; D. Wortmann, *Bonner Jb.*, 166, 1966, 65 f. and 95.

bull of Apis. He was a popular god.[48] But why did Tibullus mention him? First, the poet imitates a pentameter of Callimachus who mentions the Nile and the Egyptian woman "skilled in lamenting the white bull,"[49] that is, the bull Apis with a blaze.

But the fact that Tibullus imitates a verse of Callimachus does not absolve us from asking what Tibullus intends in the context of his hymn when he points to the Apis-bull. It was again Friedrich Klingner who gave the right answer. The dead Apis-bull became Osiris when it was mummified. Apis as well as Osiris were embodiments of the powers of fertility and, as was Osiris, so was Apis connected with the Nile flood.[50] Therefore the lamentation for the bull Apis has the same ritual significance as the lamentation for Osiris. Apis and Osiris were two different aspects of the same deity; the miracle of the Nile flood represented yet a third aspect of the same divine being, at least in the beliefs of the late period. Tibullus understood this: after he calls his god Nile and Osiris, he unveils his third name—Apis.

We should go a step further. Osiris-Apis, that is, Osorapis of Memphis, was the Egyptian god who became Sarapis under the Ptolemies.[51] Originally Sarapis was the god of the Ptolemaic dynasty, but later this god became the god of the Egyptian mysteries which conquered the ancient world. By the identification Osiris-Apis, Tibullus points to Sarapis as to the god of the mysteries.[52] Tibullus does not mention the name Sarapis, and one may guess his reasons. The name Osiris has the full color of a strange country, whereas Sarapis was a name rather common among the Greeks. In Rome political reasons might have stood against the use of the name of Sarapis, after all the god of the Ptolemies, at least in the time of Tibullus. And this might have furthered the theological

[48] See the formula used in letters τὸ προσκύνημά σου ποιῶ καθ᾽ ἑκάστην ἡμέραν παρὰ τῷ κυρίῳ Ἄπιδι (E. G. Turner, *Rech. de Pap.*, 2, 1962, 117 ff. = *SB*, 9903; idem, *Studien zur Papyrologie und antiken Wirtschaftsgeschichte, Festschr. Fr. Oertel*, Bonn, 1964, 32 ff. = *SB*, 9930). It is also a significant proof of the popularity of this cult that as late as in A.D. 362 a new Apis was installed, an event which was important enough to be reported as a good omen to the emperor Julian (Amm. Marc. XXII, 14, 6 ff.; cf. A. Hermann, *Jb. Ant. u. Christent.*, 3, 1960, 34 ff.).

[49] 383, 14 ff.   Κολχίδες ἢ Νείλῳ [
λεπταλέους ἔξυσαν, [
εἰδυῖαι φαλιὸν ταῦρον ἰηλεμίσαι.

[50] See E. Otto, "Beiträge zur Geschichte der Stierkulte in Ägypten," *Unters. zur Gesch. u. Altertumsk.*, 13, Leipzig, 1938, 1 ff.; Bonnet, *loc. cit.* (n. 38), 46 ff. and 751 ff.

[51] U. Wilcken, *UPZ*, I, 77 ff.; P. M. Fraser, *Opusc. Athen.*, 3, 1960, 1 f.; idem, *Ptol. Alex.* (see n. 15), I, 246 ff.; A. Henrichs, *Die Phoinikika des Lollianos.* Bonn, 1972, 60 f.

[52] This was also suggested by P. Grimal (see n. 1). Cf. G. Luck, *Properz und Tibull*, Artemis, 1964, 493.

development by which the name of Sarapis became the secret name of the god.[53] "Sarapis" is the sum of the other names: Nile, Osiris, and Apis, and soon Tibullus will add the name of Bacchus.[54] Often the ancients circumscribed the power of a deity by enumerating his many names.[55] But they did not dare to mention the true name of the god which embraced all his aspects and powers at once, especially not the true name of the highest god of the mysteries which had to be hidden from the people not or not yet initiated into the last secrets.[56]

Tibullus mentions the main feast of Apis, his burial, as did Callimachus. The ritual of the burial is described by Plutarch (De Is., 35). In this description, too, Apis is identified with Osiris, and the funeral procession looks like a celebration of Bacchus. As already said, soon Tibullus will identify his Osiris with Bacchus. It is this identification which is foreshadowed by the fact that Tibullus mentions the lamentations for Apis. As Horace identifies his Venus with the Isis of Memphis (see p. 129), so for Tibullus, Bacchus̄ became the Osiris-Apis of Memphis.

THE ARETALOGY

There follows a relatively long passage of ten distichs, the aretalogy, in

[53] In Ps. Call. the god himself reveals his name to Alexander, but even then he hides it behind figures 200 + 1 + 100 + 1 + 80 + 10 + 200 (ΣΑΡΑΠΙΣ). In Apuleius, Lucius undergoes three initiations: (1) the initiation of Isis, (2) that of Osiris ("magni dei deumque summi parentis invicti Osiris sacra," 11, 27, 2), and (3) for the last initiation the name of the god is not mentioned, but Lucius has a vision of the "deus deum magnorum potior et maiorum summus et summorum maximus et maximorum regnator Osiris," who admits him for the initiation and calls him into the college of his pastofori (11, 30, 3 ff.). Surely this higher form of Osiris is Sarapis, whose true name remains in the dark. This seems to fit the dates: the second initiation took place probably in the night of December 24–25, a date very suitable for "Osiris invictus" (R. Merkelbach, Aegyptus, 49, 1969, 89 ff.). Shortly after this initiation ("post pauculum tempus"; 11, 29, 1) Lucius began with the fast of ten days in order to prepare himself for his third initiation (11, 30, 1), and after a few days, obviously during his fast (11, 30, 3), he had the vision of Osiris most high. So the third initiation may have taken place after a few more than ten days, that is, possibly in the night of January 5–6, the feast of Osiris-Sarapis (see p. 135). Before Lucius was called for his second and third initiation, he was not informed that there were separate initiations to each of the three gods. One may note that the name "Osiris" was used slightly more often in Roman times than before; see Vidman, Isis (n. 15), 13 f.

[54] In the verse we read in Macrob., Sat. I, 18, 18, the deity of Sarapis is expressed by the sum of the gods who represent his different aspects: εἷς Ζεύς, εἷς 'Αίδης, εἷς Ἡλιός ἐστι Διόνυσος. And that the true name of this Dionysos is Sarapis is shown by Iulian (Or. 4, 136 A), who substitutes Sarapis for Dionysos: ἐστὶ Σάραπις.

[55] E. Norden, Agnostos Theos, Leipzig, 1923 (repr. Darmstadt, 1956), 143 ff.

[56] Merkelbach, Roman (see n. 15), 92.

which the deeds and miracles—the aretai—of Osiris are celebrated. First of all, Osiris-Nile is praised as a bringer of culture:

29 primus aratra manu sollerti fecit Osiris
    et teneram ferro sollicitavit humum,
    primus inexpertae commisit semina terrae
    pomaque non notis legit ab arboribus.
33 hic docuit teneram palis adiungere vitem,
    hic viridem dura caedere falce comam;
    illi iucundos primum matura sapores
    expressa incultis uva dedit pedibus.

[Osiris was the first to construct a plow with skillful hand, to turn up the tender earth with iron; he was the first to sow the earth, which had not experienced that before; and he was the first to gather fruit from trees not known before. He it was who taught man to bind the tender vine to stakes and to cut the green foliage at the top with a cruel pruning hook. He was the first to whom the ripe grape yielded her flavorful drink, pressed out by feet not trained before.]

Tibullus's Osiris is the discoverer of agriculture, arboriculture, and viticulture: he is the "heuretes," as the Greeks expressed it,[57] or "the one, who did it for the first time," as Egyptian thought would phrase it.[58] Hecataeus of Abdera likewise stated that Osiris taught men how to plant grain and grapes; in this he was followed by Diodorus Siculus.[59] And indeed Tibullus's "non notis . . . ab arboribus" corresponds to Diodorus's ἀγνοούμενον δ' ὑπὸ τῶν ἀνθρώπων, where the grain is meant.[60] For the

[57] A. Kleinguenther, πρῶτος εὑρετής, Philologus, Suppl., 26, 1, 1933; Cl. Préaux, Chron. d'Eg., 42, 1967, 370.

[58] At Dendera Horus is called "the one who first made all things" (LD, IV, 53), an expression which comes surprisingly near to Tibullus's "primus . . . fecit." Osiris is called in his official title as king: "The Discoverer of Mankind in the Primeval Time" (The Contest of Horus and Seth, XIV; ANET [see n. 39], 16; G. Lefebvre, Romans et contes égypt., Paris, 1949, 199; G. Roeder, Mythen und Legenden um ägyptische Gottheiten und Pharaonen, Zürich and Stuttgart, 1960, 67). In the same story Osiris addresses Ra: "you discoverer of the Ennead (sc. the nine gods)" (XV). For the Egyptians, every deed was a repetition of the deeds done by the gods in the beginning of time. The ploughing farmer did what the gods had done in the beginning; this beginning was called "the first time" (sp tpj). See D. Müller, "Ägypten und die griech. Isisaretalogien," Abh. Leipzig, Phil.-hist., Kl. 53, 1, Berlin, 1961, 23 ff.; S. Morenz, Ägyptische Religion, Stuttgart, 1960, 175 ff.; J. Bergman, loc. cit. (see n. 14), 289.

[59] Diod. I, 17, 1; cf. 14, 1 = Hecat. 264 F 25; Kore Kosmu (Stob. I, 49, 44, p. 406 W. = Corp. Herm., fr. XXIII, 68 Fest.) οὗτοι μόνοι τὰς κρυπτὰς νομοθεσίας τοῦ θεοῦ παρὰ Ἑρμοῦ μαθόντες τεχνῶν καὶ ἐπιστημῶν καὶ ἐπιτηδευμάτων ἁπάντων εἰσηγηταὶ τοῖς ἀνθρώποις ἐγένοντο καὶ νομοθέται, sc. Osiris and Isis. See also p. 146.

[60] 264, F 25 = Diod. I, 14, 1. As late as in Pinturicchio's ceiling-paintings of the Sala dei Santi in the Appartamento Borgia (Vatican) Osiris teaches agriculture and viticulture, and Isis the use of fruits (P. Ehrle-H. Stevensohn, Les fresques de Pinturicchio, Rome, 1898, pl. 40a and b, 41a); see A. Hermann, loc. cit. (n. 48), 47 f.

Greeks it was of course Dionysos who had discovered viticulture, and it was Triptolemos who had invented the plow. But Dionysos had been identified with Osiris since the time of Herodotus, and no later than the early Roman period Osiris was in turn identified with Triptolemos. As a consequence, Osiris carried out the united functions of both Dionysos and Triptolemos.[61]

That corresponded to Egyptian conceptions, because the Egyptians also worshipped Osiris not only as the giver of wine but as the giver of grain as well. So in one hymn Osiris is said to boast of himself: "I am he that created barley . . . no other god or goddess could be found to do it."[62] One also may recall the hymn to the Nile cited above (see p. 138), since Tibullus's Osiris is identified with the Nile. It is the god of the Nile "who makes barley and brings emmer into being." He is "the bringer of food, rich in provisions, creator of all good." It is he "who fills the magazines and makes the granaries wide," and it is he "who makes every beloved tree to grow."

Nevertheless Osiris gives not only the blessings of nature, but also the benefits of culture:

> 37   ille liquor docuit voces inflectere cantu,
>   movit et ad certos nescia membra modos,
>   Bacchus et agricolae magno confecta labore
>   pectora tristitiae dissolvenda dedit.
> 41   Bacchus et adflictis requiem mortalibus adfert,
>   crura licet dura compede pulsa sonent.

[Taking the form of wine, he taught man to raise his voice in song, to move his limbs, untrained before, in the fixed measures of the dance. He, Bacchus, enabled even the peasant[63] to free his breast of cares, tired though he may be

[61] Herod. II, 42 and 144. Osiris-Triptolemos: P. Antinoop. 18 = R. Merkelbach, *APF*, 16, 1956, nr. 1141 (confessions of the dead before Triptolemos); Serv. Auctus on Verg., *Georg*. I, 19 ("uncique puer monstrator aratri"): "alii Triptolemum, alii Osirim volunt; quod magis verum est, ut dicit . . . Tibullus" (= Th. Hopfner, *Fontes hist. rel. Aeg.*, Bonn, 1924, 616); see also [Probus] *ad loc*. (Thilo-Hagen, 352 = Hopfner, 618): "quidam putant Triptolemum Atticum dici . . . sed constat multis annis ante et fruges in Aegypto inventas esse et arasse primum Osirim duobus bubus, quorum nomina sunt sacra sub eis qui religionis causa eodem vocabulo appellati coluntur, Apis et Mnevis, quorum alterum Memphitae colunt Apim, alterum Heliopolitae Mnevim." Also *Anon. brevis expositio*, p. 206 Thilo-Hagen = Hopfner, 618; Serv. on *Georg*. 1, 147 = Hopfner, 616; Isidorus, *Etym*. XVII, 1 = Hopfner, 726; *Myth. Vat*. III, 7, 1 = Hopfner, 746; cf. Diod. 1, 18, 2. In Mart. Cap. viticulture is taught by Dionysos and Osiris, agriculture by Isis and Triptolemos (II, 158). For Triptolemos-Horus s. Merkelbach, *loc. cit*. (n. 36), 119, n. 12.

[62] A. H. Gardiner, *The Library of A. Chester-Beatty*, Oxford-London, 1931, XIV, 12; A. M. Blackmann, "Osiris as the Maker of Corn . . .," *Studia Aeg.*, I, Rome, 1938, 1 ff.; D. Müller, *loc. cit*. (n. 58), 32; Lefebvre, *loc. cit*. (n. 58), 200; Grimal, *loc. cit*. (n. 1), 44.

[63] One looks for a dative connected with "dedit": (a) "tristitiae" could be corrected into "laetitiae" (A. E. Housman, *Cl. Rev.*, 17, 1903, 309): "He, Bacchus, consigned to

by his hard work. He, Bacchus, brings respite to suffering mortals, even when cruel chains clank about their feet.]

The beginning of this passage is usually translated differently: "That drink taught men to sing." Then in the following lines the Bacchus who frees the peasant from his cares and gives mortals respite from their sufferings is said to be used metonymously for wine.[64] Osiris creates wine, and wine teaches men to sing and dance and enables them to forget their exhaustion and their cares. If this interpretation is right, lines 37–42 form a digression directly praising the wine, not Osiris.

In our translation we have chosen a rather different interpretation. In line 37 "ille" resumes the "illi" of line 35, and in this line 35 "illi" is Osiris. Accordingly, the "ille" of line 37 also stands for Osiris; in this case "liquor" should be taken as apposition: "he, the wine," "he in the form of wine," not simply "that wine." By means of the apposition "liquor," Osiris is identified with the wine. The liquor is Osiris himself. Bacchus in lines 39 and 41 is then likewise a name for the god. Osiris-Bacchus, manifested as wine, gives song, dance, freedom from care, and inner contentment.

The two interpretations are not contradictory: they are complementary. But one may remark that the hymnic style here rather suggests that one should think of Bacchus as the deity and not the metonym. Moreover, it is part and parcel of the Osiris faith that one regarded the drink as a manifestation of the god, as is barley, trees, and the Nile.[65] According to Plutarch, not only the Nile, but generally the entire principle producing moisture is called Osiris.[66] The old Egyptians thought of the Nile as of being beer and later also wine. For example, in a text at Edfu it is the sun

---

pleasure the farmer's breast ..., that it might be freed"; (b) "agricolae" may be dative: "He, Bacchus, granted the farmer ... a breast to be freed from his depression." If so, "Bacchus et agricolae" corresponds exactly to "Bacchus et adflictis" (mortalibus), and "pectora tristitiae dissolvenda dedit" echoes Euripides's *Bacch.* 378 ff. (Διόνυσος τάδ' ἔχει) ... ἀποπαῦσαί τε μερίμνας (see n. 81). See also the translations, e.g., of M. Ponchont, W. F. Lenz (Reclam), R. Helm, and P. Grimal (see n. 1), p. 42: "Bacchus, il a donné au laboureur le moyen de dissiper l'accablement de son coeur épuisé par un long travail.' For the genitive of separation see the commentaries, which try to construct "dedit" without a dative: "Bacchus hat auch des Bauern Herz ... von Trauer und Kummer befreien lassen" (Klingner, *loc. cit.* [n. 46]).

64 For this interpretation see, e.g., K. Fl. Smith in his commentary (*ad loc.*) and F. Levy (alias Lenz), *St. It. Fil. Class.*, N.S., 7, 1929, 108, who states that Bacchus here means the wine but that the listener is supposed to associate it with the god as well. Grimal thinks rightly of Bacchus the god (*loc. cit.* [n. 1]).

65 Bonnet, *loc. cit.* (n. 38), 571.

66 Plut., *De Is.*, 33, p. 364 A; Sallust., *De diis et mundo* 4.

god who refers to the Nile flood and says to victorious Horus: "You poured grapes into the liquid,"[67] that is, you changed the water into wine; for the Greeks, Dionysos caused springs of wine.[68] It refers to such beliefs when in a Greek hymn the river Nile is asked to make drunk the fruit-bearing land by its floods.[69] There was a ritual in the mysteries of Isis in which people took water from the Nile and drank it in the faith that it was wine, thus re-enacting the discovery of Osiris.[70] Similar ideas also were current among the Greeks: Timotheos, for example, called wine "the blood of Bacchus."[71]

In addition, the formal structure of Tibullus's wording imitates liturgical language. There is the series: 29 primus . . . Osiris . . ., 31 primus . . ., 33 hic . . ., 34 hic . . ., 35 illi . . ., 37 ille . . ., 39 Bacchus . . ., 41 Bacchus. At the beginning stands the name of Osiris; at the end, the name of Bacchus. Between these names one finds "hic" and "illi" as well as "ille"; all the pronouns apply to the god Osiris-Bacchus, who is mentioned by his name at the beginning and the end of the passage. I called this passage an aretalogy, a praise of the deeds of the god. In the aretalogies of Isis, the goddess herself tells her believers: ἐγώ εἰμι ἡ καρπὸν ἀνθρώποις εὑροῦσα (M 7), ἐγώ εἰμι ἡ ἐν τῷ τοῦ κυνὸς ἄστρωι ἐπιτέλλουσα (the bringer of the Nile flood; 9), ἐγώ εἰμι ἡ παρὰ γυναιξὶ θεὸς καλουμένη (10), ἐγὼ ἐν ταῖς τοῦ ἡλίου αὐγαῖς εἰμί (44), ἐγὼ τοὺς ἐν δεσμοῖς λύω (48), ἐγώ εἰμι ἡ θεσμοφόρος καλουμένη (52).[72] All sentences start with ἐγώ εἰμι or ἐγώ; but we find such aretalogies also in the third person: οὗτός ἐστιν or simply οὗτος. For example, in one of the Hermetic writings called Κόρη κόσμου Isis and Osiris are praised as follows: οὗτοι βίου τὸν βίον ἐπλήρωσαν, οὗτοι τὸ τῆς ἀλλοφονίας ἔπαυσον ἄγριον. τεμένη προγόνοις θεοῖς οὗτοι καὶ θυσίας καθιέρωσαν. νόμους οὗτοι καὶ τροφὰς θνητοῖς καὶ σκέπην ἐχαρίσαντο (65) . . . οὗτοι πρῶτοι δείξαντες δικαστήρια εὐνομίας τὰ σύμπαντα καὶ δικαιοσύνης ἐπλήρωσαν (67), and so on.[73] There are long series of οὗτοι . . . οὗτοι . . . οὗτοι πρῶτοι. Isis and

---

[67] M. Alliot, Le culte d'Horus à Edfou au temps des Ptolémées, II, Cairo, 1954, 722.

[68] E. R. Dodds in his commentary on Euripides's Bacchae (ll. 704–711); Merkelbach, Roman (see n. 15), 221 n. 2.

[69] Milne, loc. cit. (n. 43), 239, 27: καὶ γῆν καρποφόρον μέθυσον τοῖς σοῖσι ῥεέθροις (as the verse has been reconstructed; cf. Merkelbach, loc. cit. [n. 24], 16).

[70] Epiph., Pan. haer. 51, 29, 7 ff. (II, 301, Holl); cf. Chron. d'Eg., 73, 1962, 170, n. 3; Merkelbach, loc. cit. (n. 24), 55 ff.; D. Wortmann, "Das Blut des Seth," ZPE, 2, 1968, 229.

[71] Fr. 7; for more references see A. Henrichs, loc. cit. (n. 51), 74 ff., under the heading "Blut und Wein."

[72] R. Harder, "Karpokrates v. Chalkis und die memphitische Isispropaganda," Abh. Berl., Phil.-hist. Kl., 14, 1943, 20 f.; D. Müller, loc. cit. (n. 58) and now OLZ, 67, 1972, 117 ff.; J. Bergman, loc. cit. (n. 14) with a reprint of the text on p. 301 ff.

[73] For the Kore Kosmu cf. n. 59.

Osiris are praised just as the Osiris-Bacchus of Tibullus; the Roman poet copies a form of religious praise which was used in the worship of Isis and Osiris.

To sum up, there can be little doubt that "ille liquor" is meant as the god Nile-Osiris. With these words Tibullus does not embark on a digression but continues the praise of his god. Osiris, then, alias Sarapis, was the teacher of song and dance. In the cult of Sarapis at Tanagra, literary and musical ἀγῶνες were performed.[74] According to Diodoros, Osiris was a friend of laughter and delighted in music and dancing. In his train came the nine muses together with their leader Apollo; and satyrs too were there, these beings who, as Diodoros tells us, particularly rejoiced in dancing, singing, refreshment, and amusement of every sort.[75] Osiris's son Harpocrates, who was identified with Apollo, claims in his own aretalogy that he invented the sistrum of Isis, the flute, and reed pipes, and that together with the muses he invented hymns and dances.[76] Osiris himself was reputed to be the inventor of the flute and the trumpet.[77] Flute-players of "Great Sarapis" took part in the Isis procession recounted by Apuleius (11, 9, 6). According to Propertius, the playing of flutes was particularly appropriate for the Nile god.[78] A well-known mosaic at Leptis Magna shows how the Nile flood is welcomed by trumpets and cymbals. For the celebrations people hired dancers.[79]

In the festivals of Osiris music and dancing played prominent roles. This is an ancient concept in Egypt where dances and music, especially the playing of harps, took place at all festivals, even at the banquets in the

[74] Vidman, *SIRIS* (n. 15), 48 (97–95 B.C.). For athletic contests in the cult of Isis and Sarapis at Lycia, see Vidman, *SIRIS*, 343 and 344.

[75] Diod. I, 18, 4 f. According to P. Oxy. 1380, 62, Isis is called μουσαναγωγός (see also line 128).

[76] Vidman, *SIRIS* (see n. 15), 88; for this aretalogy cf. also n. 72. According so S. Schott (*Mél. Maspero*, I, Cairo, 1935–1938, 475 ff.) it was Harueris, the elder Horus, who was worshiped as god of harping; but the elder Horus, the falcon-god, and the younger Horus, the son of Isis and Osiris (Harsiesis), are different aspects of the same deity (see Morenz, *loc. cit.* [n. 58], 278). It fits to these two aspects, when in his aretalogy Carpocrates is called son of Sarapis and Isis (Harsiesis) as well as brother of Dionysos (Harueris).

[77] Iuba Mauritanus ap. Athen. IV, 175 E = Hopfner, *Fontes* (see n. 61), 167; Iul. Pollux, *Onom.* IV, 77 = Hopfner, 355; Eustathius, *Comm. ad Il.* XVIII, 219 = Hopfner, 754.

[78] Prop. IV, 8, 39; cf. Claudian, *Paneg. de IV cons. Honorii Aug.* (c. 8), 576 f.

[79] For example Bonneau, *loc. cit.* (n. 24), pl. VI, gives a picture of the mosaic of the Villa del Nilo. For hiring dancers see P. Oxy. 519, 10 = M. Vandoni, *Feste pubbl. e priv. nei documenti Greci*, Milano-Varese, 1964, nr. 36.

necropolises and, of course, at the feasts of the Nile.[80] In the Nile hymn mentioned above one reads: "Men began to sing to thee with the harp, and men sing to thee with the hand," that is, they clapped rhythmically. But at the same time the verses are suitable for Bacchus, the god who according to a chorus in Euripides rejoices at the banquets and causes his followers to dance, to laugh to the music of flutes, and to rest from their cares.[81] They are suitable also for Dionysos in whose cult for the first time the friends of Ikarios drunk and danced round a slaughtered goat. And this is how Eratosthenes explained the origin of Greek tragedy.[82] In the Osiris-Bacchus (Sarapis) of Tibullus, Egyptian and Greek concepts are united.

Tibullus's Osiris-Bacchus is further a releaser of cares through wine. "Bacchus shall be here the giver of joy," as Vergil puts it (Aen. 1, 734). The ancients valued wine as an escape from troubles.

In the choral song of Euripides mentioned already, Bacchus exercizes his role as liberator from cares when the cheering wine is served at the banquets of the gods and the wine vessel causes the ivy-crowned men to sink into sleep.[83] And earlier in the play, Teiresias had said that Dionysos discovered wine, which frees tired mortals from their sorrows and brings sleep and forgetfulness of suffering (280 ff.). As late as the fifth century A.D. we hear practically identical statements from Nonnos, who came from Panopolis in Egypt, and from Rutilius Namatianus born in Gaul.[84] For the Roman poets wine was above all a means of relief from the pangs of love and worry about the future.[85] The so-called "Vatican mythographer" explains the epithet of the Roman wine god Liber: "servi ebrii

---

[80] For the banquets in the necropolises see S. Schott, "Das schöne Fest im Wüstensande," *Abh. Mainz*, 1952, 11, esp. 64 ff.; Bonnet, *loc. cit.* (n. 38), 490 f.; below, p. 149; for the joyful feast of the Nile see Bonneau, *loc. cit.* (n. 24), 361 ff., esp. 413 ff.

[81] Eurip., *Bacch.* 378 ff. (cf. n. 63): ὃς τάδ' ἔχει, | θιασεύειν τε χοροῖς | μετά τ' αὐλοῦ γελάσαι | ἀποπαῦσαί τε μερίμνας (to be continued in n. 83), 416 f., ὁ δαίμων ὁ Διὸς παῖς | χαίρει μὲν θαλίαισιν . . .

[82] Fr. 22 Powell; cf. K. Meuli, *Mus. Helv.*, 12, 1955, 226 f.; W. Burkert, "Greek Tragedy and Sacrificial Ritual," *Greek Roman and Byzantine Studies*, 7, 1966, 93; Merkelbach, *loc. cit.* (n. 45), 471 f. and 494 ff.

[83] Eurip., *Bacch.* 382 ff. (continuation of the passage quoted in n. 81): ὁπόταν βότρυος ἔλθῃ | γάνος ἐν δαιτὶ θεῶν, κισ|σοφόροις δ' ἐν θαλίαις ἀν|δράσι κρατὴρ ὕπνον ἀμ|φιβάλλῃ.

[84] Nonnus, *Dion.* VII, 78 f.: ἀρχέγονος δὲ | ἄχνυται εἰσέτι κόσμος, ἕως ἕνα παῖδα λοχεύσω. 87 νηπενθὴς Διόνυσος, ἀπενθέα βότρυν ἀέξων. 96 Διόνυσον ἀλεξητῆρα γενέθλης. 367 f. (Σεμέλη) ὀλβίη, ὅττι θεοῖσι καὶ ἀνδράσι χάρμα λοχεύσεις, | υἱέα κυσαμένη βροτέης ἐπίληθον ἀνίης. Rut. Nam. I, 373 (reg. Osiris).

[85] Prop. III, 17, 3 f.; Hor., *Ep.* 9, 37 f.; cf. Tib. I, 2, 1; Sen., *De tranqu. an., Dial.* IX, 17, 8; A. Otto, *Die Sprichwörter der Römer*, Leipzig, 1890, 1899; K. Fl. Smith, in his notes on Tib. I, 7, 39 ff., also J. André.

Egyptian Influence in Tibullus 149

liberi sibi videntur" (III, 12, 1). And such a liberator is Tibullus's Bacchus, even for the men whose chains rattle about their feet. This god ignores social differences; as Euripides puts it: ἴσα δ' ἔς τε τὸν ὄλβιον | τόν τε χείρονα δῶκ' ἔχειν | οἴνου τέρψιν ἄλυπον.[86] Wine and the companionship of the bottle free man of his cares. It is therefore only natural that Dionysos himself, the god of wine, should be considered as Lyaios or Lysios, the "releaser." In mythology, and in Euripides, the god releases not only himself but also the maenads from chains and imprisonment.[87] He releases the imprisoned (Paus. 9, 16, 6). But one thinks of Sarapis too in just this way. In many a community, from the end of the third century B.C. on, it was to Sarapis that freedmen were dedicated upon their emancipation from slavery.[88] Plutarch recites an aetiological tale to the effect that even in the last days of Alexander the Great Sarapis released a young man named Dionysios from his chains.[89] But in Tibullus we find not this physical release, but rather a spiritual one, as is appropriate for the god of the mysteries. One observes that Servius, in a note to Vergil's Georgics, says that Father Liber, identified with Osiris, frees and purifies the soul of man in mysteries.[90] Just as a dead man was—according to the Egyptian concept of the after-life[91]—freed from the chains which shackled him hand and foot, so did the god of mysteries endow the soul of his follower with inner freedom, in this world— even if, externally, he lived as a slave in chains. One thinks of the philosophical trends of the time: for the Stoics human freedom was independent of earthly position; they thought exclusively of spiritual freedom. But in

[86] Eurip., *Bacch.* 421 ff.; for ἴσα see no. 44.

[87] Cf. E. R. Dodds's remarks on Eurip., *Bacch.* 498; idem, *The Greeks and the Irrational* (paperback), 273 and 279; O. Weinreich, "Gebet und Wunder," *Genethliakon W. Schmid* (Tüb. Beitr. z. Altertumsw. 5), Stuttgart, 1929, 285 (repr. in *Religionsgesch. Studien*, Darmstadt, 1968, 123).

[88] Boeotia: Vidman, *SIRIS* (see n. 15), 55, 56, 60. Phocis: *SIRIS*, 64, 67, 69. Locris: *SIRIS*, 70, 71. Hyrcania: *SIRIS*, 369; see P. M. Fraser, *Opusc.* (see n. 15), 43 f.; also Isis confesses that she frees the bound ones.

[89] Vita Alexandri 73; see Grimal, *loc. cit.* (n. 1), 46.

[90] Serv. on Verg., *Georg.* I, 166 (p. 171 Thilo; Hopfner, *Fontes* [see n. 61], 617): "animas purgat"; cf. J. Harrison, *Prolegomena to the Study of Greek Religion*, London⁴, 1961, 526 ff.

[91] J. Zandee, *Death as an Enemy*, Suppl. to *Numen*, 5, Leiden, 1960, 78 f. Damned men are bound; see E. Hornung, "Altägyptische Höllenvorstellungen," *Abh. Leipzig*, Phil.-hist. Kl., 59, 3, Berlin, 1968, esp. 17 ff. The liberation of the bound ones in Hades is still mentioned as late as in the "Teachings of Cleopatra," a book connected with the mysteries (M. Berthelot, *Coll. des anc. alchim. grecs*, Paris, 1888 [repr. Osnabrück, 1967], II, 292, 18); and the early Christians thought that Christ liberates from the chains of Hades (see *APF*, 17, 1960, 71).

Tibullus it is, for example, not human nature which enables man to live in spiritual freedom but a gift from the god of the mysteries.

Tibullus's Nile-Osiris-Apis-Bacchus is the god of the Egyptian mysteries. Tibullus continues:

> 43 non tibi sunt tristes curae nec luctus, Osiri,
> sed chorus et cantus et levis aptus amor,
> sed varii flores et frons redimita corymbis,
> fusa sed ad teneros lutea palla pedes
> 47 et Tyriae vestes et dulcis tibia cantu
> et levis occultis conscia cista sacris.

[Not for you, Osiris, are sad cares and sorrows, but dances and songs and easy love, various blossoms and a garland of flowering ivy worn around the forehead, further the flowing garment of saffran that hangs to your tender feet, robes of Tyrian purple, the sweet sound of flutes, and the easy burden of the box that knows the secret instruments of the mysteries.]

As in Tibullus, cares and sorrows are not appropriate to Osiris, so Diodorus's Osiris is a god of pleasures and entertainment; not a god of war plunging people into dangers but one offering them his benefits (see note 75). When Osiris died the vegetation dried up and the Nile carried but little water. Then it was time for lamentations. Again, when Osiris was found and revived together with the vegetation and when the Nile brought his flooding waters, then it was time to forget all sorrows, to rejoice, and to dance. In an Egyptian hymn Osiris is called "Lord of the Jubilations" at which people danced; a few lines later they are reminded of the joyful feast called "wag" on which the god was worshiped as "Lord of the Wine-Cellar" (Pyr. 820a). At the "haker" feast which at Abydos was celebrated for the dead presumably in connection with Osiris, people danced during the night.[92] Especially the Nile feast mentioned above was a joyful festival (p. 147). In the hymn to the Nile god we hear of joy (see p. 138): "He who was sorrowful is come forth gay. Every heart is gay." Dionysos had the same jolly character. In Smyrna it was nefast to approach the altars while wearing black garment during the mysteries of Dionysos; black was the color of sorrow, and the mysteries must be a celebration of joy.[93]

[92] For the hymn to Osiris see M. A. Moret (*BIFAO*, 30, 1931, 725 ff., l. 2, cf. ll. 5 and 8), who already compares the pleasures of the mysteries of Isis (p. 737). For the "wag" feast and similar frolicsome celebrations see Kees, *loc. cit.* (n. 47), 121; Grimal, *loc. cit.* (n. 1), 47; and for the "haker" feast see Bonnet, *loc. cit.* (n. 38), 574; cf. the Pamylia at which women accompanied by flute players and singers carried Dionysos (Osiris) through the villages; this Dionysos had a large, erectable phallus (Herod. II, 48; cf. Bonnet, *loc. cit.*, 580).

[93] Sokolowsky, *LSAM*, nr. 84, l. 10; cf. M. P. Nilsson, *Dion. Myst.*, Lund, 1957, 133 ff.; A. D. Nock, *Harv. St. Class. Phil.*, 63, 1958, 415 ff. (= *Essays on Relig.*, II, Oxford, 1972, 847 ff.).

Tibullus thinks of this joyful Dionysos, this joyful Nile-Osiris and Sarapis, who in a hymn is called χρυσοστέφανος and for whom a Roman inscription makes the wish: [- - -] ἐπ' ἀγαθῷ σοι γένοιτο, Νειλάγωγε· | [- - -] καλή σου πᾶσα ὥρα, εὐεργέτα Σάραπι.⁹⁴ The darker sides of this god are naturally forgotten at Messalla's birthday party.

Tibullus further connects this joyful god with a kind of light-hearted love which causes no one suffering or worry. Without Dionysos, without wine, there would be no love. That sentiment we can read as early as the Nestor cup, from about 700 B.C.: ὃς δ' ἀ⟨πὸ⟩ τοῦδε π[ίη]σι ποτηρί[ου], αὐτίκα κεῖνον | ἵμερ[ος αἱρ]ήσει καλλιστε[φάν]ου 'Αφροδίτης.⁹⁵ And we find something similar for example in Euripides's Bacchae; for these bacchants yearn for Cyprus, the land of Aphrodite and her miracles (403 ff.). Later in Apuleius a wine jar is greeted: "ecce, Veneris hortator at armiger Liber advenit ultro."⁹⁶

Love fits in with wine, and it fitted in with the mysteries, which were often not so much "mysterious" as festive and pleasurable, as is shown, for example, by the easy living in the gardens of Canopus⁹⁷; and even the afterlife of the mysteries was a place of joy and love, pictured by Tibullus in I, 3.⁹⁸ That love had a place in the afterlife was a thing the Egyptians

⁹⁴ Vidman, SIRIS (see n. 15), 458; cf. 363. The hymn is SIRIS, 325.

⁹⁵ For the reconstruction of this text see A. Dihle, Hermes, 97, 1969, 257 ff.

⁹⁶ Apul. 2, 11, 2; that wine is the helper of Aphrodite and her desires is a commonplace (see, e.g., Achill. Tat. 2, 3, 3; Lollian fr. B, 1, v. 20 ff. Henrichs [see n. 51]; Diod. 4, 6, 1; cf. Henrichs, loc. cit., 46 n. 9); but, of course, people had the opposite experience in antiquity too.

⁹⁷ The gardens of Canopus were love-gardens connected, I think, with the cult of Isis and Sarapis (see Strabo 17, 1, 16 f.). According to Amm. Marc. 22, 16, 14 the place is so charming and the air so healthy, especially when the summer wind blows, that one believes oneself outside of this world, that is, in the elysium which was famous for the soft blowings of the wind. One is not surprised that the joyful landscape of the Nile with erotes and psychai, and a temple of Isis were depicted on a sarcophagus of an initiate of Isis (Vidman, SIRIS [see n. 15], 542). The ἀπόψεις mentioned by Strabo represented an Egyptian "m₃rw", that is literally translated "viewing place," "place of being viewed" (Brugsch, Wb., V, 525, and Levi, Vocab., III, 35); Amenophis III called the m₃rw he dedicated to Amon "a place of recreation at his beautiful feast"; it designates a small building in a garden connected with a lake in which the sun-god made his appearances (cf. A. Badawy, JEA, 42, 1956, 59 ff.), and Sarapis, who had a famous temple in Canopus, was a sun-god, who was addressed as Ζεὺς Ἥλιος μέγας Σάραπις ἐν Κανώβῳ (A. Bernand, Le Delta égypt. d'après les textes grecs, Cairo, 1970, 242 ff., nr. 13 = SB, 8281 = SEG, 24, 1192; Bernand, 14 = SB, 8452; Bernand, 25 = SB, 8094 = SEG, 8, 435; cf. Bernand, 24 = SB, 431). For the religious character of these gardens cf. also Dio Cass. 50, 27. A. Bernand (Alexandrie la Grande, Paris, 1966, 298 ff.) gives a detailed description of entertainments at Canopus; P. Roussel compares it with modern Lourdes (loc. cit. [n. 15], 168); cf. also Fraser, Alex. (see n. 15), I, 200 f., and Merkelbach, loc. cit. (n. 15), 118 n. 3.

⁹⁸ I, 3, 57 ff.; cf. Prop. I, 19, 13 f. (cf. the commentary of P. J. Enk) and such ideas of

had believed for time immemorial.⁹⁹ And, of course, love suits the theme and tone of Tibullan amorous verse.

The god wears a robe that reaches his feet, a robe that was worn by women in the cult of Dionysos.¹⁰⁰ Its color is saffron: in Aristophanes, too, Dionysos wears a saffron robe, and, according to Plutarch, statues of Osiris were draped in a robe "the color of fire." As a matter of fact, the initiates of Isis and Osiris, even the male ones like Lucius in the novel of Apuleius, wore such robes at their initiation ceremony.¹⁰¹

But the most unmistakable characteristic of the god is the "cista," because this light "cista" is the basketwork container in which the sacred instruments and symbols were kept, both in the mysteries of Dionysos and those of Isis and Osiris. Such a cista, "secretorum capax penitus celans operta magnificae religionis," was carried in the Isis procession portrayed by Apuleius.¹⁰² The god to whom Tibullus turns is really the god of the mysteries in whose person Dionysos and Osiris are united; his true name, it turned out before, is Sarapis.

Tibullus opened his hymn to Nile-Osiris-Apis by questions about the Nile and its flood, which were much discussed in antiquity, but at the

the afterlife and its amusements as found in an epigram added to a representation of the banquet of the dead: εὐφρανθείς, παίξας, γελάσας, ῥοδίνοις στεφανωθείς, | νήδυμον ὕπνον ἔχων ἐς Ἀίδην ἐδόθην (2029, 8 f. Peek; third century A.D.). It is at such ideas that Lucian scoffs (v. hist. II, 19); the Greeks believed in banquets and garlands of the afterlife since the sixth century B.C. (K. Kircher, Die sakrale Bedeutung des Weines im Altertum, Rel. Vers. u. Vorarb., IX, 2, Giessen, 1910, 58 f.). The hope for love in the afterlife does not exclude doubts and admonitions to enjoy life so long as one is on earth. In a Roman inscription of the third century A.D. dedicated to the dead husband of an initiate of Isis and allegedly spoken by him we are told: "amici, qui legitis, moneo, miscite Lyaeum/ et potate procul redimiti tempora flore/ et Venereos coitus formosis ne denegatis puellis" (Bücheler, CLE, 856 = Vidman, SIRIS, 451.

⁹⁹ The Egyptian dead had statuettes of women at their disposal; cf. S. Morenz, "Die Wöchnerin mit dem Siegelring," ZÄS, 83, 1958, 138 ff.; H. Kees, loc. cit. (n. 47), 95, 130, 262, 264, 286.

¹⁰⁰ Aesch. fr. 59 N.; Prop. III, 17, 32; the god wears the smyrna (Sen., Oed. 423; Herc. fur. 475). For the following cf. the commentaries of K. Fl. Smith and J. André.

¹⁰¹ Saffron: Aristoph. Frogs 46; cf. the saffron-colored girdle in Sen., Oed. 421. Osiris: Plut., De Is. 51: ἀμπεχόνη δὲ φλογοειδεῖ στέλλουσιν αὐτοῦ τὰς εἰκόνας. For Lucius's long robe see Apul., Metam. 11, 24, 2. See also Henrichs, loc. cit. (n. 51), 115. According to Grimal (loc. cit. [n. 1], 45), the robe described by Tibullus does not fit the representations of Osiris, but Sarapis, whose iconography has been influenced by Dionysos. This statement cannot be applied to Osiris, the god of the mysteries, whose alias is Sarapis. And that in Tibullus Sarapis hides behind the name of Osiris is exactly what Grimal wants to demonstrate.

¹⁰² Apul., Metam. 11, 11, 3; for the cista see O. Jahn, Hermes, 3, 1869, 317 ff.; M. P. Nilsson, loc. cit. (n. 93), 96; W. Burkert, Technikgeschichte, 34, 1967, 293; for representations see V. Tran Tinh, loc. cit. (n. 21), 107, 130, 144, 153.

same time concerned secret teachings of the Egyptian priests, since the answer was given by the death and the resurrection of Osiris. The implications of this statement are clearer now, after it turned out that Tibullus's Osiris is the god of the mysteries. In the initiations the mystai were asked questions to which the answer revealed a secret of the mysteries.[103] This may be true of Tibullus's opening questions. His audience, being intimate with the mysteries, their teachings, rites, and customs, and not forced to pick up dispersed pieces of information as we do, may have immediately understood these questions not as trivial allusions to a very common unsolved scientific problem but as questions concerning the central secret of the mysteries.

THE HYMNOS KLETIKOS

The section concerning the deeds and greatness of the god is followed by a prayer for his appearance.

49   huc ades et Genium ludis Geniumque choreis
         concelebra et multo tempora funde mero;
         illius et nitido stillent unguenta capillo,
         et capite et collo mollia serta gerat.
53   sic venias hodierne, tibi dem turis honores
         liba et Mopsopio dulcia melle feram.

[Come and celebrate the Genius with us, celebrate the Genius in games and dances; pour streams of wine about his brows. His glistening hair must drip with ointment, he must wear soft garlands around forehead and neck. Come to me today in order that I may honor you with the smoke of incense[104] and bring you sacrificial cakes sweet with the honey of Attica.]

Osiris is asked to appear at the birthday party of Messalla, as in the Aeneid Dido asked Dionysos and Iuno to appear at her banquet: "adsit laetitiae Bacchus dator et bona Iuno" (I, 734). Sarapis was συμποσιάρχης as well as Dionysos. It became clear that Tibullus in this poem honors

[103] Merkelbach, Roman (see n. 15), 334, 162, 168. Cf. the questions which had to be answered by the Egyptian dead (The Book of the Dead, at the end of Chapter 125) and which were inherited by Egyptian gnostics (Epiph., Pan. haer. 26, 13, 2 = I, 292, 13 ff. Holl); but also Greek women asked and answered riddles in the cult of Dionysos (Plut., Quaest. conv. 8, 1, 717 A; M. P. Nilsson, Griech. Feste, 274 n. 1).

[104] For the construction "sic . . ., tibi dem . . ." cf. Hor., Ode I, 3, 1 ff., Cat. 17, 5 f., Tib. 2, 5, 121 and the parallels collected by Kiessling-Heinze and C. J. Fordyce; normally this "sic" prepares for a condition expressed by an imperative or adhortative subjunctive ("under this condition"), but in Tib. I, 7, 53, it announces a subjunctive wish ("to this intention come: I shall give you"). For "hodierne" see the literature collected by Lenz (third edition by G. C. Galinsky, 1971).

154   Illinois Classical Studies, I

Sarapis under the name of Osiris, and Sarapis did participate at private banquets in Egypt, as we know mainly from invitations written on papyrus, and in other places as well where communities of mysts were living, as in Augsburg and Cologne. The god was at once guest and host at these banquets, including that which was given to celebrate the birth of a child or a young man's coming of age.[105] This was the most important "birthday party" of one's life. Also, Messalla was celebrating a birthday, which, because of his triumph, had special significance. Tibullus summoned this god to appear at the party as guest, but as host he is to grant his gifts to the genius of Messalla. This is the same situation as at the Sarapis banquets in Egypt.

But Tibullus unites Egyptian ritual with the Roman practice of honoring a man's genius on his birthday. For the Romans this genius was the essence of the person of the individual man; it existed apart from one's corporeal being but resembled it exactly in appearance. It was born with one, and originally died with one as well. Only when the belief in an afterlife developed in philosophy and in the mysteries did the genius come to play a central role in the concept of human immortality—it became man, surviving in the afterlife.[106]

Osiris is to pour wine over the forehead of Messalla's genius and give him ointment and garlands. Garlands, ointment, and wine are likewise gifts for the genius in Tibullus II, 2.[107] In I, 7 it is Nile-Osiris who gives these gifts. Already in the ancient Egyptian Nile hymn the Nile looks after

[105] Birth of a child: P. Oxy., 2791; coming to age: P. Oxy., 1484 = Vandoni (see n. 79), nr. 138. The clinae were celebrated at private and religious festivals; they took place in temples (e.g. P. Oxy., 2592, 2791), but also in private houses (P. Oslo, 157 = Vand., 143; P. Oxy., 523 = Vand., 142; P. Oxy., 1755 = Vand., 145; P. Yale, 85; cf. P. Fouad, 76 = Vand., 141; cf. L. Robert, "Inscript. d'Athènes et de la Grèce Centrale," Arch. Ephém., 1969, 7 ff.). For the clinae of Sarapis at Cologne see Vidman, SIRIS (n. 15), 720 (cf. G. Grimm, Die Zeugnisse ägyptischer Religion und Kunstelemente im römischen Deutschland, Leiden, 1969, 83 f.), at Augsburg see Grimm, loc. cit., 81 and pl. 44, 39 f. (G. J. F. Kater-Sibbes, Preliminary Catalogue of Sarapis Monuments, Leiden, 1973, nr. 857). Sarapis as guest and host: Ael. Arist., Hymn to Sarapis 27; as host the god himself invites the guests (ZPE, 1, 1967, 121 ff. = SB, 10496). See H. C. Youtie, HTR, 41, 1948, 9 ff. = Scriptiunculae, I, Amsterdam, 1973, 487 ff.; L. Castiglioni, Acta Ant., 9, 1961, 287 ff.; Vidman, Isis (see n. 15), 116, 121, and 170; F. Dunand, Le culte d'Isis, Leiden, 1973, III, ind. V. s.v. Banquets; P. Köln I (in press).

[106] K. Latte, loc. cit. (n. 21), 103 f.; W. F. Otto, RE, VII, 1155 ff.; F. Cumont, After Life in Roman Paganism, New York², 1959, 142; idem, Recherches sur le symbolisme funéraire des Romains, Paris, 1942, 115 n. 1; G. Dumezil, La religion romaine archaique, Paris, 1966, 351 f.; E. Rohde, Psyche, Tübingen⁶, 1910, 320, II, n. 1; see also K. Fl. Smith and André.

[107] See also the gift of wine for the genius in Hor., Ode III, 17, 14; Epist. II, 1, 144; ad Pis. 209 f.

ointment. Osiris is a god of wine and wears garlands himself. So he makes the genius of Messalla a drinking companion.

In return for his appearance, Tibullus promises Osiris the smoke of incense and ritual-cakes sweetened with Attic honey.[108] For it is this god to whom l. 53 is directed; "sic venias" repeats the request of l. 49, "huc ades," and there it is addressed to Osiris.[109] Incense and sweet cake are suitable gifts for Osiris-Dionysos; according to Ovid's *Fasti*, Dionysos was regarded as the discoverer of incense and of honey (III, 731 ff.). The maenads of Greece caused honey to drip miraculously from their thyrsoi (Eurip. *Bacch.*, 710 f.). And cake was given to Dionysos in Attica.[110]

Dionysos was offered cakes, because he liked sweet food to eat (Ov. *Fasti*, III, 731 ff.). But on the other hand, incense and cakes were characteristic gifts for household gods. They are offered to the genius also in Tibullus's other birthday poem[111]: there the wish "ipse . . . genius adsit" (5) corresponds to the request to Osiris in our elegy, "huc ades" (49) and "sic venias" (53). Osiris therefore is treated as a genius. He is called upon as "hodierne" (53), that is, as the god who appears at today's birthday celebration as a second genius. The two beings, Osiris-Dionysos alias Sarapis and the genius, have become very similar here. They belong together.

And just this is known from Pompeii and Herculaneum. There in the shrines of the lares we find the gods of the Isis mysteries in company with the traditional gods of the household. Sarapis, Harpokrates, and Anubis can even replace the traditional gods.[112] Nile, Osiris, Sarapis, and Agathos Daimon, the Greek equivalent of the Genius, were in fact related. They all adopted the shape of a serpent, as did Amon, one of the gods amalgamated in the deity of Sarapis. A canal in Alexandria called Agathodaimon was represented as a snake, also Sarapis, whose human head sometimes was combined with the body of a snake. Isis was depicted similarly. As the snake Isis-Thermuthis corresponds to the Greek Ἀγαθὴ Τύχη and the Roman Fortuna, so does the snake Sarapis to the Greek

108 "Mopsopio" echoes again Callimachus (fr. 709) as does l. 51 f. (fr. 7, 12; *hymn* II, 38 f.; cf. Bulloch, *loc. cit.* [see n. 34], 77).

109 It is significant that J. P. Postgate proposed his conjecture "hodierne Geni, tibi . . . feram" in order to avoid the conclusion drawn above.

110 A. Pickard-Cambridge, *The Dram. Fest. at Athens*, Oxford, 1953, 27; M. P. Nilsson, *Arch. Jb.*, 31, 1916, 331 (= *Op. sel.*, Lund, 1951, I, 201); A. S. F. Gow in his commentary on Theocr. 26, 7; A. Henrichs, *ZPE*, 4, 1969, 231.

111 II, 2, 3 ff.; see also *Corp. Tib.* III, 11, 9 (incense).

112 V. Tran Tinh, *loc. cit.* (n. 21), 106 ff., cf. 23 n. 2; Merkelbach, *Latomus*, 26, 1965, 145; see also Vidman, *SIRIS* (n. 15), 535 (Rome).

156 Illinois Classical Studies, I

Ἀγαθὸς Δαίμων and the Roman Genius.[113] The similarity in the appearance as snakes reflects similar theological ideas. Osiris-Sarapis of the mysteries was not only a tutelary god of the initiates as long as they lived, but in addition he guaranteed an afterlife for them; just the same functions were fulfilled by the genius of the Romans who believed in life after death. Osiris, from an Egyptian standpoint, can be regarded as the "ka" of a man, as they called one of their concepts of the soul. And this Egyptian "ka" corresponds to the Roman concept of the genius. The Egyptians translated Agathos Damon-Genius by the word "schai," which denotes the concept of man's fate; but "fate" could be expressed also by "ka," and in this sense the term "schai" could be replaced by "ka." Further, they used a word "ka" for "bull," and it is most likely that the term "ka" denoting a concept of human soul is derived from "ka" meaning "bull." If so, "ka" literally denotes the generative power of man; and the term "genius" is derived from the stem "gen" (gignere).[114]

Genius and Osiris-Sarapis, alias Nile, alias Apis, personify the same concept. But in Tibullus, Osiris and the Genius remain distinct beings, at least in lines 49–51. The assimilation is carried out only insofar as Osiris

[113] For Osiris as snake see Kákosy, loc. cit. (n. 32), cf. here p. 135; Wortmann, loc. cit. (n. 47), 89 on Juv., Sat. VI, 538 ff. (also on the Nile as snake); Kater-Sibbes, loc. cit. (n. 105), nr. 418. For Sarapis see W. Kaiser, Ägyptisches Museum Berlin (Stiftung preußischer Kulturbesitz), Berlin, 1967, nr. 997 and plate = Kater-Sibbes 425 (together with Isis depicted also as snake with human head; tails enlaced; in bronze, from Cyzicus); a marble relief found at Rome shows also a Sarapis head on the body of a snake (Kater-Sibbes, 686 and pl. XIX); three similar terracotta representations though with variations in details are in the Coll. Fouquet (found at Kasr Daoud, Kater-Sibbes, 100), in the Museum of Alexandria (nr. 22971, Kater-Sibbes, 174), and in my private collection (from Egypt, unpublished); a fourth one was found at Heracleopolis Magna (Kater-Sibbes, 97). Also on coins the snake Agathos Daimon had the head of Sarapis (R. S. Pole, Cat. Greek Coins Brit. Mus., Alexandria, p. 88 (Hadrian), 130 (Antoninus Pius), and cf. 56 (Trajan, see A. Bernand, Le Delta [see n. 97], 87). Cf. also the marble figure of Sarapis wrapped by a snake which was discovered at Arles (Kater-Sibbes, 802 and pl. XXVII). For Isis-Thermuthis as snake with a human head see Fr. Dunand, BIFAO, 67 1969, 9 ff.; for the serpent Agathos Daimon representing the Nile see A. Bernand, Alexandrie (see n. 97), pl. 24, opposite p. 296, and idem, Le Delta (see n. 97), 89.

[114] For the term "schai" replacing the "ka" see W. Spiegelberg, ZÄS, 49. 1911, 360; for "schai" as translation of Agathos Daimon see S. Morenz, "Untersuchungen zur Rolle des Schicksals . . .," Abh. Leipzig, Berlin, 1960, 26; the "schai" was especially the Agathos Daimon of Ptolemaios I., who founded Ptolemais: its Egyptian name was Psoi = Schai. See also Grimal, loc. cit. (n. 1), 47; H. Frankfort, loc. cit. (n. 47), 65: "The best equivalent for the Ka is the genius of the Romans, though the Ka is much more impersonal. But in the case of the genius, as well as in that of the Ka, there is the recognition of a power which transcends the human person even though it works within him." As the Roman gods had a genius, so the Egyptian gods had one or more kas. Similar ideas are found elsewhere too.

gives his gifts of wine, ointment, and garlands, thus making the genius his drinking companion. In wine, the god gives himself; and ointment and garlands are symbols of immortality.[115] In giving these things to the genius, Osiris makes it immortal and shares with it his own divinity. Just in this way the Osiris of ancient Egypt animated the "ka" of a departed man and resurrected it as Osiris himself. The Egyptian dead was absorbed by Osiris and lived on as Osiris. Such an absorption may be indicated in lines 53 f., which direct the request for appearing to Osiris and treat him at the same time as if he were the genius; at this point the genius disappears. One may conclude that after Osiris offered his gifts of immortality to the genius, he and the genius are amalgamated. But there remains a fundamental difference from the Egyptian concept of the dead becoming Osiris. Tibullus does not think of the god of the underworld, but of Sarapis, the god of the mysteries, who gives man a claim to immortality even during his earthly life.

In his prayer that the god appear at the birthday celebration, Tibullus attempts to harmonize Egyptian thought with Roman. Osiris makes not the man himself immortal, but rather his genius. The strength and power of the god increase the strength and power of the man who stands under his protection. Thus in praising the might of Osiris, Tibullus praises the might of Messalla, who is devoted to the god.

A FINAL REMARK ON THE STRUCTURE OF THE WHOLE POEM

If the hymn to Osiris honors Messalla, too, as I argued, then it is an appropriate theme for his birthday elegy; it stands in the middle of the elegy and is consequently no unbalanced excursion, as Wilamowitz expressed the opinion of his time,[116] but rather the center of the whole poem, as F. W. Levy alias Lenz recognized.[117]

This becomes still clearer when one considers the structure of the elegy as a whole. At the beginning of the poem stands Messalla's triumphal

---

[115] For the ointment see Merkelbach, *Roman* (see n. 15), 47 f. There was a consecrated oil called μυστήριον also used by the magicians in the ceremony of making immortal (*PGM*, IV, 741 ff. and 770 f. = A. Dieterich, *Eine Mithrasliturgie*, Leipzig and Berlin, 1923, 17 f.; cf. Th. Hopfner, *Griech-ägypt. Offenbarungszauber*, II, Leipzig, 1924, 62, §121); see also Firm. Mat., *De err. prof. rel.* 22 f. (cf. R. Reitzenstein, *Hellen. Mysterienreligionen*, 400 f.) and the novel *Joseph and Asenoth* (8, 5, and 15, 4, χρίσματι τῆς ἀφθαρσίας; ed. M. Philonenko). The garland is a sign of the mystai (Apul., *Metam.* 11, 24, 4; Merkelbach, *Roman*, 35; cf. his index, s.v. "Kranz").

[116] *Hellenistische Dichtung*, II, 301 n. 1: "anorganische Einlage"; cf. I, 238: "Abschweifung"; see also M. Schuster, *Tibull-Studien*, Wien, 1930, 20 ff.

[117] *Loc. cit.* (n. 64), 439 f.; cf. L. Dissen in his edition of 1835, XCII f.

procession in Rome, in which the triumphator comes on stage as Jupiter and in which, according to the Roman concept, his superhuman might became manifest. The Osiris hymn is the Egyptian counterpart to this picture: the true strength and hope of Messalla is the god Osiris. At the same time, of course, the world of Osiris, with its joyful festivities, is more comfortable and familiar to Tibullus than is the ceremonial glitter of the triumphal procession. At the end of the poem we have again very Roman ideas: may Messalla survive after death in the person of his sons and in the benefaction he gave to his countrymen by repairing the via Latina. These concluding scenes correspond to the opening picture of the triumph. The Osiris hymn is, as it were, the focal point around which the Roman themes, the triumphal procession, and the closing scenes are centered.

This central position of the hymn to Nile-Osiris is reflected also in details of composition. Even in the portrayal of the triumph, Tibullus concentrates on the rivers; and when he mentions Cilicia and Syria, he concentrates on the miraculous. Thus he foreshadows the miracle of the river Nile. Tyre invented ships; in the hymn Osiris is celebrated as the great inventor. Tibullus remains steadfast to his associations, and from the very start of the poem he directs us straight toward his hymn to the Nile. There is similarly a direct transition from the celebration of the genius to the conclusion of the poem. The genius is a symbol of human reproduction, and its mention is immediately followed by a wish for progeny. The last distich celebrates the dies natalis, as did the first distich, and so Tibullus returns at the end to the opening theme.[118]

MESSALLA AND OSIRIS

Let us likewise return to the opening theme of our interpretation. It was made clear, I hope, what a central position has the hymn to Nile-Osiris in I, 7 and how the song of praise to Osiris was at the same time a song of praise to Messalla. Messalla had been in Egypt. Tibullus was clearly aware of how deeply the Egyptian cult had impressed him. Perhaps Messalla had even become an initiate. But the biographical question is unimportant for our understanding of the poem. In any case,

[118] "Natalis" may be understood as a genius who is invited to come still brighter in the years ahead (cf. II, 2); but even so the birthday celebration is meant. In the first line "dies" seems to designate the day of Messalla's triumph, which was announced by the Parcae. Only in l. 49 it becomes clear that in reality the birthday was meant. The birth of Messalla, on which occasion the Parcae fixed his fate, comprehends already his victory over the Aquitanians. There is no need to conclude that Messalla won his victory or had his triumph on his birthday. See also André.

Tibullus was able to speak as if Messalla included Osiris among his household deities and regarded him as his special protective god.

The pro-Egyptian mentality of Messalla may have induced Tibullus to write a poem full of allusions to the Egyptian world and to give his poetic picture of this strange world. At the same time Delia, his beloved mistress, was initiated into the mysteries of the Egyptian gods. Tibullus could be sure of pleasing her exactly with this kind of poetry. Therefore he follows Egyptian religious thoughts also in the second and third elegy of his first book. Propertius was in a quite similar position with regard to his mistress; Egyptian influence can be traced with him too.[119]

One is inclined to ask whether this special situation of Greek-educated Roman poets being in love with the initiates of the Egyptian gods was not one of the factors which changed Greek elegy and gave birth to the Roman love elegy. The answer to this question cannot be given here. We are satisfied with having seen how the Roman poets interwove Egyptian and Greco-Roman religious thoughts. People may find fault with this syncretism. But on the other hand one may admire the power of poetic imagination which in the new cosmopolitan time of Augustus combined Greco-Roman thought with the religious world of the Egyptians.

University of Cologne

[119] For the time being see p. 129.

13

Structure and Meaning in Propertius Book 3

HOWARD JACOBSON

Like many others who have discovered new approaches to old problems, Otto Skutsch has not always been fortunate in his *epigonoi*. His key to the elaborate, intricate, and complex structure of the Propertian *Monobiblos* has since been appropriated by others.[1] One scholar has recently attempted, following Skutsch, to disclose the structure of Propertius' third book but has met with little success. In a brief article published in 1967, A. Woolley argued that Book 3 shows an interlocking paneled structure of essentially the same sort as Skutsch revealed for the *Monobiblos*.[2] The relationships that Woolley sees between poems are often contrived and forced and unlikely to convince anyone not already a believer in the virtual omnipresence of the Skutschian *schema*. In contrast, E. Courtney's article in *Phoenix*, 1970, disagree as one may on specific points, is entirely persuasive in its general view that the movement of Book 3 is linear.[3] Using Courtney's essay as a starting point, I shall examine in some detail the nature of direct and immediate linear continuity in this book by focusing on two groups of poems within it, namely, 12–13 and 21–24, in each of which the meaning of any individual poem is defined and developed by the poem or poems which immediately follow.

In this connection, W. R. Nethercut has argued that 3.12–14 are a unified group, bound together by the theme of female participation in

---

[1] *CP*, 58 (1963), 238–239. I am indebted to Professors David F. Bright and John Vaio who read an early draft of this paper and made helpful suggestions.

[2] *BICS*, 14 (1967), 80–83. More recently, H. Juhnke, *Hermes*, 99 (1971), 91–125, has made an elaborate and complex attempt to combine the architectonic view with a linear one.

[3] *Phoenix*, 24 (1970), 48–53.

military exercise and by the "war" between *aurum* and *fides*.[4] Though Nethercut sees the group as interlocked, with 12 and 14 framing 13, the linear movement from the problems posed in 12 and 13 to the "solution" in 14 is apparent in his scheme. Leaving aside the question of the validity of this thesis, I would like to suggest a quite different relationship between 12 and 13.

"*Postumus* has gone with the army to the East. Propertius reproaches him for leaving his *Galla* (1–14); affirms that *Galla* will be faithful to him in his absence (15–22); and compares her . . . with Penelope (23–38)." So Camps in his introduction to 3.12.[5] But this summary oversimplifies and misses the poem's nuances and colorings. The matter is not so clear-cut. The opening rebuke, with the distance between the two lovers made concrete by the separation of their names, is rather light-hearted and may contain a note of humor in the combination of plosives and liquids: *Postume, plorantem potuisti linquere Gallam* (1). Little more serious in tone is the juxtaposition of the generalization that soldiering implies avarice (5–6) to the precise portrait of poor Postumus wrapped in a cloak and compelled to drink wearily from a helmet (7–8). A brief catalogue of the possible disasters that may befall Postumus in the East, as Galla imagines them, follows (9–14). Here a sharp break occurs, and *modo Propertiano* we are abruptly wrenched into a new world: *ter quater in casta felix, o Postume, Galla!* (15). No connection to the preceding is immediately apparent. Until now the focus has been on the villain Postumus and his disloyalty to the erotic ideal. Now Galla becomes prominent, and the focus, un-expectedly, is on her chastity. We sense suddenly that in Propertius' rebuke and warning of Postumus there is more than meets the eye: "Postumus," runs the unspoken message, "by venturing off to the East you risk losing Galla." And from this point the poem wavers between two poles, the explicit declaration that Galla is a paragon of virtue, and the implicit suggestion that Galla is not more trustworthy than any other woman.

If *moribus his alia coniuge dignus eras* (16), then the inverse is equally true—Galla deserves another lover, one who will not abandon her. Indeed, *quid faciet nullo munita puella timore,/ cum sit luxuriae Roma magistra suae?* (17–18): there is little reason for Postumus to expect Galla to be faithful. The irony in *munita* is clear: Postumus goes off to war—but it is Galla whom he should be defending! Propertius then seems to back away and cheer

---

[4] *CP*, 65 (1970), 99–102. For an interpretation of 3.12 that is completely different from mine, see F. Cairns, *Generic Composition in Greek and Roman Poetry* (Edinburgh, 1972), 197–201.

[5] W. A. Camps, *Propertius: Elegies Book III* (Cambridge, 1966), 112–113. I have used Camps' text of Propertius throughout.

Postumus: *sed securus eas: Gallam non munera vincent,/ duritiaeque tuae non erit illa memor* (19–20). Yet even here the explicit is confronted by the implicit. *Non munera vincent* suggests the picture of lovers wooing Galla in Postumus' absence and is hardly calculated to raise his hopes. *Vincent* is pointed: while Postumus is away playing soldier, others in Rome are usurping his role as soldier-lover. Similarly, verse 20 skillfully hints quite the opposite of what it says. The condemnation of Postumus' *duritia* gives Galla the justification to be faithless as a kind of revenge; and if Propertius cannot forget Postumus' *duritia*, it is unlikely that Galla will. But again any qualms Postumus may have are allayed: *nam quocumque die salvum te fata remittent,/ pendebit collo Galla pudica tuo* (21–22). *Galla pudica*, as earlier *casta Galla* (15) and later *casta uxor* (37; an implicit reference to Galla). If Postumus (or the reader) feels that Propertius doth protest too much, who can blame him?

Here the theme of chastity takes a new form. Galla will prove to be an *altera Penelope*. Lines 23 ff. recount at length the heroic adventures of the original Penelope's husband during the period of her virtuous endurance, a passage which Rothstein considered totally alien to the main topic of the poem.[6] But the elaborate narrative of Ulysses' exploits, emphasizing at once the vast and manifold difficulties he encountered and also the greatness of his achievement, is quite to the point. For while Propertius *prima facie* presents Postumus as a modern-day Ulysses, he subtly undermines the equation by the specific and detailed account of the Greek warrior's feats. That Postumus is another Ulysses cannot be taken seriously. But if Postumus is no Ulysses, there is one inescapable inference. As little as he could be another Ulysses, so little could Galla be another Penelope. Postumus would hardly leave a Calypso, if he found one, nor would he be able single-handed to overwhelm a crowd of suitors.[7] And Galla would not endure loneliness and reject the attractive offers of her seducers. The poem ends with another ambiguity, in which the explicit points in one way, the unspoken in another: *vincit Penelopes Aelia Galla fidem* (38). This bald-faced assertion is made all the more brazen and ridiculous by its direct simplicity, its complete lack of artifice and grand language. Thus we leave 3.12 with an unresolved doubt, debating whether to accept the assertions at face value or to consider the poem a playful piece in which the explicit declarations are designed to be denied and rejected in favor of the underlying implications.

3.13 resolves the issue. As Camps observes, this poem is a "discourse on a

---

[6] M. Rothstein, *Die Elegien des Sextus Propertius* (Berlin, 1924²), vol. 2, p. 102. Camps too (pp. 112–113) expresses dissatisfaction with this section of the poem.

[7] The reference to the suitors in 35 suggests, as did verse 19, that Galla is being wooed.

general theme."[8] Yet, it is not—as he also implies—association run wild, because the generalization here grows out of the preceding poem. Rome is corrupt, especially her women. The condemnation is all-inclusive— Galla cannot escape. The leitmotif of 3.12, that Galla is another Penelope, is shown here for what it is worth. Even if she were another Penelope, it would not matter: *haec etiam clausas expugnant arma pudicas,/ quaeque gerunt fastus, Icarioti, tuos* (9-10). Not even Penelope can maintain her virtue in Rome. At all events, Galla is no Penelope: *hoc genus infidum nuptarum, hic nulla puella/ nec fida Euadne nec pia Penelope* (23-24)—no Roman lady can make such a claim. This is the essential interplay between poems 12 and 13. But the relationship is maintained in many details too. The theme of the greedy soldier, exemplified in 12 by Postumus, is translated here into that of the greedy girl, *Quaeritis, unde avidis nox sit pretiosa puellis,/ et Venere exhaustae damna querantur opes?* (1-2); and by the poem's end we are quite ready to identify this girl with Galla.

Mention of a *puella* eliciting gifts from her prospective lovers recalls the hint of such gifts to Galla at 12.19. The elaborate catalogue of luxuries in 5-8 contains just the sort of *munera* that indeed *vincent* Galla. Verses 9-10 are to be interpreted in the light of the similar language of poem 12. Not only are the girls *pudicae*, like Galla, but the military language parallels that used in 3.12: *haec etiam clausas expugnant arma pudicas* (3.13.9)/ *nullo munita puella timore* (3.12.17), *Gallam non munera vincent* (3.12.19). Neither the girls of 13 nor Galla of 12 can defend and maintain their virtue.[9] In a final summation, the theme is reiterated: *aurum omnes victa iam pietate colunt* (48). *Pietas* suggests Penelope (cf. 3.12.37; 3.13.24) and *victa* recalls the *vincent munera* of Galla. In Rome there is no *pietas*, no Penelope, and of course no longer a faithful Galla.[10]

Furthermore, two important themes of 13 are related to the "irrelevant" account of Ulysses' adventures in 12. First, the list of exotic, foreign places in 13.5-8, the lands producing those gifts which plague and please Roman womanhood, corresponds to the catalogue of Ulysses' exploits in which strange people and places are prominent. The following correspondences may be noted: *cinnamon* (13.8) is an auditory doublet of *Ciconum mons* (12.25),[11] and "mountain" may be present again in *cavis . . . metallis* (13.5). The allusion to the "Red Sea" (13.6) recalls Ulysses' desperate swimming (12.32), and the *pastor . . . Arabs* (13.8) will make us think of

---

[8] P. 115.   [9] We might also note the theme of *spolium* at both 12.3 and 13.12.

[10] One is tempted to see a double entendre in *sed nulla fides* (13.61) and read 12.38 in its light.

[11] Camps reads *mors*, but there seems to be no substantial reason for doubting the genuineness of the MS tradition. (Camps *ad loc.* thinks *mons* "colourless.")

Lampetie tending (*paverat*) the cattle of the Sun (12.29–30). The people and places enumerated in 3.12 prove to be obstacles which hinder Ulysses (*prima facie* = Postumus), those of 3.13, temptations and evils which persecute Penelope (*prima facie* = Galla).

On the other hand, the Ulyssean catalogue is also mirrored in the panegyric of the Indian women who undergo self-immolation out of devotion to their lost husbands. Like the Greek hero the virtuous Indian wife *sequatur coniugium* (19–20); indeed, both Ulysses and the Indian women pursue their devotion to the ultimate degree, by willingly going to the Land of the Dead (note *viva sequatur*, 3.13.19, just as Ulysses travels alive to the Land of the Dead; cf. 3.12.33). It is, in the end, only these inhabitants of an alien world who can be likened to the great heroes and heroines of mythological Greece, not the corrupted heroes manqués of Augustan Rome.

Finally, the link between 3.12 and 3.13 is further developed by the concluding association of Propertius' Rome with the ancestral fatherland, Troy (3.13.60–66). For, like Troy, Rome stands on the verge of decay and collapse. But more than the genetic connection between Troy and Rome is involved here. The mention of Troy's fall inevitably restores us to the world of Ulysses and Penelope (3.12), most notably in the calculated allusion to the wooden horse (64), Ulysses' stratagem which overthrew Troy. Far in the mythological past it was Ulysses who negotiated the destruction of Troy from without. Now it will be those within the city who fail to measure up to Ulysses (and Penelope) who will precipitate the death of Rome.

In sum, there is an interaction between 3.12 and 3.13 which compels us to interpret each in the light of the other. Thus, the generalizations of 13 prove directly relevant to the limited subject of 12 and demonstrate the validity of interpreting the latter as ironic. But the interaction is reciprocal, for 12 clarifies and expands the context within which 13 is set and thereby provides the framework for its interpretation.

We turn now to the latter part of Book 3, specifically elegies 21–24. Here Courtney has made some brief but important observations on the interrelation of these poems, and my arguments take off from his.[12]

In 3.21 Propertius declares his intention to break off with Cynthia and travel to Athens. 3.22 is an appeal to his friend Tullus to return home to Rome from Cyzicus. In 3.23 the poet laments the loss of his writing tablets, and in 3.24 he proclaims his final liberation from Cynthia. Though these poems appear somewhat disconnected, Courtney notes that they are tied together, in linear progression, by the theme, explicit or implicit, of

[12] See too R. J. Baker, *AJP*, 90 (1969), 333–337.

Propertius' decisive and in the end successful struggle to free himself from Cynthia. Courtney's general argument is convincing, and I should like to develop more specifically the view that this calculated sequence of poems is also unified by a leitmotif (or leitmotifs) that links all four poems. To summarize briefly my general argument, I do not think that Propertius here ever contemplated—or meant his readers to think he did—a journey to Athens. The voyage is a metaphor with a double significance. The ship of poetry and the ship of love coalesce in the metaphorical assertion that Propertius is at once rejecting Cynthia and the writing of love poetry. The metaphors (ship of love, ship of poetry) have a long history and go back at least to Pindar and Theognis.[13] More relevant, they are part of the stock-in-trade of the Latin love poets of the first century. When Ovid comes to the end of the *Remedia amoris* he describes it as the conclusion of a sea voyage (811–812), and when he refers to his propensity for the lesser genres of verse he does it with images of small bodies of water and humble crafts (*ex Ponto*, 2.5.21–22; *Trist.*, 2.329–330). Horace, when on the verge of composing epic, is confronted by Apollo: *ne parva Tyrrhenum per aequor/ vela darem (Carm.*, 4.15.3–4). No less frequent is the ship of love. Catullus' lovers are sometimes, so to speak, shipwrecked (64.97–98; 68.3, 63–64). So, too, Horace saved from Pyrrha (*Carm.*, 1.5.13–16). When Ovid tries, to no avail, to give up love, *Ut subitus prope iam prensa tellure carinam/ tangentem portus ventus in alta rupit,/ sic me saepe refert incerta Cupidinis aura/ notaque purpureus tela resumit Amor (Am.*, 2.9.31–34). Similarly, when a young man, intent on ridding himself of love, attempts to follow Ovid's advice, he almost succeeds *inque suae portu paene salutis erat (Rem. am.*, 610) before falling back again. Of the same metaphorical order are verses 368 and 373 in the *Ars amatoria* Book One. Propertius 2.14.29–30 is a fine instance of his use of this metaphor. Examples need not be multiplied. The Roman audience was clearly attuned to mentions in Latin poetry of seas, ships, sailors, voyages, and the like which were not meant to be taken literally but often enough as metaphors for poetic creation and for the world of love.[14] Often the metaphor will involve details of concreteness and precision, e.g., the name of the sea, the rigging of the ship, that have in fact no one-to-one correspondence with the general realities being suggested; yet this was an accepted aspect of the utilization of such metaphor. It is then around this metaphor and allied themes that these

[13] Theognis 457 ff.; Pindar, *Pyth.* 11.38 ff., etc.

[14] We should remember that there is not a consistent set of correspondences between the various nautical facets of the metaphor and the different aspects of the worlds of love and poetry. The poets did not practice strict uniformity in applying these metaphors.

four poems find their focus, connection and unity.[15] Nor would a somewhat novel application of the metaphor have escaped Propertius' audience,
especially since Propertius alternates the metaphor here with explicit
declarations of his rejection of Cynthia.

In the opening lines of 3.21 Propertius declares his intention to take a
magnum iter ad doctas Athenas and hopes by so doing to end his love affair
with Cynthia. At line 11 details sharpen: *nunc agite, o socii, propellite in
aequora navem,/ remorumque pares ducite sorte vices,/ iungiteque extremo felicia
lintea malo:/ iam liquidum nautis aura secundat iter* (11–14). The language is of
the same order as in Propertius' address to Maecenas, *quid me scribendi tam
vastum mittis in aequor* (3.9.3), where the metaphor is obvious: Maecenas
impels Propertius in a certain poetic direction. *Propellite in aequora navem*
need be no more literal.[16] In this poem, however, the intimate connection
between Cynthia, Propertius' darling, and Cynthia, Propertius' inspiration
(cf. 2.1.4: *ingenium nobis ipsa puella facit*) unites the two potential facets of
the metaphor. This is a journey away on the one hand from Cynthia and
on the other hand from the genre of erotic elegy. The ship voyage is at
once Propertius' poetic creativity and his career as a lover. When the ship
is launched he is on his way in his attempt to reject both Cynthia and
erotic elegy in favor of new worlds. In his valedictory, *Romanae turres et
vos valeatis, amici* (15), Propertius declares his farewell to the friends who
have been associated with his relationship to Cynthia since the very first
poem of the *Monobiblos*.

But why Athens? Perhaps we need not ask this question. After all, the
ship metaphor in Latin poetry often uses concrete details which transcend
the system of precise correspondences. Still, here we may note an interesting parallel. There is good reason for believing that Horace's *propemptikon*
addressed to Vergil (*Carm.* 1.3) is not literal, that Horace addresses Vergil
as he prepares to embark on some new path of poetic endeavor.[17] As in
Propertius 3.21, Horace describes the difficulties of the journey and calls
attention to the Adriatic. Most remarkably, Vergil, like Propertius, is
sailing to Athens. Just as one can conjecture why Vergil's metaphorical
journey ends in Athens, so one can with that of Propertius. As the revered
seat of artistic creativity, Athens symbolizes and represents many forms
of art, but erotic elegy was certainly not one—as is also indicated by the

15 In support of this view one notes that Propertius was especially interested in the
ship/poetry-love metaphor when writing Book 3. See, e.g., 3.9.3–4, 35–36; 17.1–4. For
additional examples of the ship/love metaphor in Hellenistic and Roman poetry, see
A. La Penna, *Maia*, 4 (1951), 202–205.

16 Similarly, the *fessa vela* of verses 19–20 reminds one of Ovid's *fessa carina* (*Rem. am.*,
811), his poem-ship.

17 See, e.g., C. W. Lockyer, Jr., *CW*, 61 (1967), 42–45.

list of artists and arts enumerated in verses 25ff. So perhaps the trip to
Athens signifies an abandonment of the uniquely Roman genre of erotic
elegy[18] for some other genre of poetry more commonly represented by
Greek poets. The association of Theseus with Athens in the metonymical
use of the adjective *Theseae* (24) = Athenian may reflect essays into epic
or aetiological poetry. That Athens is immediately identified as *doctas
Athenas* (1) and two of its representatives are called *docte* (26, 28) gives
some indication that the journey is a creative voyage into a new form of
artistic activity (as perhaps evidenced in Book Four).[19]

In brief, I shall argue that 3.21–24 are unified by the metaphor of the
ship voyage and by a network of related themes that are associated with
it, e.g., home/foreign land, place names, travel, bodies of water, and
water.[20] To see the unity of the last poems of Book 3 in these terms is
particularly suggestive when one considers that Nethercut has argued that
the *opening* poems of this book (1–5, 7, 9) are unified by a number of
themes, one of the most important of which is (again) water.[21]

On the surface 3.22, which calls on Tullus to return to Rome from
Cyzicus, seems unrelated to the preceding poem. But Courtney observes
that beneath the apparent dissimilarity there are important ties: Propertius is being driven from Rome, Tullus can return with happy prospects.
The Greek world which appeared so appealing to Propertius is now a land
of monsters, while Italy is attractive. The contrast between 21 and 22
emphasizes the humiliation love has brought on Propertius. All this is
insightful, but I should like to approach the question in a somewhat
different manner and also to elaborate the problem and solution.

In the first place there are so many verbal and substantive echoes of 21
in 22 that it is clear that the two poems are meant to be considered together and not as isolated pieces. The very opening distich picks up a
number of themes from 21. The reference to the *isthmos* of Cyzicus recalls

[18] I forgo becoming involved in the question of the relation of Latin erotic elegy to
Greek genres of verse and think it suffices in this context merely to note that there is no
evidence for a form of erotic elegy as found in the first century Latin elegists before them.

[19] Is it possible that the crossing of the Isthmus (21–22) into the Saronic gulf, within
sight of Attica, may be a metaphor within a metaphor, the isthmus perceived as a symbol
of that which separates two worlds, two kinds of life, two forms of poetry? The only
metaphorical use of *isthmus* I know before Propertius is at Soph. fg. 145 N^2 = 568 P. For
later instances of *isthmus* as a poetic image, see the similes at Lucan 1.99–106 and Silius
15.152–157, and the discussion by M. v. Albrecht, *Hermes*, 91 (1963), 364–365. Perhaps of
interest is Lucretius' strange metaphorical use of *fretum* (4.1030).

[20] Water, even without the theme of voyage, is an important image for the realm of
ancient Greco-Roman poetry because of the waters of inspiration the poet imbibes. See,
e.g., Prop. 2.10.25–26; 3.3.51–52.

[21] *TAPA*, 92 (1961), 389–407.

the Corinthian *isthmos*; the mention of a long period of time in absence from home recalls 21.31, *spatia annorum*, and the allusion to water reintroduces an important theme of 21 (*Propontiaca . . . aqua* occurs in essentially the same position in the pentameter as *placida . . . aqua*, 21.20). That *frigida* (22.1) sometimes has erotic connotations may be more than a coincidence given the final verse of the poem and the poem's connection to the preceding elegy which dealt with an *amor* now *frigidus*. Verse 3 mentions one of Cyzicus' marvels, a statue of Cybele carved from a vine stock. As sculpture, this returns us to the art of Athens mentioned at 21.30, *sive ebore exactae, seu magis aere, manus.*[22] And it might not be stretching the probable too far to suggest that the allusion to a *raptoris . . . via* (22.4: Pluto's rape of Proserpine) looks back to the *Theseae viae* at 21.24, because, even more than Pluto, Theseus was a famous *raptor* of women (Helen, Ariadne), among whose exploits was an attempt to steal Proserpine. Further, the rape of a woman seems particularly significant in relation to the theme of 21, the rejection of a woman. Thus Cyzicus has been miraculously transformed by the proximity of 3.22 to 3.21 into another Athens, a city noteworthy for its works of "art" and associated with famous womanseizers.

Let me briefly consider a few more allusions and themes present in 22 that at least appear to recall motifs of 21 or to be in counterpoint to them. Verses 7–10 are usually—and rightly—taken to refer to hypothetical journeys to North Africa and points west where the recounted wonders took place. But the language is suggestive. No verb indicates any movement or travel; there is only *aspicias*. Further, many of the objects of *aspicias* are puzzling since no contemporary of Propertius, even traveling to the said locations, could actually see them (not Atlas, unless this refers merely to the mountain; not the Gorgon's head or the *choros* of Hesperides, unless one understands this to mean not choruses but dancing places, a meaning *chorus* never has elsewhere in Latin literature). Rather, underlying the passage is the idea of viewing works of art, an idea emphatically suggested by the odd use of *signa*—moreover, Greek (or Athenian) works of art, as is implied by the reference to the Gorgon's head which could be seen in Athens set in Athena's aegis. Thus we return to the world of 21, where Athenian works of art are a seductive highlight of the Greek *polis* (29–30). But here, in a reversal that dominates the whole poem, the "Greek" attractions and wonders are deemed inferior to the Roman alternatives.

When the language becomes that of a nautical voyage (11 ff.), we

[22] *Fabrico(r)* is indeed found as a term for artistic creation, e.g., Cic., *Off.* 1.147; Ov., *Fast.* 5.137.

again sense a mirror image of 21. Tullus' craft is launched with the same language as was Propertius' (*propellite navem/ propellas Phasim*). When Tullus' voyage calls to mind that of the Argo, this archetypal journey is seen to have a contemporary analogue in Propertius' venture (*rudis vehar*, 21.17; *rudis natat*, 22.13).[23]

But probably the most striking coincidence of the poems is in regard to bodies of water. We have noted already the similar phrases *placida aqua/ Propontiaca aqua*. To this we might add the references to the Cayster (15) and the Nile (16) where *unda* (again at 28) may make us think of *undisonos* at 21.18. But the significance of this emphasis on water (especially in 22) lies deeper. Consider some of the poem's mythological allusions. The region of Cyzicus is termed *Helles Athamantidos urbes* (5), which will recall for the reader at least the story of Helle, who drowned in the strait, and perhaps even the legend about Athamas who pursued Melicerta and Ino into the sea. These are the first hints in this poem of the very real and frightening dangers of the sea and of sea travel, a theme of little relevance here but of importance in 21. Then there is Andromeda (29), exposed to die at the hands of a sea monster, and the Greek fleet waiting to set sail for Troy (34), an expedition fraught from the very beginning with death and destruction.[24] Finally, the allusion to Sciron (37–38) once again may involve violent death by drowning. In the context of poem 21 all this is of real import. Whereas in 3.21 Propertius is quite prepared to make little of the perils of sea travel, in this poem both the language and the mythological allusions emphasize its dangers, notably in the Greek (Eastern) world—or rather in that world inhabited by Greek myth. And the sea dangers of Greece are magnified by other dangers implicit in 33–38. One major exception is striking and helpful. When Propertius turns to proclaim the virtues of Rome, he describes its beauties strictly in terms of water:

> hic Anio Tiburne fluis, Clitumnus ab Umbro
> tramite, et aeternum Marcius umor opus,
> Albanus lacus et socia Nemorensis ab unda,
> potaque Pollucis nympha salubris equo.
> at non squamoso labuntur ventre cerastae,
> Itala portentis nec furit unda novis.   (23–28)

---

23 Note the similarity of sound between *Romanae terrae* (22.17) and *Romanae turres* (21.15), the latter phrase a vocative like the *Roma* of 22.20.

24 There is almost certainly a lacuna after verse 36. I think it highly likely that it contained a reference to Ariadne. This would produce the following series of "heroines," Andromeda, Bacchant, Io and Ariadne (29 ff.), just as in 1.3.1–20. Further, the movement from Ariadne to Sinis would provide a typically allusive Propertian transition, with both Ariadne and Sinis having close ties to the myth of Theseus.

The inferences are clear-cut. The waters of the world are hazardous and untrustworthy outside Italy; Greek and Eastern waters are menacing and destructive; those near Rome are peaceful and healthful. For the poet of 3.21 this can be but a single message: do not leave Italy, forget your trip to Athens. Or, to translate the metaphor, give up your plans of abandoning Cynthia and erotic elegy.[25] We should note that in his praise of Rome's natural splendors, Propertius cites first the Anio, which was tributary to the Tibur. No wonder that this stands first here, for it was a trysting place for him and Cynthia (cf. 3.16.4).

One last aspect of the poem reinforces the view presented here. The protracted account of the wonders of the foreign world (7 ff.) turns out to be, by and large, a résumé of mythological material traditionally used in Epic and Drama (exploits of Heracles, the Argonauts, etc.). This, however, is declared inferior to the Roman possibilities, *omnia Romanae cedent miracula terrae* (17), in literary terms, to erotic elegy. That is, whereas Propertius had in 21 announced his abandonment of Latin love elegy in favor of other genres, here he reverses himself and reaffirms the superiority of his elegy to other forms of literature.

One might reasonably object that such an interpretation extends the poem beyond its obvious bounds, i.e., a simple appeal to Tullus to return from Cyzicus to Rome. But if the scope of the poem is so narrow, why is there so clear a shift from the limited perspective and situation of Tullus in Cyzicus to a view that embraces much of the geographical and mythological worlds? Surely, to move the poem beyond the narrow frame that it *prima facie* inhabits. And the final distich of the poem incorporates an unexpected "erotic" note, which is the explicit bond which links 22 to 21: *coniunx* and *amor*; the very reasons which in 21 motivated the need to leave Rome here become the best inducement to stay.

In sum, we might even think of 22 as a palinode to 21. In the latter Propertius resolves on a journey away from Rome (that is, he seeks to reject Cynthia and love elegy). In the former, under the guise of advice to a friend, he shows himself unable (or unwilling) to act on his plan of 21 and "rationalizing" his change of mind: after all, travel is risky, foreign

[25] That such a contrast between Greece (the East) and Italy is present is substantiated by a structural parallel. When Propertius praises the Italian landscape, the language recalls the very opening of the poem with its description of the region of Cyzicus. In both, the key words are *fluit* (*fluis*; 2 and 23); in both, references to divinities and horses are important (3-4, 26). The two passages are thereby linked, but for purposes of contrast. And, by the way, this triad of motifs (water, horses, divinities) can scarcely help but call Hippocrene to mind. Indeed, the very notion of good waters versus improper waters recalls the choice of water the poet must make, i.e., the choice of type of poetry (see Prop. 3.3).

lands have their dangers and, all in all, Italy (= Cynthia and love poetry) is best.

That poem 23 is a metaphor is beyond serious question. While the very fact that the poet still uses and desires his tablets demonstrates the failure of his earlier resolve (3.21), nevertheless the loss of his tablets clearly signifies that Propertius' activity as lover-poet is approaching its end. Moreover, the fact that the tablets' absence can be attributed either to Cynthia's failure to return them or to her loss of them is emblematic of her responsibility for the failure of their relationship.[26] In a number of places the language used of the tablets and their condition is such as to clarify the metaphorical value. The tablets had been worn down by *usus* (3), language unmistakably sexual in the erotic context (cf. Ov. *Rem. am.*, 357; Tib., 1.9.55).[27] They have always been *fideles* (contrast Cynthia).[28] The *poeta disertus* is replaced (note *sine me*, 6) by his tablets (*verba diserta loqui*, 6). In effect, "Propertius" and "Propertius' art" become interchangeable terms, each designating the creative poet.

This metaphoric meaning would probably suffice to explain the poem's place and relevance in this series. If poem 21 was a decision to leave love and love poetry and 22 a rejection of 21, 23 displays the next stage wherein the poet has indeed resumed love poetry but is patently on the verge of breaking off again, though not yet fully resolved. Such a view, while sufficing to clarify the place of the poem on the level of external situation, still leaves us wondering what has happened to the thread of the guiding metaphor that was present in 21 and 22. Perhaps it is not totally unreasonable to see it partially in the very essence of the theme of "being lost," in the question of the relative desirability of different "residences" for different people or things.[29] In poems 21 and 22 the fundamental question was whether Propertius and Tullus were in their proper and most suitable places; here the question devolves upon Propertius' tablets: should they best reside with the poet or with some energetic businessman, *his aliquis rationem scribit avarus/ et ponit diras inter ephemeridas!* (19–20). At any rate, it is the final verse, with its emphatic geographical note, that restores us to the world of 21 and 22, *et dominum Esquiliis scribe habitare tuum* (24). Not only does the poet now opt for the desirability of the tablets' being at the Esquiline but, as the language itself shows, the emphasis is on

26 I do not consider the absence of Cynthia's name in 3.23 of any importance.

27 While I do not know any example of *detero* with erotic value, there are such instances of *tero*, e.g., Prop. 3.11.30; 3.20.6.

28 Note the illuminating parallel of 21.16 (of Cynthia) to verse 9, *qualescumque mihi semper mansere fideles.*

29 A commonplace of sorts among the ancients. Cf. Hor., *Sat.* 2.6, *Epist.* 1.11; Lucr. 3.1057–1070.

where Propertius himself now resides—and the answer must be taken in light of elegies 21 and 22: It is not in Greece; it is not in the East. Propertius remains in residence at Rome.

Finally, let us consider the last elegy of the series which is its ultimate resolution (3.24). Two devices stress the sense of finality here. First is the abrupt and intense opening, *falsa est ista tuae, mulier, fiducia formae* (1); second are the constant reminders of 1.1, which implies that, as that was a beginning, so this is an end. After some ten lines, mostly of castigation, we begin to see where we are: *haec ego non ferro, non igne coactus, et ipsa/ naufragus Aegaea vera fatebar aqua* (11–12); we are back in the world of sea-faring and shipwrecks. It is hard not to hear in this couplet (whatever its precise meaning, which is a matter of much debate)[30] an echo, both in its hint of death and in its structural form, of the final distich of this series' opening poem: *seu moriar, fato, non turpi fractus amore;/ atque erit illa mihi mortis honesta dies* (21.33–34). And, to move ahead, the poem ends with a recollection and a resolution of 3.21:

> ecce coronatae portum tetigere carinae,
>   traiectae Syrtes, ancora iacta mihi est.
> nunc demum vasto fessi resipiscimus aestu,
>   vulneraque ad sanum nunc coiere mea.
> Mens bona, si qua dea es, tua me in sacraria dono!
>   exciderant surdo tot mea vota Iovi.   (15–20)

The journey planned in 21, then delayed and postponed, has at length been accomplished: Propertius has reached harbor safely, the love affair with Cynthia is over, as is Propertius' dedication to writing love poetry about her.[31] Indeed, earlier verses here had anticipated the point of the metaphor:

> noster amor talis tribuit tibi, Cynthia, laudes:
>   versibus insignem te pudet esse meis.
> mixtam te varia laudavi saepe figura,
>   ut, quod non esses, esse putaret amor;
> et color est totiens roseo collatus Eoo,
>   cum tibi quaesitus candor in ore foret.   (3–8)

---

[30] See recently Camps, *ad loc.*; A. W. Bennett, *CP*, 64 (1969), 30–35; G. L. Koniaris, *CP*, 66 (1971), 253–258.

[31] I note additionally that *vasto aestu* (17) continues the nautical imagery, while *vulnera* (18) commonly alludes to the "wounds" of love, e.g., Prop. 2.12.12; 2.22.7. *Coronatus* (15) and *corona* are frequently found in contexts of both lovers and poets, e.g., Prop. 3.3.47; 3.1.10. For an example of *Syrtes* (16) in an erotic context, see Ov., *Rem. am.* 739.

It is relevant to observe that H. Akbar Khan, *AAHung*, 16 (1968), 253–256, has sought to explain Prop. 1.11 in terms of sea symbolism, and E. W. Leach, *YCS*, 19 (1966), 211–232, has discussed the metaphorical nature of the voyage at Prop. 1.17.

At once we discern in these verses the resolve to reject both love and erotic poetry. Each pentameter is a rejection of Propertius' poetry as reflected in the preceding hexameter.

In brief, 3.21–24 can be seen as a metaphoric drama in four acts. On one level, the movement is (1) Propertius resolves to leave Rome, (2) Propertius realizes that it is, after all, best to stay, (3) Propertius affirms explicitly that he still lives at Rome, but there are hints that a change is coming, and (4) Propertius has finally completed his journey.

Or, to translate the metaphor: (1) Propertius decides to leave Cynthia and give up erotic elegy, (2) he changes his mind and affirms that the best course is to continue his relationship with Cynthia and erotic elegy, (3) he affirms that his affair with Cynthia and elegy abides, but there are indications that the end may be in sight, and (4) Propertius resolutely proclaims his rejection of both Cynthia and love elegy.[32]

In sum, whatever other structural patterns may be discerned in Propertius' third book, it is clear from an analysis of 3.12–13 and 3.21–24 that, at the least, significant portions of this book are built on the principle of linear progression.

University of Illinois at Urbana

[32] I do not wish to enter into the question of the relation of 3.25 to 3.24, but would simply observe that 3.25 seems to me a kind of summary epilogue rather than a part of the sequence of poems beginning at 3.21. It is an explicit farewell that serves, so to speak, as a seal on the Book. It is, however, fascinating to consider, as Professor Bright points out to me, that 3.24 and 3.25 contain together 38 lines, which suggests that the pair may be a counterweight to 1.1 (38 lines) and as such an inseparable poetic couple. The implications could be significant and far-reaching. For discussions of 3.24 and 3.25, see L. Alfonsi, *Orpheus*, 3 (1956), 59–65; E. Burck, *Hermes*, 87 (1959), 191–211.

14

Juvenal's Fifteenth Satire

SIGMUND C. FREDERICKS

Juvenal's Fifteenth Satire is an unpopular and misunderstood poem, largely because it has been studied too often in order to document the satirist's alleged exile in Egypt.[1] The merits of the satire therefore remain unexamined even though it is his last complete poem. My reconsideration will discuss two unexplored characteristics of the poem: first, the vocabulary carefully elaborated by Juvenal and, second, the structure of the satire, which develops a paradox because the satirist begins by stating that men should not act like animals but ends by using the natural sociability of animals as a standard to criticize human depravity. In this satire as in his earliest works, Juvenal's wit and literary artistry will resist a one-dimensional interpretation which treats a complex, ambiguous poem as a moral tract or rhetorical declamation on a conventional theme. When Juvenal moralizes, we must be prepared for irony and paradox; and when

[1] The exile is mentioned explicitly in the manuscript *vitae*, but the best scholars are now disposed to believe that they do not provide authentic, independent biographical data about Juvenal. They suggest that the events described in them are based partly on conjecture from the contents of the satires themselves and partly on *topoi* from the biographical literary tradition established by Suetonius. See P. Wessner, *Scholia in Iuvenalem Vetustiora* (Leipzig, 1931; *BT*), XXXVI, who insists that the *vitae* are historically unacceptable and most likely originated as a fiction of a *homo semidoctus*. G. Brugnoli, "Vita Iuvenalis," *Studi Urbinati*, 37 (1963), 5–14, though casting doubt on every other event mentioned in the *vitae*, does accept the notice of the exile as perhaps the single event related which antedates the formation of the scholiastic tradition on Juvenal, although even this notice was expanded on the basis of references in the Fifteenth Satire (27–28 and 44–46) as well as *Sat.*, 4.38. However, U. Knoche, *Die römische Satire* (Göttingen, 1971[3]), 91, is more extreme and interprets the exile as a legend developed in the second half of the fifth century. His views are supported by M. Coffey, "Juvenal 1941–1961," *Lustrum*, 8 (1963), 169–170, who also remarks that literary form and satiric conventions may explain much of the content of the satires without references to biographical motives or social context. R. Syme, *Tacitus* (2 vols., Oxford, 1958), 499, note 9, assesses Juvenal's exile as "a fictitious construction."

he resorts to rhetorical commonplaces, we must look for creative adaptation.

A successful interpretation of the poem must begin by reading the satire in its entirety. For example, in his brief but useful chapter Gilbert Highet[2] overemphasizes the personal element, the historicity, and the topicality of the satire, because there is much more to the poem than the historical event mentioned in lines 33–92. Similarly, the commentaries, although they regard the satire as a conventional attack against "Egyptian cannibalism," put the stress on "Egyptian" and tend to view the satire as a document which is meant to criticize the horrible practice of the Egyptians from the ordinary Roman point of view.[3] This interpretation ignores Juvenal's positive exhortation to *humanitas* in the later part of the satire. Other more limited views of the poem have been offered which either read the satire as an instance of a rhetorical *locus de crudelitate*,[4] or interpret it as a parody of aretalogy.[5]

My own reading of the satire follows a recent suggestion by W. S. Anderson that the poem modulates between a vice labelled as *ira*, which is attacked in the first half (1–92), and the virtue, *humanitas*, which is espoused as an ideal in the second half.[6] This view has the advantage of accounting for the second half of the satire as integral to the work. Here Juvenal goes beyond the incident of Egyptian cannibalism, generalizes his attack against the practice, and delivers a protreptic argument for *humanitas*. In the light of the second half, then, the real thesis of the first half of the satire is that cannibalism is a corrupt and malignant practice because it reduces men to the level of animals, as illustrated by recent events at Tentyra. Cannibalism is by this view more important to the overall meaning of the satire than the qualifying adjective, "Egyptian."

---

[2] *Juvenal the Satirist* (Oxford, 1954), 149–153 and notes, 284–286. J. Lindsay, *Daily Life in Ancient Egypt* (London, 1963), 109–121, offers a credulous and confused attempt at a biographical interpretation of the satire.

[3] See, e.g., the commentaries of J. E. B. Mayor (2 vols., London, 1880–1881[2]), 355–356; L. Friedlaender (Leipzig, 1895), 574; J. D. Duff (Cambridge, 1898; newly edited by M. Coffey, 1970, with introduction), 434–435.

[4] J. De Decker, *Juvenalis Declamans* (Ghent, 1913), 50–54.

[5] R. Reitzenstein, *Hellenistische Wundererzählungen* (Leipzig, 1906), 27–29, followed recently by E. C. Witke, "Juvenal III: An Eclogue for the Urban Poor," *Hermes*, 90 (1962), 247, note 2. Witke seems unaware that Reitzenstein was opposed long ago by P. Vollmer in *RE*, 19 (1918), 1047 (who like De Decker emphasizes the declamatory nature of the poem). Reitzenstein's argument has again been revived by A. Scobie, *More Essays on the Ancient Romance and its Heritage* (Meisenheim am Glan, 1973; *Beiträge zur klassischen Philologie*, 46), 53–63. Characteristically the first thirteen lines of the poem are ignored, and an inadequate account is given of the entire second half of the poem (93–174).

[6] "The Programs of Juvenal's Later Books," *CP*, 57 (1962), 151 and note 12.

The poem begins with a rhetorical question, *quis nescit?* which implies that the entire satire is to be construed as an elaborate response to a question whose answer ought to be common knowledge. The question also reveals Juvenal's attitude of cynicism, because he assumes everyone must be aware of Egyptian religious insanity. From the outset he rhetorically prejudices the case with the phrase *demens Aegyptos*.

Juvenal exhibits his artistry at its best in the first thirteen lines, a brilliant prologue which establishes a grotesque scene and tone for the entire poem (particularly grotesque is the description of the truncated statue of Memnon at Thebes in lines 5–6). First he lists the exotic animals that the Egyptians worship. These (*portenta*, 2) include the crocodile, ibis, monkey, cat, fish, dog, sheep, and goat. But, as the satirist says in a typically radical generalization, not one soul worships Diana (*nemo Dianam*, 8), a goddess who is notably anthropomorphic and normal in contrast to the Egyptian theriomorphic deities.[7] She also possesses a proper name, which is not true of the strange animal species that Juvenal presents as gods of the Egyptians. In some instances the satirist has reduced well-known Egyptian theriomorphic divinities to the class of beasts, no longer gods with animal features and distinctive names and characteristics, like Thoth, Osiris, and Anubis. In other cases he has deliberately exaggerated certain Egyptian dietary taboos and promoted these animals also to a divine level. Finally, he adds two humble garden vegetables (*porrum et caepe*, 9) and concludes that the Egyptians must be a holy race indeed to be able to pick their gods from their own gardens! Juvenal has thus debased the objects of Egyptian piety, has transformed the gods into animals and vegetables, and has converted Egyptian religion into something grotesque. The prologue is immediate evidence that Juvenal's work is truly satire, a poetry which distorts and exaggerates the facts for effect, and not accurate anthropology.[8]

Further, Juvenal makes use of religious terminology: *portenta, colat*, and *adorat* (2), *pavet* (3), *effigies* and *sacri* (4), *venerantur* (8), *nefas violare* (9), *sanctas* (10), *numina* (11), *nefas* (12). Much of the wit in the opening passage of the satire lies in the contradiction between the religious language and bizarre animals and lowly vegetables which are the objects of reverence.

---

[7] Duff, on line 8, suggests a contrast between the dog as an animal sacred to the Egyptians and Diana as mistress of the hunt at whose altars dogs were often sacrificed.

[8] The references to this satire in J. G. Griffiths, *Plutarch's De Iside et Osiride* (Cambridge, 1970), support this view. Especially see 272, where the author remarks that the native evidence does not confirm that Egyptians abstained in general from animal flesh; the suggestion is in fact that only in certain places did there exist an animal taboo and this for special reasons, in a limited sense, and for a limited group. For onions as an object of religious veneration, see *op. cit.*, 280, though this did not always mean dietary abstinence.

With *carnibus humanis vesci licet* (13) the prologue concludes rudely and abruptly, and the last clause marks a change in direction. Yet the first five words in line 9 (*porrum et caepe nefas violare*) introduce three parallel contrasts: between vegetables and human beings (the wrong ones being eaten), between *violare* and *vesci* (each applied to the wrong object), and between *nefas* and *licet*. The satirist here laconically underscores the ridiculous contradiction inherent in "sacred animals and vegetables."

The mention of cannibalism is a proper climax to this opening passage since from the very earliest references in Greek literature it was considered a fundamental distinction of man from the animals that he did not practice cannibalism.[9] Hesiod, an author to whom Juvenal often refers, makes the explicit statement that man is a species which does not eat members of its own kind, whereas the rest of animal creation does (*Works and Days*, 276–281). Like their worship of beasts, cannibalism shows that the Egyptians have given up their humanity.

Juvenal does not maintain the high style and emotional intensity of his indignant attack against the Egyptians, but turns (13–26) to mythological allusion, and whimsically makes reference to the banquet of Alcinous in *Odyssey* 7 and 8. In Juvenal's version, Ulysses' stories of Polyphemus and the Laestrygonians are rejected because cannibalism is so monstrous a crime that the hero must have made it up; it is far easier to accept the other outrageous stories, like those of Scylla, Charybdis, Aeolus' winds, and Circe. The continuity between these lines and the opening of the satire

---

[9] See H. D. Rankin, "'Eating People is Right': Petronius 141 and a *Topos*," *Hermes*, 97 (1969), 382–383, for the most ancient references to cannibalism; especially *Iliad* 22.346–347, where Achilles claims he could eat Hector raw and this declaration simply indicates that wrath has carried the hero outside of normal humanity, and *Odyssey* 9, where the cannibalism of the Cyclopes is intimately connected with their lawlessness and godlessness.

As late as Diodorus Siculus (1.14.1 and 1.90.1), the view remains that man is a progressive species and does not eat his fellows which in itself constitutes one source of his superiority over the animals. For a list of passages in Greek literature and philosophy on the theme, see W. K. C. Guthrie, *In the Beginning* (Ithaca, N.Y., 1957), 95 and 142–143, note 1; for cannibalism in Diodorus' myth of progress, see E. A. Havelock, *The Liberal Temper in Greek Politics* (New Haven, 1957), 83–89.

One can also trace the theme as a *topos* in Greek anthropological and geographical writers, beginning with Herodotus (4.18 and 106); for these, see the passages discussed in Tomaschek's article, "Androphagoi," in *RE*, 2 (1894), 2168–2169. In these references cannibalism suggests barbarian men who are lawless and primitive, hence not fully human, as opposed to the fully civilized humanity of the Greek city-states (as, e.g., Aristotle, *Politics*, 1338b, 20–30, who argues that true manly courage is not inculcated by animal ferocity).

is also clear, despite the shift in both content and mood. The first word, *attonito*, "thunderstruck," is the perfect word to mark the reaction of a sane and sober man who is the opposite of the lawless, godless, cannibalistic Cyclopes and Laestrygonians. Alcinous is therefore the prototype of the courteous and humane host, and his affable, civilized reception of Odysseus with a banquet in the *Odyssey* is the exact contrary of the savagely cannibalistic reception given by Polyphemus in Book 9.[10] Homer's Alcinous properly serves Juvenal as inspiration for a model of human behavior which is the reverse of the bestial conduct of the Egyptians.

Alcinous' refusal to believe must also be interpreted both in the context of the entire satire and especially in the light of the opening phrase of the satire, *quis nescit*. Juvenal has deliberately juxtaposed contemporary life and society, where perverted horrors are commonplace, with the world of epic myth, a nobler age of mankind in which even the thought of such perverted actions was outrageous. Juvenal represents contemporary man in his cynical rhetorical question, *quis nescit?*; Alcinous, in his astonishment, the lost age of mythical virtue. Juvenal will use myths for this purpose again in the satire, a technique he had exploited effectively before in the Sixth and Thirteenth Satires.[11] The passage also anticipates the major event of the poem, the act of cannibalism at Tentyra, for the banquet of Alcinous is indeed a *cena* (14), a humane and noble one, contrasted with the drunken *cena* (41) at Tentyra.

So far the satirist has stated his case generally. Juvenal completes the first half of the satire (27–92) with a concrete and vivid illustration of Egyptian religious insanity, which is one of his finest examples of *enargeia*. We should not forget that Juvenal intends this passage to be a particular instance of a more general truth, and we must not regard its narration as the essence of the satire. However, there is more poetry in the narrative itself than has been generally recognized, and this helps to integrate the passage into the structure of the entire satire.

Juvenal in a brief introduction (27–32) insists that the Egyptians have

---

[10] For Alcinous and his exceptionally civilized Phaeacians as the antitheses of the man-eating and primitive Cyclopes and Laestrygonians, see G. S. Kirk, *Myth: Its Meaning and Functions in Ancient and Other Cultures* (Cambridge and Berkeley, 1971; Sather Classical Lectures, 40), 162–171. For the significance of Alcinous in the *Odyssey* see also W. Jaeger, *Paideia*, trans. G. Highet (3 vols., Oxford, 1945²), vol. 1, 20; and M. I. Finley, *The World of Odysseus* (New York, 1965²), 92–93 and 105–107.

[11] I agree with M. Morford's insistence that in the Sixth (1–20) and Thirteenth (38–59) the satirist's use of mythology serves a dual function: it not only criticizes the corruption of present times but also naive moralizers who live with outdated attitudes. See "Juvenal's Thirteenth Satire," *AJP*, 94 (1973), 27–28 and note 6.

committed such an act of cannibalism (*gesta*, 28)—recently in the consulship of Iuncus (A.D. 127)[12]—an act so terrible that it outstrips the worst imaginings of reasonable men (*miranda*, 27) and is more horrible than the events that are described in that most brutal and explicitly violent literary form, tragedy. Juvenal has chosen his words very carefully. There is a deliberate tension between *gesta* and *miranda*, reminding us that this preternatural and wondrous act was actually committed by an entire populace. We remain, therefore, in Juvenal's cynical universe where the crimes of one race of contemporary mankind—no matter how commonplace their vices are from one point of view (*quis nescit?*)—are more horrible and incredible than the primitive nastiness related in the ancient myths. The satirist even insists that the crime *committed* by the Egyptian populace outdoes what was permitted by other peoples to be *portrayed* in tragedy.

This passage contains two echoes of Juvenal's own earlier satires. The reference to the horrors narrated in tragedy reminds us of the close of the Sixth Satire (634–661) where Juvenal insists that the crimes of contemporary women have taken on the dimension of tragic myth. The epilogue in the Sixth therefore breaks down the distinction between myth and contemporary reality (as Mark Morford has recently noticed),[13] whereas the Fifteenth heightens it. On the other hand, the mention of Pyrrha in line 30 recalls the First Satire (81–86), but while the passage in the earlier poem definitely suggests a temporal continuity in human affairs (and in human vices) from the time of the Flood to the present age, the line in the Fifteenth implies that contemporary life (*nostro aevo*, 31–32) can furnish examples of vice that are worse than the most outrageously bloodthirsty events of mythology and literature.

The description of the event at Tentyra as *dira feritas* (32) is a key expression and the focal point of the first half of the satire. *Dira*, a word of religious significance often associated with portents and other exceptional phenomena,[14] here looks back to *portenta* (2) and the other religious terms clustered in the opening passage. The preternatural, even monstrous, quality of Egyptian religion is thereby reinforced. *Feritas* looks forward to the act of cannibalism, viewed as pathology, to imply that the Egyptians

---

[12] The date of A.D. 127 for Iuncus' consulship was established by B. Borghesi, "Intorno all' età di Giovenale," *Oeuvres Complètes* 5 (Paris, 1869), 49–76. More recent scholarship has tended only to confirm it. See, e.g., Coffey, 169; Knoche, 90; Syme, 775 (all cited above, note 1).

[13] "A Note on Juvenal 6.627–661," *CP*, 67 (1972), 198.

[14] See *TLL*, s.v. "*dirus*" in its older, stricter usage (vol. 5, pars 1, cols. 1268–1270).

who behave like animals are reduced to the level of the beasts by their savagery.[15]

The poet then introduces the story of Ombi and Tentyra (33–44) and assures us that the rivalry between the two cities (*vetus atque antiqua simultas,* 33) is not eveh of the human order because he characterizes it hyperbolically as *immortale odium* (34). Juvenal once again has deliberately clustered his terms to indicate that this *simultas* is a horrible and inhuman pathology. He uses the metaphorical phrase, *numquam sanabile vulnus* (34), to describe it, but a series of other terms reinforces it: *ardet,* 35; *summus furor,* 35–36; *odit,* 37; and *inimicorum,* 40—a language of hatred and enmity that contrasts strongly with the satirist's description of the inhabitants of the two cities as *finitimos* (33) and *vicinorum* (36). In addition, Juvenal makes no distinction between the two cities when it comes to this *odium; utrimque* (35) and *uterque locus* (37) make that certain. Consequently, although Tentyra was the special cult center of Hathor, goddess of love and gaiety, it is no less guilty of embittered and exclusive religious passions than Ombi, the religious center of Set, god of darkness, and the more aggressive city in Juvenal's account.

The satirist establishes a second set of terms in opposition to the vocabulary of *odium* when he sets the scene at Tentyra's seven-day religious festival and describes it as a public banquet for its animal god. The scene is, in brief, a *cena: tempore festo,* 38; *laetum hilaremque diem* and *magnae gaudia cenae,* 41; *positis ad templa et compita mensis,* 42; and *pervigilique toro,* 43. Here we have a feast, a religious one, where men ought to enjoy pleasurable company and civilized affection. Yet Juvenal interlaces the passage with words for hostility and impending conflict so that the festive atmosphere is perverted by horror and cruelty.

Juvenal again announces his own personal attitude toward these events (44–46):

---

[15] See *TLL,* s.v. *"feritas," "ferus,"* and *"fera."* In its narrow sense, when applied to men, *feritas* concerns habits and characteristics that belong by nature to beasts; in a wider sense the term refers (as it also does when applied to animals) to concepts like *vehementia, atrocitas, crudelitas,* and *rabies.* See vol. 6, pars 1, col. 602, line 24; and col. 519, lines 10–11 and 71–73, respectively.

For Seneca's *De ira* as the philosophical background to Juvenal's literary presentations of emotional pathologies in this and other satires, see W. S. Anderson, "Anger in Juvenal and Seneca," *UCPCPh,* 19 (1964), especially the section entitled "The Angry Man," 160–165, where the author refers to Seneca's refutation of *ira* as a virtue (163): "Similarly, when (his) *adversarius* invokes spirited beasts such as lions to exemplify the nobility of wrath, Seneca lets him convict himself. Lions and wolves do possess *feritas* and *rabies* that can be considered as analogous to *ira,* but only because *ira* itself debases Man to the level of the beasts (cf. *De ira,* 2.16)."

horrida sane
Aegyptos, sed luxuria, quantum ipse notavi,
barbara famoso non cedit turba Canopo.

In the first place, this transitional passage suggests a poetic reminiscence of earlier views of Canopus in the Sixth Satire (83–84), where Eppia the wife of a senator has committed an act so shameful in running off with a gladiator that even Canopus, ill-famed though it is, can condemn the morals of Roman women. In the second place, we should consider these lines in the light of what the satirist had already said about the most notorious product of Canopus, Domitian's pretorian prefect, Crispinus. As early as the First Satire (26–29), he is portrayed as an outrageous example of the vice of *luxuria*; in the Fourth (1–33), his *luxuria* in paying an inordinately large amount for a fish to grace his table is an effective prelude to Juvenal's later attack on the Emperor in precisely the same matter of a large fish. At the rhombus-council the satirist again has Crispinus parade his *luxuria* (108–109):

et matutino sudans Crispinus amomo
quantum vix redolent duo funera, . . .

Therefore, the reference to Egyptian *luxuria* echoes the earlier satires of Juvenal where Canopus served as a typical example of the vice.[16]

The phrase, *quantum ipse notavi*, creates a different problem. Since the time of Friedlaender's commentary, *quantum* has been commonly interpreted to mean "as." The lines are then rendered "as I myself have noticed"—which naturally suggests that the satirist had had personal experience of the Egyptians; and this in turn might serve to confirm the notice in the *vitae* that Juvenal had spent time in Egypt as an exile.[17] However, if *quantum* can possess its original, more usual, and classical meaning "as much as," the entire phrase would suggest a limitation in the satirist's experience: "as much as I myself have noted." I propose that we not emphasize the significance of the phrase in order to have it add an element of topicality to the satire or furnish a tempting autobiographical

---

[16] Cf. Seneca, *Epistulae Morales*, 51.3, for Canopus, like Baiae, as *deversorium vitiorum*.

[17] Friedlaender, on line 45, following Müller, translates *quantum* as "*was*" or "*wie*," but his major witnesses are Apuleius, the *Historia Augusta*, Augustine, and other writers who are even later. In this interpretation of *quantum* he has been followed by Duff, *loc. cit.*, and most recently by P. Green in his English translation (Penguin Books, 1967), 290, n. 10.

For the usual classical sense of the adverb, *quantum*, in a limiting sense, see the list of passages from Terence in S. Ashmore, *The Comedies of Terence* (New York, 1908), on *Andria*, 207; confirmed by Lewis and Short, s.v. "*quantus*," and Forcellini, s.v. "*quantus*," No. 31. The Loeb translator, Ramsay, renders the Juvenalian phrase, "so far as I myself have noted." This is preferable to Friedlaender's forced and artificial interpretation.

reference in a poet who otherwise tells us little about himself. The phrase does not necessarily mean that Juvenal traveled to Egypt to acquire knowledge of Egyptian vice. The satirist states a commonplace: Canopus is infamous (*famoso*) and—to the best of his knowledge—the rest of the Egyptians are no better. Using the passage in the satire to substantiate the legend of the exile mentioned in the *vitae* improperly reverses the logic of interpretation because the theory of his exile probably originated in these lines of the satire.[18]

But beyond the issue of Juvenal's autobiographical remark, these lines are important to the poetry of the satire because of the paradoxical way in which the adjective *horrida* and the noun *luxuria* are equally applicable to the Egyptians. The only other passage in Juvenal where *horrida* is applied to a nation is in the Eighth Satire (116), where the satirist advises his addressee, Ponticus, that he may properly despise the Greeks and other effeminate and unmilitary races if he becomes governor of a province, but that *horrida Hispania*, a martial and vigorous land, should be avoided. The word *horrida* well describes a barbarian region like Spain, one of whose tribes is contrasted with the Egyptians in the second half of the Fifteenth, but which is so primitive that the term *luxuria* is inapplicable. Juvenal's comment here at 44–46 anticipates the distinction he later makes betwen the Egyptians as cannibals and other barbarians as cannibals: the former alone display *luxuria*.

Luxuria is readily associated with drunkenness, as it was previously in the Sixth Satire (300–313), and the description of the stupor of the Tentyrans (47–50) serves as a transition. At this point the *cena* is transformed completely into a *rixa* (51–62), which the satirist depicts as a *bellum* using military language: *sonare*, 51; *tuba*, 52; *clamore, concurritur,* and *teli*, 53; *volnere*, 54; *certamine*, 55; *agmina*, 56; *exercere acies*, 60; *turbae*, 61; and *impetus*, 62. This is, in exaggerated terms, a battle that brings to fully developed form the earlier identification of hatred as a *volnus: paucae sine volnere malae*, 54; *nulli . . . nasus integer*, 55–56; *voltus dimidios*, 56–57; *alias facies*, 57; *hiantia ruptis ossa genis*, 57–58; and *plenos oculorum sanguine pugnos*, 58. Juvenal here succeeds perfectly in giving us a vivid physical portrayal of pathological emotion (the latter also set forth, in the terms *odium*, 51, *animis ardentibus*, 52, and *saevit*, 54).

Then he turns again to the world of myth (65–68) for a comparison and imitates a Homeric formula which describes one of the heroes picking up a

[18] See above, note 1. Scobie (above, note 5), 54, also rejects Friedlaender's autobiographical interpretation of *quantum ipse notavi*, but further notes, 59, how Juvenal describes his own account of the act of cannibalism as a *fabula* in line 72, which suggests a tongue-in-cheek attitude toward the event.

great stone to hurl at his enemies, a feat that not two men could *now* (in the time of the narrator) perform.[19] But Juvenal has also expanded the formula (69–70):

nam genus hoc vivo iam decrescebat Homero,
terra malos homines nunc educat atque pusillos;

The satirist is comparing the Egyptians of his day to the heroes of the *Iliad* in an unfavorable light, but generalizing (line 70 refers to all contemporary men, not just to the Egyptians), Juvenal also says mankind has degenerated a long way from Homer's own time.[20] Alluding to Hesiod's description of his own times as an Iron Age (*Works and Days*, 174–201), Juvenal had employed an analogous myth of human degeneration in the programmatic Thirteenth Satire (28–30) where he referred to the contemporary world, satirically and hyperbolically, as a *nona aetas*, an age so bad that there was no metal base enough to describe it.[21]

The satirist now climaxes the scene of battle between the two towns at the central moment in the satire (72–92): the Tentyrans are forced into flight, one unfortunate citizen slips and falls in his frenzy to escape, the Ombians tear him limb from limb and devour him on the spot. At once comical and horrible,[22] the episode sums up *ieiunum odium* (51): the Ombians' hatred is literally starved. The cannibalistic banquet is described with words like *voluptatem* (90) and *gustat* (92), and the victim has been transformed into victuals (*hac carne*, 88). The picture of those Ombians who were too slow to get any of the meat scraping the ground with their fingers for the last drops of blood is a vivid illustration of the adjective *ieiunum*. Figuratively, the act of cannibalism is the culmination of insane anger, and it proves that the Egyptians have abandoned their humanity.

For good reasons, then, Juvenal inserts another allusion to myth (84–87), the story of Prometheus' theft of fire from the gods on behalf of mankind. Juvenal rejoices because fire, the use of which distinguishes men

19 This formula appears in the *Iliad* at 5.302–304 (Diomedes) and 20.285–287 (Aeneas); with variation at 12.381–383 (Ajax) and 12.445–449 (Hector). For the Vergilian imitation which refers to Turnus, see *Aeneid*, 12.896–900.

20 I also note that *hoc genus* in line 69 refers generally to "the race of man" (translating with Ramsay in the Loeb); confirmed in Mayor's comment on line 70.

21 See my earlier study, "Calvinus in Juvenal's Thirteenth Satire," *Arethusa*, 4 (1971), 220 and 229, note 8.

22 Twice in this satire Juvenal seems to propose that our reaction to evil should maintain a paradoxical balance between anger and laughter. In line 15 he speaks of *bilem aut risum* as a listener's choice of reactions to Ulysses' stories of cannibalism. At line 71 he says that god himself *ridet et odit* when he views the Egyptians, men who are simultaneously evil and puny (*malos atque pusillos*, 70). Throughout the satire, Juvenal's own narrative moves back and forth between the two responses to correspond to what he says in these two quasi-programmatic lines.

from the beasts according to the myth, was not polluted by the Egyptians since they ate their victim raw! This paradox is a perfect way of topping off the first half of the satire and of reinforcing the conclusion to be drawn from the practice of cannibalism: these Egyptians are inhuman. The cumulative effect of Juvenal's imagery and mythological references is to identify the Egyptians with beasts, and this is the overall consequence of the first half of the satire.

At line 93, Juvenal's argument begins to reflect on itself, and while I certainly agree with Highet[23] that the second half of the satire is to be divided into two parts, 93–131 and 131–174, I would go one step further and also suggest that 93–131 are closely related to 33–92 and 131–174 must be linked to 1–32. Consequently, the opening and closing passages of the satire are related.

When he refers to the Celtiberian Vascones (93–106), Juvenal keeps to the theme of the previous section, cannibalism, but he introduces several obvious and important differences (res diversa, 94). To begin with, this passage contrasts the "active" cannibalism of the Egyptians with the "passive" cannibalism of the Vascones who were reduced by a siege to eating their own dead. This latter type of cannibalism is mentioned, for example, in Plutarch's Lucullus (11), where Mithridates' troops are described as forced into this practice in the war against Cyzicus, and in Pseudo-Quintilian's twelfth declamation, Cadaveribus Pasti, in which a legate in command of the grain supply is supposed to defend himself against the charge that he was derelict in his duty and caused an entire town to devour corpses in order to survive. Although a distinction between these types of cannibalism might be sufficient for a moral tract, Juvenal's poem is not just one-dimensional moral philosophy, and so he makes other contrasts which relate to the themes and language established earlier in the satire.

The cannibalism takes place as a last resort during a siege in a real war between two martial peoples, yet even their own enemies felt pity for their misfortunes (hostibus ipsis . . . miserantibus, 100–101). Juvenal is even more explicit: the gods themselves (103) and the dead who were devoured (105) could forgive them. And this must contrast with the Egyptian towns who expressed only odium toward each other.

Juvenal does not abandon the vocabulary of anger which he had used so effectively to characterize the Egyptians; he transforms it. He speaks of invidia (95), but it is an impersonal envy due to misfortune and war, and he uses the expression vacui ventris furor (100), meaning that it was real physical starvation that compelled the horrible, crazed cannibalism of the

23 Above (note 2), 285, note 2.

Vascones. In the case of the Egyptians, bestial and pathological fury led to cannibalism since starvation was only a metaphor for inhuman passions (*ieiunum odium*, 51; reiterated at line 131, *similes ira atque fames*). So Juvenal employs the key phrase *dira egestas* (96) for the Vascones to correspond to his earlier description of Egyptian anger as *dira feritas* in line 32.

Juvenal marshals every poetic resource to reinforce the ideas of *invidia fortunae* (95) and *dira egestas* (96), because these barbarian tribesmen have been reduced *physically* in every possible way. Terms like *pallorem, maciem,* or *tenuis artus* (101) or *lacerabant* (102) vividly express how these men were physically reduced by their sufferings. This contrasts with the normal physical puniness of the Egyptians, a theme stated in lines 126–128:

> hac saevit rabie inbelle et inutile volgus,
> parvula fictilibus solitum dare vela phaselis
> et brevibus pictae remis incumbere testae.

This is a brilliant synecdoche, scornfully characterizing the pettiness of the Egyptians by means of their tiny earthenware craft fitted out with little sails and oars, and it should be contrasted with the two preceding lines where various barbarian nations (not just those of Spain) are described with the terms *terribiles, truces,* and *immanes.*

Another contrast is suggested by line 104: *ventribus . . . dira atque immania passis*, which describes how the tribesmen have suffered. But Juvenal insists that the Egyptians have committed terrible acts: *detestabile monstrum audere* (121–122; restated with *monstra* in line 172 which refers again to the act of cannibalism at Tentyra).[24] This clarifies Juvenal's argument that the barbarians of Spain can be pardoned since they passively endured to commit a monstrous act when they were forced to cannibalism, while the Egyptians actively committed a monstrous crime.

With the phrase *mollissima corda* in line 131 we reach the final section of the satire and the final transformation of Juvenal's argument. He makes a

---

[24] For Juvenal's use of *monstrum* (altogether thirteen times in the satires), see J. R. C. Martyn, "A New Approach to Juvenal's First *Satire*," *Antichthon*, 4 (1970), 61, note 31: four times for sexual perversion (2.122, 143; 6.286; 9.38); twice for monstrous individuals (4.2, 115); twice for murderesses (6.645, 647); twice for cannibalism (15.121, 172); and once for unnatural honesty (13.65). Martyn categorizes these eleven references as "unnatural perversions of *human* behavior." The two remaining occurrences (4.45 and 14.283) refer clearly to real "monsters."

I would, however, go beyond the literal meaning of the word, and I would interpret it here in the light of other words that Juvenal uses for the preternaturally horrible religion of the Egyptians (*portenta*, 2) as well as his description of their passions as *dira feritas* (32). The overall idea of "preternatural monstrousness" encompasses the monstrous objects of their religious passions, their pathological anger, and the actual monstrous act of cannibalism.

positive plea for pity and fellow-feeling which represent the best human emotion (*optima sensus*, 133) and which define us as *men* and distinguish us from the animals (142–143). In contrast to *ira* and kindred terms he used earlier, Juvenal now develops another set of words: *lacrimas*, 133; *plorare*, 134; *fletu*, 136; and *gemimus*, 138. This not only generalizes what was said earlier for the particular instance of the Vascones in lines 93–106, but twice Juvenal states explicitly that *natura* itself (132 and 138) justifies his argument that pity is fundamental to human nature. Unlike anger, which is a mutually exclusive and divisive emotion, *lacrimae* express a principle of universal inclusion, something which belongs to all men as part of their natural being and which can be shared by all: *quis enim bonus . . . ulla aliena sibi credit mala?* (140–142).

In lines 143–147, Juvenal describes man as a creature who raises his face to the heavens while animals look at the ground. This seems to be a reminiscence of Ovid's story of Prometheus' creation of man (*Met.*, 1.76–88), which makes the same distinction between man and the rest of the animals.[25] C. P. Segal has made an interesting observation on the Ovidian passage which can shed light on its parallel in Juvenal. Segal remarks that it "presents an essentially Stoic view of man as *sanctius animal* formed in the image of the all-ruling gods, standing erect and beholding the heavens and the stars (I, 76–88). Yet the ensuing narrative of the Four Ages dwells not on man's kinship with the divine, but rather on his capacity for evil and violence."[26] The statement can be applied also to this satire, because Juvenal develops the same contrast between the best and worst in man's capabilities, although the negative side is emphasized in most of the satire.

In subsequent lines (147–158), Juvenal represents the human race as having a community of shared interests based on a sense of universal fellow-feeling (*mutuus adfectus*, 149–150). Here the satirist's portrayal of how men originally joined together, built homes and cities, and aided one another in war and peace is in accord with traditional views in Graeco-Roman culture:

> The standard set by the Greeks for the true man varied to some extent according to the point of view of the thinker, but always, with one notable

[25] The connection between the two passages has been noticed by G. Highet, "Juvenal's Bookcase," *AJP*, 72 (1951), 385, and by E. Thomas, "Ovidian Echoes in Juvenal," in N. I. Herescu, *Ovidiana* (Paris, 1958), 508. In a later article, "Some Aspects of Ovidian Influence on Juvenal," *Orpheus*, 7 (1960), 35, Thomas has commented that Juvenal's debt to Ovid in choice of subject-matter, theme, and philosophy becomes more marked from the Tenth Satire onwards.

[26] "Myth and Philosophy in the *Metamorphoses*: Ovid's Augustanism and the Augustan Conclusion of Book XV," *AJP*, 90 (1969), 262.

exception (the Cynics), it involved the idea that a man really worthy of the name is one fitted to be a member of human society and play his part in the life of the community. Homer's Cyclops, Protagoras' "misanthrope," and Aristotle's "cityless" man all stand outside the true human pattern because they are incapable of social and political association with normal men.[27]

Lines 149–158 accumulate examples of *concordia*. As a definition of man this *concordia* is also the exact contrary of *odium*, but Juvenal goes beyond literary and philosophical commonplaces through his emphasis on *lacrimae* as a concrete, physical anticipation of the more abstract and intellectual *adfectus*. If irrational anger turns men into beasts, it is reasonable for the satirist to look upon the *sensus* (146)[28] the gods gave us at our creation as our special way of identifying ourselves with the gods, instead of with the beasts as the Egyptians did.

At lines 159–164 Juvenal's poem achieves a humorous contradiction when he defends the ideals of *concordia* and *communitas* with an appeal to the natural nobility of the animals! Previously Juvenal had tried to argue against our identifying with animals, beginning with the catalogue of exotic beasts worshipped by the Egyptians in lines 1–13; here, using this menagerie—lions, boars, tigers, and bears—he insists that the beasts are morally superior to man in his present degraded state. He is most cynical and paradoxical when he states that serpents have a *maior concordia* than contemporary men do (159), because *concordia* ought, on the basis of the preceding lines of the poem, to be the human virtue *par excellence* and the distinguishing characteristic of the human species.

The conclusion of the satire (165–174) may be analyzed into three brief components. In the first (165–168), Juvenal alludes to the end of Saturn's Golden Age when men committed a primeval crime by forging weapons.[29] Even war is too little (*parum*, 166) for the Egyptians, and they must go one step further in their degeneracy. In his second comment (169–171), Juvenal returns specifically to the act of Egyptian cannibalism not mentioned since line 131 because he intended to present a contrasting view of human nature. Again the connection is made between *ira* as an illegitimate

[27] H. C. Baldry, *The Unity of Mankind in Greek Thought* (Cambridge, 1965), 202, a passage which also summarizes what Roman thought adapted from the Greek. *Concordia* is an equivalent of the Greek *homonoia* (cf. *op. cit.*, 154), whereas *humanitas*—a term that Juvenal does not use—translates the Greek *philanthropia* (for which cf. Jaeger [above, note 10], vol. 3, 310, note 75). Baldry further notes, 201, that Cicero (who like Juvenal also uses *genus humanum* for the species, "man") specifies "humanity" in the sense of "mankind" with the phrases *communitas* and *societas generis humani*.

[28] The word in 146 may repeat its use and meaning in line 133. Duff, on 146, comments that "*sensus* must here mean much the same as *communis sensus*, 'sympathy,'" as in 8.73, too.

[29] Vergil, *Georgics*, 2.539–540, mentions that under Saturn there were neither wars nor forged weapons, a theme restated in Ovid, *Met.*, 1.97–99.

emotion and the reduction of men to a form of food (*genus cibi*, 171, not *genus humanum* as at 132; with a reminiscence of *carnibus humanis* in 13). Finally, the third comment is the coda of the satire which reflects upon the first thirteen lines in several ways (171–174):

> quid diceret ergo
> vel quo non fugeret, si nunc haec monstra videret
> Pythagoras, cunctis animalibus abstinuit qui
> tamquam homine et ventri indulsit non omne legumen?[30]

The Pythagoras of popular lore was believed to have maintained taboos regarding both animal flesh and beans, so he is analogous to the Egyptians as they appeared in the opening passage of the satire. Yet for Pythagoras the abstentions were based on a belief that beans and animals were equal to men (*tamquam homine*), and his views therefore promoted the lower forms to higher ones; Juvenal says of the Egyptians that their practices demote higher forms (men) to lower (food).

It is significant for the structure of the entire poem that it ends as it began, with a question. This rhetorical technique must be viewed as Juvenal's means of framing the entire content of the poem,[31] so that at its conclusion the poem remains ambiguous, balanced between two contrary impulses: one in the original *quis nescit?* suggesting that corruption is a commonplace in corrupt times, and the other revealed in the human and humane morality of Alcinous and Pythagoras, for whom the only reaction to such inhuman horrors must be speechlessness or flight.

---

[30] Juvenal's Pythagoras is an allusion to what R. A. Swanson has called "Ovid's Pythagorean Essay" (*CJ*, 54 [1958–1959], 21–24) in *Met.*, 15.60–478, a passage which, it must be remarked, reflects on Ovid's creation story in *Met.* 1. W. R. Johnson, "The Problem of the Counter-classical Sensibility and its Critics," *CSCA*, 3 (1970), 138–143, has an important interpretation of Ovid's Pythagoras and his views on vegetarianism as a caricature because the legendary philosopher's morality—however much it accurately criticizes the predatory nature of man—is pathetic in the context of a depraved world. Segal (above, note 26), 287, has recognized that Ovid's purpose throughout the *Metamorphoses* was to disclaim myth as offering a picture of a better, more moral world.

[31] I borrow the idea of a "frame" technique from W. S. Anderson, "Juvenal 6: A Problem in Structure," *CP*, 51 (1956), 74: "in the conclusion (or epilogue), often hyperbolic, often, too, deprecatingly humorous, the satirist rounds off the structure by reverting to some of the ideas of the prologue as clarified in the heart of the satire." I suggest, too that *monstra* (172) is related to *portenta* (2) as discussed above, note 24.

For Juvenal's rhetorical questions throughout the satires, see De Decker (above, note 4), 177–186, whose list includes lines 1–2 but not 171–174, despite the hyperbole in *quo non fugeret* and the humorous effect produced by ending the satire with a question. As early as the Second Satire (1–3), the satirist had proposed a fantastic escape from unbearable immorality. J. Adamietz, *Untersuchungen zu Juvenal* (Wiesbaden, 1972; *Hermes Einzelschriften*, 26), 42 and note 96, has also made this thematic connection between 2.1–3 and 15.171–174.

There seems to be no answer to the satirist's paradox: mankind (not just the Egyptians; Juvenal's theme has become general by lines 131–164) can neither remain where it is, in a corrupted state inferior to the beasts, nor return to the ideal virtue of a bygone and lost age. The mythical worlds of Alcinous and Pythagoras do not seem to offer suitable models for contemporary man.[32]

Cynical common knowledge or inapplicable moral attitudes? Juvenal leaves the question and his satire unresolved, just one more example of the irony that had increasingly become the satirist's forte since the Seventh Satire and had practically become a mannerism with the Thirteenth. In its total significance, then, the poem is not simply a satire on the Egyptians or a moral tract on the commonplace theme of cannibalism or for that matter a definition of "mankind" based on the emotion of pity. With self-contained ambivalence, Juvenal's poem does seem to modulate between two possible reactions to evil in the world, outrage and astonishment on the one hand and cynical worldly wisdom on the other. In this final manifestation of his craftmanship, Juvenal offers a satire that is thoroughly structured in whole and in part, a satire that is carefully organized in terms of special vocabularies and repeated key terms, but as a moral statement the poem is anything but explicit, concluding as it does in witty self-effacement.

Indiana University

[32] See above, notes 11 and 30. Cf. D. Wiesen, "Juvenal and the Intellectuals," *Hermes* 101 (1973), 482–483, who speaks of the satirist's "simultaneous use of a double point of view" in Satires 2, 6, 7 and 13; Juvenal not only mocks the corruption of his own times but the conventional interpretations of myth and history which pictured a more virtuous world.

15

The Second Medicean Ms.
and the Text of Tacitus

From 1846 to 1951 everyone knew that codex Laurentianus LXVIII.2, commonly known as the Second Medicean of Tacitus, was the unique source of *Annales* XI–*Historiae* V, and no dictum in the *Überlieferungs-geschichte* of classical texts was more generally accepted as unquestioned orthodoxy. Heretical doubts were first aroused[1] by C. W. Mendell, who discovered in Leidensis 16.B the manuscript that unkind souls had thought a fiction imagined by Theodorus Ryckius in 1687 to lend authority to his own ingenious conjectures. Mendell's work culminated in his *Tacitus* (1957) and in the photographic reproduction of the Leidensis in the monumental series of *Codices Graeci et Latini photographice depicti* (1966).

Few were convinced by Mendell's arguments, but among the few was Erich Koestermann, who had the courage to use the Leidensis as a witness independent of the Medicean in his next editions of the *Annales* (1960) and the *Historiae* (1961). His temerity, as he wryly remarked in 1964, "animos virorum doctorum magnopere movit nec non paululum perturbavit." It brought down upon him a landslide of reviews and articles, most of them sceptical, many of them hostile, and some denunciatory. One gentleman went so far as to describe Koestermann's work as "well-intentioned idiocy,"[2] and a number of others were content to intimate as much in

---

[1] It is true that Félix Grat, *Mélanges d'archéologie et d'histoire*, XLII (1925), 31–66, argued that Vaticanus 1958 was a copy independent of the Second Medicean, but no one paid any attention to him. His subsequent publications, so far as I know, dealt chiefly with the methodology elaborated by Dom Quentin. Since it is now customary to follow fashion or indulge vanity by citing and discussing every publication conceivably relevant to the subject that one has seen or heard about, I remark that, in the interests of the reader's patience and the printer's time, I have strictly limited myself to citations that seemed to me essential to the argument.

[2] N. P. Miller, *Journal of Roman Studies*, LII (1962), 280 f.

more decorous terms. Considerable heat was generated, but not enough light for the disputants to see that Mendell had imposed on the learned world an obligation, regrettable, perhaps, but inescapable, to make a thorough collation of all the extant manuscripts of this part of Tacitus' great work and to establish, if possible, a *stemma codicum.* This task, arduous but imperative, was at last undertaken by Rudolph Hanslik, who set his doctoral candidates to work on the compilation and publication of complete collations of portions of the text. Two of these, *Historiae* II and *Annales* XI–XII, are now available.[3]

It would be premature to attempt at this time to outline, even tentatively, the interrelationship of manuscripts which show a dismaying amount of "horizontal transmission," but it may be apposite to call attention to certain aspects of the problem that I have discussed with my seminars on Tacitus and in private correspondence since 1958 and 1961 but which, so far as I know, have not yet appeared in print.

I

The Second Medicean was copied at Monte Cassino between the years 1038 and 1058,[4] and if it was not copied directly from what remained of an ancient codex in rustic capitals, there cannot have been many intermediaries between it and that unique archetype.[5] The fate of this manu-

[3] *Historiarum* liber II, adnotationibus criticis ex omnibus codicibus qui exstant haustis instruxit Ingeborg Schinsel. Wien (= *Wiener Studien,* Beiheft 3), 1971. *Annalium* libri XI–XII, . . . instruxit Horst Weiskopf. Wien (= *Wiener Studien,* Beiheft 4), 1973. Rudolf Hanslik contributed prefaces to both; see his admirably judicious and concise summary of the manuscript-tradition of all of Tacitus' works in the *Anzeiger der österreichischen Akademie,* CIV (1967), 155–162. It is not clear to me whether Kenneth Wellesley's edition of Book III of the *Historiae* (Sydney, 1972), which contains an excellent and extremely valuable historical commentary (far more useful than Heubner's), was also intended to fulfill his agreement with Hanslik and provide adequate collations for that book; it certainly does not provide them, as Wellesley would surely admit (p. 29).

[4] E. A. Lowe's fundamental study has now been reprinted in the posthumous edition of his *Palaeographical Papers, 1907–1965,* edited by Ludwig Bieler, Oxford, 1972, Vol. I, 289–302.

[5] This is still true. In my study of the First Medicean and the early history of the Tacitean corpus in *Transactions of the American Philological Association,* LXXXII (1951), 232–261, I very tentatively accepted (notes 4, 87, and 88) the orthodox view of the Second Medicean as a unique source of Books XI–XXI of the consolidated work, to which someone had given the title, *Historia Augusta.* I now think it *certain* that there was *at least* one intermediary between the ancient codex in rustic capitals and the Second Medicean. Hanslik (in the article cited above) agrees that the one copy of Tacitus to survive the Dark Age must have been a codex of the Fourth Century in *capitalis rustica.* He believes that the surviving parts of it reached Fulda and were there copied, which is quite

script during the next four centuries has been confidently determined on the basis of conjectures and inferences that we shall consider later, but we have *no* positive information about what happened to it between the time it was written and September 1427, when it was in the possession of the famous Florentine collector, Niccolò de' Niccoli, who had obtained it clandestinely as stolen property or, at least, as property of disputed ownership. That Niccolò had obtained the manuscript surreptitiously is quite clear from the letter written to him by Poggio Bracciolini, who was then in Rome and wanted to borrow it: "Cornelium Tacitum, cum venerit, observabo penes me occulte. Scio enim omnem illam cantilenam, et unde exierit, et per quem, et quis eum sibi vindicet, sed nil dubites: non exibit a me ne verbo quidem."[6] On October 21, Poggio acknowledged receipt of the manuscript in terms that permit us to identify it: "Misisti mihi . . . Cornelium Tacitum, quod est mihi gratum, at is est litteris Longobardis et maiori ex parte caducis, quod si scissem, liberassem te eo labore."[7]

Poggio's description of the manuscript as one written in the Beneventan script and with ink that had flaked off in various places, and as having

possible, even if we insist (as he does not) on an Insular intermediary between the ancient codex and the Carolingian minuscules of the First Medicean and of the lost copy from Fulda that, on this hypothesis, was sent to Monte Cassino, and became the source of the Second Medicean. Michaela Zelzer, *Wiener Studien*, LXXXVI (1973), 185–195, would transfer the honor of preserving what we have of Tacitus from Germany to Naples. I fear that at least her reliance on a reference to "Historiam Cornelii cum Omero" is illusory; as Lowe saw long ago (*Palaeographical Papers*, Vol. I, p. 292), the reference is to the Latin version of Dares Phrygius. She certainly errs in assuming that the ancient codex was in uncials and comparable to the extant manuscripts of Livy. Of the examples of misreadings that she gives, the only one that would not fit rustic capitals better than uncials is a single P/C, and this, if significant, would raise the question of transmission of the text at some point through the so-called "cursive majuscule" script, as was suggested long ago by M. L. Constans, *Comptes rendus de l'Académie des Inscriptions et Belles-Lettres*, 1927, 36–38. Miss Zelzer finds traces of "cursive majuscules" in the text of Livy: *Antidosis, Festschrift für Walther Kraus*, Graz, 1972, pp. 487–501.

[6] *Epist.* III.14 (Vol. I, pp. 212 f., in the standard edition by Thomas de Tonellis, Florentiae, 1832–1861).

[7] *Ibid.*, III.15. *Litterae Longobardae* are, of course, what we now call the Beneventan script. The humanists, naturally, did not use such terms with the precision of modern palaeography, but we now have the invaluable work of Silvia Rizzo, *Il lessico filologico degli umanisti*, Roma, 1973, based on a very extensive reading of the Humanists, and wherever possible, identification of the codices to which they refer. The references in Poggio are to Beneventan, but other Humanists occasionally call "Lombard" writing in Insular minuscules and in a cursive hand now assigned to the Fifth or Sixth Centuries. Although we deduce from the First Medicean that there must have been a copy of Tacitus in an Insular hand at Fulda in the Ninth Century, we can scarcely imagine that it came into the hands of Niccolò!

several lacunae,[8] entitles us to identify it as the Second Medicean, which, as is attested by an endorsement on it, was owned by Niccolò de' Niccoli, who left it by will to the library of San Marco, whence it eventually passed into the Medicean Library. To be sure, it is theoretically possible that more than one copy of Tacitus was made at Monte Cassino. One thinks at once of the possible analogy of the two major manuscripts of Apuleius, of which the first, cited as F in critical editions, was copied at Monte Cassino a few decades after our Second Medicean, with which it is now bound in Laurentianus LXVIII.2, while the second, known as ϕ, was copied from F around the year 1200 in Beneventan script and probably at Monte Cassino and is now Laurentianus XXIX.2.[9]

Since we have mentioned the two manuscripts of Apuleius, we may here notice in passing two facts about them that may be relevant to our own study, viz., (1) unless the editors of Apuleius[10] are grievously mistaken, one or more manuscripts now lost were copied from F, presumably at Monte Cassino, before one leaf of that manuscript was mutilated and before ϕ was copied from it, so that the portions of the text lost in the mutilation can now be supplied from the extant descendants of those copies and (2) the scribe of ϕ, when he, presumably at Monte Cassino, copied from F, which was then more than a century old, was often negligent and impatient and, as Lowe remarked, "did not hesitate to write what he did not actually see."[11] Therefore, we cannot exclude the possibility that Tacitus was similarly copied (and miscopied) at Monte Cassino.[12]

Although there may have been two Beneventan copies of Tacitus, we are surely justified in considering it highly improbable that *both* would have come into the possession of Niccolò de' Niccoli between 1427 and his death in 1437 and that one of them would have disappeared without

---

[8] *Ibid.*, III.17: "in tuo Cornelio deficiunt plures chartae variis in locis."

[9] Lowe's article is reprinted in his *Palaeographical Papers*, Vol. I, 92–98.

[10] See D. S. Robertson's preface to his edition of the *Metamorphoses* in the Budé series (1940), pp. xxxviii–liv; Robertson's conclusions are accepted by Frassinetti in his revision of Giarratano's edition in the Corpus Paravianum (1961). Neither editor considers the theoretical possibility that the later manuscripts were derived from the lost codex that was the ancestor of F rather than from F itself.

[11] Note that this scribe more or less consistently imposed his own notions of orthography (usually erroneous) on the text and frequently transposed words. Lowe identifies some of his changes as ignorant emendations rather than mistakes in reading his exemplar.

[12] The superimposed writing that on some pages of the Second Medicean restores the text where the original writing had become evanid is identified by Lowe as "thirteenth-century Cassinese characters." If this is correct, one could imagine that the need for such restorations was perceived when a copy was to be made.

leaving some trace of its existence. We may conclude, therefore, that the manuscript borrowed by Poggio was the Second Medicean.

As is well known, Poggio, unable to find a scribe who could decipher the Beneventan script and unwilling to undertake himself a task which he thought unnecessarily arduous, returned the manuscript to Niccolò without copying it, since it was not the manuscript that he had intended to borrow: "Legi olim quemdam [sc. codicem Taciti] apud vos manens litteris antiquis, nescio Coluciine esset an alterius. Illum cupio habere vel alium qui legi possit. . . . Cura ut alium habeam, si fieri potest; poteris autem, si volueris nervos intendere."[13] So far as I know, the significance of this request has not hitherto been understood.

Like all the Humanists of his time, Poggio was not an impeccable Latinist, but he was accurate and consistent in his use of tenses. He said *esset*, not *fuisset*. It follows, therefore, that he saw the manuscript, which he describes as written *litteris antiquis*, during the lifetime of Coluccio Salutati, who died in 1406, and furthermore that he saw the manuscript before the end of November 1403,[14] when he, then an obscure youth of twenty-two, left Florence armed with letters of recommendation from the influential Chancellor to seek his fortune in Rome, whence he did not return to Florence until long after the death of Salutati.

The date is of great importance. As has long been known, in the usage of the early Humanists the term *litterae antiquae* designates either (1) the Carolingian minuscule or (2) the revival of that style of writing by the Humanists, who properly disdained the Gothic and semi-Gothic hands that the late Middle Ages had called *litterae modernae*.[15] Now B. L. Ullman has shown in his fundamental study, *The Origin and Development of the Humanistic Script*,[16] that the Carolingian minuscule was revived by Poggio himself under the patronage of Coluccio Salutati, that the oldest known manuscript in the new *litterae antiquae* is a copy of Salutati's essay *De*

---

[13] *Epist.* III.15. Whether Niccolò exerted himself with success is not known.

[14] On 23 December, 1403, Salutati replied to a letter (now lost) in which Poggio announced his success in making the acquaintance of certain prominent men and, characteristically, enclosed a copy of his first collection of ancient inscriptions. Salutati's letter may be found in Vol. III, pp. 653–656, of his *Epistolario*, a cura di Francesco Novati, Roma, 1891–1911. Novati's copious notes and appendices are a mine of information about the earliest Humanists.

[15] Silvia Rizzo, *op. cit.*, 114–122.

[16] Roma, 1960; in this fundamental study Ullman notes (12–19) that Petrarch and Salutati preferred and sought Carolingian manuscripts, and complained that the contemporary Gothic and *bastarda* were ugly and hard on the eyes—a complaint with which we may certainly sympathize. It seems to have remained for Poggio to denounce the *moderna* as barbarous.

verecundia made by Poggio in 1402 or 1403, and that other scribes do not use that new style in datable manuscripts before 1405.[17]

It is obvious that if Poggio had himself copied in 1402 or 1403 the Tacitus to which he refers, he would know more about it, and if, as is not likely, he trained other scribes to write in that elegant style before he left Florence, he would in all probability have known what important commissions they had executed and for whom. We are thus forced to conclude that unless Poggio's memory was sadly at fault or he used the term *litterae antiquae* with some unparalleled meaning in 1427, long after the designation had become standard in the Humanists' vocabulary, there was extant in Florence between 1401 and 1403 a manuscript of Tacitus that had been copied between the ninth and the twelfth centuries and may well have resembled the First Medicean, which is the unique source of *Annales* I–VI.[18]

There are other indications that a manuscript of Tacitus containing *Annales* XI–*Historiae* V became known in Florence at the very end of the fourteenth century. In a letter that was probably written in 1392, Salutati lists Tacitus among the great historians whose works had perished, an "inexcusabile damnum . . . de quo quidem mecum nequeo consolari."[19] Given Salutati's known interests and the high position he held as Chancellor of Florence, we may be certain that he would have been told, had any literate Florentine known that, as we shall see later, there was a copy of Tacitus somewhere in a heap of unwanted books stacked up in some obscure lumber room of a Florentine monastery. In August 1395, however, Salutati described Tacitus as a decadent writer, "qui, licet eruditissimus foret, . . . a Livio, quem non sequendum solum historiae serie, sed imitandum eloquentia sibi proposuit, longe discessit."[20] Salutati is not given to making judgements without knowledge, and I can call to mind no ancient or Mediaeval writer whose opinion he could have been echoing.[21] I think it likely, therefore, that Salutati had either seen some

17 *Op. cit.*, 21–57, 80–82.

18 The only escape from this conclusion, it seems to me, is to posit that Poggio could have applied the designation *litterae antiquae* to some particularly clear Gothic or bastard hand, but Poggio, who was an accomplished calligrapher himself, was so proud of his revival of the Carolingian minuscule and so conscious of its elegant contrast to the scripts that he called barbarous that I cannot believe that he, of all Humanists, would have used the term so loosely.

19 *Epistolario*, Vol. II, pp. 296 f. For the date, see Novati's closely reasoned discussion in his note, pp. 289 ff.

20 Vol. III, pp. 81 f.

21 The short quotations in Orosius would surely have been an insufficient basis for this stylistic judgment. After Tacitus, who is his prime example, Salutati lists *en bloc* later writers (Suetonius, Pliny, the Scriptores Historiae Augustae, Apuleius, Macrobius)

text by Tacitus or heard a report from someone who had and in whose stylistic sense he had confidence.[22] Since Salutati does not later mention Tacitus—not even in his tractate *De tyranno* written around 1400[23]—it is unlikely that he ever owned such a manuscript, although he must, at the very least, have had an opportunity to see one in 1403, when it must have been available to two of his close associates. His pupil and protégé, Leonardus Arretinus (Bruni), quoted from it in the *Laudatio Florentinae urbis* which he composed in the summer of 1403, i.e., a few months before Poggio left Florence.[24] And it was probably in the same year that Salutati's friend and intellectual parasite, Domenico di Bandino, doubtless using the same manuscript, quoted Tacitus in his discursive *De civitatibus*.[25]

The manuscript that was available in Florence in 1403 is almost certainly the one that Poggio saw and remembered, and if, for example, he saw it when it was temporarily in the hands of his fellow protégé, Leonardus, who must have borrowed it, since he was then too young and poor to own many books, we can understand why Poggio was uncertain who owned it. That manuscript cannot have been the Second Medicean,

---

whose works show "quantum maiestas illa prisci sermonis, quae cum Cicerone summum apicem tenuit, imminuta est." It is to the point that he owned copies of all the later writers he names (see B. L. Ullman, *The Humanism of Coluccio Salutati*, Padova, 1963, pp. 215–252) and so is presumably expressing his own opinion.

[22] Ullman, *op. cit.*, p. 252, repeating an earlier conclusion, says that it is not likely that Salutati ever saw any part of Tacitus, but, apart from the general consideration that Salutati probably would not have named as his prime example of stylistic decline an author of whom he knew nothing, it seems to me that his statement that Tacitus intended to continue Livy was most probably suggested by the exordium of the *Historiae*, supplemented by either an inference drawn from the part of the *Annales* transmitted with them (he could have supposed that the missing Books I–X began where Livy had stopped) or from Jerome's statement in his commentary *In Zachariam* (of which Salutati owned a copy) that Tacitus' work began *post Augustum*. I think it likely that Salutati read at least enough of Tacitus—a page or two would have sufficed—to see the great difference of his style from Livy's.

[23] Most conveniently available in Francesco Ercole's *editio minor*, Bologna, s.a. [1942].

[24] The date of Bruni's treatise was determined by Hans Baron, *Humanistic and Political Literature in Florence and Venice*, Cambridge, Massachusetts, 1955, pp. 69–107.

[25] Miss Hankey, in her article on Domenico in *Rinascimento*, VIII (1957), says (p. 182) that the work was "written c. 1400," but later (p. 207) decides that certain chapters of it "were presumably written about 1403." It cannot have been completed earlier if Domenico used in it the information supplied, evidently for this particular work, by Salutati in a letter of July, 1403 (*Epistolario*, Vol. III, pp. 622–628). Domenico seems habitually to have pumped Salutati for the erudition that he displays (without acknowledgment) in his dismayingly voluminous writings. (He may have felt that he repaid the debt by writing a eulogy in which he concludes that "Colucius . . . solus est arcanae naturae conscius, qui divina solus et humana complecti animo et eloqui stilo possit adeo exuberanter quod [!] omnes laudatos veteres antecedat.")

which Poggio obviously did not see before he borrowed it from Niccolò de'
Niccoli and which is written in the Beneventan script that neither Leonardus nor Domenico di Bandino is likely to have been able to read with
any ease; and if the manuscript was correctly described by Poggio as
written *litteris antiquis*, it could have been as old as the Ninth Century and
could not have been produced later than the Twelfth.

That is a fact that should give pause to the most obstinate votary of the
Second Medicean.

II

It is now universally believed that the Second Medicean migrated from
Monte Cassino to Florence in the way that Rostagno described in his
introduction to the lithographic reproduction of that manuscript (1902),
which is concisely summarized by Koestermann in the preface to his latest
edition of the *Annales* (1965): ". . . codex Laurentianus 68.2, quem medio
saeculo XI monasterio in Casinensi formis litterarum Longobardis
scriptum . . . Iohannes Boccaccius ante a. 1370 inde surripuisse videtur,
cuius bibliotheca[26] postea in possessionem Nicolai de Nicolis (1363–1437)
pervenit, qui codicem una cum reliquis suis libris Conventui S. Marci
Florentino legavit; inde codex in bibliothecam Laurentianam transiit."

This is the accepted story and, at least until Mendell came to disturb
orthodoxy, it was further believed that the Second Medicean, saved from
Monte Cassino by Boccaccio's glorious theft, was the exemplar from which
in the fifteenth century all other extant manuscripts of this part of Tacitus'
work were copied, with many strange corruptions, presumably caused
by the difficulty of reading a Beneventan hand, and with some very strange
mutilations of some of those copies early in the fifteenth century, so that
the extant manuscripts now fall into three clearly defined classes: (I)
those which end where the Second Medicean ends, (II) those which end
abruptly in *Hist.* V.23.2 with the word *potiorem*, which occurs in the middle
of line 16 of the second column of f. 103^r of the Medicean—there being no
perceptible reason why a copyist should have stopped at that point, and
(III) those which end in *Hist.* V.13.1 with the word *evenerant*, which
occurs in line 8 of the first column of f. 102^r of the Medicean—there being
no conceivable reason why a copyist should have thrown down his pen
after transcribing the first word of a sentence.

---

[26] The word *bibliotheca* is, of course, merely a *lapsus calami*, for as Koestermann well
knew (see his article in *Philologus*, CIV [1961], p. 94), Boccaccio's library was left to the
convent of Santo Spirito, and it was never supposed that more than a few of his books had
been obtained by Niccolò.

This codicological tale has always been intrinsically implausible. Since 1961 it has been demonstrably false.

Fairly early in his career, Boccaccio was inspired by the example of Petrarch, for whom he conceived the utmost admiration and veneration, to turn from vernacular poetry and prose to Latin and scholarship, and it was probably not long thereafter that he began to compile the work that he was to regard as his surest claim to immortality, the *De genealogia deorum*, which was to be at once a comprehensive manual of mythology and a contribution to Latin literature. He completed his first version of that work before 1359,[27] but after he learned as much Greek as the Calabrian adventurer, Leonzio Pilato, could teach him in 1360–1362, he undertook a thorough revision of his work to incorporate information from the parts of Homer that he had read and from such other instruction as Pilato had given him. He doubtless intended this revision to be the definitive text, because his autograph manuscript, now Laurentianus LII.9, must have been written slowly and laboriously, with the most painstaking effort to produce regularly formed characters, precise margins, and uniform columns on each page.[28] In this fair copy, Boccaccio made no use of Tacitus and probably had not yet read him.[29]

[27] He dedicated the work to Hugo IV of Lusignan, King of Jerusalem and Cyprus, who died in 1359. It is characteristic of Boccaccio that he preserved that dedication in all of his subsequent revisions of his work, and although he continued to improve the text for fifteen years thereafter, he neither replaced the dedication nor altered the passages in which he addressed the king as alive.

[28] I saw the manuscript at a time when I had no particular interest in it and even noticed the marginal addition that I am about to mention, but without perceiving its significance. Photographs of some pages, with enlargements of small portions to show changes in Boccaccio's handwriting, are included in P. G. Ricci's article, "Studi sulle opere latine e volgari del Boccaccio," *Rinascimento*, X (1959), 3–32, and in Ricci's half of the book that he wrote in collaboration with Vittore Branca, *Un autografo del Decameron*, Padova, 1962. The autograph manuscript is the basis of the edition, *Genealogie deorum gentilium libri*, a cura di Vincenzo Romano, Bari, 1951, which contains, Vol. II, pp. 789–864, a detailed discussion of the various manuscripts and of the stages of composition shown by Boccaccio's revisions in the autograph. Romano believes that the fair copy was begun late in 1363 and completed early in 1366 but that Boccaccio probably began to make further revisions in the early books, by erasure and rewriting, before he completed the later books.

[29] That is Romano's conclusion (p. 843), which I see no reason to doubt. That Boccaccio knew Tacitus much earlier was believed by Hecker and other scholars, whom Rostagno followed in his preface to the photographic reproduction of the Second Medicean, and this has most recently been maintained by Ricci, who has identified ("Studi," pp. 12–21) six successive revisions and rewritings of Boccaccio's *De mulieribus claris* and assigns a date before 1362 to the version that contains stories based on Tacitus. That Boccaccio dedicated his work to Andreola Acciaiuoli at an opportune time, when he hoped for favors from her brother, I can well believe but, with the example of his dedi-

This recension, however, was far from definitive. Boccaccio soon felt impelled to make revisions and additions and, indeed, he continued to review and improve his work until his death. He erased and rewrote long passages in his fair copy, and when this would no longer serve he added supplements in the once ample margins. In one such marginal addendum he cites Tacitus as his authority for information taken from *Hist.* II.3. This addition must have been made before 1371, because Boccaccio, when he set out on the last of his journeys to Naples in search of his vanished youth, took with him either the extant autograph or a copy of it now lost,[30] and near the end of his brief sojourn in Naples lent it to Hugo, Count of San Severino who, violating a promise,[31] permitted the making of copies from which, it is agreed, were derived numerous manuscripts and the early printed editions, all of which contain the passage derived from Tacitus.[32] It follows, therefore, that Boccaccio obtained and used a manuscript of Tacitus before January 1371. (Whether this was the manuscript that was in his possession when he arrived in Naples is a question that we shall consider later.)

In Chapter 23 of Book III of his *De genealogia*, Boccaccio, after some discussion, concluded that the story that Venus had been born from the sea near Paphos was if not exactly an allegory a mythical expression of the fact that the inhabitants of the island of Cyprus were reputed to be most extraordinarily addicted to erotic pleasures. After he read Tacitus, it

cation of the *De genealogia* (note 27 *supra*) before me, I cannot see why the presence of that dedication (which Boccaccio never cancelled) suffices to date that version. I think the stories from Tacitus were added long after the dedication was written, because it seems to me unlikely that Boccaccio was so tactless as to present to the lady, who had become by her second (or third) marriage the Countess of Alteville, a version of his book that included his sketch of Pompeia Paulina (wife of Seneca) which he obviously elaborated from Tacitus only because it gave him an opening for a long digression on the *libidinosa prurigo* of women who marry a second time and, like whores, take pride in having had sexual relations with more than one man, which proves that they are whores at heart, even though they go through a marriage ceremony to keep up appearances. As for Ricci's extremely minute and discerning analysis of changes in Boccaccio's handwriting, the dating of those changes is partly based on the supposed date of the autograph manuscript dedicated to the Countess of Alteville and containing the stories from Tacitus.

[30] Which it was does not matter for our purposes, so we need not enter into a question that has been the subject of long and lively debate between Romano, G. Martellotti, D. Peraccioni, P. G. Ricci, and perhaps others whose contributions I have not seen.

[31] The circumstances are stated by Boccaccio in a letter published in his *Opere latine minori*, a cura di Aldo Massèra, Bari, 1928, pp. 198–203.

[32] This I infer from Romano's study of the manuscripts and early printings cited in note 28 *supra*. Texts derived from the copies made by Hugo of San Severino are easily recognized because they contain certain passages (none of which concerns us here) that are not in the autograph manuscript.

occurred to him that the myth might reflect an historical event, so he added in the margin the passage which I quote from the text edited from the autograph manuscript by Vincenzo Romano, who has introduced modern capitalization and punctuation, but has retained Boccaccio's ugly misspellings.[33]

> Verum hoc potius ad hystoriam quam ad alium sensum pertinere ex Cornelio Tacito sumi potest. Qui velle videtur Venerem auspitio doctam armata manu conscendisse insulam bellumque Cynare regi movisse; qui tandem, cum inissent concordiam, convenere ut ipse rex Veneri templum construeret, in quo eidem Veneri sacra ministrarent, qui ex familia regia et sua succederent. Confecto autem templo, sola animalia masculini generis in holocaustum parabantur, altaria vero sanguine maculari piaculum cum solis precibus igneque puro illa adolerent. Simulacrum vero dee nullam humanam habere dicit effigiem, quin imo esse ibidem continuum orbem latiorem initio et tenuem in ambitu ad instar methe exurgentem, et quare hoc nullam haberi rationem.

A strange story, certainly, and one more worthy of Semiramis than of the golden Aphrodite. I now transcribe the relevant passage in Tacitus (*Hist.* II.3) from f. 60ʳ of the Second Medicean, resolving contractions but making no other change.

> Conditorem templi regem uerianus · uetus memoria · quidam ipsius deae nomen Idperibent · fama recentior tradit · acinyra sacratum templum · deamque ipsam conceptam mari huc adpulsam · sed scientiam artemque aruspicum accitam · et cilicentamiram Intulisse · atque Ita pactum ut familiae utriusque posteri caerimoniis praesiderent · mox ne honore nullo regium genus peregrinam stirpem antecelleret · ipsam quam Intulerat scientia hospites cessere · tantum cinyrades sacerdos consulitur · hostiae ut quisque uouits& · mares deliguntur · certissima fides haedorum fibris · sanguinem arae obfundere uetitum · precibus et Igne puro altaria adolentur · nec ullis Imbribus quamnquam Inaperto madescunt·,· Simulacrum deae · non effigie humana · continuus orbis latiore Initio tenuem Inambitu meta modo exsurgens · et ratio in obscuro·,·

It is quite obvious that Boccaccio could not have extracted his story from that text—not even with the aid of a flagon of *spumante*.

I now transcribe the text from f. 110ᵛ of Mendell's Leidensis.

> Conditorem templi regem venerianum vetus memoria. quidam ipsius deae nomen id perhibent · fama recentior tradit a cinara sacratum templum deam que ipsam conceptam mari huc appulsam : sed scientia arte que aruspicum accitam et cinarae certamina intulisse atque ita pactum vt familiae vtriusque posteri cerimoniis presiderent · mox ne honore vllo regium genus peregrinam stirpem antecelleret · ipsa quam intulerant scientia hospites cessere · tantum cinarides sacerdos consulitur · hostiae vt quisque vouisset mares deliguntur · certissima fides edorum fibris · sanguinem arae offundere vetitum · precibus et igne puro altaria adolentur. nec vllis imbribus quamquam in aperto

[33] Vol. I, p. 151.

madescunt · simulacrum deae non effigiae humana continuus orbis latiore initio tenue in ambitu metae modo exurgens. et ratio in obscuro. Now we see whence Boccaccio derived the notion of a bellicose Venus, who practiced augury, led an army against a king named Cynara, and founded a family on Cyprus. His manuscript of Tacitus was not the Second Medicean: it was a manuscript that could have been the ancestor of the Leidensis.

I consider this one example probative, and I accordingly refrain from adducing the supporting evidence that could be elicited from the stories derived from Tacitus that Boccaccio added in some revision of his *De mulieribus claris*,[34] but only at the expense of a long analysis of his literary purposes and techniques to distinguish between details that he probably derived from readings not in the Second Medicean[35] and details that he added to make more vivid and dramatic stories that he selected as illustrations of the wide variety of feminine character and conduct.[36]

The glaring discrepancies between Boccaccio's account of the Paphian Venus and the accepted text of Tacitus must have been apparent to most readers of the *De genealogia deorum* since the Renaissance, but they probably assumed (as I did) that Boccaccio had contaminated the report in Tacitus with information drawn or inferred from some source now lost, perhaps the strange mythology or theology of the mysterious Theodontius.[37] It was

34 Cf. note 29 *supra*.

35 For example, in his story of the younger Poppaea Sabina, taken from *Ann.* XIII.46, Boccaccio suggests, as one of the alternative explanations of Otho's fulsome praise of his wife to Nero, a wish to be rid of her ("seu nequiens petulcae mulieris tolerare mores et ob id eam in Neronis concupiscentiam trahere conaretur"). He could have deduced this from the readings of the Leidensis, *si . . . femina potiretur . . . eam duceret*, understanding the subject of the verbs to be Nero. In the absence of complete collations for this part of Tacitus, I do not know whether Boccaccio could also have found in his manuscript *vitium impotentiam* instead of *vinculum potentiam*, which would have clinched the matter.

36 For example, he expands Tacitus' brief mention of what *quidam* said about Triaria (wife of Lucius Vitellius) into the story of a woman who, with Amazonian courage, took up sword and shield and fought amid the vividly described horrors of a city taken and sacked by night. He attributes this conduct to a determination to assure her husband's victory, and he thus can expatiate on the nature of women, who, though often terrified by the sight of a mouse, can be inspired by their devotion to a man and so find the courage to affront perils and horrors that would daunt many a robust and valiant soldier. He concludes that Triaria, who showed the devotion that he had read into a few words in Tacitus, must have been *longe aliis meritis spectabilis*, although history has failed to record her other virtues.

37 I commented briefly on the problem of Theodontius in *Speculum*, XXXIII (1958), 150–153, but I now think that we should consider the possibility that this work, whether or not related to the Theodotius mentioned by Servius, was circulated in late Byzantine times in the interests of the secret Neo-Platonic religion, on which see François Masai, *Pléthon et le platonisme de Mistra*, Paris, 1956.

not until 1961, when Koestermann's new edition of the *Historiae* made available the readings of the Leidensis, that it became apparent that Boccaccio was merely interpreting the text of Tacitus that he had before him.

I will confess that when Koestermann's edition reached me, I thought the problem solved and Mendell's position vindicated—and that ten years later, when I examined Ingeborg Schinzel's collations for Book II, I felt a sensation of mild vertigo.

I list below the decisively disjunctive readings that underlie the elements in Boccaccio's story shown in parentheses, and then, for each of the three classes of manuscripts,[38] I give Hanslik's sigla for the manuscripts that show all three of the readings, and I indicate, after a plus sign, the number of other manuscripts of that class that have the one reading under consideration:

cinara (= Cinara)   I. YO_3 + 10
                      II. L + 2
                      III. N21, O_48 + all four of the others.
deam . . . scientia arteque aruspicum accitam (= Venerem
auspicio doctam)   I. YO_3 + 2
                      II. L + 7
                      III. N21, O_48 + 1
Cinarae certamina intulisse (= bellum . . . regi movisse)
                      I. YO_3
                      II. L
                      III. N21, O_48 + 2

Even allowing for extensive "horizontal transmission" between classes, it seems clear that if the manuscript that was the source of these readings belonged to Class I, its text was apocopated in some of its descendants, and if it belonged to Class II or Class III, the text was supplemented in one or two of its descendants.

III

We have shown that Boccaccio's manuscript was similar to the Leidensis and others. We have yet to consider the possibility that he may also have had his hands on the Second Medicean at some time.

Of the three bits of evidence that have been used to connect him with

[38] See above, p. 197. Note that I use the classification given by Koestermann in the preface to his edition of the *Historiae* and followed in the collations by Hanslik's pupils and *not* the classification given by Mendell in his *Tacitus* (pp. 337–342) and Hanslik in the article cited above (p. 159), in which the order is reversed. In other words, in the classification that I use here, the Second Medicean belongs to Class I, *not* III.

that manuscript, one may be summarily dismissed. The Second Medicean is now bound with the Beneventan manuscript of Apuleius known as *F*, and there is also in the Laurentian Library (LIV.32) a copy of Apuleius in Boccaccio's handwriting. It is certain, however, that *F* was not Boccaccio's exemplar. On the basis of a minute study of all the major manuscripts, D. S. Robertson concludes[39] that Boccaccio's copy was made from a contaminated copy of a manuscript now in the British Museum which was a direct copy of Ambrosianus N.180 sup., which in turn is an early fourteenth century copy of a copy of *F* that had been made before 1200.

It is certain that Boccaccio visited Monte Cassino and inspected its library at least once. For this we have his own statement as reported by his younger friend and pupil, Benvenuto da Imola, who succeeded him in the lectureship that Florence tardily established for him. Benvenuto, who venerated Boccaccio as a new Chrysostom[40] and was proud of having had a *praeceptor* so illustrious for wisdom and eloquence, reports the story in the execrable Latin of his commentary on Dante:[41]

> Venerablis praeceptor meus, Boccaccius de Certaldo, dicebat . . . quod dum esset in Apulia, captus fama loci, accessit ad nobile monasterium Montis Cassini . . . et avidus videndi librariam, quam audiverat ibi esse nobilissimam, petivit ab uno monacho humiliter, velut ille qui suavissimus erat, quod deberet ex gratia aperire sibi bibilothecam. At ille rigide respondit, ostendens sibi altam scalam, "ascende quia aperta est." Ille laetus ascendens invenit locum tanti thesauri sine ostio vel clavi, ingressusque vidit herbam natam per fenestras, et libros omnes cum bancis ['bookcases'] coopertis pulvere alto; et mirabundus coepit aperire et volvere nunc istum librum, nunc illum, invenitque ibi multa et varia volumina antiquorum et peregrinorum ['pagan'] librorum, ex quorum aliquibus detracti erant aliqui quaterni, ex aliis recisi margines chartarum, et sic multipliciter deformati. Tandem, miseratus labores et studia tot inclitissimorum ingeniorum devenisse ad manus perditissimorum hominum, dolens et illachrimans recessit, et occurrens in claustro petivit a monacho obvio quare libri illi pretiosissimi essent ita turpiter detruncati. Qui respondit quod aliqui monachi, volentes lucrari duos vel quinque solidos, radebant unum quaternum et faciebant psalteriolos, quos vendebant pueris, et ita de marginibus faciebant evangelia et brevia [i.e., short quotations, used as periapts and charms], quae vendebant mulieribus. Nunc, vir studiose, frange tibi caput pro faciendo libros!

[39] *Op. cit.*, p. xlvii. Frasinetti reprints the preface of Giarratano, who dismisses Boccaccio's manuscript as a much contaminated copy of the Ambrosian codex. At all events, it is certain that Boccaccio cannot have copied from either of the Beneventan manuscripts and, so far as I know, there is no indication that he could even read the Beneventan script.

[40] Benvenuti de Rambaldis de Imola *Comentum super Dantis Aldigherij Comoediam*, editum sumptibus Guilielmi Vernon, curante Jacobo Lacaita, Florentiae, 1887, Vol. V, p. 164.   [41] *Ibid.*, pp. 301 f.

The story is, of course, as well known as Poggio's account of the German *ergastula* from which he liberated classical authors, but it is worth citing in the original. It certainly suggests that a man of Humanistic piety should have abstracted what he could from the moldering library or, if very scrupulous, have given some monk a few *solidi* or even a florin to carry selected manuscripts out and load them on his sumpter-horse, but it does not say that Boccaccio did so. On the contrary, since Benvenuto is writing some years after Boccaccio's death but before ancient manuscripts became so valuable as to incite strenuous efforts to reclaim what might have been taken from Monte Cassino, we may suppose that Benvenuto would not have failed to report an act that he would certainly have regarded as highly creditable to his teacher.

Despite Benvenuto's silence, it has been assumed Boccaccio "liberated" Tacitus on this visit, because (1) the probable occasion for such a visit was one or another of his journeys to Naples[42] and (2) on the last of these, he certainly arrived in Naples with a Tacitus in his possession, and one, moreover, that seems to have been unbound, whence we could infer that he had removed the manuscript from its binding to facilitate asportation or to lighten his luggage.

To estimate the probabilities, we must take some notice of one aspect of Boccaccio's mentality. As every reader of his early works in the vernacular, especially the *Filostrato, Amorosa visione,* and *Fiammetta,* well knows, Boccaccio regarded Naples as a land of felicity. It was the land in which he, supported by his wealthy father, had spent the greater part of his adolescence, and the combination of youth and prosperity had made his life a season of happiness to which he ever afterward looked back as to a lost paradise.[43] When his father suffered financial reverses, probably as an aftermath of the bankruptcy in 1339 of the great Florentine banking houses of the Bardi and Peruzzi, who had rashly lent Edward III of England the then prodigious sum of 1,075,000 florins, Boccaccio, who was probably

[42] In middle life Boccaccio traveled extensively in northern Italy and southern France on special diplomatic errands for the Florentine Republic (some of the diplomas accrediting him as ambassador are extant and were published by Francesco Corazzini in his edition of Boccaccio's *Lettere edite e inedite,* Firenze, 1877, pp. 387–411), but none of these errands took him as far south as Rome. Monte Cassino was situated on what was at that time the principal road between Rome and Naples (hence its strategic importance to both the Papacy and the Norman kings and their successors), and Boccaccio must have passed it, at least, every time that he traveled to and from Naples.

[43] According to Vittore Branca, P. G. Ricci, and other Italian scholars, Boccaccio embellished his ostensibly autobiographical statements with poetic licence, but it does not matter to us whether his most cherished mistress in Naples was really the illegitimate daughter of King Robert, nor need we inquire whether she discarded him or was left disconsolate by his departure.

twenty-eight, was compelled by sheer economic necessity to leave Naples, the home of light and life and laughter, where men and women lived in elegant leisure and devoted themselves to love, poetry, and learning; and he had to return home to Florence, a gloomy city inhabited by money-grubbing businessmen, saturnine, uncouth, dishonest, greedy, and pusillanimous. If the contrast seems overdrawn, remember that Boccaccio was young and a poet.

He returned to Naples as soon as a revival of the family fortunes permitted, but that visit was abruptly terminated when his father, whom he had never forgiven, inconsiderately died and left an inadequate estate. In 1362, when he was forty-nine, Boccaccio received cordial but perhaps insincere invitations from two of his friends, and he delightedly set out to recapture his youth. He appears to have packed up all of his books and valued possessions and, taking his young brother with him, to have migrated to Naples with roseate expectations that were bitterly disappointed. His hosts, probably embarrassed by his acceptance of their invitation, did not receive him with the cordiality that was due a friend, a poet, and a scholar. They gave him lodgings that he describes as a stinking hole, permitted their servants to be insolent, and neglected him themselves. Boccaccio left in April 1363 and went to Venice, whence he addressed to his former friends a vehement and mordant letter of denunciation.[44]

He could have visited Monte Cassino on the way either to or from Naples, but there is no mention of Tacitus, an author whom he evidently did not know when, after his return home, he made the fair copy of his *De genealogia* that we mentioned above.

We might suppose that Boccaccio would have learned a lesson from his disappointment and chagrin in 1362, but late in 1370, when he was vexed by some act of "ingratitude" on the part of the Florentine government, he remembered cordial invitations from his old friend, Niccolò da Montefalcone, who had become Abbot of San Stefano in Calabria, and he set out again. Whether he stopped at Monte Cassino on the way, we do not know, but he had a copy of Tacitus with him when he descended on his surprised and doubtless embarrassed host's home in Naples.

History repeated itself. Niccolò, probably dismayed by the acceptance of his invitations and even more by the contrast between his status as abbot of a poor monastery and the glowing descriptions of his prosperity that he had evidently sent his friend, after a day or two, in which there

---

[44] Only a small part of Boccaccio's text has survived, but the substance of the letter is preserved in a fifteenth-century Italian translation, which occupies thirty pages of small type in Massèra's edition of the minor Latin works cited in note 31 *supra*.

must have been some time for literary conversation, stole out of his own house by night and had a boat carry him off to his monastery. Boccaccio sent after him an indignant letter which concludes with the demand, "Quaternum quem asportasti Cornelii Taciti quaeso saltem mittas, ne laborem meum frustraveris et libro deformitatem ampliorem addideris."[45]

It was generally assumed that this manuscript was the Second Medicean, which Boccaccio had acquired on the way. But is it not conceivable that the aging man, when he again sought the place of his happy youth, again traveled with a mass of impedimenta, including at least his most prized books? I think it is, if we consider the state of mind that we have adumbrated above. It is true that Boccaccio, after he had returned to his *patrius agellus*, no doubt chastened by his second humiliating disappointment, pretended that his short sojourn in Naples had been merely a casual visit,[46] but his irate letter to Niccolò da Montefalcone leaves no doubt but that he had intended or hoped to make the supposedly opulent monastery his *latebra*, in which he could reside indefinitely and enjoy the "nemorum amoenam solitudinem, quorum circumsaeptum aiebas coenobium tuum, librorum copiam, fontes limpidos, et ipsius loci devotionem et commoda— sino rerum abundantiam et caeli benignitatem."[47] It would have been only reasonable to bring with him at least the books that he could not expect to find in even the well-stocked library he had been led to expect. We have, therefore, no reason to suppose that the Tacitus of which the runaway abbot abstracted a fascicle was other than the manuscript we have described as similar to the Leidensis.

IV

When Boccaccio returned to Florence and his home in Certaldo, he undoubtedly took with him his Tacitus (with or without the purloined *quaternus*), and we have every right to assume that it remained in his possession until his death and was among the books that he willed to the monastery of Santo Spirito with the proviso that they be catalogued and placed in a library.[48] The holy men of Santo Spirito evidently saw no profit in the bequest, and the books were simply piled up in chests and

45 In Massèra's edition, pp. 183–185.

46 E.g., in a letter of 1372 (p. 189): "quia laboriosam magis quam longam anno praeterito peregrinationem intraverim et casu Neapolim delatus sum."

47 Pp. 183 f.

48 Whether Boccaccio intended to establish a public library, as is sometimes stated, is uncertain. In the autograph draft of his will in Italian (*ap.* Corazzini, *op. cit.*, p. 416), the custodian of his library "debba . . . far copia ad qualunque persona li volesse di quegli libri," but the text of what appears to have been the legal document (*ibid.*, p. 428)

closets,[49] no doubt in out-of-the-way places, so that it is not remarkable that in 1392, eighteen years after Boccaccio's death, Salutati, although he had friends in Santo Spirito whom he frequently visited, did not know that the works of Tacitus had not been totally lost.

Boccaccio's books may have lain unnoticed in some lumber room until Niccolò de' Niccoli, probably a number of years after 1400, insured their preservation by having a special room added to the monastery and fitted up to house them suitably,[50] stipulating that all learned men have access to them, and doubtless making provision for their safekeeping.[51] The Tacitus, as we shall see in a moment, was among the books placed in that library, and since we have decided that it was not the Second Medicean, we have eliminated a point that always troubled me and, I hope, others. While I have no doubt but that Niccolò would have had no scruples about buying the Second Medicean as stolen property, I did not like to think

---

restricts the privilege of consultation to the monks of Santo Spirito ("ut quilibet de dicto conventu possit legere et studere super dictis libris"). This may correspond to a lacuna in the draft.

[49] In "casse e armari," according to Vespasiano da Bisticci in the passage quoted below. Vespasiano, who spent almost all of his life in Florence, where he was said to be the world's largest and most highly reputed producer of beautiful manuscripts, especially accurate copies of Greek and Latin books, retired from his business when it was ruined by the banausic and vulgar art of printing, and around 1485, when he was sixty-four, settled down in his country villa to write his *Vite di uomini illustri del secolo XV*, which is now regarded as one of the minor Italian classics and is available in many editions. He knew personally and intimately the literary world of his time, and his evidence about matters pertaining to books cannot reasonably be questioned. He distinctly implies that Boccaccio's books were preserved only by the intervention of Niccolò de' Niccoli. In his life of Pope Nicholas V, §8, he says: "È ancora oggi in Santo Spirito . . . una libreria che si chiama del Boccaccio . . . la fece far Nicolao Nicoli, e fecevi mettere i libri del Boccaccio, acciocchè non si perdessino."

[50] Vespasiano, "Nicolao Nicoli," §7: "sendo morte messer Giovanni Boccaccio, e avendo lasciati tutti i sua libri a Santo Spirito, sendo posti in casse e armari, parve a Nicolao ch'egli stessino bene in sua libraria che fusse publica a ognuno; e per questo delle sue sustanze fece fabricare una libraria, a fine che così potessino mettere i detti libri, sì per loro conservazione, il simile ancora per onore di messer Giovanni, e a fine che fussino comuni a chi n'avesse di bisogno; e fece fare le panche da tenere i libri, le quali si veggono infino al presente dì."

[51] Francesco Novati, in his rigorous study of the fortunes of this library, *Giornale storico della letteratura italiana*, X (1887), 413–425, notes that in the contemporary list of books in the library of the monastery itself there is listed a manuscript of one of the polemical diatribes of St. Augustine which the monks particularly prized because it was given them by a Pope, and the entry is followed by the notation, "Propter periculum latronum positus est in parva libreria." If the little library built by Niccolò was a safer place for a valuable book, there must have been some provision for what is now called "security."

that he would have had the manuscript stolen from the very library that he had established in honor of Boccaccio and for the use of scholars.

The library that Niccolò established seems at first to have borne Boccaccio's name, but it later became known as the Parva Libreria, probably, I conjecture, because it was housed in a small building adjacent to the monastery.[52] It included Boccaccio's Tacitus, which was still there in September 1451 as is attested by an inventory made at that time and preserved in Laurentian manuscript, from which it was first published by A. Goldmann in 1887.[53] The inventory is quite explicit: "Istud est inventarium parve librerie . . . in quo scribentur omnes libri qui ibi reperientur. Factum et inceptum die XXᵃ mensis Septembris m.⁰cccc.⁰LI." Note the future tenses: we have no reason to doubt but that the compiler did proceed to enter the titles of the books that he actually found on the shelves.[54] Books from other gifts and bequests had been added to the collection, but Boccaccio's books remained together as the central part of the library, and we may be certain that the contents of *Bancus V* came from his bequest: of the twelve books in it, six are by Boccaccio, four are by Petrarch. Book No. 7 is thus described "Id quod de Cornelio Tacito reperitur conpletus copertus corio rubeo cuius principium est 'nam valerium agiaticum.'"[55] Finis vero in penultima carta 'machina accessura

[52] Novati refers to it as an *aula* and says that it was demolished ("l'aula eretta in S. Spirito dalla pietà del Niccoli, caduta da qualche tempo [i.e., prima del anno 1570] sotto il piccone demolitore"), doubtless in the course of some alterations in the conventual buildings. No large structure would be necessary to house less than two hundred books.

[53] *Centralblatt für Bibliothekswesen*, IV (1887), 137–155. The inventory, which begins on p. 144, lists 107 codices, of which about fifty certainly come from Boccaccio's collection, and about thirty-five more probably do. Novati believes that a considerable part of Boccaccio's collection disappeared before Niccolò de' Niccoli arranged for the preservation of what was left.

[54] Goldmann reports changes in the color of the ink, which show that the entries were not made at one sitting. It is absurd to suggest that the compiler merely copied an earlier inventory and that the Tacitus was the Second Medicean, which had therefore been missing for a quarter of a century in 1451.

[55] The spelling is not a mistake in Goldmann's transcription: Oskar Hecker, *Boccaccio-Funde*, Braunschweig, 1902, minutely collates Goldmann's printing against the manuscript (pp. 38–42), noting that the penultimate word in the entry I quote is spelled *acessura*, but does not question this word. Most of his corrections of Goldmann's text merely show that the compiler's spelling was even worse than appears from Goldmann's printing, and it would be mere fantasy to deduce from *agiaticum* anything about the hand in which Boccaccio's manuscript was written. The numerous misspellings show that the compiler had an assistant, and that one wrote while the other read from the books and dictated the entries. It is worthy of note, however, that Boccaccio's manuscript evidently bore the title (as distinct from a colophon) that, according to Mendell's descriptions, is now found only in Vat. Lat. 2965 (Hanslik's V65): *Cornelii Taciti quod reperitur*. This manuscript belongs

erat.'" The *explicit* has been recognized as coming from Vitruvius, X.16.7. It is obvious, therefore, that Boccaccio's Tacitus was bound with an incomplete copy of Vitruvius; it is also obvious that the compiler of the inventory merely examined the first and last pages of the volume and that we can attach no significance to his statement that the Tacitus was "conpletus," which probably means no more than that the binding was unbroken.

How long after 1451 Boccaccio's Tacitus remained in the library, we have no means of knowing. The little building that housed the collection, and perhaps the entire convent, escaped damage when the church was completely destroyed by fire in 1471,[56] and Boccaccio's books could still be consulted in Santo Spirito at the end of the century, but the collection was largely or entirely dispersed, for reasons and in circumstances unknown, before 1570, perhaps when the structure that Niccolò de' Niccoli had built was demolished.[57] Some of Boccaccio's books have been found in the Laurentian and various other libraries, but many seem to have disappeared, Boccaccio's Tacitus among them. Barring the remote possibility that it may still be found in some obscure and uncatalogued collection, we must assume that, since all known manuscripts of this part of Tacitus' work, with the sole exception of the Second Medicean, have

---

to Class III, and of the disjunctive readings I listed above, it lacks only the third, for which it has *e mare certamina intulisse*, which would less precisely fit Boccaccio's paraphrase, but would not exclude it.

[56] This is certain from the evidence presented in Novati's article, to which Hecker, *op. cit.*, pp. 7 f., adds a few details. Goldmann's statement (p. 138) that Boccaccio's books were destroyed in the fire, though based on statements made by a number of earlier Italian *cognoscenti* (who copied one another), is a gross error—and one that should never have been made, given the explicit statement of Vespasiano da Bisticci, quoted above, that the library built by Niccolò de' Niccoli was still there when he wrote, in 1485 or later. Hecker himself located and identified (pp. 29–37) a number of codices still extant that came from Boccaccio's library and were in Santo Spirito. He believes that Boccaccio's books were zealously protected by the monk to whose care Boccaccio had left them, and only after that man's death thrown into some corner in conditions which fully account for the fact that many of them did not reach the shelves of Niccolò's library: "So blieben denn die Bücher, die Boccaccio mit so opferfreudigem Eifer gesammelt und mit so warmer Liebe gehegt und behütet hatte, in mangelhaft verwahrten Kisten der Habgier und den Mäusen und Würmern zur willkommenen Beute jahrzehntelang unbeachtet liegen, bis im ersten Viertel des XV. Jahrhunderts . . ."

[57] It is possible that some of the books may have been destroyed in 1497 and 1498, when Savonarola's followers had particularly acute fits of piety in the carnival season, but that seems unlikely, because quite a few of Boccaccio's autograph copies of his own works are still extant. No disaster to the city or to Santo Spirito between 1485 and 1570 is recorded, so the most reasonable assumption is that priors of Santo Spirito sold the books, quietly and a few at a time, no doubt to raise money for pious purposes.

been identified as of the fifteenth century or later, it is no longer extant. We have shown, however, that this lost manuscript had a text similar to that of the Leidensis, and I hope that we have permanently deleted from the record the generally accepted[58] and incredibly fantastic story that the Second Medicean was stolen from Monte Cassino by Boccaccio; presumably went to Santo Spirito, whence it was stolen for Niccolò de' Niccoli; was not bound with any other work when it was lent to Poggio in 1427, but was bound with Apuleius before it passed to San Marco in 1437 or shortly thereafter; was amazingly taken from San Marco and hustled back to Santo Spirito to be bound with a Vitruvius before 1451; and was thereafter carted back to San Marco and rebound with the Apuleius before it, together with many other books in San Marco, was transferred to the Medicean Library. *Pro deûm atque hominum fidem!*

V

But the Second Medicean? If not Boccaccio, who?

A new candidate was brought forward in 1953 by the learned Giuseppe Billanovich: Zenobi da Strada.[59] Billanovich seems to take it for granted that the Second Medicean reached Florence in the time of Boccaccio, but he argues that Boccaccio was not a man of sufficient prestige and authority to remove manuscripts from Monte Cassino—although no prestige, other than a handful of *soldi*, would have been needed, according to Boccaccio's report, which we have quoted in full above, and of which we have no reason to doubt the essentials, although it may well be that Boccaccio yielded to the universal human impulse to make a good story better by pointing up some of the details. Zenobi da Strada, we are told, lived at Monte Cassino from 1355 to 1357 and, since he had status as the vicar of a bishop, could have carted off codices to which he took a fancy. And finally, Zenobi has been identified by his handwriting as the author of marginal notes in both of the Beneventan manuscripts of Apuleius,[60]

---

[58] Even by Mendell, *Tacitus*, pp. 238–241, 295–297.

[59] *I primi umanisti e le tradizioni dei classici latini*, Friburgo, 1953; pp. 29–33, 40. If the promised work on Zenobi has been published, I have missed it. Billanovich's conclusions were accepted by Ricci, "Studi," p. 20, who thinks them confirmed by his dating of the *De mulieribus claris* (cf. note 29 *supra*), i.e., Zenobi must have brought the Second Medicean to Florence in time for Boccaccio to use it for that work.

[60] So Billanovich, *loc. cit.*, who recognizes Zenobi's handwriting also in the margins of the surviving portions of a third Beneventan manuscript of Apuleius, which Luigi Pepe, *Giornale italiano di filologia*, IV (1951), 214–225, 279–280, thought independent of *F*. He is to be credited with having provoked a masterly refutation by D. S. Robertson, *Classical Quarterly*, L (1956), 68–80, whose model exploration of the relevant phase of the text

including the so-called *spurcum additamentum*. If the handwriting of Zenobi can be identified with such assurance, it is still possible that Zenobi made the annotations while residing at Monte Cassino and decorously left the two codices there when he departed.

Boccaccio certainly knew Zenobi, and while it may not be fair to judge from the few letters that have survived of Boccaccio's correspondence, I note that in one letter, written while Boccaccio was in Forlì in 1348, Zenobi, then in Florence, was in some way concerned in having some book copied for Boccaccio by a scribe named Dionysius, who evidently wanted assurance that he would be paid. It was Boccaccio who had found somewhere a copy of Varro—possibly, though not necessarily, the Beneventan manuscript, now Laurentianus LI.10, that is believed to be the unique source of what remains of the *De lingua Latina*[61]—and was having it or an apograph of it sent to him in Forlì.[62] In later life Boccaccio described Zenobi as an elementary school teacher who, after winning undeserved honor with a few verses, "tractus auri cupidine in Babylonem occiduam abiit et obmutuit,"[63] i.e., abandoned literature and went where the money was, in the service of the Papacy, then in Avignon. Granted that there may have been some personal rift between the two men that still rankled in Boccaccio's mind eleven years after Zenobi's death, I doubt that Boccaccio

---

tradition may suggest useful analogies to editors of Tacitus. Robertson reports E. A. Lowe's judgment that this third manuscript was written about the time of *F* or earlier, i.e., nearer the date of the Second Medicean. The surviving portions of the eleventh-century Beneventan manuscript come from leaves that were cut up for use as covers for documents by an Italian notary in the middle of the sixteenth century. If Zenobi annotated all three manuscripts, as Billanovich reports, he must have been an early specialist in Apuleian studies.

61 On which see the preface to Goetz and Schoell's edition, pp. xi–xxvi. On Varro at Monte Cassino, see Roberto Weiss, *Medium Aevum*, XVI (1947), 27–31.

62 In Massèra's edition, p. 128. It would be interesting to know whether the Varro that Boccaccio was expecting was the Beneventan manuscript or an apograph. He made a copy that he gave to Petrarch, who thanked him in his *Ep. de rebus fam.*, XVIII.4: "Recepi ... a te librum ex Varronis ac Ciceronis opusculis [*sc.* Pro Cluentio, etc.] ... Accessit ad libri gratiam quod manu tua scriptus erat." Boccaccio would surely have kept a copy for himself, but nothing of the sort appears in the inventory of 1451. Boccaccio has been credited with having "liberated" Varro, too, from Monte Cassino (cf. Lowe, *Papers*, Vol. I, p. 296), and Billanovich would transfer the aureole to Zenobi's head, but if the copy that Boccaccio says he was *habiturus in brevi* was the Laurentian manuscript, his letter to Zenobi proves (1) that Zenobi had nothing to do with it and (2) Boccaccio did not himself take it from Monte Cassino. He does not say whence the copy of Varro is to come, but he says that he may not be in Forlì to receive it because he is likely to go south to the Campania (i.e., much nearer Monte Cassino) as a military observer, and that suggests that the expected copy was coming from some other direction.

63 Massèra's edition, p. 196.

would have spoken with such disdain of a man whom he knew to have been a great student and discoverer of ancient literature.

Pending further studies, therefore, I remain unconvinced, and I think prudence requires us to conclude that, so far as we now know, the Second Medicean could have been taken from Monte Cassino soon after it was copied around 1050[64] or it could have remained there until 1427 when it passed into the possession of Niccolò de' Niccoli.

VI

Since Boccaccio's Tacitus is no longer extant and the few readings that we can identify are common to a number of manuscripts of different classes, we can *know* nothing more about it. It could have been a copy made around the middle of the fourteenth century or one made much earlier; it could conceivably have been the copy in Carolingian minuscules that Poggio saw in Florence around 1403. We do not know whether the *deformitas* of which Boccaccio complained was the incompleteness of the Tacitean text, as seems likely, or referred to deterioration or mutilation of the parchment. It may have been unbound when Boccaccio brought it to Naples; if it was bound, the fact that a fascicle was loose enough to be detached would suggest that the codex was fairly old—or that it had been severely damaged.

In the absence of facts, one may spin theories; so come, let us speculate together.

It is highly improbable that Boccaccio ever recovered the *quaternus* that had been removed from his manuscript. Unless Niccolò da Montefalcone had the temperament of either an angel or a slave, the verbal flaying that he received in Boccaccio's letter cannot have disposed him to return pages that he had thought worth filching in the first place.

We do not know enough about Niccolò's character to discern his motive. It could have been one of the most common of human motives, malice—a desire to injure as best he could a friend who had disconcertingly accepted an unmeant invitation and to frustrate the *labor* on which he was then engaged, which could have been anything from transcribing the text to finding material for further additions to the *De genealogia*, the *De mulieribus claris*, or other literary works. Even so, how-

---

[64] K. J. Heilig, *Wiener Studien*, LIII (1953), 95–110, has shown that Paulinus Venetus, Bishop of Pozzuoli, who died in 1344, used in his own work extracts from Tacitus, most of which correspond to marginal marks in the Second Medicean. Granting that he made the marks, this does not prove that he went to Monte Cassino to consult the codex, which he could have seen elsewhere. Or perhaps it was he who stole it!

ever, it seems likely that Boccaccio exhibited his Tacitus to Niccolò soon after he arrived, and that when they parted, perhaps for the night, Niccolò retained a loose fascicle that particularly interested him, perhaps on the plea that he wanted to copy all or part of it.

We have no means of knowing what would particularly interest Niccolò but, given his occupation, one distinct possibility is *Hist.* V.13, in which Tacitus enumerates the *prodigia* that kept the Jews in Jerusalem agog during the siege by Vespasian and Titus, and particularly the statement that even during that siege the Jews entertained notions of world conquest: "pluribus persuasio inerat antiquis sacerdotum litteris contineri, eo ipso tempore fore ut valesceret Oriens profectique Iudaea rerum potirentur." With only a modicum of imagination, Niccolò could have seen in that statement a veridic prophecy of the ultimate victory of Christianity[65] or, for that matter, Boccaccio, who had in him a strain of highly emotional religiosity,[66] could have proudly claimed to have discovered that meaning in the passage. If that happened, we can understand why the abbot purloined the *quaternus* containing that part of the text, and carried it off to his monastery, either as substance for his own pious meditations or to dazzle his monks.

Now if, for the sake of an hypothesis, we assume that Boccaccio's manuscript belonged to Class I and had as much of the text of Tacitus as is preserved in the Medicean and in Hanslik's YO3, the amount of text from the beginning of V.13 to the end was equivalent to 253 lines of Teubner text. In the Second Medicean, this text begins near the top of the first column on f. 102[r] and extends to near the bottom of the first column on f. 103[v], i.e., occupies four pages with a blank space at the end. The number of pages that would be needed in other formats is easily calculated. If we assume that in Boccaccio's manuscript one quaternion or

---

[65] It is a little odd that Orosius did not think of this when, with Tacitus before him, he composed his anamorphosis of Roman history.

[66] As Hecker observes, *op. cit.*, p. 300: "Boccaccio ist sein lebenslang religiös gewesen," but with emotional fluctuations. When he was in his late forties he was visited by some holy man who claimed to be a messenger sent from on high to threaten him with death and damnation if he continued to read the wicked pagan writers, who were then being fried for their sins, and the message was evidently delivered in such thunderous tones that poor Boccaccio was frightened into a kind of nervous prostration, from which Petrarch had to rescue him with a vigorous letter (*Epistulae seniles,* I.4) that concluded with an ironic offer to buy the baneful books. Our knowledge of the incident comes entirely from Petrarch's letter, which Hecker could have used as the most dramatic proof that Boccaccio's protestations of Christian faith in the *De genealogia* are to be taken seriously. It would have been quite in keeping with Boccaccio's character to have discovered with excitement a prophecy in Tacitus' text, and the *labor* of which he speaks could have been some plan to exploit his sensational discovery. If so, Niccolò neatly frustrated it.

other gathering ended with the last word of V.12, then, if each page contained as much text as an average page of the Leidensis, the remaining part of the *Historiae* would have required seven full pages with four to seven lines on the eighth page. If the manuscript resembled the First Medicean, in which the Carolingian minuscule shows some variation in density, the remaining text would have required either ten or eleven pages, with only a few lines left blank on the last page.[67]

Now unfortunately we do not know how many pages were in the *quaternus* that Niccolò da Montefalcone purloined. In the usage of the Middle Ages and early Renaissance, *quaternus* does not mean quaternion: it designates sheets folded in the middle as for binding in a codex, and it was even applied to a single sheet folded to form four pages, although there are only a very few instances of its use in this sense, possibly only with reference to such a sheet when associated with larger signatures in a bound book, or possibly only in error.[68] Although the word was used with

---

[67] I am stating the problem in its simplest terms, considering only the loss of the text after V.12, and accordingly I do not complicate this speculation by adding a second, viz., that if Boccaccio's manuscript in its original state corresponded in length to Class I, it contained the text of *Hist.* IV.16–52, which is now missing in all the manuscripts of Class III, which, however, have at the very end (i.e., following *evenerant*) two separated "excerpts" from that missing portion (the facts are summarized by Mendell, *Tacitus*, pp. 305, 309–311, 315–317, 337–338). Since Boccaccio's manuscript was in such a state that the *quaternus* stolen by Niccolò was detached, it is likely that other gatherings were loose from the binding, and it is possible that the gatherings that contained IV.16–52 were lost except for the pages containing the "excerpts," which are of about equal length, so that each presumably corresponds to one leaf (two pages) or one sheet (four pages) of the manuscript. From this datum we could proceed to calculate from the amount of text lost before, between, and after the "excerpts" the size of the pages in Boccaccio's manuscript, which we would thus regard as the origin of Class III. This is quite likely, if the speculation in which I here indulge has merit, but the two losses are not *necessarily* connected, so I avoid what would be a circular argument.

[68] It may well mean a single sheet in the passage from Benvenuto (Boccaccio's pupil) quoted on p. 203 above; the palimpsest *psalterioli* that the monks sold for a few coppers obviously contained only a few selected psalms, perhaps those that the *pueri* were to memorize, and to make one of them it would have sufficed to remove from a codex and erase a single sheet of parchment (four pages), so it seems likely that that is what is meant by *unum quaternum*. Silvia Rizzo, *op. cit.*, pp. 42–48, has an example that shows that as early as the sixth century *quaternio* had come to mean a gathering of sheets folded for binding and had lost a numerical meaning. She notes the Mediaeval use of the word even "per un solo foglio," but she gives no example in which that meaning is indubitable, nor do I find one in the works that she cites, although in some, as in the passage from Benvenuto I have mentioned, it is quite probable. If we could be sure that Boccaccio would not have used *quaternus* to refer to an unio, we could disregard the chances that his manuscript contained some text after Tacitus and thus infer that the manuscript was not written in a dense hand with two columns to a page, such as we find in the Second Medicean

precise meaning in commerce and a few library catalogues, *quaternus* in Mediaeval usage was applied to any gathering of from two to six sheets folded in the middle to form from eight to twenty-four pages. The portion of the text that Niccolò da Montefalcone abstracted according to our hypothesis could easily have been a gathering of two or three sheets at the end of the book, and Boccaccio could have called it a *quaternus*. It could, of course, have been a quaternion in the correct sense of that word, with the pages following the end of Tacitus utilized, as was customary, for some short text in prose or verse that Boccaccio did not mention.

In other words, if the last gathering of Boccaccio's manuscript began with *Evenerant prodigia*, with *evenerant* as the *custos* at the bottom of the last page of the preceding quaternion, or if it simply began with *prodigia*, Niccolò da Montefalcone's theft could have been the origin of Class III of the manuscripts and would explain the strange apocopation of their text at that point.

So far as we can tell from the little that we know of its readings, Boccaccio's manuscript could have been the archetype of Class III. As is obvious from the many readings they have in common as well as from the apocopation of the text, the six manuscripts of this class are closely related. Although, as I have indicated above, only two of them have all three of the crucial readings presupposed by Boccaccio's story of Venus, the only significant difference is found in the last instance, where four of the manuscripts (N21, O48, V64, O22) have *et cinarae certamina* and one (V65) has *e mare certamina*, which obviously came from *etcinare* misread as *exinare/exmare* and corrected.[68a] *K*, however, has *e cilicia miram*, which must be a correction of the reading *e cilicenta miram* that is common to the manuscripts of the Genevan[69] group (V58, BO5, G, H, Mal, Prm, J). This is not remarkable,

---

and in Boccaccio's autographic *De genealogia*, but was instead in some hand and format that would have required more than an unio to transcribe the remaining part of the *Historiae*, and therefore could have resembled the First Medicean. This, I fear, we cannot do. Any codex might have had an unio at the end, and if in Boccaccio's mind *quaternus* meant nothing more than a signature (i.e., a unit of one or more sheets folded for binding), he could have used that word instead of *folium*, which would probably have been his usual term for a single sheet.

[68a] V65 is the manuscript that has the title, *Cornelii Taciti quod reperitur*, that was on Boccaccio's copy; see note 55 above. If that copy was the source of Class III, the misreading *e mare* could, of course, have come from some intermediary.

[69] I do not understand why this group of manuscripts is commonly called "Genoan" or "Genoese," as though there were some connection with Genoa in Italy. The locative *Genuae* found in colophons is, of course, ambiguous, but V58 and some others have the marginal note that is quoted by Mendell, *Tacitus*, p. 316: "generales nundinae ut genuae allobrogum urbis hodie sunt." Genua Allobrogum is, of course, Geneva in Switzerland, which was so designated by the Humanists, who believed *Genua* to be the correct name

however, because K is clearly a copy of a Class III manuscript now lost (conceivably Boccaccio's!) which Ludovicus Rex of Imola revised in 1488 by collating some manuscripts of the Genevan group and using his own ingenuity.[70] So far as we can test it, therefore, our hypothesis is valid.

Our theoretical exercise has produced what is, so far as I know, the first plausible explanation of Class III. I need not remark, however, that unless the hypothesis can be supported with evidence that I cannot now adduce, it is mere speculation.

VII

The foregoing discussion, I believe, has demonstrated that in addition to the Second Medicean there were manuscripts which had a markedly different text and which we may call "Mediaeval" to distinguish them from the thirty-two that are now collectively called *Humanistenhandschriften*. One such manuscript, which was certainly written before 1370 and *could* have been the ancestor of Class III was, during the second quarter of the fifteenth century and probably for a few years earlier and several decades thereafter, in a public library in Florence in which it was presumably available to anyone who wished to use it. In the first years of the fifteenth century there was in Florence and (at least temporarily) in private possession a manuscript in Carolingian minuscules and, although we cannot be certain, the chances are that this was not the same as the the one we have just mentioned. Given the existence of one or more "Mediaeval" manuscripts now lost, it is, of course, possible that there were others.

From this determination follow four obvious consequences:

(1) It is probable that most, if not all, of the "Humanist" copies were derived from the "Mediaeval." In 1427 Poggio could not find in Rome a professional scribe who could read Beneventan, and it is not likely that there were many scribes in fifteenth century Italy who learned to copy

---

of the city, because it is so spelled in all of the old manuscripts of Caesar (where the text is corrected to *Genava* by modern editors) and in the *Cosmographia* of the Anonymus Ravennas (ed. M. Pindar & G. Parthey, Berolini, 1860, p. 237). The Swiss city was sometimes designated as simply *Genua*, but *Allobrogum* was added (Caesar describes it as an *oppidum Allobrogum*) when necessary to distinguish it from Genoa, which, in turn, was sometimes distinguished as *Genua Ligurum*, *Genua Superba*, or *Ianua Ligurum* (following the reading in some manuscripts of Mela).

[70] Rex's editorial note, copied by the scribe of K, is quoted by Mendell, *Tacitus*, p. 305: "Hic liber visus et ut accuratius ex incuria temporum potuit emendatus est per me" etc. His use of a Genevan manuscript will be evident from even a cursory inspection of the apparatus provided by Hanslik's pupils. Since the Genevan manuscripts are all of Class I, we are left with the mystery why Rex did not use his to supplement the curtailed text.

from that script. As for the Humanists themselves, they certainly shared Poggio's preference for a manuscript "qui legi possit," and would not have transcribed a text from Beneventan when they had available a copy in a more familiar and less "barbarous" hand.

(2) It is no longer certain that the second sheet in the eighth quaternion of the Second Medicean, containing *Hist.* I.69–75 and I.86–II.2, became detached and lost after 1452. On the contrary, it is highly probable that those folia were lost before Poggio noticed that *plures chartae* were missing and that our text of the chapters now wanting in the Medicean comes from the "Mediaeval" manuscripts.

(3) In the numerous passages on the flesh side of sheets in the Second Medicean where the original writing became evanid and was "retraced" in a thirteenth century Beneventan hand or supplied interlinearly by a Humanistic hand, it now becomes possible that the restorations were made with the aid of another manuscript and that the errors in those restorations come from that manuscript rather than a misreading of the faint characters of the original. In those passages, therefore, it would be desirable to ascertain whether the original writing can be read by application of the techniques now used with palimpsests.

(4) It is no longer true that "il est absolument démontré que le Mediceus II est notre source unique."[71] The "Humanist" manuscripts are not oddly garbled and interpolated copies of the Medicean; some of their peculiar readings certainly come from the "Mediaeval" manuscripts, and it thereby becomes probable that many of those lections come from the same source. In this sense Mendell, Koestermann, and the other defenders of the Leidensis have rendered an inestimable service to Tacitus, because although the collations by Hanslik's pupils have now shown that the Leidensis does not have the unique value that Mendell attributed to it, they have also shown that some of the fifteenth century manuscripts, especially the Genevan group but including the Leidensis, preserve readings that are certainly right and could not have been derived from the Medicean.[72] The most reasonable explanation is that there was at least

[71] Henri Goelzer in his Budé edition of the *Annales* (1923), p. xxvii.

[72] See Hanslik's preface to Horst Weiskopf's collations, pp. viii–xi, and his "Versuch einer Wertung der Handschriften von Tacitus" in the *Festschrift* for Walther Kraus (Wien, 1972), pp. 139–149, which became available after the present article had been accepted for the press. Although one or two of his numbered theses may require support from further collations (which I hope his pupils will provide for all of the remaining books of this part of Tacitus's work), it is impossible, I think, to dispute his conclusion that all existing editions of the *Annales* and *Historiae* are now obsolete, and that the long contemned and disregarded *recentiores* represent at least one tradition of the text that is independent of the Second Medicean.

one other "Mediaeval" manuscript—one that was in Geneva around 1440
and had a text that differed markedly from the text of the "Mediaeval"
manuscript then in a public library in Florence.[73]

Now that we have regretfully consigned to oblivion the long accepted
story about the Second Medicean which was, in its way, as romantic as
anything that Boccaccio imagined in his *Amorosa visione*, it becomes
imperative that we determine the relation of the "Mediaeval" manuscripts
to the Medicean. It is likely that it will be years before we are able to re-
write the *Überlieferungsgeschichte* of this part of Tacitus's work, but in the
meantime it may be profitable as well as interesting to consider the possible
source or sources of the "Mediaeval" tradition.

I. It is certain that each of the two parts of Tacitus's historical work
that we now have come from a single archetype, and it is virtually certain
that archetype was a codex in rustic capitals of the fourth or possibly even
of the third century and represented an edition in which the *Libri ab
excessu Divi Augusti* and the earlier work that we call *Historiae* had been
combined, probably in the third century,[74] into a single sequence of thirty
or more[75] consecutively numbered books. If we wish gratuitously to assume
that there were two such codices, both of which had been dismembered,
so that the first part of one and a section from the middle of the other
survived the Dark Ages, our problem is not significantly changed. It is
not likely that any extant manuscript was copied directly from that
archetype.[76]

[73] Where we can check, the Genevan MSS. have a text different from Boccaccio's:
p. 202, *supra*.

[74] See the article cited in note 5 *supra*. C. Poghirc, in an article in the Rumanian
periodical, *Studii Clasice*, VI (1964), 149–154, writing independently of my article (his
note 16), concluded that the two works of Tacitus were most probably combined when
the emperor, M. Claudius Tacitus, gave orders for the preservation of the works of his
supposed ancestor; he neatly impugns Syme's objections to that hypothesis. Poghirc
further observes that the phrase in the biography of the emperor (10.3), "librum . . .
scribi publicitus . . . iussit," implies that the works had been united in a single corpus,
i.e., *librum scribi* must stand for *codicem describi*.

[75] We must remember that the number thirty depends entirely on the reference in
Jerome's *Commentarius in Zachariam*, 3.14. We must regret that the new edition of that work
by M. Adriaen in the Corpus Christianorum, Turnholti, 1970, has what is obviously a
very select apparatus and has no note on the passage that interests us, so that we are still
left in ignorance whether all the manuscripts read *triginta* or *XXX* or show variations that
would render the figure suspect. It would be easy, for example, to conjecture that the
archetype may have read XXXVVOLVMINA.

[76] Lowe's theory that the Second Medicean was copied directly from the rustic-
capital archetype must be discarded, since the inversions in the text, caused by misplace-
ment of sheets when the exemplar was bound, could scarcely have occurred in such an
archetype. There also are errors of the eye that could scarcely have occurred in copying
from rustic capitals, e.g., *uerian(us)* for *aerian* in the passage quoted above, p. 200.

II. Since there are indications, which we need not now reexamine, that the First Medicean was copied from an exemplar in Insular script,[77] we may posit that the ancient codex, doubtless sadly mutilated and fragmentary by that time,[78] was copied by an Insular scribe whose work, possibly after mutilation, reached Fulda in the ninth century. This manuscript was presumably the ancestor of all extant manuscripts. It is possible that some of the "Mediaeval" manuscripts were derived from the Insular copy through intermediaries of which there is now no trace. That does not now seem very likely, but we are not yet in a position to estimate the likelihood with any confidence.

III. Since the observation of Dom Quentin was confirmed and amplified by Walter Allen, Jr.,[79] it seems certain that the well-known inversions in the Medicean text came from an exemplar that closely resembled the First Medicean in format, so that it seems probable that the Second Medicean was copied from a manuscript in Carolingian minuscule that had been brought from Fulda. Since it is unlikely that Fulda would not have retained a copy, it is obviously possible that there was at Fulda a manuscript that could have been the copy in Carolingian minuscules that was seen by Poggio in Florence around 1403 or the copy, of unknown date and script, that was in Geneva around 1440 or earlier.[80]

IV. The copy in Carolingian minuscules that was presumably sent to Monte Cassino also could have reached Florence in the early years of the fifteenth century. Since it was presumably the exemplar from which the

---

[77] The examples given by Rostagno in his preface to the photographic reproduction of the First Medicean seem probative.

[78] Walter Allen, Jr., in his searching analysis of the readings of the Leidensis, *T.A.P.A.*, CI (1970), 1–28, argues that "the losses in *Annals* V and VI" indicate "a time when the text was in the form of a *volumen* for each book and when each *volumen* confronted its own destiny." I do not follow the argument. Those parts of text could easily have been lost when folia became detached from a codex or the surviving portion of a codex that had already been dismembered, whereas it seems to me that a papyrus roll that had been broken or torn would have been copied or discarded at a time when the *volumen* was still the normal (and inexpensive) form of books.

[79] *Op. cit.*, especially pp. 22–25.

[80] Hanslik's B72, according to Mendell, *Tacitus*, p. 299, bears the date "MCCCCX," but "the Bodleian interprets this . . . as originally MCCCCXL." I do not know whether that "interpretation" is based on traces of an erased L or merely on the assumption that this manuscript should have been written about the time of the other dated manuscripts of the Genevan group. In the *Festschrift* cited in note 72 above, Hanslik says (p. 143) that in B72 "als Jahreszahl 1410 angegeben ist, was aber wahrscheinlich richtig 1490 heißen muß," but does not explain why he assigns so late a date. If he is right, V58 is the earliest Genevan manuscript that is specifically dated in the colophon (Mendell, p. 316); it was copied at Geneva (*Genuae*) in 1449 from an exemplar that its scribe describes as "inter cetera de quibus scitur non est neque pessimum neque mendosissimum."

Second Medicean was copied, it cannot have been the manuscript in Geneva, which had a markedly different text.

V. It is entirely possible that the Second Medicean was not the only copy made at Monte Cassino from the codex sent from Fulda. Such a copy, not *necessarily* in a Beneventan hand, could have had correct readings at points where the scribe of the Second Medicean erred, and if its text was at other points corrupted in passing through several inter- mediaries, it could have been the parent of the Genevan manuscripts and, perhaps, others.

VI. Although it has come to seem unlikely, it is still possible that the Second Medicean was, after all, the ancestor of all extant manuscripts and that we need revise the orthodox view only to the extent of deriving the fifteenth century copies from "Mediaeval" copies that were in turn derived from one or more copies of the Second Medicean made in the twelfth, thirteenth, or possibly the early fourteenth century. The principal objection is that this hypothesis requires us to assume the existence of Mediaeval Bentleys and Housmans, who emended correctly the text where it is corrupt in the Second Medicean.[81]

VIII

The possibility that we last suggested is, of course, the crucial one, and I shall conclude by suggesting one test by which we may tentatively estimate its probability. Mendell's famous "third inversion" remarkable for its absence in the Leidensis and Koestermann's "*Ti*tios, Ve*tt*ios, Plau*ti*os" from the same source, have not, indeed, lost their relevance to the problem, but there are other readings that are now more conspicuous criteria.

One of these is at *Ann.* XI.4.1, where, according to the generally re- ceived text, we are told that after the judicial murder of Valerius Asiaticus

[81] We may seriously underestimate the likelihood of sound emendations before the time of Valla and Pontanus. I am impressed by what D. S. Robertson, *C.Q.*, L (1956), 74, reports of an obscure fourteenth-century secretary, Antonio da Romagno (c. 1360–c. 1408), whose manuscript of the *Apologia* of Apuleius contains emendations of which "the number and quality . . . is, indeed, astonishing," including an "admirable correction" that Robertson particularly discusses. He says that H. E. Butler adopted about seventy of Antonio's emendations in his text of the *Apologia* (1914), some of which had previously been attributed to "such scholars as Casaubon and Lipsius." Butler's apparatus is selective, but he reports from the same source some very stupid emendations, especially *rubram spinam* in *Apol.* 59. Robertson, for reasons not apparent to me, says that "it is impossible to doubt that Antonio da Romagno is responsible" for the emendations that first appear in a manuscript written in his hand. Could he not have copied from a lost exemplar corrections made at an earlier date?

and the maliciously induced suicide of Poppaea Sabina, "Vocantur post haec patres, pergitque Suillius addere reos equites Romanos illustres, quibus Petra cognomentum. At causa necis ex eo, quod domum suam Mnesteris et Poppaeae congressibus praebuissent. Verum nocturnae quietis species alteri obiecta, *e.q.s.*" Here we have what seems to be at first sight a perfect example of corruption and interpolation that we can trace clearly through Horst Weiskopf's collations. The original presumably read MNESTERIS, and we assume that it is only by coincidence that the fullest traces of that reading appear in a manuscript (YO1) that was written around 1475: *in nesteris.* The Medicean has *nesteris,* which was corrupted to the *uesteris* and *nestoris* of certain other codices, and some sagacious scribe, seeing that those readings were meaningless, studied the context and boldly wrote *Valerii,* which is the reading of the Genevan manuscripts (V58, BO5, G, H, Mal, Prm, J, B72), the Leidensis, and some others. By no sequence of hands known to palaeography could *nesteris* have come by successive corruptions from *ualerii,* so the latter must be an interpolation. Q.E.D.

The case, however, is not really so simple, and it was not without reason that Mendell thought *Valerii* the correct reading[82] and Koestermann reported it in his apparatus with the comment, "nescio an rectius." It is easy to accept *Mnesteris* and then infer, with the confidence for which we censure such scholiasts as the Pseudo-Asconius, that in the lost part of Book XI Tacitus *must* have explained that Messalina suspected that Poppaea was sharing Mnester's probably phenomenal services and then, invoking the well-known adage that Hell hath no fury, etc., to use that guess to explain Messalina's animus against Poppaea and Asiaticus, thus attributing to her a pathological jealousy that she may also have shown in her demand that Silius divorce his wife—unless the latter was merely preparation for her marriage to him. As Mendell points out, however, there is no slightest indication of all this in the later references to Mnester; on the contrary, we are told that the actor, believing himself under orders from a crack-brained ruler of the world, was at Messalina's disposal until her downfall. What is more, Cassius Dio (LX.28.3) informs us that she τὸν Μνηστῆρα ἀποσπάσασα ἀπὸ τοῦ θεάτρου εἶχε, and that when people complained that the actor had disappeared, Claudius fatuously swore ὅτι μὴ συνείη αὐτῷ—a statement which (since a pun is most unlikely in the circumstances) must be a denial that the actor was living in concealment in the imperial household. The implication certainly is that Messalina kept him virtually in confinement at home as a domestic convenience so that he could come running whenever she whistled. Furthermore, one

[82] *A.J.P.,* LXXV (1954), 258; *Tacitus,* 331.

need not venture far into the turbid murk of sexual pathology to see in our
evidence indications that Mnester was so precious to Messalina because
he added a special variety to her multiplex amusements and enabled her
to savor a sadistic spice that other paramours could not provide; and the
most likely identification of Mnester's peculiarity is one that would render
a liaison with Poppaea or any other women most unlikely.[83]

It is also relevant to the reading *Mnesteris et Poppaeae congressibus* that
congressus is not an euphemism for sexual intercourse. According to Gerber
and Greef's *Lexicon*, this is one of the thirteen occurrences of the word in
Tacitus, and in all of the other twelve a sexual implication is categorically
excluded by the context. The word, however, does fit perfectly the kind
of statement that we should normally expect to find at this point.

In the first century, as today, when judicial procedures are used to
eliminate persons whom it would be simpler to assassinate, the trials are
staged to mislead public opinion, and some specious allegations of criminal
conduct are obviously requisite for the performance. At Rome the need
for such pretexts was felt so strongly that Augustus, when he exiled Ovid
by use of a discretionary power and without even a semblance of a public
trial, felt obliged to publish the absurd story that he was belatedly expressing disapproval of the *Ars amatoria*. For public proceedings in the
Senate, more plausible pretexts would be needed, especially when the
action was initiated by a *delator*.

It is quite obvious that the formal charge against Valerius Asiaticus

[83] At the end, Tacitus tells us (XI.36.1), Mnester pled for his life, "dilaniata veste
clamitans, adspiceret verberum notas." This, of course, is long after the beginning of his
services to Messalina, so she obviously has had him whipped frequently. Although in our
progressive society some fashionable males who can afford the fun find females much more
appetizing after they have been well bloodied with a buggy whip, sadism in females seldom
takes the form of thus inflicting pain on a submissive male—and we have no reason to
suppose that tastes differed in cosmopolitan Rome. In such societies, however, certain
females find a morbid satisfaction in obtaining sexual services from reluctant or resisting
males. Noteworthy, therefore, is Mnester's initial and extreme reluctance to entertain
Messalina who, according to Dio (LX.22.4), was unable to seduce him by any means
until she obtained an order from Claudius: ἐπεί γε μηδένα τρόπον μήθ' ὑπισχνουμένη τι μήτε
ἐκφοβοῦσα αὐτὸν συγγενέσθαι αὐτῇ ἀναπεῖσαι ἐδύνατο, διελέχθη τῷ ἀνδρί, κ.τ.λ. Messalina was,
by all accounts, an attractive and superficially elegant woman and, given her notorious
promiscuity, it is hard to believe that the popular pantomime's obduracy was caused by
mere timidity or prudence. He had been one of Caligula's playmates (Suet. *Cal.*, 36.1:
"M. Lepidum, Mnesterem pantomimum, quosdam obsides dilexisse fertur commercio
mutui stupri." 55.1: "Mnesterem pantomimum etiam inter spectacula osculabatur,"
e.q.s.), and Dio tells us, in the passage cited above, that Messalina was particularly aware
of Mnester's relations with Caligula. All this suggests that Mnester may have had a
morbid aversion to sexual relations with women and that this accounted for Messalina's
extraordinary interest in him.

when he was arraigned in Claudius's star chamber was treason: a plan for a military revolt, possibly involving use of Claudius's son, Britannicus.[84] This much is clear from Tacitus; Cassius Dio (LX.29) adds the interesting detail that, as sometimes happens today, the prosecutors were inefficient in coaching the perjurers whom they had hired to support their case. Poppaea can have been involved only through a claim that she was Valerius's confederate, and this is further implied by the statement that she was driven to suicide *terrore carceris*, i.e., the fear that she would be strangled in the *carcer* by an executioner, the traditional punishment for *perduellio*. The talk about her sexual irregularities and those of Valerius was clearly no more than rhetorical embellishment by Suillius and can have had no legal force.

Now when Suillius before the Senate involved the brothers Petra[85] in the case against Valerius and Poppaea (*addere reos*), both of whom were dead, he must have accused the two men of complicity in treason, and he must have supported the allegation with some circumstantial evidence, however flimsy. According to the accepted text, Tacitus does not tell us of what Suillius accused the brothers, because it is obvious, of course, that whether or not Poppaea had really sampled Mnester's private artistry, Suillius would not have dared to mention an allegation that was not only irrelevant to his case but would inevitably have focused attention on Messalina's own patronage of the esoteric arts. The most obvious accusation that Suillius could have brought against the two brothers was that it was at their home that Valerius and Poppaea met for the conferences (*congressūs*) at which they plotted a revolt against Claudius, doubtless following the business meeting with a recreational hour of *adulterium*. To support a claim that the brothers knew that the object of those private meetings was more than fun, Suillius would have adduced the dream,

84 The rôle of the boy's *educator*, Sosibius, in the plot against Valerius Atticus, and the lavish reward given him "quod Britannicum praeceptis, Claudium consiliis iuvaret," may be some indication that the scenario that Suillius composed for his accusation made some mention of the child, and a scheme to present Britannicus to the German armies as the eventual heir could have been made the subject of a plausible tale. On the other hand, Sosibius's warning about *opes principibus infestas* suggests an effort to "restore the Republic," which might have seemed plausible in the light of the prominence of Valerius in the effort to restore Senatorial rule after the assassination of Caligula, although Valerius, as an intelligent man, must have learned from that experience. As an Allobrox, Valerius, however wealthy and influential, could not rationally have aspired to the principate himself.

85 Koestermann in his commentary *ad loc.* is wrong in saying "Ritter mit dem Namen Petra sind sonst unbekannt." It is possible that the two brothers were sons of T. Pomponius T.f. Petra, who was "praefectus equitum Germanici Caesaris," and is commemorated by an inscription, *C.I.L.*, XI, 969.

described by Tacitus, to which one of the brothers had superstitiously and imprudently given an interpretation unfavorable to Claudius when he assuaged his human itch to narrate his dreams to others.

Now can we believe that Tacitus failed to mention the principal charge against the two brothers, inserting instead a parenthetical explanation that the true reason for their condemnation was Messalina's secret and (at the time) unmentionable animus, and then gave considerable space to the dream, which can have been only a secondary and merely substantiating part of the official accusation? Having looked through all of Tacitus's reports of trials before the Senate without finding a parallel for such an illogical sequence of statements, I think it unlikely that he did. Every consideration of historical probability, it seems to me, is in favor of *Valerii* as the correct reading.

I have elaborated this point because I think we must, sooner or later, choose between the two alternatives, with all that they imply:

(1) *Valerii* is the true reading. Since *nesteris* cannot be a palaeographical corruption of that word,[86] it must either (a) have entered the text from some marginal comment, and that is unlikely because we have no reason to believe that the text was annotated or commented upon before modern times, or (b) be an alteration intentionally or inadvertently made by someone who had the *histrio* much on his mind, and there seems to be no good reason for such preoccupation, or (c) be a remnant of a considerable lacuna in our text, coming from some mention of Mnester, perhaps as an informer or as having some relation to the brothers Petra or, conceivably, as having met Messalina at the home of the indulgent pair, and all these suggestions seem rather farfetched, or (d) be a chance collocation of syllables that were merely the débris of two or more words in a statement defining the location of the house or the time of the meetings or of a statement preceding *at*, and it would be a remarkable coincidence that thus produced a reading so closely resembling the name of Mnester.

(2) *Valerii* is an interpolation. In this case, I think we should still pay

---

[86] Subject to the proviso that scribes are sometimes capable of what surpasseth all understanding. In *T.A.P.A.*, LXXXIX (1959), 216, I give a collation of a fifteenth-century manuscript in which a simple statement of commonplace Stoic doctrine reads: "Si personam induisti supra Aesopi vires, neque eam substines et quod implere poteras omisisti." *Aesopi* is, of course, an error for *tuas*, and there is nothing in the entire discourse that even remotely suggests Greek fables or Roman actors. Obviously, the blunder cannot be palaeographic, and the only possible explanation is that the scribe inadvertently wrote down a word that he heard spoken in the room in which he worked or that was brought to his mind by some private train of thought that engaged his consciousness while he performed the mechanical task of copying from his exemplar. With that example before me, I shall call no scribal aberration impossible.

sufficient regard to historical probability to assume a lacuna before *at*, i.e., the loss of a passage in which Tacitus indicated the basis of Suillius's accusation, whether or not that had anything to do with the house in which the Petras resided—an accusation that certainly involved Valerius and possibly Poppaea in some way. This statement disappeared by homoeoteleuton or in some other way before our archetype was copied, leaving only the statement about Mnester and Poppaea that Tacitus added to show that the principal charge was so flimsy that it succeeded only because Messalina had a secret reason for using her influence against the brothers. This is possible, of course, but if *Valerii* is an interpolation, it was no impulsive scribal expedient. It must have been a change deliberately made after careful study of the context by someone who either did not recognize the name of Mnester or, more probably, decided, by following the reasoning that we set forth above, that the historical situation required mention of Valerius. A man who gave that much thought to the text would also have been capable of making such emendations as *capiendis pecuniis* ⟨*posuit*⟩ *modum* in XI.7.4, ⟨*bo*⟩*leto*⟨*rum*⟩ in XII.67.1, and {*vi an*} *vinolentia* in the same section[87] and, so far as I can see, he could have made all the other emendations required to make the Genevan manuscripts give an apparently correct text in place of the corruptions that appear in the Medicean. On this hypothesis, however, we are faced with the paradox that a scholar so competent and diligent was also too stupid, indifferent, or lazy to do anything about the gross corruptions in the same manuscripts, where a patently unintelligible text could have been mended with much less effort.

Either alternative, in other words, is open to objections so grave as to make it seem improbable. It will require prolonged, meticulous, and discriminating work to extricate us from this dilemma.

University of Illinois at Urbana

[87] See Hanslik's preface to Weiskopf's *Annales XI–XII*, pp. viii–xi.

16

Aldus Manutius' *Fragmenta Grammatica*

JOHN J. BATEMAN

Scattered through the various editions of Aldus' Latin Grammar are several references to a work with the title *Fragmenta* or, occasionally, *Fragmenta Grammatica*. This title seems to be abbreviated. The full form, and first reference, occurs in the dedicatory letter to Alberto Pio for the first printed edition of the Latin Grammar, the *Institutiones Grammaticae*, published for Aldus by Torresano in Venice in 1493.[1] Aldus, describing the pains he devoted to the *Institutiones*, mentions some other grammatical works he wrote during the same time. They are: "graecas institutiones: & exercitamenta grammatices: atque utriusque linguae fragmenta: & alia quaedam ualde (ut spero) placitura."[2] Light is thrown on this sentence by a passage in a letter from Aldus to Caterina Pio, mother of Alberto and Leonello Pio, princes of Carpi, whom Aldus was tutoring from about 1483 to 1489. The letter is dated March 14, 1487.[3] Aldus produces a list of his writings and indicates that they were made especially for the instruction

[1] The letter is reproduced by C. S. Scarafoni, the discoverer of this previously unknown edition of the Latin Grammar, in *Miscellanea Bibliografica in memoria di Don Tommaso Accurti* a cura di Lamberto Donati (Rome, 1947), 197.

[2] The *atque* suggests that the *exercitamenta* and the *fragmenta* formed a single work. Scarafoni apparently makes the same assumption since he paraphrases the title as "esercitazioni su ambedue le lingue classiche" (*op. cit.*, p. 198). However, the references to the work are always simply to the *Fragmenta* with one exception, where in a discussion of the verb *mutuor* Aldus refers to the fuller treatment in his *exercitamentis grammaticis* (see No. 13).

[3] By Ester Pastorello, "L' Epistulario Manuziano," *Biblioteca di Bibliografia Italiana*, 30 (Florence, 1957), No. 4. C. F. Bühler, however, argues for a date prior to January 1, 1485, in his "The First Aldine," *Paps. of the Bibl. Soc. of America*, 42 (1948), 273–277.

[4] The *de accentibus et Latinis et Graecis opusculum* seems never to have been printed. Its contents are probably to be met with in the Letter to Students appended to the 1501 edition of Virgil and in the section on accents in Book IV of the third edition of the *Institutiones Ling. Lat.*, Venice, 1508.

of children. In addition to the *Grammaticae Linguae Latinae Institutiones*, there is a work on Greek and Latin accents,[4] the *Panegyrici Musarum*,[5] a *libellus graecus tamquam isagogicus*,[6] and a work on the writing of poetry.[7] These *libelli* are doubtless the *alia quaedam* referred to in the later letter to Alberto Pio. Having used these works as textbooks, Alberto at least would understand the reference; the uninitiated purchaser of the *Institutiones Grammaticae* could take pleasure in the thought that his Aldus had more to offer him soon.

Aldus, dissatisfied, as he tells us, with all the textbooks then available, prepared these *opuscula* in connection with his duties tutoring Caterina's children in Carpi, and perhaps some other children too at the time.[8] They all found their way into print sooner or later in one form or another except the *Exercitamenta grammatices atque utriusque linguae fragmenta*. Aldus, it seems, never found the time either to perfect it to his own satisfaction or to see it into print. The manuscript disappeared after his death; stolen, according to his son Paolo.[9] All that survives are the tantalizing references found mainly in the successive editions of the Latin Grammar and in the *De literis Graecis*. The partial treatment of these references to date has produced a certain amount of confused comment about the *Fragmenta* in the scholarship on Aldus. Therefore, in order to offer a better picture of this lost work, I have collected all of these references, arranged them according to their content, and by comparing them with other contemporary grammatical texts have tried to divine a little of what the *Fragmenta* may have contained.

The title and the extant "fragments" suggest a miscellany of grammatical problems in the Greek and Latin languages whose discussion was intended both to inform and to instigate (*exercitare*) the mind to further

---

[5] First printed in Venice at the press of Baptista de Tortis sometime between May 1487 and March 1491; cf. Bühler (above, note 3), pp. 277–278.

[6] Julius Schück, *Aldus Manutius und seine Zeitgenossen in Italien und Deutschland* (Berlin, 1867), p. 7, thought this work was the *De literis graecis* which was first published in 1495 as an appendix to Constantine Lascaris' *Erotemata*. Pastorello (above, note 3), p. 285 identifies it with the *Breuissima Introductio ad Graecas Literas*, which she believes was first printed in 1494. But C. F. Bühler shows that the *Breuissima Introductio* is a condensed reprint of the 1495 Appendix and was probably contemporary with the 1497 edition of the Greek *Horae*; cf. *PBSA*, 36 (1942), 18–23.

[7] *De componendis carminibus opusculum*; this work was apparently never printed separately though its contents may have been employed in Aldus' later writings on metrical subjects.

[8] Cf. Schück (above, note 6), p. 7, n. 1.

[9] Cf. Paolo's letter of November 8, 1565, to Mario Corrado (Epist., VII, 7): Fragmenta patris mei quod requiris: apud me nulla sunt: furto ablata, quo ille tempore uita excessit, creditum est.

study.[10] Aldus had before him such models as Valla's *Elegantiae*, Perotti's *Cornucopiae*, and Politian's *Miscellanea*, different though they may have been in size, scope, or specific purpose. Aldus' own purpose was to give instruction in grammar. The *Fragmenta Grammatica* must then be considered in relation to Aldus' *Grammaticae linguae latinae Institutiones*.[11] The fifteenth-century humanistic Latin grammars were modeled on and to a considerable extent derived from the ancient grammars some of which, like Terentianus Maurus, were again coming to light. Special works like the Ars Minor of Donatus apart, these grammars tended to contain a considerable amount of detail. The humanistic grammars sought to eliminate a good deal of this detail, but even a relatively simple grammar like that of Sulpitius Verulanus offered many an obstacle to the beginner. On the other hand excessive simplicity was also pernicious since grammar was a science and the major subject of study by the child until he was ready for oratory and poetry. As mentioned above, Aldus was led to his grammatical writings by his dissatisfaction with currently available textbooks. He says in the epilogue of the *Institutiones*: "I had to teach young children and I was not able to do it as effectively as I wished. No one in my judgment had yet written a grammar suitable for instructing children. One was quite short and concise, another exceedingly diffuse and ostentatious, a third utterly inept and indigestible [he is describing perhaps in order Donatus, Priscian, and Alexander's *Doctrinale*]. Although there exist works which are carefully and learnedly written [presumably humanistic grammars], still I must confess none of them satisfied me. . . . I have sought what I most felt the need of, a grammar to teach children quickly and effectively."[12]

To achieve this end Aldus simplifies the standard pattern.[13] He reduces the amount of illustrative material, eliminates the extended treatment of

[10] Aldus derived the notion and perhaps part of his title from Quintilian 1, 4, 6, which he quotes in Book IV of the *Institutiones* where he exhorts the student to read and reread his remarks on the letters and related material in Book I (Venice, 1523, 101b). Quintilian says grammar is a "subject of great subtlety which is calculated not merely to sharpen the wits of a boy, but to exercise (*exercere*) also the most profound erudition and knowledge." Aldus' own fascination with language and the intricacies of grammatical description surfaces in many places in his writings and occasional comments of which the prefatory letter in his 1496 *Thesaurus Cornucopiae. & Horti Adonidis* (*2ᵛ) is very typical.

[11] The *Graecae Institutiones*, written in the 1480's and published only posthumously in 1515, was never used by Aldus for the same purposes as the Latin Grammar and contains nothing pertinent to this study.

[12] This passage occurs in the first edition, published in 1493, is revised slightly for the second edition of 1501 and is eliminated from the subsequent editions.

[13] Represented, for example, by the *Ars Maior* of Donatus and Perotti's *Regulae Sypontinae* [*Rudimenta grammatices*], Venice: Christophorus de Pensis, November 4, 1495.

complex subjects, and introduces several passages of mnemonic verse (not of course in itself an innovation). He reveals his rationale in a remark made when he comes to heteroclite nouns: "We have considered these few things about genders to be sufficient for those who are learning the first rudiments of grammar. But we shall treat copiously of genders in our *Fragmenta* because the child will have progressed by then."[14] The *Institutiones* contain the rudiments—hence the title of the 1501 edition.[15] Advanced material is reserved for the *Fragmenta*. We can perhaps perceive here the role of the *Fragmenta* in Aldus' plan of instruction. The various works listed in the letters to Caterina and Alberto Pio make a graded series of textbooks from the first step of learning simultaneously the Greek and Latin alphabets through the mastery of the two languages and the eventual writing of poetry in classical forms. Aldus is thus the forerunner of modern pedagogical practice and textbook preparation and publication.

We shall never really know why all of these writings did not eventually appear in print as some of them did. No doubt the demands of time and money made by the printing business were a factor: priority had to be given to other publications. More important perhaps were the changes in Aldus' own views and intentions as he advanced in years and learning.[16] Our knowledge of the *Exercitamenta Grammatices atque Utriusque Linguae Fragmenta* is derived, as noted above, chiefly from the four editions of the Latin Grammar published by Aldus during his lifetime, from the various editions of the *De Literis Graecis*, and from a famous insert made in the 1512 edition of Constantine Lascaris' *Erotemata* in order to fill two blank pages. Inference also may be drawn from remarks in sundry other publications edited or supervised by Aldus, most notably the 1509 edition of Horace's *Carmina*. These works are in chronological sequence:

A: (Institutiones Grammaticae; no title page). Colophon: Vtilissimae ac per quambreues (sic) Institutiones grammaticae. Venice. March 7, 1493 (no printer named).

B: Rudimenta Grammatices Latinae Linguae. Venice: Aldus Manutius, February 1501 (Venetian style; 1502 actually).

C: Institutionum Grammaticarum Libri Quatuor. Venice: Aldus Manutius, April 1508.

---

[14] See Fragment No. 1, below.

[15] *Rudimenta Grammatices Latinae Linguae*. The return to the original title of *Institutiones* etc. for the revised edition of 1508 also signals a new attitude on Aldus' part to the function of the grammar and his own role as teacher through the printed word.

[16] The evidence may be found primarily in the shift in the kinds of books Aldus undertakes to print—a new direction is taken in 1501—and in the revisions and expansions made in the third edition of the Latin Grammar of 1508. As remarked in note 15 above, it no longer purports to offer only the rudiments of the language.

Cd: De literis graecis, ac diphthongis, & quemadmodum ad nos ueniant. Etc. Appended to the Latin Grammar but separately signed.[17]

D: Q. Horatii Flacci Poemata. Venice: Aldus Manutius, March 1509.

E: (De vitiata vocalium ac diphthongorum prolatione πάρεργον.) Pages &2ᵛ–3ᵛ in Constantine Lascaris' [Erotemata], Venice: Aldus Manutius, October 1512.[18]

F: Institutionum Grammaticarum Libri Quatuor. Venice: Aldus Manutius, December 1514.

Fd: De literis graecis, etc. Appended to the 1514 edition of the Institutiones Grammaticae.[19]

The Institutiones Grammaticae was written during the 1480's when Aldus was at Carpi, as is evident from the letter to Caterina Pio. But the work was being revised as late as 1492, probably as it was being prepared for the press, since Aldus refers in it (p. m2ᵛ) to the capture of Granada by Ferdinand and Isabelle on January 2. The dedicatory letter to Alberto Pio, perhaps written shortly before the book went to press, implies that the Fragmenta Grammatica was ready for publication in the near future. The verbs which Aldus uses in the 1493 text to refer to the Fragmenta/Exercitamenta are all in the future tense. These futures can be interpreted to indicate the relationship of Aldus the teacher speaking to his students (that is, you are now studying this point of grammar in a rudimentary fashion, you will take it up again in a more advanced form in the future in my Fragmenta); or Aldus the author addressing his wider public: I am now writing the rudiments of the grammar, I shall presently discuss the

[17] This work is actually a collection of separate, short pieces on the Greek alphabet and the ways of writing it, prayers and poems which together constitute a Greek Primer. It first appears in print as an appendix (ALPHABETUM GRAECUM) to the 1495 Aldine edition of C. Lascaris' Erotemata and was subsequently appended in revised versions to all the other editions of Lascaris' Grammar as well as to his own Latin Grammar published by Aldus. It probably originated as the libellus graecus tamquam isagogicus mentioned in the letter to Caterina Pio (above, note 6).

[18] See Fragment No. 19 below for further information about this item. The title Aldi Manutii, De Vitiata Vocalium ac diphthongorum prolatione, πάρεργον, first appears in an edition of Jacobus Ceratinus' De Sono Literarum, Praesertim Graecarum libellus, published by Johann Soter in Cologne in 1529, pp. B3ʳ–4ʳ. Soter or his editor apparently extracted the material from the 1512 Lascaris Erotemata and gave it this title. It was frequently reprinted thereafter, including several times by the Aldine Press late in the sixteenth century, and thus enters the bibliographical records as a minor opusculum of Aldus Manutius.

[19] Matter pertinent to this study appears first in the version of the De literis graecis which was prepared by Aldus for publication with the 1508 edition of the Latin Grammar. It was reprinted without revision in the 1512 Lascaris Erotemata. Several minor changes and additions were then made in the text for the publication with the fourth edition of the Latin Grammar in 1514.

topic in detail in the (not yet written) *Fragmenta*. These future tenses remain in the second edition of 1501 (1502), which could mean either that Aldus overlooked them in revising the text or, more likely, that they fitted the actual circumstances: despite the announcement in the letter to Alberto Pio the work was not really finished and in a form suitable for publication. Final revisions were perhaps never completed: hence the failure to publish. But some advance was certainly made during the six years between the publication of the second edition of the Latin Grammar in February 1502 and the third edition in April 1508. In the third edition five of these future tenses (see Nos. 7, 8a, 9, 10, 11a below) are changed to the perfect tense. This change in tense could be taken to mean that the *Fragmenta* was now finished.[20] However, four other verbs in the future are left unchanged (Nos. 12, 13 *bis*, 14a below). These are probably oversights on Aldus' part. But the use of the future in No. 18 which first appears in the 1508 edition of the *De literis Graecis* (though the sentence itself could have been written several years earlier) suggests a third possible relationship: that of Aldus the publisher to his prospective customers. This possibility may receive some support from the change of tenses in No. 11b. The future *erit* in the phrase *mihi cum illis erit hac de re certamen* of the 1493 and 1501 editions is changed to *est* in the 1508 edition and then back to *erit* in the 1514 edition. In changing *est* to *erit* (unless this is due to the compositor), Aldus seems to be contemplating future publication since all the other indications suggest that work on the *Fragmenta* is now finished.

It is possible that these changes from future to perfect or present tense in the third edition of the Latin Grammar should be correlated with the times, otherwise unknown, during the six-year period when Aldus was revising the text for the third edition and simultaneously working on the *Fragmenta*. The perfect tenses would imply that the *Fragmenta* was finished before Book III of the *Institutiones* went through the press in 1508.[21] The future tense which appears in the passage on the diphthongs in Book I (No. 15a) would have been added by Aldus closer to 1502 than to 1508.

---

20 Engelbert Drerup seems to have been the first scholar to notice the implication of these changes in tense; cf. his *Die Schulaussprache des Griechischen* (Paderborn, 1930), I, 35. Drerup was comparing the use of the future tense in a reference in the 1508 edition of the *De literis graecis* and the perfect tense on page &3ᵛ of the 1512 *Erotemata*. He had not examined the texts of the Latin Grammar and was consequently not aware of all of the ramifications of his observation; and he would not of course have known about the existence of the 1493 edition and the letter to Alberto Pio. He was thus led to infer that the *Fragmenta* was contemplated by Aldus in 1508 and finished in 1512.

21 The four Books are printed so that each book ends with a gathering. This procedure suggests that the work was printed in sections and not continuously. Aldus was very likely working on it even as it was going through the press.

Revisions in the text of the *De literis graecis* which was also being prepared for publication with the new edition of the Latin Grammar in 1508 bear almost entirely on the subject of correct pronunciation though other matters enter too. One of these latter is a quotation from Lucian's *Iudicium Vocalium*. Since the second edition of Lucian appeared in June 1503, this date could be taken as a *terminus post quem* for the start on the revisions of these writings. However, the earliest actual evidence of Aldus' interest in the correct pronunciation of the classical languages and the first reference to the *Fragmenta* in this connection occurs in the 1501 edition of the Latin Grammar (14ʳ; cf. No. 14a below).[22] The question of the correct pronunciation of the classical languages was obviously a subject of continuing interest with Aldus. There are references to his discussion of the sound of eta in the *Fragmenta* in Book IV of the 1508 *Institutiones* (No. 14c, d below). This book, whose contents are largely a new addition to the Latin Grammar, is centered on metrical matters and was probably being written in 1507 or 1508.

Aldus, like most humanist grammarians, had long had an interest in classical metrics. One result of this interest is the metrical introductions to the lyric poems in the second edition of Horace's *Poemata*, published in March 1509. Moreover, Aldus was stimulated, perhaps on the spur of the moment, to add some notes on the text which involve metrics and a sketch of Horace's lyric meters which together occupy the first two sheets (gatherings) of the book. The signaturing of the book suggests that Aldus had originally intended to use only one sheet for the front matter, and after the presswork on the body of the book was begun or even finished decided to include his annotations and suggested new readings. For instance, in his note on *Carmina*, 1, 27, 5, he justifies his change of the

---

[22] Aldus' concern for a good pronunciation of Latin in the sense of being fluent and not improperly affected by contemporary sounds of the vernacular dialects is already evident in the opening pages of the 1493 edition where he apologizes for his exercises on syllabification and observes (a2ᵛ): Nam si bene didicerit puer: & quot syllabarum sint dictiones: easque tum in libro tum ad digitos syllabatim connectere: nec scribet: pronuntiabitque caelli caellorum: & allius allia alliud per geminum ll ut plurimi in Gallia cisalpina solent: quod ipse saepe & uidi & audiui nec ubi una esse debet consonans duas ponet: nec ubi duae unam. ubi eadem in Gallia perpauci sunt qui non errent. Quod si sub litterarii ludi magistro cum essent paruuli didicissent ad digitos plurima uerba syllabicare: quod fieri in Latio assolet: non toties & scribendo & loquendo Barbarismum facerent. His sensitivity to dialectical differences in Italian and indeed his deep interest in these linguistic features may be observed in the preface to the *Thesaurus Cornucopiae. & Horti Adonidis*, published in 1496, where he remarks that the language and pronunciation are quite different in Rome, Naples, Calabria, Florence, Genoa, Venice, Milan, Brescia, and Bergamo and cites some examples of common words which are pronounced very differently in these places.

received *acinacis* to *acinaces* on the ground that the erroneous pronunciation of η as i [i:] had influenced the transmission of the text since the customary Latin equivalent of Greek eta was a long e. He then says: *Sed de hoc alius erit tractatus.* The *tractatus* is certainly the *Fragmenta Grammatica.* The future tense again points more likely to the act of printing than of writing. It would thus accord with the uses of the future notes above in Book I of the 1508 *Institutiones* and in the *De literis graecis* appended to it.

In conclusion, then, the 1512 edition of Lascaris' *Erotemata* provides the evidence of a *terminus ante quem* for the completion of the *Fragmenta*. Parts of it were being worked on simultaneously with the revision of the Latin Grammar for the new edition which appeared in 1508. Completion and publication were being contemplated in 1509. Aldus' abiding interest in grammatical questions began early and lasted right up to the end of his life in 1515. His awareness of the differences between contemporary and ancient pronunciations of Greek and Latin first becomes evident in 1501, though it is only in 1508 that he begins to make forthright statements about contemporary errors and the need to correct them.[23] It seems to be this new interest in correct pronunciation of the classical languages which continued to delay the completion and publication of the *Fragmenta* and which perhaps eventually frustrated Aldus' plans altogether.

THE FRAGMENTS

What follows is a collection of the actual and possible references to the *Exercitamenta Grammatices atque Utriusque Linguae Fragmenta* found in the works listed on pp. 229 f. I have separated and organized the "fragments" according to subject matter, beginning with morphology, then syntax, and finally pronunciation. This is roughly the order of Aldus' Latin Grammar and the Appendix On Greek Letters and may have been the order followed in the *Fragmenta Grammatica*. However, it is possible that since the grammar traditionally began with the letters (*de litteris*), Aldus may have begun the *Fragmenta* with his views on pronunciation. This would have required a revision of the order which evidently obtained in the earliest version(s), and as I have suggested above, may have been one reason for the long delay in completing the work. In any case the topics of the different

[23] It was precisely at this time that Erasmus came to Venice to work with Aldus. The implications for this association have been traced by Deno Geanakoplos, *Greek Scholars in Venice* (Cambridge, Mass., 1962), pp. 256–278; see also my article, "The Development of Erasmus' Views on the Correct Pronunciation of Latin and Greek," *Classical Studies Presented to Ben Edwin Perry* (Urbana, 1969), pp. 50–53.

passages in each broad category will give some idea of the scope of the lost work and the range of Aldus' interests in grammar.

The alphabetical sigla identify the work from which each passage has come; the rest of the reference indicates the location of the passage by signature, page number, and recto or verso. (Pagination, even if it does exist in any of these Aldine books, is not a reliable guide.) Variant readings are noted after each passage. In general, I have reproduced the text of the original edition as closely as seemed feasible. Thus I have kept the orthography of the copy text except that abbreviations have been resolved and the ampersand replaced by *et*. I have capitalized words according to modern practice and have similarly brought the punctuation into accord with modern usage, but only to the extent of replacing periods and sometimes commas with semicolons (which were not in the Aldine roman fonts) within the sentence. The notes are intended to explicate the overly succinct references and to set the fragment into some context.[24]

A. General Grammar and Morphology

1. A: a8ᵛ–b1ʳ; B: a8ᵛ–b1ʳ

There is on these pages a section of the Grammar containing a brief summary of the rules on gender of nouns. At the end of the section is the statement:

> Haec perpauca de generibus satis esse duximus iis, qui prima discunt rudimenta grammatices. Sed in fragmentis nostris de generibus, quia tunc iam profecerit puer cumulate tractabimus.

This statement disappears from the third (1508) and subsequent editions of the *Institutiones Grammaticae*. The reason apparently is because the brief compendium of rules is now replaced by some six pages *De Generibus* (CF: b5ʳ–7ᵛ). The new section is completely rewritten and contains material from the earlier editions only by coincidence. In addition to the general rules on gender, it consists mostly of lists of nouns and adjectives which are arranged alphabetically according to their nominative singular endings.[25] There is nothing novel or unusual about the contents of this section or

---

[24] I have used the following copies of these Aldine publications: A: Biblioteca Nazionale di San Marco, Incunabuli V. 632; B: British Museum, G 7581; C: British Museum, 625. c. 14; Cd: Idem; D: University of Illinois Library (uncatalogued); E: University of Illinois Library, 485. L33g. 1512; F: British Museum, 625. c. 15; Fd: Idem.

[25] The head words, for example, are B (the letter), Epigramma, Cubile, Libye, Gerundi, Sermo, Cornu, Lac, Lupercal, Mel, Pugil, Consul, Delubrum, Carmen, Torcular, and so on with -er, -or, -ur, -as, -es, -is, -os, -us, -ix, -ps, and -ns. This method of classifying nouns by their endings is common in mediaeval and humanistic grammars alike and probably comes from Priscian. Cf. also Pompeius, *GLK*, 5, 164, 28–165, 18.

their presentation. It would appear that Aldus has introduced into his revised edition of the Grammar the detailed discussion which he had at an earlier time thought unnecessary and indeed unsuitable for beginners in grammar. The material presumably came from the *Fragmenta*.

2. (a) A: b7^r; B: b4^v

> Singulariter. haec Dido, huius Didus et Didois, huic Didoi, hanc Dido et Didoem, o Dido, ab hac Didoe. Pluraliter. hae Didoes, harum Didoum, his et ab his Didoibus, has Didoes, o Didoes; sine n. Sed inflecte iam tu cum litera n sic, haec Dido, huius Didonis, haec Calypso, huius Calypsonis, sicut haec Iuno, huius Iunonis. Sed de his multa dicemus in fragmentis.

(b) C: d1^r; F: d1^r

> Singulariter. haec Dido, huius Didus et Didonis, huic Didoni, hanc Dido et Didonem, o Dido, ab hac Didone. Pluraliter. hae Didones, harum Didonum, his et ab his Didonibus, has Didones, o Didones; sic haec Calypso, huius Calypsus et Calypsonis, sicut haec Iuno, huius Iunonis. Sed de his multa in fragmentis.

Leaving aside the matter of the elimination of the question and answer format between the second and the third editions, Aldus has evidently moved somewhat in his thinking about this particular kind of declension between 1501 and 1508. The grammatical question under consideration here is whether Greek nouns like *Dido* and *Calypso* are to be declined in Latin on the Greek stem (Dido- + us, i, etc.) or whether the stem too had to be Latinized as *Didon-* before using Latin endings. The grammarians usually preferred the second approach.[26] However, Aldus found a dissenting voice in Phocas who says the forms in -*nis* etc. are repudiated by the harshness of the sound and the authority of the ancients (*GLK*, 5, 424, 19–24), a view to which Quintilian seems to give some support (I. 5, 63 f.). Aldus quotes these passages together with Priscian in C (e3^v; F: e3^v–4^r; the passage does not occur in AB):

> Licetne nomina in o ut Dido, Sappho latine declinare ut Iuno? licet secundum Priscianum, qui antiquos huiusmodi declinatione usos ostendit. Actius, Custodem assiduum Ioni apposuit. Ennius, Poenus Didone oriundos. Plautus, Vidit Argum, quem quondam Ioni Iuno custodem apposuit. Qua ratione declinandi etiam C. Caesar secutus antiquos usus est, quod indicat tetrastichon hoc in Romulo.
>
> > Vatibus Ausoniis Tyriam dat Graecia Dido.
> > Fecit Didonem romula uox Taciti.
> > At Calypsonem Latiis das inclyte Caesar.
> > Quodque decor patitur Quintiliane iubes.

---

[26] Cf. Priscian, *GLK*, 2, 209, 14–210, 13; Probus, *GLK*, 4, 9, 34–36 and 10, 16–18.

Sed errant, ait Foca grammaticus, qui Didonis, aut Mantonis genitiuum dicunt, cum et uocis asperitas, et ueterum autoritas eiusmodi declinationem repudiet; nam translata in Latinam linguam, nihilominus Graece declinantur, sic Dido, Didois, Didoi, Didoem, Didoe. Idem sentire uidetur Quintilianus his uerbis: Nunc recentiores instituerunt Graecis nominibus Graecas declinationes potius dare, quod tamen ipsum non semper fieri potest. Mihi autem placet Latinam rationem sequi, quousque patitur decor; neque enim iam Calypsonem dixerim, ut Iunonem.[27]

The changes made in the presentation of the declension in the third edition of the Grammar do not make it entirely clear whether or not Aldus followed Quintilian's suggested *via media*. Phocas is clearly the source of the forms *Didois, Didoi*, etc., which appear in A and B and which were presumably justified in the *Fragmenta*. Their suppression in the 1508 edition, which thus bows to tradition and perhaps the authority of Quintilian, need not reflect Aldus' own solution to this question. His predilection for things Greek may have ultimately made him side with Phocas.

3. A: b8ᵛ; B: b6ᵛ; C: d2ʳ; F: d2ʳ

Haec anus, huius anus cuius declinationis? quartae. Quare? quia nomina quarti declinatus etiam in uis syllabas inueniuntur prolata in casu patrio, ut dicemus in fragmentis grammaticis.*

---

* ut . . . grammaticis AB] ut supra est dictum CF

The removal of the reference to the *Fragmenta Grammatica* suggests, as in No. 1 above, that the new material on this grammatical point in the 1508 edition was taken from the *Fragmenta*. Aldus has inserted here in Book I between the section on gender and a section entitled *Quaestiones de nomine*[28] some ten pages of material under the heading *De nominum declinatione* (b7ᵛ–c5ʳ in C). In these pages he takes up the morphology of the noun, case by case, singular and plural, through the five declensions. The reference, *ut supra dictum est*, is therefore to this prior discussion of the genitive case and specifically to pages b8ᵛ–c1ʳ. He says here:

Genitiuus quartae declinationis quot terminationes habet? treis, ut haec manus huius manus, hic fructus huius fructus; uis diuisas, ut haec manus huius manuis, hic fructus huius fructuis, haec anus huius anuis. Terentius eius anuis opinor causa, quae mortua est. M. Varro in primo de agricultura Contra ut Mineruae caprini generis nihil immolarent propter oleam, quod

[27] Priscian, *GLK*, 2, 209 f. is the source of the citations from Accius, Ennius and Plautus; Quintilian, 1, 5, 63, that from Caesar. I do not know the source of the tetrastich. Phocas is paraphrased rather than quoted directly; cf. *GLK*, 5, 424, 19–24.
[28] *Examen in nomine* in A, *Interrogationes in nomine* in B.

eam quam laeserit fieri dicunt sterilem; eius enim saliuam esse fructuis uenenum. A quo genitiuo uis in frequenti usu est datiuus ui. Nam a genitiuuo manus huic manu est datiuus. Item u ut hoc cornu huius cornu.[29]

Aldus' starting point for his discussion of this topic in the *Fragmenta* was undoubtedly Priscian, who says the ancients produced a genitive ending *in uis divisas* and cites the passage of Terence (*GLK*, 2, 362, 24–363, 5). Aldus was familiar with this passage in Priscian since he quotes the line from Terence elsewhere in the 1493 edition in a second note on *anus* (a curious doublet, A: c1^r; B: b6^v). The additional material probably comes from Aulus Gellius either directly or through an intermediate source like Sulpitius Verulanus.[30] Gellius (4, 16) says Varro and P. Nigidius used the forms *senatuis, domuis,* and *fluctuis.* He also cites the line of Terence. Gellius does not actually quote Varro. Aldus may simply have read through the *De Re Rustica* until he came upon one of these forms in the passage cited; it comes from near the beginning of the work. Gellius is also the source for Aldus' comment on the endings of the dative case in the fourth declension.[31]

C: c1^r f.; F: b8^v (not in AB)

Datiuus quartae declinationis quot terminationes habet? duas, ui syllabas ut huic senatui, huic manui; u, ut huic senatu, huic manu. Vergil, Teque aspectu ne subtrahe nostro. Idem, parce metu cytherea. Caesar grauis autor linguae Latinae in Dolabella, In aedibus fanisque et honori et ornatu erant. In libris analogicis omnia huiusmodi sine i litera dicenda censet. lege .A. Gel. Vtimurne huiusmodi datiuis per apocopen, ut cursu pro cursui dicamus? minime inquit Seruius. Quomodo igitur? per rationem artis antiquae, quia omnis nominatiuus pluralis regit genitiuum singularem. Item a genitiuo* singulari datiuus singularis regitur, nec eo maior esse debet. Est igitur cursui datiuus a cursuis genitiuo, et huic cursu a genitiuo cursus.

---

* Item a genitiuo F] ~ datiuo C

The starting place for this note is likewise Priscian who cites the Virgilian phrase, *parce metu cytherea* (*Aen.*, 1, 257), in his discussion of the dative forms of the fourth declension (*GLK*, 2, 363, 10). The reference to

[29] Terence, *H. T.,* 287, Varro, *De re rust.,* 1, 2, 19.

[30] Aldus was acquainted with Gellius before 1493 because the term, *patrius casus,* for the genitive case comes from Gellius. Sulpitius, *De arte grammatica* (ca. 1480; Hain 15142), b4^v says, for example: Genitiuus ergo in us. terminatorum exit in us productum ut Hic visus. huius visus. Vetustissimi tamen in uis. syllabas terminabant, et datiuum in u. vt senatus. huius senatuis. huic senatu. Hic metus. huius metuis. huic metu. Huius rei Aulus gellius est approbatus assertor.

[31] The odd phrase, *lege .A. Gel.* (read Aulus Gellius), in the middle of this passage looks like a marginal note which Aldus wrote to himself and which was included in the printed text by the compositor. The reference is still to Gellius, 4, 16.

238   Illinois Classical Studies, I

Caesar comes from Gellius. The rule on the length of the genitive and dative cases is taken from Servius' *Commentary on Aeneid*, 1, 156: "curru" non, ut quidam putant, pro "currui" posuit, nec est apocope, sed ratio artis antiquae, quia omnis nominativus pluralis regit genetivum singularem et isosyllabus esse debet, ut "hae musae, huius musae," "hi docti, huius docti." Item a genetivo singulari dativus regitur singularis, ut isosyllabus sit, ut "huius docti, huic docto." The view of Servius seems to have been originally formulated against the position advanced by Priscian who views these texts as instances of the use of the ablative in place of the dative and hence from another perspective as figures of speech.[32] Aldus' use of *cursus* here instead of *currus* seems to be a *lapsus memoriae*. *Cursu* in the ablative occurs in the very next verse of the *Aeneid*.[33] The direct connection of the form of the dative in -ui with the genitive in -uis, and of the dative in -u with the genitive in -us, which would flow from the Servian rule, seems to be Aldus' own idea. Such matters were evidently reserved for the advanced discussions in the *Fragmenta*.

4. (a) A: c1^v; B: b7^v; C: d3^r; F: d3^r

> Dies huius dies, huius die, huius dii cuius declinatus? quinti. Quare? quia quintae inflexionis nomina etiam in es et in e et in ii inueniuntur prolata in casu patrio apud antiquos ut ostendemus abunde in fragmentis.*

> * ut . . . fragmentis AB] ut ostendimus superius, ubi de genitiuo quintae declinationis scripsimus [scribimus C] CF

The reference in CF, as in No. 3, is back to the discussion on c1^r (b8^v–c1^r in F). We may again assume that material from the *Fragmenta* has been introduced here.

(b) C: c1^r; F: b8^v–c1^r

> Genitiuus singularis quintae declinationis quot terminationes habet? quatuor, ei ut dies huius diei, ii ut huius dii, es ut huius dies, e ut huius die. Vergilius in primo aeneidos, munera laetitiamque dii pro diei. M. Tullius pro S. Roscio, Quarum nihil pernicii causa diuino consilio sed ui ipsa et magnitudine rerum factum putamus pro perniciei. Vergilius in georgicis, Libra dies somnique pares ubi fecerit horas pro diei. Item M. Tullius pro P. Sestio, Equites uocaturos illius dies poenas. Salustius dubitauit acie pars, inquit, pro aciei. Ouidius in tertio Metamorphoseon, Prima fide uocisque

---

[32] Cf. *GLK*, 2, 366 f. Forms like *curru* or *die* (for *diei*) are discussed in various contexts by the grammarians. The handle, as here, is usually offered by the text of Virgil; cf. Servius on *Georg.*, 1, 208, and Priscian, *GLK*, 3, 189, 8 ff.

[33] prospiciens genitor caeloque invectus aperto
flectit equos, *curru*que volans dat lora secundo.
Defessi Aeneadae, quae proxima litora *cursu*
contendunt petere . . . (155–158)

ratae tentamina sumpsit pro fidei. Idem in sexto, Vtque fide pignus dextras
utriusque poposcit pro fidei pignus. Caesar in secundo de analogia huius die
huius specie dicendum putat.[34]

(c) C: c1^v; F: c1^r

Datiuus quintae declinationis quot terminationes habet? treis, ei ut huic diei,
ii ut huic facii, e ut huic facie. Lucilius in satyris, ut citat Gellius, Primum
inquit facie honestas accidit. Idem qui te diligit, aetati facieque tuae se
fautorem ostendat. Sunt tamen inquit Gellius non pauci, qui utrobique facii
legant.[35]

The citations from Virgil's *Georgics* and from Sallust and Ovid are used
by Priscian (*GLK*, 2, 366, 9–18); the Sallust passage is also cited by
Servius in his note on Georgics, 1, 208. These texts and the use made of
them in discussing the variant forms of the fourth and fifth declensions are
thus part of the common tradition. The rest of the forms and passages
used to illustrate them are taken from Gellius, *N.A.*, 9, 14. Gellius had
already been incorporated into the humanistic grammars and commentaries on Virgil in the fifteenth century. Thus Sulpitius Verulanus
cites him in his account of the fifth declension forms of the genitive and
dative,[36] and Antonio Mancinelli cites him by book and chapter in his
annotation on *Georgics*, 1, 208, and quotes from him the examples from
Virgil, *Aeneid*, 1, 636, Cicero's *Pro Sestio* and Caesar. None of the illustrative
material, therefore, is really original with Aldus or the result of his own
reading of the classical authors. What is new perhaps is the organization
of the material and the way in which the different forms are accounted
for. That is probably what was "abundantly shown" in the *Fragmenta*.
However, there is no reason to assume that insofar as illustrative matter
was concerned, Aldus went beyond his immediate sources in the grammatical tradition.

5. A: d7^v; B: c6^v

Quot species deriuatiuorum uerborum? quinque. inchoatiua, meditatiua,
deminutiua, frequentatiua, desideratiua, ut Inchoat, arcesso, uiso; meditatur,
amasco; sorbillo minuit; legitoque et curso frequentant. Parturit est partum
desiderat, esurit esse. Sed de his cumulatissime in fragmentis.

The reference to the *Fragmenta* is suppressed in C, and the brief account
of A and B is expanded into one and a half pages of material. Presumably

---

34 Virgil, *Aen.*, 1, 636, Cic., *Rosc.*, §131, Virg., *G.*, 1, 208, Cic., *Sest.*, §28, Sall., *Hist.*, 1,
41 M, Ov., *M.*, 3, 341 and 6, 506. Cf. Gellius, *NA*, 9, 14.
35 Gellius 9, 16.
36 *De arte grammatica* (ca. 1480), b5^r.

the added matter is again taken from the *Fragmenta*. This additional material consists chiefly of a longer list of examples under each type of verb, the rules for their formation and conjugation, and a brief discussion of the past tense of "meditative" (that is, inchoative in modern terminology) verbs. All of this material is traditional and can be found, though with some variation, in Diomedes, Donatus, Servius, and Priscian above all and, following Priscian, in the humanistic grammars of Perotti and Sulpitius Verulanus. Since the *Fragmenta*, in its original conception, was to contain advanced grammar, it was certainly appropriate to reserve this somewhat complicated material for it. Its inclusion in the revised edition of the *Institutiones Grammaticae* implies a change in Aldus' view of the purpose and educational functions of his Latin Grammar and also perhaps of the *Fragmenta Grammatica*.

However, what had originally necessitated a very detailed (*cumulatissime*) treatment of these verbs in the *Fragmenta*, which was apparently retained in it, was Aldus' acceptance of the position of Lorenzo Valla on this question. Valla severely criticized the traditional account in his *Elegantiae* (I, 22–24) and in effect turned it upside down. He centers his attack on Priscian, who gives the fullest exposition of the subject. Priscian presents a five-type classification of inchoative, meditative, frequentative, desiderative, and diminutive verbs.[37] Inchoative verbs end in -sc-, are mostly derived from intransitive verbs, do not have perfect tenses or a supine stem, and belong to the third conjugation, like *calesco, fervesco*. Meditative verbs end in -uri-, are derived from the supine in -u but lack their own supine stem, and belong to the fourth conjugation. Frequentative verbs end in -to, -so, or -xo, are derived from the supine in -u except those verbs having a stem in -gi (like *legito*), and all belong to the first conjugation. Desideratives end in -so or -sso and signify "to be eager to do something," as *viso, facesso, capesso*.[38] Diminutive verbs end in -lo.

Valla claims to be disputing with all the ancient grammarians, but in fact is dealing primarily with Priscian and secondarily with Servius in his

---

[37] *GLK*, 2, 427–431, 508, 535, 559–560; cf. also Diomedes, *GLK*, 1, 343–346, Donatus, *id.*, 4, 381–382, Servius, *id.*, 4, 412–413, whose accounts differ from Priscian's in a few respects. For example, they do not recognize Priscian's desiderative type. Donatus and Servius also have an "absolute" or "perfect" type (known to Diomedes, but not considered by him) which is the base form in a sequence like *lego, legito, lecturio*.

[38] Verbs of this type are more often considered in the tradition a subclass of frequentative verbs. It was the fact that they have perfective forms and do not belong to the first conjugation which led to their separate classification as desideratives. Priscian was not responsible for this treatment since it was already known to Servius; see his note on *Aen.*, 8, 157. There are traces of an ancient dispute among the grammarians on this point; cf. Servius, *GLK*, 4, 413, 1–3.

role as commentator on Virgil.[39] His procedure is to begin with a text used by Priscian or Servius, show how the interpretations based on their grammatical theories are false, and by citing other texts construct his own view of the correct signification of these verb forms. For example, he refutes Priscian's interpretation of the verb *aegrescit* in the Virgilian phrase, *aegrescitque medendo*, as meaning "he begins to be ill," and supports his refutation with parallel examples from Virgil, Cicero, Quintilian, Plautus, and the Vulgate. These verbs in -sco, he argues, do not signify "beginning" but "becoming." They are thus complementary to verbs compounded with fio like *calesco: calefio*. Verbs in -sco are different because they imply that the source of their action or passion is in their subject while those in -fio imply that it is outside. These verbs therefore have a perfective tense. Valla subtly discriminates the perfect tenses of verbs in -sco and -fio on the basis of meaning and retorts Priscian's view by arguing that if verbs in -sco have perfect tenses, then they cannot have an inchoative meaning. The success of his arguments on inchoative verbs no doubt lent credence to his subsequent arguments and interpretations of desiderative and meditative verbs. He again employs the same critical procedure. By refuting Priscian's interpretation of specific texts, Valla overturns the grammatical theory on which it rests. Additional citations are then used to support his own view of their signification. Verbs like *viso* and *facesso* signify a physical action and mean "to go to do something." Verbs in -urio are more aptly called desiderative or optative because they signify an emotional, not an intellectual or physical, aspect of the action they denote. Valla concludes his reinterpretation of the traditional grammar by saying:

> If we want to give appropriate names to each of these types without disregarding the usual terminology, we may call verbs in -sco "meditative," that is "exercising," because someone who is becoming warm (*calescit* or *calefit*) is, so to speak, meditating and exercising to make himself warm. We may call those in -so "inchoative," those in -rio "desiderative." And these, I think, were the true and real meanings of these terms. But posterity depraved the meaning assigned to them in antiquity.[40]

Aldus completely accepted Valla's interpretations and suggested terminology. His presentation of these verbs thus appears to be unique

---

[39] The only ancient texts he seems familiar with are Priscian, the *Ars Minor* of Donatus, and Servius' Commentaries; he is in effect really disputing with the contemporary school tradition.

[40] *Elegantiae* in *Opera . . . in unum uolumen collecta*, (Basle: H. Petri, March, 1540), p. 31; reprinted by photoreproduction in "Monumenta Politica et Philosophica Rariora," Ser. 1, No. 5 (Torino: Bottega d' Erasmo, 1962), Vol. I.

among fifteenth century school grammars. Other grammarians like Sulpitius Verulanus certainly knew Valla's work, but still followed Priscian,
perhaps for the reason given by Sulpitius: De nominibus et significatione
horum verborum aliter et argutius sentit Valla. sed nos tritiorem usum
secuti sumus non paruo consilio.[41] Aldus was clearly not one to follow
tritiorem usum. However, his actual discussion, insofar as it can be detected
from the succinct presentation in C, is an amalgam of Priscian and Valla.
Format and examples from Priscian are accommodated to the views of
Valla.

6. C: f8ᵛ; F: 8ʳ

> Diomedes tamen separatim declinat sic, tempore praesenti utinam amem,
> imperfecto utinam amarem, perfecto utinam amauerim, plusquamperfecto
> utinam amauissem, futuro utinam amem. sed de his in fragmentis plura.

This statement is not found in A or B but occurs here as an addendum
to the customary conjugation of the verb in the optative mood. Aldus lists
these tenses in the usual way, as it is, for example, found in Donatus and
Priscian,[42] thus:

(a) present and imperfect: utinam amarem, etc.
(b) perfect and pluperfect: utinam amauissem, etc.
(c) future: utinam amem, etc.

Between 1501 and 1508 Aldus evidently became familiar with Diomedes
or some statement on the optative purportedly derived from him. Diomedes (*GLK*, 1, 340, 4–22) takes note of three divergent views on the
optative. Some deny that there can be a present tense of the optative
mood. Others admit the present tense, but combine it with the future.[43]
The third group, which Diomedes himself follows, join the present and
imperfect together. Similar disputes revolve around the past tenses for
some grammarians had evidently raised the question: How could one
wish for something in the past. Diomedes has a suitable answer. In his
own conjugations of the optative Diomedes then distinguishes four tense
forms: present and imperfect (*amarem*), perfect (*amaverim*), pluperfect
(*amassem*), and future (*amem*).[44]

Aldus' report in the *Institutiones Grammaticae*, whatever he may have said
in the *Fragmenta*, does not square with the transmitted text of Diomedes.
He has either wrongly reported Diomedes or he has erroneously ascribed
to Diomedes the paradigms of some other grammarian. Probus, for in-

---

[41] (Above, note 30), d3ʳ⁻ᵛ.   [42] *GLK*, 4, 360, 27–33; 2, 407, 10–408, 17.
[43] Cf. [Sergius], *in Donatum, GLK*, 4, 509, 1–17.   [44] *GLK*, 4, 352, 9–18.

stance, gives the forms of the optative which Aldus here assigns to Diomedes.[45] I have been unable to discover an exact source for Aldus. In any case his discussion of the tenses of the optative in the *Fragmenta* probably followed the outline of Diomedes.

As well as Book IV, which is completely new, there are several other insertions of new material in the third edition of the Latin Grammar. For example, in the first two editions Aldus had printed some seventy mnemonic verses in dactylic hexameter on heteroclite nouns in order that children though they are learning only the rudiments of the language may not be wholly ignorant of the fact that some nouns are declined in different ways. This poem is revised for the third edition and, as noted above, is preceded by fourteen new pages on heteroclite nouns. While for the most part containing mere lists of nouns, these pages have occasional grammatical disquisitions. Similarly the treatment of the verb is reorganized and nine new pages of general information on its morphology are added before the quiz and paradigms. A considerable amount of new material on syntax also appears in Book III. It is not apparent at first sight whether any of this new material comes from the *Fragmenta* in the way postulated above. A careful study of the text of the four editions of the Latin Grammar might answer this question, at least in part. Such a study would certainly prepare the way for a better estimate of Aldus' own scholarship and a deeper insight into his mind at work.

B. Syntax

7. A: i7^{r-v}; B: i2^r; C: m4^r; F: m4^v

Quomodo construuntur impersonalia uocis passiuae? cum ablatiuo agente cum praepositione a uel ab, ut a me studetur, id est, ego studeo; a te dormitur, id est, tu dormis. Post se uero regunt casum uerborum si a neutris tertiae et septimae speciei deducta fuerint, ut seruio tibi, a me seruitur tibi; eo ad templum, a me itur ad templum. Nam quae ab actiuis ueniunt ego non memini legisse cum casu patiente. Non enim legi unquam apud doctos quale est amatur Socratem, aratur terram, sed passiue semper, amatur Socrates, aratur terra. Quod ne apud Graecos quidem fieri deprehendi nec quiui inuenire qui legerit. Illud enim apud Priscianum λέγεται Διογένην τὸν κυνικόν hoc est dicitur Diogenem Cynicum, si non subauditur ποιῆσαι ἢ τύψαι uel aliud infinitum Graeci non approbant. Negant enim dici apud eos στέργεται τὸν Σωκράτην hoc est amatur Socratem. Docetur uero grammaticam et petitur gratiam ita dicitur ut donatur tibi, turbatur agris, a me accipitur a te.

[45] *GLK*, 4, 160, 28–161, 4. Aldus presumably did not know this particular work which was first published by Angelo Mai in 1833. But in view of the way manuscripts of grammatical treatises were written and circulated, even in the fifteenth century, it is not impossible that he could be acquainted with the contents.

Non enim in his pati aliquid significamus. Ponuntur frequentius absolute,
ut amatur, statur. Sed quare non liceat dicere amatur Socratem ostendimus*
in fragmentis nostris.

* ostendimus CF] ostendemus AB

The construction, impersonal verb with retained object in the accusative
case, criticized here by Aldus is accepted in both mediaeval and humanistic
grammarians. Alexander, for instance, says,

> quae [sc. verba] sine persona sunt atque gerundia iungis,
> si tamen a verbo, quod transeat, illa creabis:
> Matthaeum legitur; psalmos erat ante legendum.
> (*Doctrinale*, 1262–1264)

Sulpitius Verulanus uses the same example of *Matthaeum legitur* and gives
the rule justifying the contruction: omnes dictiones quibus significatus, id
est, modus significandi est idem regunt eundem casum. However, he also
points out that in learned (that is, classical) authors the accusative with
such verbs is found only with prepositions.[46] It is not clear from this limited
context just what Aldus' arguments against this construction in his
Fragmenta might have been other than its absence in classical authors. But
even this point may have been open to question. A sentence in a letter
of Antonio Codro to Aldus shows that Aldus was seeking the help of his
friends in exploring this problem. Codro writes: Impersonale uerbum,
quod est apud Ouidium cum accusatiuo, cum inuenero, ad te scribam,
nunc οὐ δύναμαι.[47] It is possible that Codro told Aldus that the construction was classical and used by Ovid, but on being asked for the source
was unable to supply it. Or Aldus may simply have been asking Codro's
help on this point as well as on several others since this particular sentence
occurs in a series of such replies in the letter.

8. (a) A: i8ᵛ; B: i3ʳ; C: m5ʳ; F: m5ᵛ

Et notandum horum uerborum nominatiuum semper neutri generis esse
oportere, quemadmodum Laurentius Valla praestanti uir ingenio docet,
cui ego facile assentior, quia nusquam aliter memini legere* quam cum
nominatiuo neutri generis. Sed an uerbum aliquod sit impersonale, osten-
dimus† abunde in fragmentis grammaticis.

* legere CF] legisse AB   † ostendimus CF] ostendemus AB

Aldus is describing the syntax of *interest* and *refert* (the *horum uerborum* of

[46] Cf. Diomedes, *GLK*, 1, 398, 31–399, 12; Priscian, *id.*, 2, 425, 13–19, 3, 231, 10–21,
238, 25–234, 9.
[47] Printed by Julius Schück (above, note 6), p. 118.

the first sentence). The reference to Valla is to his discussion of these two
verbs in *Elegantiae*, II, 1. There Valla remarks about the construction,
Hoc interest mea, that, hoc uerbum habere ante se nominatiuum, sicut sum,
es, est. Sed in neutro genere quis dubitet, quum omnia plena sint exem-
plorum?[48] But Aldus' reference to the *Fragmenta* here seems to point to a
larger question about personal and impersonal verbs than just the proper
constructions with *interest* and *refert*. But I do not see just what he has in
mind.

(b) A: k1^r; B: i3^v; C: m5^v; F: m6^v

> (A text) Notandum etiam dici latine tua discipuli interest libros legere etsi
> sunt qui negant: sed de his in fragmentis.
> (BCF text) Praeterea tua discipuli interest libros legere, sunt qui negant dici
> posse* latine, sed tua, qui es discipulus. sed de his in fragmentis.

---

* posse *om.* CF

The use of *notandum* to introduce these two topics and the references to
the *Fragmenta* in the text of A suggest that these two passages are in fact
notes added to the original text of the *Institutiones*. The reference in *sunt
qui negant* is probably primarily to Valla who in this same chapter of the
Elegantiae (II, 1) says about joining a substantive and a pronominal adjective: Adeoque uerum est, hos ipsos genitiuos respuere consortium
substantiui, ut ne in possessiuorum quidem forma illud pati uelint.
Vidimus licere dicere, meam unius operam, tuum solius studium: non
tamen dicemus, meum Laurentii studium, suum Prisciani praedium, sed
meum studium, qui sum Laurentius, praedium suum, qui est Priscianus.[49]
The text in A suggests that Aldus, contrary to Valla, believed that the
construction of *tua discipuli interest* was legitimate. He would have found
justification for this point of view, and a criticism of Valla, in Perotti who
explained the form of the possessive adjective with *interest* and *refert* as
modifying the noun *re* which is compounded with the verb *rē-fert* and
(apparently) *inter-rē-est*. Thus the construction, *mea Platonis interest*, is the
equivalent of *in re mea Platonis*. By analogy *tua Pyrrhi refert* is the equivalent
of *res tua Pyrrhi fert*.[50] Perotti also considered *interest* and *refert* as both personal and impersonal verbs and gives as an example of the personal use:
sermo tuus interest nostra. Aldus clearly agreed with Valla that such a
construction was erroneous. It is possible that the revision of the text of

[48] *Opera* (Basle: Petri, 1540), p. 48.

[49] *Ibid.*, p. 49.

[50] *Rudimenta grammatices* (Venice, 1480), pp. g6^{r-v}. The same view is advanced in his
Cornucopiae (Basle, 1526), p. 47.

passage (b) in B implies that Aldus is swinging toward Valla's view on this point also.[51]

9. A: K3ʳ; B: i6ᵛ; C: m7ᵛ; F: m8ᵛ

> Sed caue dicas, a me uult legi, a te uult seruiri mihi, me uult taedere tui, quia uult non unquam impersonale. quare autem non sit, in fragmentis nostris disputauimus.*

---
* disputabimus AB

This reference appears to be to the same part of the *Fragmenta* referred to in 8 (a) above. The context is a discussion of the syntax of *incipit, potest, desinit, solet, debet,* used impersonally, and *volo.* The construction Aldus has under consideration is of the type, *a me incipit legi* or *a te potest satisfieri mihi.* The inclusion of *vult* in this list and the erroneous construction which Aldus warns against here may be exemplified from Sulpitius Verulanus who gives the rule that if these verbs are joined with personal infinitives, they are used personally (*ego volo amare te*), but impersonally if joined with impersonal infinitives as in *me vult delectare dormire.*[52] Aldus, citing the authority of Priscian (*GLK,* 3, 232), insists that *volo* must be used personally: nam persona uolens semper esse in nominatiuo debet, ut ego uolo a me benefieri tibi, tu uis a te seruiri mihi, et ita in caeteris generis eiusdem. But oddly enough his list of impersonal verbs of the sixth species in the active voice still contains *uult.* Perotti on the other hand omits it entirely from his similar list.

10. A: k3ʳ; B: ibʳ; C: m8ʳ; F: n1ʳ

> Nos amabimus: nos amatumire, uel nos amaturumesse, uel per participium, nos amaturos esse; et idem significant, ut ostendimus* in fragmentis; nos amabimur: nos amatumiri.

---
* ostendemus AB

The ancient grammarians regularly give the forms of the future infinitive as (active) amatum ire or amaturum ire, (passive) amatum iri or amandum esse.[53] They are followed in this practice by the fifteenth century humanist grammarians like Perotti and Sulpitius Verulanus. The usage of the extant classical authors is of course different and, as Aldus

---

[51] One would like to think Aldus did since the construction is not classical; cf. Kühner-Stegmann, *Ausführliche Grammatik der lateinischen Sprache* (Hannover: Hahnsche Buchhandlung, 1971; reprint of the fourth edition, 1962), II: 1, p. 461.

[52] *De arte grammatica* (Venice: Christophorus de Pensis, 1488), p. e8ʳ.

[53] Cf., for example, Priscian, *GLK,* 2, 475, 18–476, 6; Diomedes, *id.,* 1, 352, 31; Donatus, *id.,* 4, 361, 5 f.; Gellius, *NA,* 1, 7. *Amaturumire, amaturumesse, amatumiri,* are written as single words to prevent, as Sulpitius says, their being taken as two words.

notes, employs the participle. Aldus writes here as though some grammarians had interpreted the construction of the future participle with the infinitive *esse* as having a different meaning from the other two constructions. But there seems to be no evidence of such a distinction in the ancient grammarians, and I have found no traces of it in later authors. Aldus must have cited in the *Fragmenta* texts, presumably from classical authors, in which the construction with the future participle is demonstrably a kind of future infinitive.

11. (a) A: k3^v–4^r; B: i6^v; C: n1^r; F: n2^r

> Amandi, amando, amandum quae pars orationis sunt? libet respondere illud Horatii in poetica de uersibus elegis: grammatici certant, et adhuc sub iudice lis est. Aliqui enim neque nomina esse uolunt, quia regunt transitiue, neque uerba propter casus quos habent, neque participia, quia sunt sine tempore, neque aliquam ex octo orationis partibus, sed partem potius per se. Aliqui affirmant esse uerba participialia, aliqui uero nomina participialia; sed et de gerundiis et de supinis abunde diximus* in fragmentis.

---

* dicemus AB

(b) Ibidem

> Quam significationem habent? tam actiuam quam passiuam ab actiuis, communibus, et neutris ut aro; a caeteris uero quam eorum uerba. Non me latet quid Laurentius et alii senserint, quod nunc ne confundamus pueros, praetermittimus. In fragmentis enim mihi cum illis erit* hac de re certamen. Satis sit nunc unum exemplum ex Iustino: Athenas quoque missus erudiendi gratia, id est, ut erudiretur.

---

* cum illis est C

The differentiation of the gerund from the gerundive and the determination of their correct usage was (and still is) an arduous and lengthy business for the grammarians. The initial stage in the recovery of the classical usage by the humanists was the separation of the grain from the chaff in the ancient grammarians whose divergent views are summarized by Aldus in passage (a). The first major effort was made by Lorenzo Valla in his *Elegantiae* (I, 27). It is evident that the subject does indeed admit of abundant discussion though what Aldus' particular contribution may have been in the *Fragmenta* is by no means clear. The point in passage (b) on the *significatio* of the gerund on which Aldus takes issue with Valla[54] is, I think, the following. Valla, in partially distinguishing the gerund from the

---

54 Among the *alii* who follow Valla is certainly Perotti, who may well be the only person Aldus actually has in mind here despite the plural. Perotti in his *Rudimenta grammatices* and even more so in his *Cornucopiae* takes phrases and illustrations virtually verbatim from Valla.

gerundive, establishes the rule that gerundives have a passive meaning when joined with nouns, but that gerunds, though sometimes passive, are usually active. After illustrating this rule in the accusative and ablative cases, he concludes his treatment with an example of a typical soloecism:

> Quidam uero indoctus hac aetate scribere ausus est: Iamiam urbs in periculo capiendi est, pro eo quod est, urbs iam in periculo est ne capiatur, siue hostis parum abest a capienda urbe. Quum semper sine substantiuo gerundium accipiatur actiue, aut si a neutro uenit, neutraliter: nisi aliquando, ut ostendimus, in ablatiuo.

Aldus' citation from Justin is evidently intended to justify the use of the gerund in the genitive case with a passive meaning. Presumably the *Fragmenta* offered other examples from ancient authors.[55]

12. A: k5^v; B: i7^v; C: ni^v; F: n3^r

> In fragmentis grammaticis ostendam supinum in um accipi etiam passiue, ut contumelia factum itur, id est datur opera ut fiat contumelia; et in u actiue, ut surgo cubitu, id est a cubatione.

Here again Valla may illustrate what Aldus has in mind. In *Elegantiae* I, 29, Valla says that the supine in -um is active, the one in -u is passive. Since he does not notice any exceptions, he could be read as laying down a universal rule. Much of Valla's energy in the two chapters on the supine (28 and 29) is spent on distinguishing the supine from fourth declension verbal nouns, criticizing Priscian's statements about the differences between supines and gerundives, and on censuring the erroneous usage of contemporary writers and teachers. An instance of this last is furnished by Sulpitius Verulanus who illustrates the supine thus: eo doctum discipulos; et eo doctum a praeceptore. Dignum doctu: id est, dignum ut doceat vel ut doceatur.[56] Sulpitius remarks that the supine of transitive verbs can be used with an active or passive meaning. Valla, however, chides the view that the supine can be indiscriminately employed with an active or passive significance. This is clearly the point at issue. In the section on supines in the Latin Grammar Aldus says flatly that supines in -um are active, those in -u are passive, and interprets several examples in this light. However, the reference to the *Fragmenta* shows that he had other views also. Presumably his discussion of supines in the *Fragmenta* ranged over all the questions concerned with this form similar to Valla's treatment in the *Elegantiae*. Valla's study was undoubtedly the starting point

---

[55] Justin, 17, 3, 11; cf. Kühner-Stegmann (above, note 51), II: 1, 728 f., who cite no other examples of this use except the passage in Justin.

[56] (Above, note 30), e8^r.

of Aldus' own discussion since his section on the supine in the Latin Grammar has several things in common with Valla and suggests close familiarity with the two chapters in the *Elegantiae*.[57]

13. (a) A: h2^r; B: g4^r; C: k5^r; F: k5^r

> Mutuo as aui atum per prestare, quod non redditur idem. Sed de mutuo abunde dicemus in exercitamentis grammaticis. Significat enim non dare mutuo, sed accipere. Valerius Maximus lib. vi, cap. ii: ac potius praesidium a libertate, quam ab innocentia mutuauit. Quemadmodum et mutuor: C. Caesar libro tertio Commentariorum de bello ciuili Pompeiano: quammaximas potuerunt pecunias mutuati perinde ac suis satisfacere, et fraudata restituere uellent.*

* Significat—uellent. *add.* F

(b) A: h5^v; B: g8^r; C: l1^r; F: l1^r

> Mutuor aris atus sum per togliere imprestito. Sed est potius deponens et mutuo neutrum, de quibus (ut dixi) dicemus in exercitamentis.

As noted above these are the only places where the *Exercitamenta Grammatices atque Utriusque Linguae Fragmenta* is referred to with the abbreviated title *Exercitamenta Grammatica* or *Exercitamenta* by itself. It is possible, of course, but unlikely that the *Fragmenta* and the *Exercitamenta* were separate works. The use of the adjective *grammatica* with both nouns and the similar form of reference suggest rather that they are different ways of designating the same work. However, there is no apparent reason why Aldus preferred the short title *Fragmenta* to *Exercitamenta*.

Both of the above passages occur in the midst of lists of verbs. Passage (a) is in the middle of a list of active verbs of the third species. The principal parts of *mutuo* are given together with the meaning in Italian and a gloss (*quod non redditur idem*) which serves to distinguish its meaning from that of *commodo*. The sentence, Sed de mutuo abunde dicemus in exercitamentis grammaticis, is in effect parenthetical. Similarly, passage (b) occurs in a list of passive verbs. The *sed* both introduces the parenthetical reference and also indicates that Aldus does not accept this view of *mutuor* which he believes to be a deponent verb. The explanation added in F states the gist of the question: *mutuo* and *mutuor* both mean "receive." The addition indicates that in 1514 or at whatever time between 1508 and 1514 Aldus inserted this comment in the text of the fourth edition of the Latin Grammar, the prospects for the publication of the *Fragmenta/Exercitamenta* were still remote.

Mutuo and *mutuor* were active and passive respectively in medieval

[57] Both cite Quintilian, 1, 4, 29, and use several of the same illustrations: miserabilis uisu, optimum factu, iucunda cognitu, obscoenum aspectu, homo dignus amatu.

Latin and usually meant "to lend" and "to be lent" as Aldus indeed glosses them in these two passages. This semantic development and differentiation in usage seems to have begun in the late Latin period.[58] In the classical period, however, both verbs mean "to borrow." The deponent *mutuor* is the standard form; *mutuo* is very rare in the extant literature. This meaning and the use of the two forms of the verb is also supported by the grammarians; Priscian includes *mutuo : mutuor* in his list of verbs which have the same meaning in the active and passive voice (*GLK*, 2, 396, 13). The classical usage, especially of *mutuor*, thus conflicted with fifteenth century usage. The humanists tried to reconcile the two.

Valla distinguishes *mutuo : mutuor* from *foenero : foeneror*, and defines *mutuo* as meaning *mutuò dare* and *mutuor* as *mutuò accipere* (*Elegantiae* V, 25). Perotti rightly criticizes Valla's description of the syntax of these verbs, but still subscribes to the same view of their active and passive meaning. He states in his *Cornucopiae*: Mutuo, et mutuor ita differunt, quod qui pecuniam dat mutuo, is mutuare dicitur; qui uero accipit, is pecuniam mutuatur.[59] Both Valla and Perotti are of course describing contemporary rather than classical usage. An attempt to combine the two can be seen in Sulpitius Verulanus' Grammar. In his first edition he says *mutuo* has the same construction as *soluo* with the accusative and dative as in *mutuo pecunias tibi*. Neither *soluo* nor *mutuo* can be used in the passive voice with a personal subject. *Mutuor* is therefore a deponent and takes the accusative and ablative as in *mutuor nummos a te*.[60] He thus classifies *mutuo* as a neuter verb (that is, a verb without a passive) like *aro* and *mutuor* as a deponent. However, in his revised edition he notes that this is a modern usage: mutuo as recentiores utuntur per prestare cose che se restituischono simili.[61] Sulpitius seems to have shifted his view somewhat in the light of Perotti's statements in the *Cornucopiae* (p. 704, 48 ff.).

Aldus evidently follows the earlier position of Sulpitius in construing *mutuo* as a neuter verb and *mutuor* as a deponent. But he must also have been more concerned about classical than contemporary usage. The two texts cited in the addition in F were probably taken from his discussion in the *Exercitamenta/Fragmenta*. The sentence from Caesar (*B.C.*, 3, 60, 5) shows that *mutuor* is a deponent. But the main point at issue was whether *mutuo* meant "lend" or "borrow." The citation from Valerius Maximus

---

[58] Cf. *TLL*, VIII, 1732, v. *mutuor*.

[59] (Basle, 1526), p. 304, 24–26; cf. also 53, 51–54, 5 and 705, 13–15. The same definitions and distinctions occur in his *Rudimenta Grammatices* (above, note 50), p. e8ᵛ: mutuamus quae non redduntur eadem. Cf. Aldus' *quod non redditur idem*.

[60] (Paris, n.d.), p. e5ʳ.

[61] (Venice, 1489), p. e4ʳ.

proves it meant "borrow." Aldus presumably then demonstrated the correct classical usage of these verbs in the *Fragmenta*.

C. Pronunciation

14. (a) B: l4ʳ; C: o7ʳ; F: o8ᵛ (not in A)

> Quanquam ῆτα duplex ε psilon, sicut ωμέγα duplex omicron esse existimo, et non i, sed e sonare debere. Quare dictiones graecas, in quibus est η litera, perperam nunc pronuntiari ostendemus in fragmentis grammaticis.

These two sentences, inserted in the middle of a paragraph on the declension of Greek words in Latin, are the earliest datable indication of Aldus' scholarly interest in the correct pronunciation of Greek and the first evidence that this subject will be treated in the *Fragmenta*. The significant factor is that he views the contemporary (Byzantine) pronunciation as erroneous (*perperam*).

(b) C: c6ʳ; F: c6ʳ

> Quanquam η non i sed e longum pronuntiasse antiquos graecos existimo. constant enim η ex duplici εε sicut ω ex duplici oo. Sed et de his in fragmentis.

(c) C: aa8ʳ; F: &7ʳ

> Quod si dixeris in quibusdam e supradictis mutari η in e longum, respondeo antiquos graecos sic pronuntiasse ῆτα, ut nos e longum in Penelope, grammatice, Aristoteles. Sed de hoc multa in fragmentis nostris.

(d) C: yı̈ʳ; F: x7ᵛ

> Perperam igitur puto haec nomina scribi per ἰῶτα, erroremque inde natum, quia aetate nostra ῆτα et ἰῶτα eodem sono pronuntiantur. quanquam ne hoc quidem probo. Sed de hoc in fragmentis nostris.

(e) D: 1 4ᵛ

> Quoniam Acinaces Graece ἀκινάκης dicitur. Suidas, ᾿Ακινάκης μικρὸν δόρυ περσικόν, non Acinacis imprimendum, ut erat in exemplaribus, sed Acinaces iussimus.[62] Et puto natum errorem, quia nunc Graeci ῆτα, non e longum, sed i pronuntiant, quanquam et ipsi meo iudicio perperam. η enim non i, sed e longi sonum habere debet. Sed de hoc alius erit tractatus. Hinc paraclitum dicimus illos imitati, cum et nobis et Graecis paracletus dicendum est. παράκλητος enim scribitur Graece.[63]

[62] At Horace, *C.*, 1, 27, 5: lucernis Medus acinaces. The MSS, which all modern editors follow, read *acinacis*. The text actually printed in the Aldine edition is *acináce*! The acute accent on the short *a*, which violates the rules of the Latin accent, is doubtless also the result of Aldus' orders. He states in his Latin Grammar (C:aa8) that the Greek accent should be kept on Greek words in Latin. Aldus similarly had *Monaeses* printed for *Monaesis* at *C.*, 3, 6, 9, which he then construes as a nominative singular.

[63] The example of *paracletus* which is not elsewhere used by Aldus for any purpose may have been suggested to him by Erasmus who was working and living with Aldus at the time the Horace edition was going through the press in the winter and early spring of

(f) Fd: aa3ᵛ

H, η nunc sonat i longum, apud antiquos puto erat e longum.

15. (a) (A?)⁶⁴; B: a6ᵛ; C: bɪᵛ–2ʳ; F: bɪᵛ–2ʳ

Ex uocalibus quot fiunt diphthongi? quinque.* ae, oe, au, eu, ei,† ut aestimo,
coepi, aula, eurus, orphei. Sed ei graeca est, quae apud antiquos in frequentissimo usu fuit, nunc autem pene exoleuit.‡
Quot scribuntur et proferuntur? duae. au et eu, ut audio, euge.
Quot scribuntur et non proferuntur? tres.§ ae, oe, ei, ‖ ut Caesar, Phoebus,
omneis. Quanquam mihi non ita uidetur; non enim ita pronuntiasse antiquos
credimus. Sed de his dicemus in fragmentis nostris grammaticis.#

---

* quinque CF] quatuor B   † ei et orphei add. CF   ‡ Sed ei - exoleuit. CF]
nam ei graeca, quae apud antiquos in usu fuit, exoleuit. B   § tres CF]
duae B   ‖ ei et omneis add. CF   # Quanquam - grammaticis. add. CF

(b) C: y6ʳ; F: y5ʳ

Heu et hei diphthongi sunt, ut eheu quam pingui macer est mihi Taurus in
eruo, et Hei mihi qualis erat. Ubi quia cum pronuntiamus hei, utraque
uocalis simul sonat, admonemur et graece et latine diphthongos prope
omneis perperam aetate nostra pronuntiari, ut obiter et hoc dixerim.

The view stated in the 1501 *Rudimenta* that there are only four diphthongs
is derived from Priscian (*GLK*, 2, 37, 13 f. and 40, 10–15) and Servius
(*GLK*, 4, 423, 30–32).⁶⁵ But the ancient grammarians also mentioned the
fifth diphthong, ei, at least in connection with the interjection *hei*.⁶⁶ Aldus,
however, after surveying these multifarious statements in the grammarians
and other authorities like Quintilian and Gellius, evidently came to a
positive conclusion about the existence and correct orthography and
pronunciation of the ancient diphthongs and especially the fifth diphthong
ei. His efforts to revive its use in contemporary Latin is a striking example
of the combination of scholarship and zealous practical endeavor that
is the peculiar characteristic of Aldus' humanism.

1509. The sentence, hinc etc., looks very much like an afterthought or addition to the
original text. Erasmus had recently edited Valla's *Annotationes in Novum Testamentum* (1505)
which were in fact the foundation of his own future annotations on the New Testament.
Valla had commented on the false accentuation of *paracletus* (or rather *paraclitus*) in Latin,
in his note on John, 14:22. Erasmus may well have drawn this point to Aldus' attention.
It was subsequently to become the place where Erasmus himself started the disputation
which was eventually to be turned into his *De Recta Latini Graecique Sermonis Pronuntiatione
Dialogus*; see note 23 above.

⁶⁴ These pages are missing from the Venice copy of A; however, it is most likely that
A had the same text as B.

⁶⁵ Cf. Diomedes, *GLK*, 1, 427, 14 f. and Terentianus Maurus, *id.*, 6, 338, 418–422.

⁶⁶ Cf. Donatus, *GLK*, 4, 368, 23 f., Beda, *id.*, 7, 229, 20–23.

The first version of the Latin Grammar while acknowledging the former existence of the diphthong *ei* accepts the view that it is now obsolete. The revised version, however, notes that it was very widely used in antiquity (*in frequentissimo usu*). This notion comes of course from statements in the grammarians and not from any external evidence of ancient orthography. Diomedes, for example, says: ei, cum apud veteres frequentaretur, usu posteritatis explosa est (*GLK*, 1, 427, 15). More significant perhaps for Aldus was the use made by the grammarians of this diphthong in their explanations of morphology and the orthography of particular classical authors. Priscian, for instance, employs the phonological development of *ei* into long *i* to account for certain verb forms which he says the ancients (*antiqui*) used to pronounce with the diphthong *ei*.[67] That Aldus understood Priscian to be referring to authors of the classical period may be inferred from his treatment of Catullus 64. 319: Catullus, Vellera uirgati custodei-bant calathisci, custodeibant pro custodiebant per ei diphthongum melius scribitur more antiquo (C:r2ᵛ). The diphthong *ei* was also discussed by the grammarians as a way of writing long *i*. Priscian says: i quoque apud antiquos post e ponebatur et ei diphthongum faciebat, quam pro omni i longa scribebant more antiquo Graecorum (*GLK*, 2, 37, 9–11).[68] Quintilian throws some light on this statement. In his discussion of orthography he remarks that e and i were used as the Greeks used ει to distinguish cases and number (1, 7, 15–17). He quotes some lines of Lucilius to illustrate this practice which Quintilian himself criticizes as unnecessary and inconvenient. Gellius mentions Nigidius Figulus as employing a similar spelling (*N.A.*, 13, 26, 4). [69]

These two perspectives would appear to Aldus to be combined in a passage like Priscian on the endings of the nominative and dative-ablative plural of second declension nouns: veteres enim i finalem, quae est longa, per "ei" diphthongum scribebant (*GLK*, 2, 298, 4 f.). This passage could be put together with Priscian's account of the accusative plural of the i-stem nouns (*ibid.*, 358, 3–362, 2) and in particular with the statement (358, 3–7): inveniuntur tamen quaedam in "is" solam pro-ductam terminantia hunc casum Graeca, quae etiam nominativo similiter in "is" desinunt: "hae Sardis has Sardīs," item "Alpīs," "Syrtīs,"

67 *GLK*, 2, 452, 24 ff., 454, 23–25, 557, 16–20.

68 The subject was disputed extensively among the grammarians; cf. Victorinus, *GLK*, 6, 8, 14 ff., 17, 21 ff., 66, 24 ff.; Ter. Scaurus, *id.*, 7, 18, 23 ff., 32, 21 ff.; Velius Longus, *id.*, 7, 55, 27 ff., 77, 1 ff. There is no way of knowing which, if any, of these authors and texts were known to Aldus.

69 Aldus would have read Gellius in the text presented in part by the MSS OXII and in part by Q. This is clear from the Aldine edition of 1515, edited by Johannes Baptista Egnatius, where the text gives forms like *magnei, amicei*.

"Trallīs," quae apud Graecos in supra dictis casibus ϵις diphthongum habent finalem. It is easy to see how Aldus could have applied this statement about the ancients' use of *ei* for long *i* to the declension of nouns and have concluded that the correct classical form of the accusative plural of words like *tres, omnes, fontes* was *treis, omneis, fonteis*. This conclusion seemed to be confirmed by statements such as that of Terentianus Maurus in his *De Syllabis* (*GLK*, 6, 338, 461–466):

> "eitur in silvam" necesse est E et I conectere:
> principali namque verbo nascitur, quod est eo.
> sic oveis plureis et omneis scribimus pluraliter:
> non enim nunc addis E, sed permanet sicut fuit;
> lector et non singularem nominativum sciet
> vel sequentem, qui prioris saepe similis editur.

It must have been considerations like the above which underlay the remarks in the letter to "Students" which Aldus placed at the end of the edition of Virgil which he published in April 1501. He begins by saying:

> Si quisquam est, qui accusandi casus in is per ei diphthongum miratur excusos typis nostris, id a nobis consulto factum ne sit nescius, tum quia facere ad eruditionem uidebatur, tum etiam, ut imitarentur antiquos, qui dandi etiam, et auferendi casus in is, nedum accusandi per ei diphthongum scripsisse leguntur, ut uieis, officieis, captiueis, pro uiis, officiis, captiuis. Sed hi nunc penitus exoleuerunt. Accusatiuos autem eorum tantum nominum, de quibus Priscianus meminit ad recti, patriique casus differentiam per ei scribere operae pretium ducimus. Praesertim in Poetis Plauto, Lucretio, Catullo, Vergilio, et antiquis caeteris. Nam in aliis nondum ausim propter Criticos.

"Learning" (*eruditio*) and "imitation of the ancients" (*ut imitaremur antiquos*)—these are Aldus' motives. The reference to Priscian is evidently to the passage in *GLK*, 2, 358, noted above; the statement on the dative-ablative endings is an inference from other passages in Priscian.[70] As is clear from the changes in spelling in successive editions of the Latin Grammar, Aldus adopted himself the orthographical practices he recommended. He had a special type for this diphthong cast for his fonts, and introduced rules like the following into the third edition of the Grammar:

(i) C: c4ᵛ

> Quare dixisti hos fonteis? quia quae genitiuum pluralem in ium faciunt, accusatiuum eiusdem numeri in eis mittunt per ei diphthongum, ut hos fonteis, has parteis et partes, hos et has omneis, treis.[71]

[70] The actual linguistic facts are set out in R. G. Kent, *The Forms of Latin* (Baltimore, 1946), pp. 27, §224, 32, §237, and 46, §268.

[71] Someone apparently raised an objection to this practice, because Aldus adds to this passage in F: quanquam A. Gellius lib. xii. capite xix docet testimonio Probi Valerii, qui

(ii) C: r8ʳ

sed quīs et accusatiui in is, tum ut differant a nominatiuo singulari, tum etiam, ut diphthongo longos esse significetur, per ei melius scribuntur, quod et antiquos fecisse legimus.

There is to be sure no explicit testimony that all these matters were reviewed in the *Fragmenta*. But as will be clear below, it seems unlikely that no mention at all was made of them in connection with the larger problem of the correct pronunciation of the diphthongs.

16. Cd: aa3ᵛ; Fd: aa3ᵛ

AI αι nunc* facit ae, olim† puto omnes diphthongi pronuntiabantur, ut 'ΑΙΓῚΣ, αἰγὶς aegis.

* nunc *add.* Fd   † olim . . . pronuntiabantur *add.* Fd

The earliest editions of the *De literis Graecis* (1495, 1497, and 1501) have here only AI αι facit e ut 'ΑΙΓῚΣ, αἰγὶς aegis. An edition which was published without date as an appendix to Lascaris' *Erotemata* (also without date), but probably in 1502 or 1503 first gives *ae* instead of *e* as the Latin equivalent of αι. Similarly Μαίᾳ (page m3ʳ) is transliterated as *maea* though it is *mea* in the earlier editions. Consistency, however, is not found. On page m3ᵛ ψελλίζομαι is transliterated *psellizome*, but changed to *psellizomae* in Fd. The difficulty Aldus had in imposing his own views upon his own texts is amply illustrated by the treatment of eta in the *De literis Graecis*. The passage given above as No. 14 (f) from Fd appears in the earlier editions thus: H η facit i longum ut ΦΉΝΗ, φήνη phini. In Fd the text and the pronunciation are revised, but not the example which is still printed as *phini*! A comparison of the texts of the *De literis Graecis* could suggest either a certain amount of confusion in Aldus' mind over the sounds of Greek or even a lack of sincerity on his part. The variations and the inconsistencies really arise from the difficulty of preparing the copy for the compositor and then of course seeing that he follows it. All of the editions of the *De literis Graecis* after the *editio princeps* in 1495 were set in type from marked up copies of a previously printed version. Aldus had to squeeze his comments and revisions into this text as best he could.

The first edition which appeared in 1495 presents a thoroughly Byzantine pronunciation, which suggests that Aldus may not yet have come to hold his new views on this subject, and in particular on the pronunciation of eta. A slight change occurs in the 1497 *Breuissima Introductio* through the

---

Aeneida manu ipsius Vergilii legit, urbis accusatiuum pluralem, per i literam scribi debere. sed de huiusmodi accusatiuis multa in annotationibus nostris in Vergilii opera scripsimus.

addition of *e longum* after Ita in the Table of Letters; however, this is only ancient grammatical doctrine and need imply nothing about pronunciation. But there is a somewhat more subtle change when the phrase η *mutatur in e longum ut* πηνελόπη *penelope* (1495) becomes η *est e longum* etc. in 1501.[72] The statement that η is also changed into *ae diphthongum ut* κήρη [κηρός 1501] *caera* σκήνη *scaena* σκηνοπήγια *scaenophegia* [sic] ἠθική *aethica* is not altered until 1514 when Aldus inserts the qualifying phrases *ut quidam uolunt* (presumably not himself) before *in ae diphthongum* and *quibus ipse non accedo* after *aethica*. Similar minor changes or additions dealing with some of the other vowels are scattered throughout the treatise and indicate a change in Aldus' views about the pronunciation of Greek. However, not every reference to the contemporary Byzantine pronunciation gets corrected. Great caution must therefore be used in drawing any inferences from this particular work about Aldus' views.[73] Nevertheless, it is abundantly clear that a shift in his point of view is taking place sometime around 1500–1501.

17. (a) Vergilius. Venice: Aldus, April 1501

Praeterea quia dictiones graecas accentu graeco pronuntiandas grammatici iubent. Idcirco Simóis, Corýdon, Amaryllída, Eurystéa, Dáreta, Ádonis, Aethéra, Didó, Mantûs, et id genus multa accentu graeco imprimenda curauimus. Quare Aristotéles etiam, Penelópe, Pentecosté, et similia accentu graeco pronuntianda existimem, alibi ostendemus.

(b) C: aa7ᵛ–8ʳ; F: &6ᵛ 7ʳ

[The Latin rules for accentuation are not observed because of] Idiomate, cum graecum uocabulum, nulla nec temporis nec literarum facta mutatione, ad nos uenit. Tunc enim seruat accentum graecum, ut Tegéa, Neméa, Créusa, Aréthusa, Amaryllís, amaryllí, amaryllída, Corýdon, Simóeis, Arcádĕs, Cýclōpĕs, cýclōpăs, Penelópe, Pentecosté, Aristotéles, Demosthénes, et id genus quam plurima ... [cf. No. 14 (c)] ... In Aristótelis autem, aristótĕli, aristótĕlem, aristótĕle accentus est in antepenultima, quia latine declinantur. Comoediă autem, Tragoediă, Sóphiă, symphóniă, et similia mutant accentum, cum corripitur ultima. Graece enim κωμῳδία, τραγῳδία, σοφία, συμφωνία dicitur. Nos comoédiă, tragoédiă, sóphiă, symphóniă, ultima correpta.

[72] Similarly the note in 1495 (A7ʳ) on the meaning of the abbreviations IHS—η cum sit ita graeca uocalis quae apud nos in e longum frequentius commutatur ut ᾽ΙΗΣΟῩΣ IESVS—becomes in 1501: cum sit η ῆτα graeca uocalis, quae est e productum tam apud nos, quam apud Graecos, ut ᾽ΙΗΣῩΣ IESVS.

[73] Two examples: the comment, η *cum i subscripto facit i longum ut* τῇ μούσῃ *ti musi*, remains unchanged in all editions. The name of the Greek letter Νῦ is transcribed *Gni* in the 1495, 1497, 1501 and undated (ca. 1502) editions; this is changed to *Ni* (!) in the 1508 edition.

The edition of Virgil with the letter addressed to the *Studiosi* from which passage (a) is extracted was finished in April 1501. The second edition of the Latin Grammar which does not contain Book IV and the discussion of accents did not appear until February 1502 (1501 Venetian style). It seems unlikely that Aldus would have published the second edition of the Latin Grammar without Book IV or at least without the passages on accents (a regular part of an *Ars Grammatica*) if this material was already written and at hand. The reference in passage (a) then is probably not to the discussion of the Greek accent as it was to appear later in the third edition of the Latin Grammar, but to a more contemporary treatment. Moreover, the remarks on the Greek accent in the Latin Grammar do not constitute an answer to the question, why I, Aldus, think Aristoteles, etc. should be pronounced with a Greek instead of a Latin accent. It thus seems more likely that the phrase, *alibi ostendemus*, is a reference to the *Fragmenta*. That the *Fragmenta* contained a discussion of the effect of accents upon vowel quantity is evident from No. 18 below. How extensive this discussion may have been and to what degree it may have been related to the treatment of accents in Book IV of the Latin Grammar cannot of course be determined from the surviving evidence. But it does seem likely that the *Fragmenta* included a detailed treatment of the effect of the (stress) accent on the contemporary pronunciation of both Greek and Latin, the nature of the accent in the two languages with ample illustration from the ancient grammarians, and probably an exhortation to restore the correct pronunciation of the ancients.

18. Cd: aa6^r; Fd: aa6^r

> Sed an diphthongos et ε, η, ο, ω, υ uocaleis ut nunc nos pronuntiamus,* antiqui quoque pronuntiauerint, in fragmentis nostris disputaturi sumus. Nam et Graeci meo iudicio suas diphthongos et nos nostras tum quas diximus, uocaleis, perperam pronuntiamus. Idem etiam pronuntiandis accentibus non seruata syllabarum quantitate fieri iudicamus, ut θρω in ἄνθρωπος corripere, et μο in σιμόεις producere uideamur propter accentum.

> * ut nunc nos pronuntiamus] pronuntiamus *add.* Fd

These sentences are added to the penultimate section, *De diphthongis improprie*, of the *De literis Graecis*. They are thus a comment on both the immediate subject of the Greek diphthongs and their Latin equivalents in loan words and on the larger question of correct pronunciation which was obviously crystallized for Aldus in the contemporary sounds of the Greek vowels. Aldus seems clearly bothered by the issue of correctness. He is just not interested in recovering the ancient sounds, but in demonstrating the errors in contemporary pronunciation of Greek and Latin alike and in revealing the sources of those errors such as the effect of improperly used accents.[74] These sentences were added to the 1508 version of the *De literis Graecis*. As Drerup noticed,[75] the future participle *disputaturi* implies that the *Fragmenta* are still in the process of being written. The next datable reference in No. 19 below suggests that the work is close to or already complete.

19. E: &2ᵛ–3ᵛ

Hoc loco non uidetur silentio praetereundum, quod de αῖ diphthongo hic scribitur his uerbis: ἡ γὰρ θέσει μακρὰ ἐλάττων ἐστὶ τῆς φύσει μακρᾶς. ἐπεὶ καὶ τὸ ᾱ τὸ φύσει μακρόν, μεῖζόν ἐστι τῆς αῖ διφθόγγου τῆς ἐχούσης τὸ ῑ ἐκφωνούμενον. ὁ γὰρ ποιῶν ἔργον δύο στρατιωτῶν, ἰσχυρότερός ἐστιν ἐκείνων. Quandoquidem uel hinc colligi potest aetate nostra, et maiorum ab hinc annos octingentos, ac plus eo, perperam diphthongos omneis, et pronuntiari, et pronuntiatumesse, praeterquam αυ et ευ apud graecos; nam apud nos et illas perperam. Si enim ῑ in αῖ diphthongo ἐκφωνητέον, ut supra est scriptum: uidelicet ᾱ natura longum maius esse αῖ diphthongo, quae, ῑ quod pronuntietur, habeat, perperam, ac barbare eam nunc proferimus, cum e legimus; nam et ᾱ, et ῑ in ea sonum habere suum debent confusum in unam syllabam, ut ab ᾱ incipias, et in ῑ desinas, quemadmodum in αῦ, et ευ diphthongis facimus. Praeterea diphthongos omneis proprias hoc modo pronuntiandum esse, patet ipso nomine. Diphthongos enim dicitur, quod duos phthongos hoc est sonos, et uoces habeat: id quod et Terentianus ait his trochaicis:

> Porrò uocalem secuta, uim tenet uocalium,
> Et sonos utrosque iungit; unde diphthongos eas
> Graeciae dicunt magistri, quod duae iunctae simul
> Syllabam sonant in unam, uíque gemina proditae.

At si αῖ ē, οῖ et εῖ ῑ, οῦ u legas, ut nunc barbare legimus, non diphthongos, sed monophthongos pronuntiando facies, cum sonum utriusque quae in diphthongo propria est uocalis iungere debeas in unam syllabam. Nam ῑ in omni diphthongo propria ἐκφωνούμενον dicitur à Grammaticis contra ἀνεκφώνητον in diphthongo impropria. Atqui si αῖ e sonat, nec ᾱ nec ῑ profertur. ῡ etiam in οῦ diphthongo ἐκφωνούμενον quemadmodum in αῦ, et ευ diphthongis, esse debet, ut ab ō paruo incipias, et desinas in ῡ. Sonum autem οῦ diphthongi idest u, ut nunc male pronuntiamus, ῡ uocalem apud antiquissimos habuisse existimo. Signum est, quod nunc quoque quod graeci δύο nos duo dicimus, et quod illi σῦς, μῦς, θύλη, ῥώμυλος, nos sus, mus, Thule, Romulus dicimus, et alia id genus sexcenta.

Eodem modo ῆ, et ō̄, et ē, et ō non recte pronuntiamus. Nam η et ε, proximum, ac penè eundem sonum habere debent, hoc est e ut ῆ proferas clarius, et sub palato, ē uero minore sono in gutture. Exempli gratia, ut ῆ

---

[74] There is no trace of this topic elsewhere in Aldus' surviving writings, but Erasmus devoted considerable space to it in his *De Recta Pronuntiatione*; cf. his *Opera Omnia* (Leiden, 1703), I, 939E–949B.

[75] (Above, note 20). The future remains unchanged in subsequent editions of the *De literis Graecis*.

proferas ut e latine loquens in dictione debes, ē uero, ut e in dictionibus hisce uulgaribus: chĕ dicĕ, chĕ panĕ mangia, chĕ uino bĕuĕ. cum barbare loqueris, ut nunc uulgus. Sic o magnum proferendum, ut o in dictione bōnō cum latine nunc loquimur. Nam apud antiquos nostros o breue, et o longum non eundem sonum habuisse existimo. O uero paruum, ut o in eadem dictione bono, si ut uulgus dixeris: e bŏnŏ hŏmŏ, et miŏ amicŏ. Sic eas literas pronuntiari debere Terentianus praecipit, cum dicit:

> Litteram nanque ē uidemus esse ad ῆτα, proximam,
> Sicut ō et ῶ uidentur esse uicinae sibi.
> Temporum momenta distant, non soni natiuitas.

ῆ praeterea non i sed ē longum sonare debere ostendit etiam Eustathius, in Homerum inquiens βῆ μιμητὸν τῆς τῶν προβάτων φωνῆς. Idem βὴ βὴ φωνῆς προβάτων σημαντικόν. Καὶ φέρεται παρ' ἀιλίῳ διονυσίῳ χρῆσις κρατίνου τοιαύτη· ὁ δ' ἠλίθιος ὥσπερ πρόβατον βὴ βὴ λέγων βαδίζει. Oues uero non ui ui, ut nunc βὴ βὴ barbare pronuntiamus. Sed be be balant, et est balant pro belant à βὴ mutatione ῆ in ā dorice, ut μήτηρ mater. Vnde et id colligimus, β sic pronuntiandum ut b apud nos profertur, non ut u consonans, uel F. digamma Aeolicum. Alpha igitur, et beta et graecis ipsis dicendum, ut nos dicimus, non alpha, et uita: id, quod ex hebræis acceptum est, qui alpha, et Beth non uith dicunt. Sed de his in fragmentis nostris longe plura. Ubi etiam γ, κ, λ, ν, sequente ῑ uel ν, uel εῑ, uel οῑ perperam à græcis nunc pronuntiari ostendimus, sicut apud nos, et diphthongos omneis, et c, et g, sequente i et e, et ti sequente uocali.

Sed de his in fragmentis nostris longe plura: the passage above is the longest and most comprehensive statement left by Aldus of the contents of the *Fragmenta*, at least on the subject of pronunciation. It exists solely by the accident of Aldus' poor planning of the presswork for the 1512 edition of Constantine Lascaris' *Erotemata* and sundry other Greek grammatical treatises printed with it. Latin translations were made, largely by Aldus himself. The Greek texts and the Latin translations were printed in separate gatherings in such a way that they could be bound together with the Latin translation facing the Greek original. Aldus ran out of material to fill all of the pages in three of these gatherings (y, z, and &) so he used these pages for a list of *errata*. But the situation is best described in Aldus' own words:

Quoniam hae duae pagellae, in medio huiusce quaternionis, uacuae, et non scriptae superfuissent, nisi quid aliud in ipsis excudendum curassem (nihil enim erat e regione, quod interpretari oporteret, ut in reliquis factum uides) placuit, ut in ipsis, et in iis, quae id genus sequuntur in medio duorum, qui deinceps sequuntur quaternionum, errata corrigenda adnotarentur, quae in his de graecarum proprietate linguarum tractatibus partim inter impressionem, partim exemplarium deprauatorum culpa, facta animaduertimus. Idque celeriter uix non credas, quam sim occupatus. non habeo certe tempus non modo corrigendis, ut cuperem diligentius, qui excusi

emittuntur libris cura nostra, summisque die, noctuque laboribus, sed ne
perlegendis quidem cursim, id, quod, si uideres miseresceret te Aldi tui,
quae tua est humanitas, cum saepe non uacet uel cibum sumere, uel aluum
leuare. Interdum ita distinemur, utraque occupata manu, atque coram, id
expectantibus impressoribus, quod habetur in manibus, tum importune,
rusticeque instantibus, ut ne nasum quidem liceat emungere. o prouinciam
quamdurissimam! diuinabam equidem id futurum, uix eam aggressus, cum in
fronte eius libri, quae κανονίσματα appellantur κίχλα χέζει αὐτῇ κακὸν scripsimus, quod sic nobis malum creaturi essemus, ut turdus sibi. Sed creauerim,
si sic iuuero: ea est haec nostra prouincia. . . . Inter errores, qui corrigendi
sunt, quaedam obiter dicturi sumus, quae, ut puto, non displicebunt, ut uel in
erroribus prosim.[76]

The approximately two pages of comment on pronunciation are thus
obiter dicta as Aldus seeks to benefit his readers even in the midst of errors.
The impact they, or rather the ideas and assumptions incorporated in
them and communicated orally through the discussions in the Aldine
Academy, had upon the history of classical scholarship and upon education
has yet to be fully explored.[77] But that is another task. I will conclude
this one by noting that the motives which Aldus voices in the middle of the
hurly-burly of the printing shop are the same ones which seemingly
inspired his first publishing venture in Greek grammar. In the preface to
the 1495 edition of the *De literis Graecis* Aldus Manucius Romanus greets
the studious and says *inter alia:*

> Omnem enim uitam decreuimus ad hominum utilitatem consumere. Deus est
> mihi testis nihil me magis desyderare quam prodesse hominibus, quod et
> anteacta uita nostra ostendit ubicunque uiximus et ostensurum speramus
> (quando id uolumus) indies magis quandiu uiuimus in hac lachrymarum
> ualle et plena miseriae. Dabo equidem operam ut quantum in me est semper
> prosim. Nam etsi quietam ac tranquillam agere uitam possumus, negotiosam
> tamen eligimus et plenam laboribus. Natus est enim homo non ad indignas
> bono uiro et docto uoluptates, sed ad laborem et ad agendum semper aliquid
> uiro dignum. Non torpeamus igitur non uitam in otio uentri somnoque
> reliquisque uoluptatibus indulgentes transeamus ueluti pecora. Nam (ut
> inquit Cato) Vita hominis prope uti ferrum est. Ferrum si exerceas, con-
> teritur; si non exerceas, tamen rubigo interficit. Ita si se homo exerceat,
> consumitur; si non exerceat, torpedo plus detrimenti affert quam exercitatio.
> Sed his omissis de re dicere incipiamus. Haec tamen multis uerbis dixi amore
> incredibili erga omnis homines incitatus meo.[78]

[76] Sig. y4ᵛ.

[77] A task initiated in the twentieth century by Ingram Bywater, *The Erasmian Pronunciation of Greek and Its Predecessors* (London, 1908). Drerup's discussion of Aldus in his
monumental history of the school pronunciation of Greek (above, note 20) is regrettably
marred by numerous errors.

[78] *De literis graecis ac diphthongis et quemadmodum ad nos ueniant* (Venice: Aldus Manutius,
1495), p. A1ʳ f.

The voice of Italian humanism sounds clear and strong. It is our misfortune that we have today only these scanty fragments of what was surely Aldus' most original work, but they are enough to attest his ingenuity and his persistent industry. Whatever it was that frustrated the author's expectations, the publisher's promises which echo in these prefaces are not devoid of meaning and sincerity.

University of Illinois at Urbana

980904B   29.95 (12.95)